NO TEA, NO SHADE

No Tea, NO SHADE

New Writings in Black Queer Studies

EDITED BY

E. Patrick Johnson

DUKE UNIVERSITY PRESS *Durham & London* 2016

Library of Congress Cataloging-in-Publication Data
Names: Johnson, E. Patrick, [date] editor.
Title: No tea, no shade : new writings in Black queer studies /
edited by E. Patrick Johnson.
Description: Durham : Duke University Press, 2016. |
Includes bibliographical references and index.
Identifiers: LCCN 2016022047 (print)
LCCN 2016023801 (ebook)
ISBN 9780822362227 (hardcover : alk. paper)
ISBN 9780822362425 (pbk. : alk. paper)
ISBN 9780822373711 (e-book)
Subjects: LCSH: African American gays. | Gay and lesbian
studies. | African Americans in popular culture. | Gays in popular culture. |
Gender identity—Political aspects. | Sex in popular culture.
Classification: LCC E185.625.N59 2016 (print) | LCC E185.625 (ebook) |
DDC 306.76/608996073—dc23
LC record available at https://lccn.loc.gov/2016022047

Cover art: Philip P. Thomas, *Sharing Tea*, 2016. © Philip P. Thomas.

FOR ALL THE QUEER
FOREMOTHERS AND FOREFATHERS

CONTENTS

FOREWORD

Cathy J. Cohen

☙

TO SAY THAT THE FIELD OF black queer studies has grown is undoubtedly an understatement. As E. Patrick Johnson notes in his introduction, it seems like only yesterday that many of us were struggling to have black LGBT folks included in discussions and articles about "the" black community. I remember helping to plan the conference Black Nations/Queer Nations in 1995 and never imagining that the future would include national and international conferences where black queer studies would be a central point of interrogation by scholars, activists, and politicians as was the case at the 2014 Whose Beloved Community?" conference held at Emory University. I remember attending the Black Queer Studies conference in 2000 planned by E. Patrick Johnson and Mae G. Henderson and never believing that the group assembled there would in a decade help to revolutionize our study and understanding of black intimacy, sex, and community. And yet, here we are, the many of us, having built the academic field of black queer studies that has come to be respected, critiqued, and institutionalized.

It is the question of institutionalization and all that comes with it that currently worries me. Of course, the readers of a volume like *No Tea, No Shade* should be interested in seeing black queer studies incorporated into the mainstream of academic studies. Such institutionalization brings with it resources to train more students, jobs for those engaged in research in this field, tenure for those willing to risk their careers to push through boundaries of what was thought to be appropriate topics for scholars studying black people, and the publication of our work across disciplines and sometimes outside the academy. The incorporation of black queer studies has the potential to transform some parts of the academy, especially African American and Gender and Women Studies. However, as we descend deeper into the ivory tower we must ask ourselves at what cost. To what degree does incorporation challenge our relevance to the same communities who find themselves at the heart of our research?

The question of relevance seems especially pertinent at this moment when a movement to declare the centrality of black lives and black communities continues to build across the country and the world. One of the defining characteristics of this movement is its insistence on reclaiming from the margins the bodies, leadership, and strength of those who have often been most peripheral in society and black communities. We are watching and hopefully participating in a movement that declares that its strategy is rooted in a black queer and feminist lens. This is a movement where black cis and trans women and men, those who are incarcerated, black immigrants, and poor black folk fighting for a living wage, are not only recognized as part of black communities, but are placed at the center of our struggles, our triumphs and our imagining of black subjectivity. This movement is the embodiment of what some of us have called a black queer nationalist politic—unapologetically black as the organization Black Youth Project (BYP100) declares, but also committed to a capacious understanding of how black communities get constituted at different historical times, in different parts of the world, and by different defining characteristics.

As I have contended before, the relevance of black queer studies is evidenced in the extraordinary and transformative work of scholars, like those highlighted in this volume, whose radical imagination insists on always recalibrating blackness, its embodiment and performance in an ever-changing political economy. Scholars of black queer studies find themselves both on the frontline of activism and informing frontline activist strategy by reminding all of us of the totality of black subjectivity. Through their work we are taught that while we must insist that black people not be the targets of state violence at the hands of the police, our demands for liberation must encompass our total humanity, including attention to the very human pursuits of pleasure, intimacy, and desire. Through their work we are reminded that the bodies and lives of black cis and trans women have just as routinely been the object of state abuse as our black brothers, including our death but also the regulation of our bodies and behaviors through a rigid labor and welfare apparatus. Through their work we are shown how the state has used a plethora of ways to threaten the survival of black people, including police violence, but also the refusal of needed support such as the slow response to HIV/AIDS on the part of the state as it ravaged black communities in the early 1980s. Through their work we are told not only of the importance of the state as a site of interrogation but also that it does not encompass all the sites of power used against black people. Through their work we are taught that we must reject simple dichotomies of us versus them, highlighting instead the complexities of power that exist throughout society and in black communities, paying special attention to the collaborations between the state and black elites.

Thus, armed with these insights, the relevance of black queer studies also extends beyond the classroom into the streets, into movements and into the ways our folk creatively and defiantly build their families, communities, and relationships. Young people who have taken classes on black queer studies and black feminist theory through ethnic studies, African American studies and gender and sexuality departments are using the lessons taught in those classes to inform the organizing practices they are deploying on behalf of and in partnership with black people who may never see the inside of our classrooms. These young activists, who blend the politics of the academy and the politics of liberation, daily make black queer studies relevant to a changing world. They are the translators of academic and theoretical discourses looking for routes out of the ivory tower, searching to breathe new life into our stagnant constructions of who we are, what we do, and what we want. These young activists, fortified with the work of such authors as those in this volume, are breaking down the doors of structural racism and polite conversation, demanding that all the contours of black life are not only protected but also embraced as we make space for a radical reimagining of how all the messy contours of black life matter.

So as we read the incredible work in this volume from a new generation of black queer studies scholars, we must remember that the world in which we receive this volume is a world at war (again) over whether black lives matter; whether black desire, especially that perceived as outside the bounds of some imposed respectable perimeter, can be pursued; whether black cis and trans women can both lead movements against and be the recognized targets of state violence; and whether the institutionalization of black queer studies means its irrelevance to black people struggling for justice and freedom. Not one of these disputes has been resolved. We must, therefore, engage in battle on many fronts, struggling for the liberation of black people and as a consequence the liberation of our theories and research. The authors in this volume seem ready and able to take up such a challenge.

ACKNOWLEDGMENTS

AS I HAVE SAID ON MANY OCCASIONS, "edited volumes are so much work!" And I have always had to follow that up with, "and the final product is worth it." I am so thankful to see this next iteration of black queer studies come to fruition, and that could not have happened without the brilliant next generation of scholars whose work is contained between these two covers. When I called, they responded with fierceness and genius. I thank all of you: Jafari S. Allen, Marlon M. Bailey, Zachary Blair, La Marr Jurelle Bruce, Jennifer DeClue, Treva Ellison, Lyndon K. Gill, Kai M. Green, Alexis Pauline Gumbs, Kwame Holmes, Shaka Mc-Glotten, Amber Jamilla Musser, Alison Reed, Ramón H. Rivera-Servera, Tanya L. Saunders, C. Riley Snorton, Kaila Adia Story, Omise'eke Natasha Tinsley, Julia Roxanne Wallace, and Kortney Ziegler. I trust that you will teach the next generation of children the way in which ze will grow!

I have had the fortune of having some of the best research assistants for this project. Shoniqua Roach and Rhaisa Williams worked their magic in helping me bring these many moving parts together. I owe both of you milk for life! A special thanks to Margaret Lebron for working on the index.

To my colleagues Dwight A. McBride and Chris Cunningham, who gave me feedback on early drafts of the introduction, thank you for your candor and critical generosity.

To my wonderful editor, Courtney Berger, thank you for always listening to my pitches for new work, watching me soar in the clouds with my ambition, but always grounding me with the realities of book publishing!

I'll never forget that breakfast at the American Studies Association conference in Puerto Rico when I pitched the idea for this book. Thanks for making it a reality.

And, as always, thanks to my life partner, Stephen J. Lewis, who is my ride or die. You always know how to give me just what I need when I need it.

Introduction

E. PATRICK JOHNSON

BLACK QUEER STUDIES HAS COME OF AGE. Following on the heels of an explosion of conferences, articles, and books over the last decade, black sexuality studies has been codified as a legitimate scholarly enterprise. While the Black Queer Studies in the Millennium Conference held at the University of North Carolina at Chapel Hill in 2000 was a watershed moment, I do not believe anyone in attendance imagined that black queer studies would proliferate the way that it has since the turn of the twenty-first century. But as John D'Emilio has observed about the 1990s as regards gay liberation, the "world turned" in relation to the study of black sexuality between 2000 and 2005.[1] Bookended by the Black Queer Studies conference in 2000 and the publication of Mae G. Henderson's and my edited volume, *Black Queer Studies: A Critical Anthology* (*BQS*), in 2005 was the publication of Roderick Ferguson's *Aberrations in Black: Toward a Queer of Color Critique* in 2003, which inaugurated yet another queer (of color) analytic and complemented very nicely the work in *BQS*, to which Ferguson also contributed an essay.

The years since 2005 have shifted the ground upon which we theorize blackness and sexuality, most notably because a whole new crop of scholars took up the mantle and ran with it. Although some of them were exposed to black queer studies through *BQS*, a few of them were actually graduate and undergraduate students who attended the Black Queer

Studies conference and are now newly minted PhDs, assistant professors, or recently tenured associate professors. These scholars had the benefit of coming of age in the academy during the emergence of queer studies and cultural studies and thus were invested in generating knowledge in these areas, but with race as a central concern. In their home departments, however, they were hard-pressed to find support for their research and were often discouraged from pursuing topics that focused too heavily on sexuality. What the conference and the scholarship that emerged thereafter did, then, was not only legitimize their research interests but also provide them with role models in the field to whom they could look for support. Most often—and perhaps more important—that support came in the way of new progenitors of black queer studies evaluating the work of these emergent scholars, clearing a path for them to do the work as well as legitimizing it to colleagues in discussions of hiring and through the tenure process.

The black queer "children" who came of age during the burgeoning stages of black queer studies also learned from the lessons of their foremothers and forefathers and avoided many (but not all) of the theoretical missteps their predecessors made, while also generating their own theorizations of racial queerness with a critical difference.[2] And while these junior scholars critically engage and critique the work of senior scholars, they do so respectfully and with a sense of deference, but with no less rigor or candor. Thus, the title of this volume, *No Tea, No Shade*, stems from the contemporary black vernacular phrase made popular by millennial black queer blogger Qaadir Howard (also known as "Timiya") on his YouTube series and then taken up in black queer popular culture by drag performer RuPaul to indicate, "I mean no offense by what I'm about to say, but I need to speak the truth." Or, in other words, "to keep it real." The ingenuity of imbricating two "old school" black queer vernacular terms—"tea" (gossip) and "shade" (disrespect)—is apropos of how today's black queer scholars build upon the theorizations that preceded their own. In this way, new black queer studies scholars embody the signifyin(g) tradition of African American arts and criticism—that of repetition and revision with a critical difference.[3]

In the introduction to *Black Queer Studies*, Mae G. Henderson and I state the aims of that volume as wanting to stage "a critical intervention in the discourses of black studies and queer studies" by creating a space for more discussion of sexuality within black studies and of race in queer studies.[4] While the essays in that volume do stage such interventions and discussions, they do so in the context of having to shoulder the burden of what is left out because the anthology was one of the first of its kind in the field. Anticipating this lack, Henderson and I tried to preempt one of the critiques: the absence of diasporic voices, save for the one essay by Rinaldo Walcott in which he encourages a "diaspora reading practice."[5] As with any body of work that emerges in a new field of study, there are always going to be blind spots and limitations, despite every effort to avoid them. While some may indeed find silences and absences in the essays in *No Tea, No Shade*, by and large they are not the same ones of a previous generation. More than a few of the essays, for example, look beyond U.S. borders to theorize black queer subjectivity not separate from, but in relation to U.S. blackness and queerness.[6]

Much of this more expansive research focus is due in part to the historical context in which these scholars came of age—both chronologically and intellectually. John D'Emilio points out that the riots at the Stonewall Rebellion of 1969, while holding mythic status as the turning point in the gay liberation movement, were barely noticed by most of the country and did not result in wide sweeping policy change. He believes that Stonewall marked the "potential" of changes still to come. The 1990s, he argues, saw the symbolism of Stonewall manifest in material gains for queers in the areas of representation (for example, print, television, and film media), same-sex corporate benefits, and local-government-designated "gayborhoods," to name a few tangible examples.[7] In some ways, the authors in *No Tea, No Shade* experienced these advances and more, given the demise of "don't ask, don't tell"; the shift of support for and legalization of same-sex marriage; the striking down of the Defense of Marriage Act; the election of the United States' first black president, who also supports LGBT concerns; miraculous advances in treatment for HIV/AIDS; professional athletes identifying as queer; and transgender people being more visible and accepted. These cultural and societal shifts in beliefs and values about queers, in addition to the policy changes enacted, in no small way affected the kinds of topics and theoretical directions that these new scholars now almost take for granted as objects and areas of inquiry.

The academy itself has also changed over the past fifteen years. In 2000, when the Black Queer Studies conference occurred, those of us doing work on black sexuality were doing so in traditional disciplines and over and against the will of some of our department chairs and colleagues. Only a handful of the presenters were housed in gender and women's studies and fewer still in African American studies. Queer theory/studies had been legitimized in the humanities and some social science fields such as anthropology and sociology; still, there were few teaching positions solely devoted to this area, let alone positions focused specifically on *black* queer studies. Over time, however, this has changed. During the past several years there have been positions advertised at elite private and large public institutions for scholars who focus explicitly on sexuality and even black sexuality.[8] While many of these positions have been in women's and gender studies departments and programs, some have been in African American studies programs and departments. In fact, in the newly formed Department of African and African Diaspora Studies at the University of Texas at Austin, there are six faculty who do work on black sexuality—two of whom have essays in this volume.[9] Indeed, a shift in the academy regarding sexuality studies manifested in a host of conferences that were interdisciplinary in nature and also had race as a central analytic optic of sexuality. These included the Race, Sex, Power conference hosted at the University of Illinois at Chicago in 2008, which brought together activists, artists, and scholars from around the country to focus on black and Latina/o sexuality; the Unleashing the Black Erotic: Gender and Sexuality—Passion, Power, and Praxis Conference hosted by the College of Charleston Avery Research Center and African American Studies in 2013; the Black Sexual Economies: Transforming Black Sexualities Research Conference in 2013 hosted by Washington University School of Law; and the Whose Beloved Community? Black Civil and LGBT Rights Conference held at Emory University in 2014, to name just a few. These conferences showcased a range of current scholarship in black queer studies and, in the case of the Whose Beloved Community? conference, policymakers and activists were integral to the list of presenters, including non-queer-identified legends such as the now deceased civil rights activist Julian Bond. In addition to the conferences, there have been several special issues of journals on black queer sexuality as well as coverage in academic professional periodicals such as the *Chronicle of Higher Education* about the increasing amount of scholarship produced in this area.[10] All of these professional and institutional shifts provide context for so many emerging new voices in the field.

But there is also a sense of daring in the current black queer scholarship that takes a different tack than earlier work. No tea, no shade, but unlike some of us black queer scholars who were part of the first "wave" of black queer studies, the current children's work, to a degree, is not bound by the same institutional, disciplinary, and publishing politics. They are not, for instance, concerned as much with "intervening" in (white) queer studies as much as they are in pursuing their own agenda despite what is going on in "traditional" queer theory and as if race and class always already matters. There are no manifestos or battle cries; there is just the work. This is not to suggest that these scholars are apolitical or naïve about what is at stake with their work or in the world around them. Quite the contrary. They simply do not allow the negative discursive and material terrain that is the academy to compel a response. Many of this new generation of intellectuals are also grassroots activists, community organizers, and community leaders, and they traverse quite easily between the front porch and the lectern as they embrace the ever-increasing need to speak to multiple audiences. Their scholarship is the fruit of the old heads' labor of beating back the brush, clearing the land for a new crop to grow. Indeed, more than a few of the essays in this volume employ the work of scholars from the *BQS* volume, such as Cathy Cohen, Charles Nero, Rinaldo Walcott, and myself. They also rethink or reconsider even canonical black queer figures like Audre Lorde and Barbara Smith while practicing those same writers' grassroots activism. The contributors to *No Tea, No Shade* are conscious of the struggles of their forebears—both those in the distant past and those still actively producing scholarship—while also acknowledging that their struggles and interests are not exactly the same. Sankofa-like, the new black queer studies pays homage to the past so that it can propel the field forward. I can locate three areas of interest that the current generation of black queer scholars has taken up that build upon or signify on the work that has come before: social media, pornography/explicit sex, and black feminism as queer theory. Below, I want to provide a few examples of the new work in these areas.

At the turn of the twenty-first century, social media forms such as Myspace and Facebook were not in existence. And, while the BlackBerry mobile device was around, it was not as sophisticated as the contemporary smartphone (that is, iPhone and Android) with apps like Grindr, Jack'd, iDate, Scruff, and Guy Spy, which provide virtual sites for LGBT folks to find one another, build community, network, and hook up. Indeed, technology has evolved so quickly that it has had an enormous impact on the ways queers enact desire. The racial and class implications of these virtual forms index long-standing discourses that position the raced and working-class body as other and the white middle- and upper-class body as idyllic. Black queer theorists of today understand this phenomenon in ways that those of an earlier generation could not because, to a large degree, their everyday existence has been shaped by the forces of social media, including their sexuality. In his book *Virtual Intimacies: Media, Affect, and Queer Sociality*, Shaka McGlotten, one of the contributors to this volume, takes up the question of how cyberspace has altered our notions of intimacy and how "the particularities of our [black and Latino gay men] racial enfleshments have operated as obvious and not so obvious drags on our erotic or romantic possibilities."[11] Trained as an anthropologist, McGlotten draws on ethnographic field research to engage black and Latino gay men (including himself) about the ways in which they theorize their own sexual pleasure, desire, and heartbreak through their engagement with social media across various platforms. The temporal and spatial arrangements of these platforms are quite different from the ones that Dwight A. McBride theorizes about in his landmark essay on the "gay marketplace of desire" in which he describes the implications of the transition from gay personal print ads to online chat rooms as a watershed moment because of the ways in which it simultaneously simplified and further privatized the placing of ads.[12]

No tea, no shade, but in today's gay marketplace of desire, with an app like Grindr, one does not have to go through the trouble of placing an ad and waiting for a response, or even go through the trouble of entering a chat room; rather, all one need do is open the app, peruse pictures, and see who is closest. Hooking up has never been so easy—except that it is complicated by the same racial and class profiling that occurs in nonvirtual spaces. In many ways, McGlotten engages the same questions as McBride in terms of how sexual desire is always already a product of cultural and social conditioning, which, in this country, always means the long shadow of white supremacy. On the other hand, what is unique about McGlotten's approach within the context of black queer studies is that it employs social scientific methods like ethnography to engage theoretical discourses that typically circulate in the humanities, such as affect theory, media studies, and cultural studies. While interdisciplinarity is far from new in black queer studies, the particular employment of these methods and theories exemplifies the ways in which black queer theorists today maneuver within various fields, often deepening the work that preceded it. In the case of McGlotten, his is the first wholesale study of contemporary social media forms and their impact on the affective economy of black queer desire.

The technological advances that have occurred in social media have also affected the ways in which black queers engage in sex and represent it. Sites such as XTube.com, Black2ube.com, blacklesbianfuck.com, sweetblacklesbians.com, and others, where everyday people post self-made videos of themselves engaged in a whole range of sex acts, have made pornography more accessible to consume for those who cannot afford to rent, buy, or download it. Thus, the broader dissemination and accessibility of black queer porn has, in some ways, made discussions of explicit black queer sex less taboo or less "shocking" than, say, when a book like *Gary in Your Pocket*, a collection of poems, diary entries, and stories by black gay writer Gary Fisher, who died of AIDS in 1993, and edited by the late Eve Kosofsky Sedgwick, was published—especially in academic circles. Fisher's candid depictions of bondage, dominance, sadism, and masochism (BDSM) with (mostly) white men from his life in San Francisco and North Carolina were challenging for even the most progressive queer theorists during the 1990s. In one passage he writes: "I hadn't seen his cock, didn't know it would be so big, so unmanageable—hadn't I always wanted to die this way? He pushed toward my throat, curled me tighter, and drove my head down on it, still talking about death like it was our only alternative. Maybe I understood this mechanism, I'd become the middle of, understood its strength, its unrelenting, its selfishness and selflessness. I tasted his salt, his ooze, and my throat jumped, but I could not dislodge him."[13]

Perhaps it was the currency of the devastating effects of HIV/AIDS that made Fisher's writing so difficult to read, or perhaps it was the sense of nihilism that seemed to haunt his personal accounts; whatever the case, Fisher's work emboldens black queer theorist Robert Reid-Pharr five years later to open the introduction of his book *Black Gay Man* with a description of his white then-lover coming on his face—a scene evocative of Fisher's writing: "When he comes, usually standing over me, jerking hard at his dick and making those strange moon faces, the liquid spills out almost like accident. He drawls, 'Goddamn, Goddamn,' as the goo hits my skin."[14] It is a passage that leads Dwight A. McBride to clutch his pearls, "put the book down and call a friend," but then later, in a self-reflexive moment, recognize that Fisher's and Reid-Pharr's provocation was more about tapping into potential readers' investments of propriety, self-censorship, and (black) respectability. McBride acknowledges: "Nothing that Reid-Pharr or Fisher had said in either instance was news to me. Nothing that they had described was thought of, lived, or talked about openly with close gay friends and confidants. I allowed myself to be shocked by the public nature of these declarations, the fact that they were out there in the world. They did not ascribe to the 'positive' representation of black life, or of black gay life, that we have been so thoroughly programmed to respect, revere, and, as critics and commentators, to produce."[15]

In his self-reflection, McBride, one of the progenitors of black queer studies, indexes the hold that black respectability politics had on many of us doing work early on in this field of study. I do not want to suggest here that every writer or critic working on black queer sexuality before the publication of *Gary in Your Pocket* censored their creative or critical work in deference to a politics of black respectability. Certainly, such black writers and critics as Bruce Nugent during the Harlem Renaissance, James Baldwin in the 1950s and 1960s, Samuel Delany in the 1960s and 1970s, and Cheryl Clarke, Marlon Riggs, Essex Hemphill, and a host of others in the 1980s were describing black queer sex in explicit terms. What is notable here, however, is that most of this work was in the realm of fiction or poetry and was published by trade presses. Yes, the "shock" of *Gary in Your Pocket* was the representation of the racialization of erotic power in explicit terms, but it was also the fact that a university press published it. Thus, what I am suggesting, as McBride does, is that for those of us who did work early on in black queer studies, especially as it became codified in the academy as a legitimate field of inquiry, the protocols and limits of what we thought would be acceptable academic discourse was always already bounded by the traditional training we received in our respective fields and graduate programs. Being provocative within certain boundaries was acceptable, but that boundary shrunk and increased based on the venue of the publication, the institution where one was located, and the particular setting. Describing explicit sex acts—let alone one's own— was, and for some of my generation and earlier still is, taboo within the realm of academic writing and presentation. Indeed, I recount these earlier instances of provocative writing and the anxiety about its production to note how many current black queer studies scholars do not think twice about critically engaging and presenting explicit descriptions of taboo black queer sex—others or their own.

Regarding explicit sex acts and their depictions, I call on the example of Marlon Bailey's work, whose essay in this volume takes up "raw sex," "barebacking," or same-sex sex without the use of a condom. In his paper, "What I'm Told, What I Want, What I Do," delivered at the 2014 Whose Beloved Community? conference, Bailey chronicles the story of "Raheim," a black queer man who attends a sex party where only raw sex is allowed. Bailey performatively renders Raheim's sexual encounter without any self-consciousness, even enjoying the retelling of his interlocutor's story as the audience listens intently:

> After Raheim takes off all of his clothes, places them into a paper bag (with his handle written on it), and gives it to a guy working the party, he enters the dark back room. As soon as he enters he smells a mixture of sweat and cologne. He sees a king size bed with dudes getting fucked all over it, some doggy style, up against the wall, and others on their backs on the bed, in every corner of the room. Everybody's fucking raw, and he neither sees nor feels condom packages on the floor. A dude comes up to Raheim, bends down [in] front of him and puts his dick in his mouth and starts to suck it until it gets hard. Then he turns around and claims a corner of the bed. He bends over and toots his ass up, signaling to Raheim to enter him raw. Soon after Raheim starts to fuck him, the guy's ass is so tight and hot that after a few pumps, Raheim feels like he is about to bust, "You gon let me cum in this booty . . . huh[?] . . . You gon let me cum in this booty?" The guy moans and starts breathing really hard, as his thighs begin to shake intensely, "Yea bust that nut nigga; give me them kids."[16]

I must say that as an old-school mother,[17] I did clutch my pearls a time or two during Bailey's presentation at the explicit nature of Raheim's adventures. The rest of the audience, who were mostly of a younger generation, however, engaged in an almost call-and-response to Bailey, as they snapped their fingers and responded verbally to his erotic performance. Harkening back to Fisher and Reid-Pharr, one might assume that this representation of black queer sex within an academic setting would be shocking, not so much because of the language used to describe the sex acts (although the language is explicitly provocative), but more so because of the *kind* of sex being narrated: unprotected same-gender sex. Given the scourge of HIV/AIDS on the black community, the notion of black people seeking out opportunities to engage in high-risk sex is indeed a hard nut to swallow (pun intended). But the point of Bailey's paper and the essay included in this volume is that desire is dangerous, and despite evidence to the contrary, some marginalized groups like black gay men are willing to take risks that might endanger their lives just so that they can experience intimacy—through touch, sweat, heat—in ways that they never experience living in white supremacist society that constantly rejects them. Indeed, Bailey's research casts a light on raw sex as a practice among the black population that has been traditionally "shaded" by other (white) queer theorists doing work in this area, such as Tim Dean.[18] Similar to McGlotten, Bailey's employment of ethnographic methods gives agency to these men that allows them to theorize "what they do" that rings true for a younger generation of scholars who did not come of age in the 1980s and 1990s and for whom HIV/AIDS is not a death sentence. The desire for intimate connections forces into the background prescriptions of safe sex and staves off the paranoia of infection so commonly articulated by black gay cultural workers such as poet Essex Hemphill when he writes in "Now We Think": "Now we think/as we fuck/this nut/might kill us. There might be/a pin-sized hole/in the condom. /A lethal leak."[19] In the raw sex community, there is no condom to contend with or think about having a "lethal leak," providing no obstacle between one's enfleshed fulfillments. Analogous to the condomless sex is the disavowal of respectability politics by the new black queer theorists who press forward with wild abandon, unencumbered by any sense of propriety or deference to "proper" academic discourse or, for that matter, sexual practice.[20] Importantly, academic book publishing has changed with the times as well. Explicit sexual language in the context of an academic book is one thing, but explicit images is quite another. In 2014 alone, Duke University Press published two books on black porn by black feminist/queer studies scholars, replete with not only explicit language but also multiple images of explicit sex acts: cum shots, fellatio, anal penetration, and so forth.[21] I could not even imagine this ten years ago.

Regarding taboo sex, deceased black queer critic Vincent Woodard takes on the topic of cannibalism and homoeroticism in his posthumously published text *The Delectable Negro: Human Consumption and Homoeroticism with U.S. Slave Culture*, in which he provocatively recounts how whites literally and metaphorically consumed black flesh—a consumption that was almost always undergirded by an erotic charge. He also describes "the hungry nigger," a trope through which he theorizes the interior lives of the enslaved black male, which entailed a hunger for selfhood, intimacy, and belonging. Further developing this line of argument, Woodard links this particular hunger to homoeroticism by "theorizing the black male orifice"— namely, the mouth and anus—as a site of particular importance in the history and genealogy of the black experience that might "hint at the range of interpretive implications of black male hunger, with hunger serving as metonymy for needing, wanting, being made to taste, lack, and the taboo desire to be filled."[22] The provocation of Woodard's theorization of black male hunger under slavery is remarkable when one considers the implications of the psychosexual dynamic he describes between master and slave, but one, nonetheless, Woodard advances with confidence and a heaping of archival evidence.[23]

This does not mean, however, that there has not been resistance from senior scholars—particular those housed in African American studies—who see this new direction as troubling and a distraction from race as the primary category of analysis. Indeed, in *A Taste for Brown Sugar: Black Women in Pornography*, her book on black women in the pornography industry, Mireille Miller-Young recounts how senior black feminists called her a "pervert" and "pornographer" "not only for writing about the history of black women's images, performances, and sex work in pornography, but for showing images from this history in various presentation formats."[24] Oh, the shade of it all. Nonetheless, the old guard's power to silence this research is waning as this new generation of scholars demonstrates its ability to showcase its knowledge of traditional scholarship *and* the most current theory. It really is the case that the new black queer theorists are honoring their forebears through a critical praxis made possible by those forebears yet are not bound by the same protocols of presentation or areas of research.

Another arena in which this phenomenon plays itself out is within what I call the centering of the black female subject within black queer studies. In *The Erotic Life of Racism*, black lesbian feminist theorist Sharon Patricia Holland surveys the history of some of the most pressing debates in critical race theory and their relationship to feminist theory and queer studies. She offers a theoretical meditation on the insidious and banal nature of racism, or what she refers to as "racial practice," to account for the ways in which it cannot be disaggregated from the erotic. Throughout this meditation she indexes a number of "anxieties" around race relative to the black (female) body in feminism, queer studies, and subsequently black queer studies. Holland uses, by way of example, the by-now-classic essay "Black (W)holes and the Geometry of Black Female Sexuality," by Evelynn Hammonds, in which she laments the historical absence of the black female subject within (white) feminism and her dubiousness about the turn to queer theory as a site of hailing the black female body.[25] Holland contends that the questions that Hammonds raises within queer studies "remain unanswered despite the emergence of black queer studies, queer of color critique, and most recently, the discourse of settler colonialism brought by native studies scholars."[26] Nonetheless, I want to point to the closing lines of Hammonds's essay to make a case for how indeed the new black queer studies scholars position the black female body as central. Hammonds closes with the following: "Finally, my search for black women's sexuality through queer theory has taught me that I need not simply add the label of queer to my list as another naturalized identity. As I have argued, there is no need to reproduce black women's sexualities as a silent void. Nor are black queer female sexualities simply identities. Rather, they represent discursive and material terrains where there exists the *possibility* for the active production of speech, desire, and agency."[27] While standing by her claims about queer theory being suspect for an analysis of the black female subject, Hammonds's last line actually opens up the "possibility" for a way to instantiate black female sexuality and, I would argue, within black queer studies. This is exemplified in the work of several contemporary black queer/feminist theorists who, through the theoretical tools of black feminist and black queer studies, produce work that focuses solely on the black female voice, desires (sexual or otherwise), and the ways in which she has agency over her own life and representation. These theorists include Omise'eke Natasha Tinsley (included in this volume), LaMonda H. Stallings, and Matt Richardson, among others. If, as Hortense Spillers has rightfully argued, "black women are the beached whales of the sexual universe, unvoiced, misseen, not doing, awaiting *their* verb," then these scholars have, in part, rescued the whale, pushed her back into the sea, unsilenced her, and given the whale her due.[28]

What I appreciate most about these particular theorists' work (and I thought I would never highly value the trait I am about to attribute to them!) is its sense of entitlement. That is, it already assumes that black women's sexuality is worthy of study; it assumes that race and gender are legitimate analytic tools; it proceeds as if it has nothing to prove to white feminists (queer identified or not) or black straight feminists. These scholars simply go about "the active production of speech, desire, and agency."

LaMonda H. Stallings's *Mutha' Is Half a Word* was the first of these books to be published of the three I mention here and employs folklore studies to engage the ways in which black women function as trickster figures in black culture. Disavowing the masculinist trickster figures in African American folklore such as "Brer Rabbit," "the Signifying Monkey," or "Stag-o-lee," Stallings expands the trickster trope to account for "the uncensoring of Black women who laugh out loud, curse, sit with their legs open, and selfishly act on their desires" and "the constructions of Black female subjectivities cognizant of autonomous sexual desires."[29]

She draws on the tradition of "trickster-troping," which emphasizes in-determinacy, unpredictability, and fluidity—traits associated with queer—to argue how black women embody difference within difference to enact agency over their sexuality. Ultimately, Stallings queers black feminist theory and criticism by redirecting its focus on the "rhetoric of sex" to a more libidinal focus on black female desire—and all through the optic of black queer studies.

Another example of this centering of the black female within black queer studies (as well as a focus on diaspora) is Omise'eke Natasha Tinsley's *Thiefing Sugar: Eroticism between Women in Caribbean Literature.* Drawing on the history of black subjugation to cite the vexed expression of same-sex desire, Tinsley turns to etymology and social linguistics to discern how the remains of the discursive and material relations between enslaved Africans during the Middle Passage provided an alternative sexual epistemology for the Caribbean—one that disavows the "closet" as an apt sexual metaphor in favor of a culture-specific nomenclature grounded in the material labor of the black (female) body and its relation to land and ocean. Making connections among sugar production in the Caribbean, the paradoxical "ungendering" of black female slaves that makes their sexual selfhood pos-sible, and the landscape of the "Global South," Tinsley carefully demon-strates that the history of the black woman's body in the African Diaspora is shrouded not just in metaphor but also in the materiality of their own world-making. According to Tinsley, Caribbean women writers reappro-priate the hegemonic metaphors of land and sea deployed to justify Afro-Caribbean women's subjugation and redeploy them to provide a clearing for these same women to have "an imagination of emancipation." The places these women imagine evoke homoeroticism, not in the Eurocentric con-structions and theorizations of that term, but rather in those embedded in the social linguistics of Caribbean cultural history.

And, more recently, Matt Richardson's *The Queer Limit of Black Memory: Black Lesbian Literature and Irresolution* unearths an underutilized archive of black lesbian literature to highlight the queerness of the black diaspora. This book contests the notion that there is no archive of black lesbian art and fiction. Drawing on U.S. and British black women's fiction, Richard-son argues that these queer writers' work not only exemplifies an archive but also rewrites the history of black letters. Part of the uniqueness of this research is the examination of contemporary black lesbian texts that have heretofore never been analyzed, such as Jackie Kay's *Trumpet,* Cherry Muhanji's *Her,* Jewelle Gomez's "Louisiana, 1850," LaShonda Barnett's

"Miss Hannah's Lesson," and SDiane Adamz Bogus's "The Champagne Lady." These texts all revise history by instantiating the black lesbian subject over and against what Richardson calls "disremembering," or the process by which black lesbian subjects are deliberately forgotten or "unmourned" in the recounting of black cultural history. In a similar vein to Toni Morrison's argument that the white literary canon is always haunted by a black presence, Richardson's text represents a major intervention in African American literary and feminist studies by suggesting that there has always already been a black queer lesbian presence in the black literary canon.[30] Richardson's work is apropos as he argues that "historically, black has been inextricably tied to the queer—the lesbian in particular."[31]

In addition to these three emergent areas in black queer studies, there is yet another nascent area of research on black transgender subjects emerging. Although, as of this writing, there is still no manuscript-length study on black transgender people, there exists a feature documentary film titled *Still Black* (2008), by trans filmmaker, scholar, and activist Kortney Ziegler (who has an essay in this volume); a number of articles, including Enoch H. Page and Matt Richardson's "On the Fear of Small Numbers"; as well as a number of self-identified black transgender or gender-variant scholars.[32] Despite the increased visibility of black trans scholars, their work does not necessarily focus on transgender research. More frequently, they are producing work on gender nonconformity and/or gender variance, including two essays in this volume. Nonetheless, there is a clear sign that black transgender studies is taking hold as a legitimate form of critical analysis in the academy.

Of course, there are numerous other new areas of inquiry in black queer studies since the publication of *Black Queer Studies*, and even more so in the social sciences. The point I am trying to make here, however, is that the promise upon which Mae G. Henderson and I (and the contributors in that volume) hedged our bets has been fulfilled.

No Tea, No Shade comprises nineteen essays from a variety of disciplines, including African American studies, American studies, anthropology, sociology, film studies, history, literary studies, performance studies, and urban studies, though most of the scholars are decidedly interdisciplinary. Apropos of the authors' background, I chose not to cluster the essays under thematic headings but rather to let each essay stand on its own—although the proximity of some essays to each other was inspired by some overlap in method or theme.

The volume opens with Jafari S. Allen's "Black/Queer Rhizomatics: Train Up a Child in the Way Ze Should Grow . . . ." Inspired by botany and Gilles Deleuze and Félix Guattari's notion of the "rhizome/rhizomatic," which moves beyond tradition and history and emphasizes the creative, promiscuous, underground, multiple, and sometimes contradictory, Allen proposes "black/queer rhizomes." The rhizome (*rhízōma* [Greek], "mass of roots") is the mode of propagation and sustenance for plants as diverse as bamboo, bunch grasses, ginger, irises, and orchids. It sends out roots and shoots from its nodes. Allen's meditation draws on this trope to read closely the important nodes of the recent past and the present moment to theorize a "new and more possible meeting" of our artists, activists, scholars, policymakers, and intellectuals. The essay simultaneously avows and disavows "same gender loving," "LGBT," "queer," and "DL" discourses in the United States and various local names and concepts used to (self) identify nonheteronormative individuals of Africa(n descent) in various other parts of the world, such that we can become "fluent in each other's histories" and conversant in others' imaginations. Given the "progress" of black queer life, Allen ultimately asks, what are the conditions of possibility for beautiful and transformative work today? Where should we look for inspiration, and to whom are we accountable? Who is this "we," anyway?

The critiques of (white) queer studies continue today but take a more nuanced approach as witnessed in Alison Reed's provocative essay, "The Whiter the Bread, the Quicker You're Dead: Spectacular Absence and Post-Racialized Blackness in (White) Queer Theory." Drawing on James Baldwin's *The Fire Next Time* as a jumping-off point, Reed engages the neoliberal bent in queer studies by highlighting the ways in which it unwittingly deploys racialized bodies as "spectacular markers of queerness," the practice of employing race as theoretical fetish. Through what she identifies as a conflation of race and racism, Reed argues that (white) queer theory often undermines the eradication of institutionalized racism and, instead, buttresses the very oppressive structures it purports to undermine through its co-optation of civil rights strategies, discourses, and theories. Ultimately, Reed suggests (white) queer theory must rethink the ways in which it engages race such that it avoids redoubling the erasure of race and systemic racism for which it has been critiqued since its inception.

From discussions of queer theorizing writ large, we move to the formation of an alternative to queer as an organizing analytic and turn to Trans*. In his "Troubling the Waters: Mobilizing a Trans* Analytic," Kai

M. Green stages a conversation between black lesbian feminism and transgender studies. Through a series of close readings of editorials by Alycee Lane that appeared in *Black Lace*, a black lesbian erotic magazine, he demonstrates how black lesbian as a Trans* modifier of feminism indexes the contradiction of (white) feminist exclusion of black women, while simultaneously forging a space for the expansion of the category "woman." Through a Trans* reading of black lesbian feminist texts, Green demonstrates how this expansion of the category "woman" allows for potential trans subjectivity, sometimes named but often not.

We are introduced to more gender trouble in C. Riley Snorton's essay, "Gender Trouble in *Triton*," in which Snorton places Samuel R. Delany's novel *Triton* in dialogue with contemporary debates in black, feminist, and trans scholarship to examine the utilities of heterotopias for making sense of racial and gender difference. As his reading of the novel bears out, heterotopias are not necessarily liberatory spaces, just as plurality and difference are not "good" in and of themselves. Thus gender's troubles on Triton in the twenty-second century and some of the concerns with gender right now are not that gender is unable to proliferate; rather, the problem is that the techniques for normativizing gender so often shape one's phenomenological experience of it. In this sense, both Delany's novel and Judith Butler's often-cited passage on drag in *Gender Trouble* suffer from similar forms of mischaracterization by equating gender electivity and performativity with freedom from (gender) identity.

In his introduction to a special issue of *Gay and Lesbian Quarterly* (*GLQ*), Jafari S. Allen argues that "black/queer/diaspora work emerges in a moment in which the terms *black*, *queer*, and *diaspora* . . . have already begun to be elaborated beyond the metaphors and concepts offered by any one of these constituencies, and beyond false dichotomies of essentialism and anti-essentialism."[33] In the next four essays, the authors provide evidence of this "current conjuncture" through their methods and objects of study and by marking black queer theory's wade into Caribbean waters. First stop, Puerto Rico. In "Reggaetón's Crossings: Black Aesthetics, Latina Nightlife, and Queer Choreography," Ramón H. Rivera-Servera takes on the dismissal of *perreo*, the doggy-style dance that anchors reggaetón choreography, in contemporary Puerto Rican feminist criticism to emphasize the feminist and queer microagencies performed by dancers who engage with this musical culture. Through examining Carolina Caycedo's video documentary of a *perreo* dancing marathon in Rincón, Puerto Rico, and ethnographic data from a Latina/o queer dance club in Phoenix, Arizona, Rivera-Servera argues that the black aesthetics of reggaetón enabled queer dance practices that exceeded the heteropatriarchal politico-economic and representational frameworks of reggaetón. In offering the on-the-ground analytic of performance as an optic, the essay features the dance skills of reggaetoneras and their understanding of the racial economies of reggaetón as queer engagements, perhaps even interventions, with the gender politics of the genre.

From Puerto Rico, we head to Jamaica to engage music and theater. Lyndon Gill's essay, "I Represent Freedom: Diaspora and the Meta-Queerness of Dub Theater," engages the life and work of black queer Jamaican Canadian storyteller, playwright, and actor d'bi.young, who currently resides in Cape Town, South Africa, as a way into reading the radical queerness of one of her seemingly least queer plays. Gill first provides a brief history and genealogy of the dub music genre, an aural aesthetic birthed in late 1960s Jamaica, followed by the history of the moment in the late 1970s to early 1980s when Jamaican poets in Kingston and London first began to distill the sound principles of the relatively new music genre into "dub poetry." He then analyzes what he refers to as "the queer middle child" of d'bi.young's three-part dub theater *sankofa trilogy*, *benu*, which has no LGBT characters. Though d'bi.young openly and courageously identifies as queer, Gill argues that she actively refuses static categories of sexual orientation, especially if they are based on parochial presumptions about sex/gender transparency and stability, which invites us to expand the boundaries of queer recognition.

Staying with the Caribbean flows of queerness is Omise'eke Natasha Tinsley's "To Transcender Transgender: Choreographies of Gender Fluidity in the Performances of MilDred Gerestant." Tinsley analyzes the 1990s Haitian American performance artist MilDred Gerestant, who ascended to fame in the drag king scene, dressing, dancing, and dragging as a smooth mackdaddy who played with and subverted stereotypes of African American masculinity. Her recent performance work, however, moves her musical citations from hip hop to Haitian Vodou: "DanceHaitianGender" and "Transcender," both of which draw on Afro-Caribbean ritual, and particularly on the Haitian lwas (divinities) Danbala, Baron Samedi, and Ezili, to meditate on culturally specific imaginations of gender fluidity. Her performances integrate masculine and feminine variations of these lwas in order to creatively embody the limits of global northern vocabularies of "transgender," suggesting an alternative in *transcender*—that is, in engagement with the submerged Caribbean epistemology of syncretic religions. Tinsley offers a close reading of "I Transcender," exploring how and why Gerestant turns to Vodou not merely as a religious practice but also as an epistemology, as the only way of knowing gender and sexuality sufficiently complex enough to choreograph the racialized and classed genders that Haitians negotiate at home and in diaspora.

Bridging the Caribbean with South America, Tanya Saunders engages the black queer world-making among lesbians in Cuba and Brazil. Drawing on her experience as touring manager for a lesbian hip hop group, Saunders uses ethnographic methods to engage the ways in which black lesbians in the diaspora mobilize hip hop as a site of feminist activism. Beyond expanding the literature on queers in Cuba and Brazil—and women in particular—Saunders disavows the common logic that women and queers are invisible within hip hop. Indeed, she argues that these queer women actively integrate their African heritage, queerness, and artistry in a context where the explicit celebration of such imbricated identities—especially in Cuba and Brazil—is not the norm. Ultimately, Saunders believes that these women's artistic and activist employment of hip hop offers a different understanding of subject formation in the African diaspora.

Drag performance has always been a sign of gender play and variance but has, nonetheless, been a site of much debate about trafficking in misogyny and heteronormativity and, more recently, racist representation. In "The Body Beautiful: Black Drag, American Cinema, and the Heteroperpetually Ever After," La Marr Jurelle Bruce focuses on three films—*To Wong Foo*, *Romeo+Juliet*, and *Midnight in the Garden of Good and Evil*—that feature black drag queens that serve a particular use value within the rhetorical mise-en-scène of each film's racial, sexual, and gender politics. Theorizing the concept of "heteroperpetuity," a hegemonic form of heteronormative power that operates insidiously within the structures of American cinema, Bruce argues that the figure of the black drag queen actually potentially disrupts heteroperpetuity's power through "her" spectacular queerness and blackness.

Shifting from cisgender males' gender play to cisgender women performing masculinity, Kortney Ziegler moves between the distant archive of the Harlem Renaissance to the less distant period of the 1960s to rethink the notion of the "black sissy." In "Black Sissy Masculinity and the Politics of Dis-respectability," Ziegler examines the Harlem Renaissance performance artist Gladys Bentley and the ways in which her manipulations of gender suggest a type of kinky politics that offers a new space of black queer possibility. Specifically, he asserts that Bentley's appropriation of a fetishized image of black masculinity conjures up notions of "sissy play"—a type of BDSM role play where a male pleasurably embodies hyperfeminine attributes in order to offset his masculinity. Although Bentley did not identify as male, Ziegler interprets her work with the knowledge that black women have always been perceived as innately masculine due to competing discourses of white racism and black respectability politics, ultimately framing them within narratives of strength. He reads Bentley's instances of cross-dressing and vocal play as representative of a "black sissy" aesthetic that makes legible the interrelation of black queer and "normative sexualities," while transforming dominant notions of black female sexuality and gender.

In "Let's Play: Exploring Cinematic Black Lesbian Fantasy, Pleasure, and Pain," Jennifer DeClue takes up Juana María Rodríguez's challenge to embrace the pleasure of "untamed erotics" and not shy away from exploring the materiality of sexuality and the problematics of sex play and fantasy among racialized subjectivities. In so doing, DeClue examines three films that feature black lesbian fantasy, BDSM play, and sexual pleasure. She focuses on the tensions engendered by visualizing black lesbian sex acts, given the history of black women's sexual exploitation, and the *politics of silence* as well as the *culture of dissemblance* used to combat degradation. The essay also examines the manner in which sexual fantasy and play works out traumas of racialized sexual violence while leaving open the possibility that these cinematic representations of lesbian sexuality may traumatize as they work to disencumber the politics of visibility and silence that always already haunt black women's sexuality.

As discussed earlier, digital media and cyberspace has had an increasing impact on black queer sexual agency, desire, and representation. Combined with the discourses that circulate in HIV/AIDS prevention—especially from official agencies such as the Centers for Disease Control and Prevention—virtuality becomes a complex "web" of contradictions when it comes to black queer sexuality and sexual health. The next two essays engage these questions. In "Black Gay (Raw) Sex," Marlon M. Bailey theorizes high-risk sexual behavior in black gay communities. Drawing on interviews and analyses of black gay men's profiles on gay sex websites, he demonstrates how HIV/AIDS prevention discourses and institutions' epidemiological surveillance of unprotected sex among black gay men actually works against their aim to stop the spread of infection because it fails to encompass black gay male sexual pleasure and desire. Arguing for a move beyond a reductive causal relationship between sexual behavior and contagion that buttresses the pathologization and surveillance of black queer sexuality, Bailey calls for a reconceptualization of prevention methods and discourse in health care that would take into account the multiple factors that account for the sexual behavior of black gay men, including the need and desire for intimacy. Given the day-to-day struggles within structures of systemic racism, classism, and homophobia, black queer men, Bailey suggests, are always already "at risk"; unprotected sex is a risky behavior that at least provides them with a form of intimacy and affection that they do not otherwise receive.

Shaka McGlotten also engages the ways black queers employ the web as part of their sexuality but examines it from the perspective of the body as "data." In "Black Data," he employs the notion of "black data" to explore the ways in which black queer people are hailed, as well as ignored or forgotten, by big data. He also explores the ways black queers trouble the increasingly invisible or taken-for-granted operations of states and corporations that seek to acquire and store detailed dossiers of citizen-consumers. Thus, "black data" evokes counter- or hidden knowledges and stealthy forms of resistance ("black ops"). In particular, McGlotten applies a materialist black queer analytic to the "deep web," the algorithms, databases, and protocols that make up the vast majority of the Internet but which are usually hidden from view. Drawing on case studies from everyday life and artistic practice, McGlotten links the deep web to the ways black bodies, and especially black queer bodies, are understood as data points, as statistical objects or deviations, rather than as ontologically material persons. In other words, how do black queers navigate the perils of data fields in online queer spaces where disclosing one's racial identity can make one vulnerable to violence?

The virtual is not only a space of contestation relative to racialized sexual desire but also as an antiblack and antiqueer mobilizing force perpetuated in the name of neighborhood "safety." Zachary Blair's "Boystown: Gay Neighborhoods, Social Media, and the (Re)production of Racism" takes up these questions by examining the response of residents to a rash of violent neighborhood muggings purportedly perpetrated by black queer youth in the Boystown "gayborhood" on the north side of Chicago. Blair demonstrates how local discourses and processes and contemporary social formations are shaped and reshaped at the dynamic interface of cultural representations, collective processes, and individual subjectivity. Through analyzing the discourses that emerged on a Facebook page created to increase communication and organization among neighborhood residents and the Chicago police, Blair highlights how issues of race, gender, class, and sexuality quickly dominated all forms of communication on the web page and became a hostile arena that shaped social relations and divided neighborhood residents.

Continuing the focus on black queer geographies and the political economic effects of gentrification is Kwame Holmes's "Beyond the Flames: Queering the History of the 1968 D.C. Riot." Traditionally, historians locate the origins of black communal violence within housing shortages, systemic unemployment, and police brutality endemic to the post–World War II American ghetto. Here though, Holmes asserts that the sexual valences of ghettoization contributed to black urbanites' willingness to eschew the rational course of liberal reform in favor of the riotous release offered by the destruction of private property. Focusing on the Shaw area of Washington, D.C., Holmes engages the metropolitan police department's sexual regulation of black commercial areas, the sexual anxieties spawned by overcrowding in slum housing, and the symbolic work queer black residents, across the sexuality spectrum performed to mark the neighborhood as in decline.

The carceral state affects both black queers as much as the heterosexual black community. In "The Strangeness of Progress and the Uncertainty of Blackness," Treva Ellison analyzes the 1994 Violent Crime Control and Law Enforcement Act, the largest federal policing bill in U.S. history, to understand how the discursive production of black nonnormativity and gender nonconformity fits into the production of blackness as existing outside juridical and ethical universality. The author argues that under neoliberal multiculturalism, antiblack racism is reproduced via inclusive reforms based on gender and sexuality. The impossibility of legal redress for black injury opens up the possibility for the production of representational spaces of convergence to talk about how multiple experiences of harm and violence cohere around the production of places of absence of ethical concern. Because blackness is at once overseen and unknown to the law, a contradiction that conditions spatial differentiation, Ellison considers what a politics of scale can do for multiple expressions of blackness in the current moment.

Audre Lorde is a much-revered figure within black queer studies. Her theorization of the erotic is often used to articulate a mode of solidarity in which people from disparate backgrounds can come together to combat oppression. In "Re-membering Audre: Adding Lesbian Feminist Mother Poet to Black," however, Amber Jamilla Musser refocuses our attention on Lorde's identity politics. She asks how Lorde's claiming of the labels *lesbian, feminist, mother*, and *poet* shift our understanding of the erotic to grapple more fully with the legacy that black lesbian feminism has left to queer studies. In particular, Musser argues that Lorde's identity politics rescript the place of the mother and lesbian sex within black queer studies. Lorde theorizes both together as an important sphere of political action, thereby enlarging genealogies of black lesbian feminism and providing new avenues with which to think queer theory.

Also paying homage to Audre Lorde, but with an eye toward popular culture and contemporary social movements, is Kaila Adia Story in "On the Cusp of Deviance: Respectability Politics and the Cultural Marketplace of Sameness," a polemic that questions the efficacy of homonormativity. The essay examines the consequences of presenting identity as an "either/or" or "and/or" dichotomy through the visual and rhetorical strategies of the "return to marriage and respectability" platforms of black heteronormativity and the whitening and sanitizing platforms of the marriage equality movement. Throughout the essay, Story elucidates how the "old" way of doing racialized sexuality work is still very much present within popular media. Further, she discusses the possessive investment in the whitening of the same-sex marriage movement and the investment in heteronormativity by black cultural icons like Tyler Perry and Steve Harvey. She urges queer people of color to continue their fight for their own agency and spaces, and to do so with a consciousness that shows how their oppression has functioned primarily through the state's racialization of their gendered and sexual identities.

Alexis Pauline Gumbs and Julia Roxanne Wallace's "Something Else to Be: Generations of Black Queer Brilliance and the Mobile Homecoming Experiential Archive" continues the tradition of their foremothers such as Audre Lorde, Barbara Smith, and Pat Parker—black lesbian activists grounded in quotidian theory. Drawing on the archive of the Mobile Homecoming Project, a cross-country project in which the authors travel the United States creating ritual for and with black LGBTQ visionaries, the essay looks at what it means to move from individual recognition (neither white nor male nor straight) to a collective "something else to be." Putting pleasurable queer pressure on the terms *generation, brilliance*, and *home*, this piece uses the concept of the "experiential archive" not to insert the value of difference into an existing narrative or to draw on normative resources but rather to generate alternative resources and narratives for coming home.

Over the past decade or so, I have mentored over a dozen graduate students, many of whom are now tenured professors and have their own monographs. It has been a privilege to watch them begin as curious students and blossom into fierce theorists, activists, and performers. And while I often tease a few of them about remaining on the teat too long and that my "milk" is all gone, the truth is, I secretly want all of them to stay close to the nest, not so that I may necessarily continue to nourish *them* but so that they may continue to teach *me*. The essays collected in *No Tea, No Shade* have done just that. They have energized me to think differently about how quickly the world can turn—for the better. To continue to throw shade on the heteronormative reproduction trope and celebrate its resignification in ballroom culture, the House of Black Queer Studies was built by mothers and fathers (and those who embody both) who were/are grand and fierce, but it is the children who are constantly remodeling the house, keeping it updated, and making it the envy of the neighbors, all the while slaying and snatching trophies as their parents watch on with a careful side eye—no tea, no shade![34]

NOTES

1. John D'Emilio, *The World Turned: Essays on Gay History, Politics, and Culture* (Durham, NC: Duke University Press, 2002).

2. "Children" is a black gay vernacular term that refers to other gay folks of any age. My usage here in particular does not necessarily refer to chronological age because some of the contributors are my contemporaries, while some are considerably younger. I do mean to suggest, however, that despite *chronological* age, all these scholars are young in the profession.

3. See Henry Louis Gates Jr., *The Signifying Monkey: A Theory of African American Literary Criticism* (Oxford: Oxford University Press, 1988).

4. E. Patrick Johnson and Mae G. Henderson, "Introduction: Queering Black Studies/'Quaring' Queer Studies," in Johnson and Henderson, eds., *Black Queer Studies: A Critical Anthology* (Durham, NC: Duke University Press, 2005), 1.

5. Johnson and Henderson, "Introduction," 2, 90–105.

6. One of the critiques of the critique of the absence of diaspora theory is that oftentimes theories of diaspora proceed as if they have no relation to U.S. imperialism, as if displacement did not and does not continue to occur within U.S. borders or, alternatively, that the diasporic subject is always already at odds with an American one. In *The Erotic Life of Racism* (Durham, NC: Duke University Press, 2012), Sharon Holland argues that this myopic definition of diaspora, paralleled with a concomitant

binary of "United States–based vs. diasporic," "is blind to the ways in which native peoples have also shaped discourse about the diasporic as well as the national, both at home and abroad" (86).

7. D'Emilio, *World Turned*, ix–x.

8. Cornell University and Dartmouth University both did searches in such areas in 2013, and Spelman College, a women's historically black institution, conducted a search for a scholar of black queer theory in 2014.

9. These faculty include Lyndon K. Gill, Omi Osun Joni Jones, Xavier Livermon, Matt Richardson, Omise'eke Natasha Tinsley, and Lisa B. Thompson.

10. See, for example, the special issue of *Gender, Place and Culture,* edited by Marlon M. Bailey and Rashad Shabazz, "Gender and Sexual Geographies of Blackness: New Black Cartographies of Resistance and Survival (Part 2)," 21, no. 4 (2014); Jafari S. Allen, "Black/Queer/Diaspora at the Current Conjuncture," *GLQ: A Journal of Lesbian and Gay Studies* 18, nos. 2–3 (2012): 211–48; and Stacey Patton, "Who's Afraid of Black Sexuality?" *Chronicle of Higher Education* (December 3, 2012): 1–25.

11. Shaka McGlotten, *Virtual Intimacies: Media, Affect, and Queer Sociality* (Albany: State University of New York Press, 2014), 3.

12. Dwight A. McBride, *Why I Hate Abercrombie and Fitch: Essays on Race and Sexuality* (New York: New York University Press, 2005), 110.

13. Gary Fischer, *Gary in Your Pocket*, ed. Eve Kosofsky Sedgwick (Durham, NC: Duke University Press, 1996), 65.

14. Robert Reid-Pharr, *Black Gay Man* (New York: New York University Press, 2001), 94.

15. McBride, *Why I Hate Abercrombie and Fitch*, 98.

16. Marlon M. Bailey, "What I'm Told, What I Want, and What I Do" (paper presented at the Whose Beloved Community? conference, Emory University, Atlanta, GA, March 28, 2014).

17. The term "mother" comes from the black ballroom scene and denotes someone who plays a motherly figure but who does not necessarily have to be a biological woman.

18. In *Unlimited Intimacy: Reflections on the Subculture of Bareback* (Chicago: University of Chicago Press, 2009), Tim Dean examines the practice of barebacking primarily among white queer men in San Francisco. The study is an important contribution to the reconceptualization of sexual desire in the context of HIV/AIDS prevention discourse and the homonormative impulse of contemporary queer culture. Curiously, Dean's study does not focus on the practice of barebacking among men of color and particularly black men. I use the term "curious" because of the statistics that suggest that black men who have sex with other men are more likely than any other group to seroconvert. Moreover, when Dean does discuss race at any substantive length, it is to take to task two black scholars—Frantz Fanon and Dwight A. McBride—for

their critiques of racial fetishism. This critique of Fanon and McBride is followed by a brief close reading of a porn film titled *Niggas' Revenge*. I leave to others to engage the merits of Dean's reading of Fanon, McBride, and *Niggas' Revenge*, but what I find troubling is how, on the one hand, Dean ignores an important racialized population, failing to get its perspective on barebacking, and, on the other, rigorously critiques (on different grounds) two black scholars' responses to racial fetish. Fanon and McBride are not beyond critique, but it seems disingenuous not to buttress a critique of the *experience* of racial fetish with counterexamples from other raced subjects, particularly when the study in question is based on ethnographic methods.

19. Essex Hemphill, "Now We Think," in *Ceremonies: Prose and Poetry* (San Francisco: Cleis Press, 1992), 169.

20. This is another point on which new theorists and older ones may diverge. In other words, whereas black queer theorists of my generation and earlier might condone the *analysis of* raw sex, some of the new black queer theorists also condone the *practice of* raw sex and sometimes acknowledge their own engagement in and enjoyment of such practices in print. I would argue that this, too, exemplifies another major shift between the generations of scholars.

21. See, for example, Mireille Miller-Young, *A Taste for Brown Sugar: Black Women in Pornography* (Durham, NC: Duke University Press, 2014) and Jennifer C. Nash, *The Black Body in Ecstasy: Reading Race, Reading Pornography* (Durham, NC: Duke University Press, 2014).

22. Vincent Woodard, *The Delectable Negro: Human Consumption and Homoeroticism within U.S. Slave Culture* (New York: New York University Press, 2014), 220.

23. Black feminist theorist Jennifer Nash also develops a provocative analytic that she calls "black anality" in order to argue "how black female sexuality is imagined to be rooted in (and perhaps generative of) certain kinds of filthy spaces, particularly the ghetto; how black sexuality is constructed as literally and metaphorically dirty; how black sexuality is posited as toxic, nonproductive, and nonreproductive; and how black sexuality is imagined as wasteful." Nash sees her argument as a critique of black feminist theory, which "has long examined the buttocks as an imagined locus of racial-sexual difference and which has developed a set of analytics that now predominate in the study of black female sexualities: spectacularity, excess, grotesquerie, and display." See Jennifer Nash, "Black Anality," *GLQ: A Journal of Lesbian and Gay Studies* 20, no. 4 (2014): 441.

24. Miller-Young, *Taste for Brown Sugar*, viii.

25. Evelynn M. Hammonds, "Black (W)holes and the Geometry of Black Female Sexuality," in *Feminism Meets Queer Theory*, eds. Elizabeth Weed and Naomi Schor (Bloomington: Indiana University Press, 1997), 136–56.

26. Sharon Patricia Holland, *The Erotic Life of Racism* (Durham, NC: Duke University Press, 2012), 68–69.

27. Hammonds, "Black (W)holes," 152 (emphasis added).

28. Hortense Spillers, "Interstices: A Small Drama of Words," in *Black, White and in Color: Essays on American Literature and Culture* (Chicago: University of Chicago Press, 2003), 152. I wish to note, however, that some black feminists of this new generation of scholars point out the tensions between black feminism and black queer theory. Brittney C. Cooper raises serious concerns about what she sees as black feminism not being taken seriously as "theory" and instead co-opted by black queer theorists (specifically black and Latino male writers) who "place us [black feminist theorists] on a pedestal, styling black feminism as a foundational stepping stone to other more exciting sites of inquiry while another group reduces our contributions to the status of the intervention, allowing them to engage in liberal acts of incorporation and inclusion, and then move on, in the name of progress" (12). See Cooper, "Love No Limit: Towards a Black Feminist Future (In Theory)," *The Black Scholar* 45, no. 4 (2015): 12–14.

29. L. H. Stallings, *Mutha' Is Half a Word: Intersections of Folklore, Vernacular, Myth, and Queerness in Black Female Culture* (Columbus: Ohio State University Press, 2007), 1.

30. Toni Morrison, *Playing in the Dark* (Cambridge, MA: Harvard University Press, 1992).

31. Matt Richardson, *The Queer Limit of Black Memory: Black Lesbian Literature and Irresolution* (Columbus: Ohio State University Press, 2013), 7.

32. *Still Black* follows the lives of six female-to-male transgender men. The film is the first of its kind to focus exclusively on the experiences of black transmen. In addition to winning the Queer Black Cinema Isaac Julien Experimental Award and the Reelout Film Festival Audience Choice Best Documentary Award, the film is taught in gender studies courses across the country. Page and Richardson's essay theorizes how black transgender people are subject to institutionalized racism that demands "from all Blacks their conformity with gendered embodiments of racially disciplined civility" (57). See Enoch H. Page and Matt U. Richardson, "On the Fear of Small Numbers: A Twenty-first-Century Prolegomenon of the U.S. Black Transgender Experience," in *Black Sexualities: Probing Powers, Passions, Practices, and Policies,* eds. Juan Battle and Sandra Barnes (Newark: Rutgers University Press, 2009), 57–81. Finally, the number of black transgender scholars who are in tenure-track positions or tenured has increased enormously over the past few years. Among these are Treva Ellison, Kai M. Green, Matt Richardson, and C. Riley Snorton, to name a few.

33. Allen, "Black/Queer/Diaspora at the Current Conjuncture," 211.

34. In ballroom parlance, "slay and snatch" means to "beat your competitors and snatch (win) a trophy." See Marlon M. Bailey, *Butch Queens Up in Pumps: Gender, Performance, and Ballroom Culture in Detroit* (Ann Arbor: University of Michigan Press, 2013), 253–54.

1

Black/Queer Rhizomatics

Train Up a Child in the Way Ze Should Grow . . .

JAFARI S. ALLEN

☺

For All of Them

WELL CHILD, I WILL TELL YOU: Audre Lorde never promised you a rose garden. Or a crystal stair swept clean of tacks, with no boards torn up, or places where there ain't been no carpet on the floor/bare.[1] Rather, she and others have bequeathed a *this or that* which promises only continued devastation and certain destruction, on one hand, or possibilities—speech, visibility (if not yet recognition), articulation, home-making, joy, love, for example—on the other, which must be worked for, and for which there are no guarantees. As enticement toward protracted struggle, Lorde offers the following:

> *. . . If we win
> there is no telling.
> we seek beyond history
> for a new and more possible meeting.*[2]

Far from a rose garden, this meditation, toward a critical pedagogical agenda, assays a renarrativization of and for Black studies—finding rhizomes rather than "roots." And, indeed, as always, routes—in and out of families, discourses, and movements.[3] Finding nourishment, as water lilies do, in deep dark muck. Persistent like bamboo and other creeping grasses. Rare and delicate like orchids. Here I want to propose a Black/queer rhizomatic *agencement*—including literatures, politics, and methodologies—as well as demonstrate a Black/queer rhizomatic way of seeing and saying.[4] In nature, rhizomes arise from underground or underwater connections/roots/routes that are neither limited to one place nor destined to go in only one direction. The rhizomatic thus represents a queer temporality and sociality that is processual—not teleological or "narrativized in advance."[5] A rhizomatic conceptualization of relations, space, and time. This temporality is one of time collapsed or at least reconfigured—not "straight time," in which, for example, what is putatively most important happens in the daytime, or in which one "grows out of" same-sex "play" or finally "settles down" into heteronormative or homonormative sociality. In this time, one can project imaginations into the future and cut into the past—all in the pursuit of an elaborated litany for thriving. In this space, desires and socialities claim family and children not merely from biological or legal means but also by a process of nurture and nourishment. In some respects, Audre Lorde has already given us this utopic vision of work, love, and struggle:

> looking inward and outward
> at once before and after
> seeking a now that can breed
> futures
> like bread in our children's mouths
> so their dreams will not reflect
> the death of ours[6]

Here I take inspiration not only from Hughes and Lorde but also from French philosophers Gilles Deleuze and Félix Guattari's notion of the rhizome—including and beyond tradition and history: creative, promiscuous, underground or underwater, multiple, and sometimes contradictory—to propose Black/queer rhizomatics. The rhizome (from the Greek for "mass of roots") is the mode of propagation and sustenance for plants as diverse as the lotus, bamboo, bunch grasses, ginger, irises, and orchids. Digging up a clump of bamboo from its so-called roots will not mean that the bamboo will not grow at that site. Deracinated never. The lotus flower seems to appear out of nowhere "without roots" but gains nutrients and information buried deeply in its dark, watery grove. In *A Thousand*

Plateaus, Deleuze and Guattari encourage us to "form rhizomes and not roots, never plant! Don't sow, forage! Be neither a One nor a Many, but multiplicities! Form a line, never a point! . . . and let your loves be like the wasp and the orchid. As they sing of old man river:

> He don't plant taters
> Don't plant cotton
> Them that plants them is soon
> forgotten
> But old man river he just keeps rollin'
> along."[7]

If that ain't "quare," I don't know what is![8] With varying intensities, Black diaspora scholars have already followed the seductive pull of Deleuze and Guattari's nomadic rhizomatic model of analysis—notably, including Paul Gilroy and Édouard Glissant. They were each, of course, searching for new ways to engage age-old experiences of forced, coerced, and free movement; connection; and difficult, materially consequential origin stories (if not "origins") in the context of modernity. Glissant held that "rhizomatic thought is the principle behind . . . poetics of relations, in which each and every identity is extended through a relationship with the other." As J. Lorand Matory reminds us, Gilroy too flirted with the notion of the rhizome/rhizomatic in *Black Atlantic*, but does not pursue this in his search for ways to read intermixture, exchange, hybridity, and doubleness through chronotypes—famously settling on the figure of the ship.[9] While I am not aware of the particular language of rhizomes previously being taken up in Black/queer or Black feminist work, the spirit of this is clearly at work in the ways scholars and artists have engaged the question of "roots" and routes—not necessarily apropos of moving place but of reckoning ancestry (in terms of claiming and recalling early same-gender-loving artists and writers) and shifting, combining, and rethinking aesthetic, intellectual, and political traditions. You may consider this both on everyday and more rarified levels. Think, for example, about Cathy Cohen's skillful and timely reversal of strategic early twentieth-century DuBoisian and Lockean politics of representation and respectability, to focus precisely on "punks, bulldaggers, and welfare queens" toward finally achieving the ends for which a preceding generation of Black scholars had also fought. The Black/queer rhizome is generative, as it inspires connection beyond a staid, linear genealogy; it rejects old teleologies of heteronormative natural "progress" from a single root or (family) tree. Feel here the ineluctable association and relatedness with "intersectionality." The ways in which African (descended) groups (dis)identify as Black (or "black"), Afro-hyphenated, Kréyol, Creole, mixed, or other ways of naming or signifying (Black) hybridity do not occur in a vacuum. These choices are conditioned by particularities of place, as well as other relations that include and simultaneously surpass the local. This of course includes Black LGBTQ/SGL hybridity which is variously and oftentimes controversially named today vis-à-vis this clumsy acronym to which we necessarily continue to add letters.

I have already suggested that in what many of us now call Black queer studies, as "outside children" of Black studies and queer studies, we claim new ways to queerly trace our emergences beyond patronymic reconstruction, to do a new dance—precipitating a shift, structuring a conjuncture. In tracing intellectual, artistic, and activist rhizomatic formations, we are compelled to envision and produce work that is deeply humane and capacious. Our analyses reflect not only "real life" on the ground but also speculate on liberatory models from the past, and project our imaginations forward, to possible futures. This call is not to imagine one single rhizome—of, let's say, bamboo—creeping all over the world, but rather a historically derived sociocultural system with political-economic structures in its "DNA." For our purposes in this meditation, the Black/queer rhizomatic *agencement* is most profitably thought of as a *habit of mind*—a way of seeing and saying as much as a mode of thinking or doing. The rhizomatic is beyond tradition and memory: creative, promiscuous, multiple, and often contradictory. Like this essay. The generative value of difference, performativity, and play in the rhizomatic, and its grounding in a commitment to address material circumstances and the metaphysical at once, parallel Black/queer poetic traditions. Like Black/queer, the rhizome, Deleuze and Guattari offer, "doesn't begin and doesn't end, but is always in the middle, between things, interbeing, intermezzo."[10] Today, this is where Black/queer studies finds itself—in medias res. That is, entering into conversations already begun—not with the intention to falsify, but rather to more fundamentally reorder, critically retell stories long told and overlooked, and compose new stories out of our word-rich grammars.

Thus, the analysis offered here emerges from close readings of important nodes of the present moment and the recent past, to theorize a "new and more possible meeting" of our artists, activists, scholars, policymakers, and intellectuals.[11] This formulation seeks to include and move beyond disagreements around language of "same-gender loving," "LGBT," "queer," and "DL" in the United States, and various local names and concepts used to (self)identify gender nonnormative, "sexual minority," or otherwise nonheteronormative individuals of Africa(n descent), in various parts of the world. Looking beyond "survival" that was *never meant* for us, toward societal transformation and thriving, will require shifting the narratives we have rehearsed, toward a future in which we are indeed "fluent in each other's histories" and conversant in each other's imaginations.[12] Scholars have already assayed jeremiads, corrections, and agendas that were warranted by the moments in which they were offered, and some of which are essential to return to consider at this important social-cultural conjuncture. While elements of each find expression here, this is not (only) a critique or a genealogy or a lament, but rather a meditation taking a hybrid form in an attempt to "say some things I think ought to be said" about Black (and) queer intellectual traditions and pedagogies.[13] After all, this is an important moment to critically reassess (and celebrate) the project we have come to know as Black queer studies. Today, the economic outlook is foggy; the political landscape is stony, contradictory, and riddled with fissures. There are reminders every day—from the banal to the spectacular—of the denial of Black beauty, Black dignity, and Black life. Further, the academic and intellectual foundations on which Black studies was built seem to shift beneath our feet (still). This is a conjunctural moment, full of complex challenges and opportunities—a few which are new (or newly configured), and others that remind us, *plus ça change, plus c'est la même chose.*

Given increased visibility, articulation, and backlash, in the wake of the Combahee River Collective Statement, the Black Nations/Queer Nations conference, books such as the *Boundaries of Blackness: AIDS and the Breakdown of Black Politics*, the Black Queer Studies in the Millennium conference and resulting *Black Queer Studies: A Critical Anthology*, and the raft of monographs produced in the last twenty or so years, for example: Whither this project that Essex Hemphill described as the "creation of evidence of being . . . powerful enough to transform the very nature of our existence"?[14] Of course, to be precise, the project that Hemphill helped create and spoke of here in his introduction to the first edition of *Brother to Brother: New Writing by Black Gay Men*, was not an academic one but part and parcel of a larger Black lesbian and gay movement, led by artists and intellectuals. What are the conditions of possibility for beautiful and transformative Black/queer work today? Where should we look for inspiration? To whom are we accountable? How should those of us located in academe respond and push the project forward?

Black/Queer Teaching in the Black Studies Classroom

I am not naïve enough to believe that scholarly work *creates* everyday resistance and survival by the most multiply vulnerable among us. But it can give light to it—helping expand recognition of those sites as legitimate political expression and providing the basis for institutional support. Moreover, despite attacks on Black studies and other reminders that the U.S. academy is an engine of racialized capitalism, just as much or more than it is a society of friends of each other's mind, teaching is clearly and incontrovertibly a site in which we can work to evidence being and to transform ourselves and our students. In any event, it is my work to do where I am. After all, as poet Marvin K. White quoted to me from his own scriptures and prophesying Black/queer genius: among our highest calling is to "train up a child in the way he should vogue, and when he is old he will turn it."[15]

So, *what if*: What if the now more than forty-year track record of Black feminist artistry, scholarship, and activism were taken seriously as the formative center of late twentieth-century and twenty-first-century Black studies? What if concepts of "normativity" and "respectability" were critically taken to task and taken back by Black studies, pushed forward and transformed? What if experimentation, affect and futurity—some of the scholarly, artistic, and activist modes and methods of early Black knowledge and cultural producers, now repackaged as new and sexy and white, were taken seriously—that is, funded, reenergized, published, hired, and promoted in Black studies?

Currently, many scholars seem to agree with the Combahee River Collective's Black feminist lesbian statement that gender, race, class, and, increasingly, sexual identities are mutually constituting and interpenetrating.[16] Still, a commitment to producing and legitimizing work that actually takes up intersectional or interstitial analyses is still ahead of us in the traditional disciplines of the academy. While it is sadly true that the uni-disciplines proceed in many cases as if Black studies had never made the contributions it has,[17] and as if we are not here today, what if Black studies wholeheartedly embraced a rhizomatic Black/queer feminist habit of mind? What if all Black studies courses on the U.S. South or on labor or religion used E. Patrick Johnson's *Sweet Tea* as a main text, or those who study African religious philosophy required students to grapple with Oshun's performativity and embodiment in the work of Omi Osun Joni Jones or Omise'eke Natasha Tinsley? What if we learned and debated and taught distinctions between DL, discreet, MSM, cisgender, transgender, femme butch bottom and top—how this self-naming and negotiation of "identity" and behavior is highly contingent and interarticulated with race, color, and nationality, for example—in Intro courses? Not only through the scholarly theorization of Matt Richardson and C. Riley Snorton, for example, but also Sharon Bridgforth's juke-joint poetic theorization of "mens, womens, some that is both, some who are neither," which likewise demonstrates a more capacious understanding and appreciation of gender expression in Black communities than current notions of sexuality, (trans) gender, or queerness can hold.[18] How might we transform our students' understanding of "family" by placing Mignon Moore's *Invisible Families* on the first-year African American studies seminar syllabus, or by continuing to explode business-as-usual U.S. centrism of who gets to be Black and where, through emerging Black/queer scholarship in and on Brazil, Trinidad and Tobago, Dominican Republic, New Orleans, Canada, Germany, Cuba and the French Department of the Caribbean, for example?[19]

What if we rose to the demand of our complex now, which of course Joseph Beam would have called "coldblooded," or the brand of truth that Hemphill deemed "ass-splitting"?[20] The practice of attending to the abject, the deviant, and the perverse incorporation of queer concepts and methodologies (and indeed bodies and personal political practices) alongside/on top/or bottoming canonical Black studies authors and concepts constitutes another "litany for survival" (and thriving!).[21] Here is a moment of particularism to complement the abstract: teaching a junior seminar in African American studies. While the official title is "Interdisciplinary Approaches to African American Studies," my students and I have more work to do than a surface understanding of "interdisciplinarity" would reveal. Beyond the elementary practice of using one or another method or following or subverting a few disciplinary conventions, Black studies currently has a strong and central rhizomatic Black/queer feminist habit of mind at work (if not always acknowledged). It allows us to see and say connections and disjuncture across time, space, genre, discipline, theme, and theoretical framework. After Ferguson/after Staten Island/after Gaza/and after and after, I renamed this course "Black Studies (What Are We Doing Here?)" to begin to seriously attend to the epistemological, ontological, and phenomenological dimensions of this question—locally at Yale, in

New Haven, and apropos the project of Black studies—more than forty-five years after the establishment of the first programs and more than thirty years following Stuart Hall's fixing query, "What is this 'black' in black popular culture?" In the course, we begin with the old story of the rise of Black studies and take a *queer look*—sideways—at narratives of a bloodless, friendly, Ford-funded emergence of African American studies at Yale.[22] Before we move on with Black studies' intellectual history, readings by Joy James, George Lipsitz, and Ann DuCille then lay down the gauntlet for those who would aspire to Talented Tenth race management, white liberal exceptionalism, or single-narrative "been-there" blackness.[23] Then, we begin. In late January, we read "A Black Feminist Statement" by the Combahee River Collective, as this work represents a central pillar of the habit of mind that animates the course and my own work and, I argue, provides foundation for the work of Black studies today, focusing on what in 1977 they theorized as "the development of integrated analysis and practice based upon the fact that the major systems of oppression are interlocking. The synthesis of these oppressions creates the conditions of our lives."[24] Despite loud and sometimes ugly disavowals of "identity politics" and recent pressure from some in queer studies to eschew "intersectionality," this stream of theorization in fact makes queer studies and women's studies and ethnic studies possible. This same week, students will watch Cathy Cohen's lecture "#Do Black Lives Matter? From Michael Brown to CeCe McDonald: On Black Death and LGBTQ Politics," in which she powerfully reminds the queer studies audience what is at stake in LGBTQ capitulation to single-issue neoliberal politics. This is followed by her "Deviance as Resistance: A New Research Agenda for the Study of Black Politics." For further reading, they can go to one of Barbara Christian's classic essays, "But Who Do You Really Belong to—Black Studies or Women's Studies?" To take seriously the propositions I set forth abstractly above, the course goes on to mash up Claude McKay's "If We Must Die" (I casually and purposefully mention that he was a man who loved men, a Marxist, and a Jamaican) with programmatic and review essays by Farah Griffin, Herman Beavers, and Elizabeth Alexander. Some of the "greatest hits" of Black studies are on this syllabus, along with new and experimental work, and work representing not only (Black studies' revolt against) unidisciplines but also political and national approaches, which form our multidimensional "interdisciplinarity," which I offer here as *rhizomatic*.

The Radical Potential of "Queer"

The word "queer" never fails to rattle, offend, or perhaps slightly annoy at least a few readers. This is understandable. Please allow me to explain why I continue to find this concept useful, albeit contingent. Apparently, the larger project of queer theory is currently experiencing an existential crisis, brought on by its limited archives, lack of engagement with on-the-ground movement, and turning away from radical feminist rhizomes that sought intersectional approaches. But also, the movement of time and growth—adding perspectives and voices—has necessitated the shifts and reevaluation many scholars pose as "crisis." Queer theory now wonders, *to be or not to be*—a grave and/or a rectum, for example, to see *no future* at all, or to imagine a *then*, or perhaps an *after*.[25] In its form most usefully aligned with Black/queer studies, it envisions (queer of color) *utopias*, *socialities*, and *queer diasporas*, and it values *failure as a queer art*.[26]

For me, as well as a number of Black/queer scholars, artists, writers, activists, and archivists, queer theorists De Lauretis, Warner, Butler, Sedgwick, Bersani, and others arrived on our bookshelves only after we had already imbibed the political and poetic nectars of intellectual activism and intersectional politics offered by Black lesbian and gay poets, essayists, and scholars. Venturing outside the college, to bars and living rooms, meeting spaces, demonstrations, and moist dark places, provided the lifesaving intellectual and political shifts scholars now reflect in Black queer studies. My introduction to such thinkers as Audre Lorde, Cheryl Clarke, Barbara Smith, Pat Parker, Essex Hemphill, and Joseph Beam came from friends I met and the intense political education I received in organizations like the African American Lesbian and Gay Organization, Coalition of African Descent, Second Sunday in Atlanta, Gay Men of African Descent, Other Countries, Audre Lorde Project, and Aya Institute in New York. It seems that many folks coming up now continue to find Black/queer theorization in essays, poetry, and political praxis most useful in their lives and political organizing, as majority white LGBT organizations and queer theory continue to resist deep inextricable intersectionality and embodied narrativization of "bulldaggers, (especially) welfare queens," and poor Black folks executed in the name of neoliberal police order.

In the 1990s and early 2000s, a number of Black and brown LGBT observers and critics warned of the mainstreaming of the LGBT and queer liberation movement—that is, reconfiguring it as a gay rights *campaign*. Since then the agendas of mainstream (read white and middle class and largely cisgender male controlled) organizations have been moving forward. The call for inclusion of gays in the military, the gay marriage movement, and the push for gay representation in corporate media have all experienced significant successes. According to "A New Queer Agenda," this has achieved primacy by hewing to two tactics: "The first is to shrink the field of LGBT politics so that it only represents a narrow strand of liberal identity politics, one that only recognizes immediately and exclusively 'gay' issues as legitimate and that sees formal, legal equality as the end goal. The second is to argue that increasing lesbian and gay representation in dominant institutions lifts all queer people—call it the trickle-down theory of gay rights."[27]

Of course, Cathy Cohen pointed this out twenty years ago.[28] In 1997, she called for "a politics where the nonnormative and marginal position of *punks, bulldaggers, and welfare queens*" is the basis for progressive transformational coalitional work.[29] By 2004 she had developed this into a new research agenda for Black studies, in which the central theoretic sees "deviance as resistance."[30] While scholars situated in the elite academy largely arrived relatively late to the Black lesbian and gay party, a significant number of folks began and remain committed to on-the-ground (political and artistic) work. Moreover, a number of scholars—too numerous and important to do justice to in this space—have made significant contributions, following this ethic of looking beyond the polite, pragmatic, or politically convenient. In "A New Queer Agenda" Black gay activist-intellectual Kenyon Farrow writes: "But whatever we think about the mainstream equality movement, it is almost finished with its agenda, and thank goodness. Most of the policy issues that the mainstream LGBT movement has made the central focus of its agenda are already won." Finally, he asks, in "a collective roar to the open skies: *Can't we do better than equality?*"[31] Today, given the current downward mobility of the 99 percent, queer theorist Lisa Duggan and the contributors to "A New Queer Agenda" propose what they hold is a new set of issues for a revitalized queer movement with a global democratic vision, reaching across lines of race, ethnicity, gender and gender expression, class, religion, and nationality."[32] In 2014, in the wake of the police executions of Eric Brown, Tamir Rice, Mike Brown, and others, Cohen pointed out that the "performative solidarity" of LGBTQ groups actually belies complicity with the selfsame neoliberal policies that support the fact that "in fact, Black lives do not matter."[33]

No Justice No Peace <Oooh>. No Racist Ass Po-lice <Oooh>.

Today, the children are turning it. They are turning inveterate politics and strategies on their heads, literally snatching the mic from stalwart crusaders who are by now perhaps too comfortably adjacent to power; the children are seizing the worldwide stage that the Internet provides; and they are turning civil rights songs and spirituals into *a vogue*. Their turn away from or, more precisely, inside out of strategies of respectability and comportment is at once innovative and traditional with respect to Black radical politics and letters. While the Great Men of the late nineteenth- to mid-twentieth-century African American letters—canonical assumed heterosexual, male writers—presented a monolithic stable, clean, and pressed vision of "home" as imposed upon or interrupted by structures of white oppression (only), Black Renaissance writers such as Wallace Thurman, Langston Hughes, and Richard Bruce Nugent exposed trouble and pleasure at home around color, class, and sexuality. They wrote about a life of poverty, drunkenness, and good times in Harlem, which Dubois and Alain Locke (who, not incidentally, was homosexual and privately supported these writers) were loath to acknowledge, given their mission of New Negro respectability at that moment. As Beverly-Guy Sheftal and others have pointed out, while we must look to an "evolution" or *longue durée* of Black feminisms, since in Barbara Smith's words, "Black women as a group have never been fools. We couldn't afford to be,"[34] and thus lived and recognized some of the tenets of what has come to be known as "womanism" and "black feminism" long before the 1970s, the critical enunciation of Black feminism in the 1970s and 1980s broke abruptly from the generation of sisters who had quietly led from the background. This revealed spaces within blackness that had previously been concealed and silenced, "yield[ing] unexpected ways of intervening and could make space for something else to be," as Roderick Ferguson notes.[35]

Early Black feminists, like those who follow them today, practiced their positions through popular education and community organizing. Their work provided the foundation and impetus for Black queer studies. So, with the late 1970s and 1980s moment of anthologies—*The Black Woman; Home Girls: A Black Feminist Reader; This Bridge Called My Back;*

In the Life; *Brother to Brother: New Writing by Black Gay Men*, among them—and in the wakes of Langston Hughes and James Baldwin, early Audre Lorde, and Ann Allen Shockley, we began *to become*. Black same-gender-loving writers—rooted in the civil rights, Black feminist, and Black liberation movements which raged between the 1950s and 1970s, and responding to important global political and social shifts of the 1980s and 1990s—thus contributed to the critical understanding, maintenance, and necessary enlargement of possibilities for various sorts of kinship and "homespaces,"[36] as well as fresh perspectives on intersections, interstices, compoundedness, coarticulations, and *conflama*.[37]

Today, the runway on which Black/queer youth turn it—new-way intellectual death drops, duck walks, and poses—is not "new" in the sense of without precedent or untraceable or cut off from its people. Theirs is another iteration emerging from legendary attitudes and grammars. Wallace Thurman's *Fire*, the Combahee River Collective, Jimmy Baldwin, and Pat Parker are all in evidence here, with new technologies and bold entitlement to the unfulfilled promise of equal protection and equal rights before the law. The Combahee River Collective is alive in the work of Hands Up United, Black Youth Project 100, and aspects of the #BlackLivesMatter campaign.

Presently, we will turn to one poetic example, Jamal Terron Lewis.[38] His/her creation and sharing of the vocal performance piece "A Vogue for Freedom" was made to *carry*—similar to the men, women, and trans, those who are both and some who are neither, with whom I marched, after the news of no indictment in Ferguson, in New Haven, Connecticut. The sister at the front with the bullhorn whom many mistook for a brother *carried* in thick dreads framing their face and righteous fire in their eyes and voice as they lead the crowd in "From Ferguson to 2-0-3, Fuck Police Brutality!" The child pushing down those three or four miles we walked and chanted, wearing their jeans as tights and rocking four-inch bolero boots, certainly carried. A protest march old head, I had worried that if things turned violent, they would be ill-equipped to run and/or fight. Then I remembered the stories I had read about Stonewall—the pumps of Black (and) Boricua queens upside the heads of brutalizing police. Timmy, my Vietnamese American former student and part-time drag queen carried too. Used to hearing his dulcet tones—*leggiero* in class or meeting for tea to discuss Sylvester, RuPaul, or discursive neutering of Asian men in gay media—I was surprised to hear the force of his booming lead, basso ostinato: "What do we do when we're under attack? Stand up! Fight back!" These folks had not come out to protest what people understand as "gay issues" but to stand against state-sanctioned (that is also "overlooked") murder. This time, the specific focus was not on the murder of yet another transgender woman of color gone uninvestigated but on Mike Brown and New Haven resident Malik Jones and others. They were protesting the local police policy of "the surge," which is essentially "stop and frisk" on steroids.[39] These children also specifically and particularly call out violence against trans and queer folks—expecting folks to carry with them. The radical promise of Black/queer work today is located in scholarship, art, and activism that has cellular and psychic connections to resistance to enslavement, which tried but failed to dehumanize our ancestors. This intellectual tradition and spirit is evident in the vogue chant of young Morehouse Man girl/boy.

Having protested in New York, Lewis exited a demonstration that he/she found "ableist" in terms of expectation to keep up the fast pace and annoying in terms of the "white kids" who seemed to insist on trying to lead. Lewis put the scene of protesting queer Black kids being as queer and as Black as they want to be to music, prose, and pose.[40] I will leave it to Black studies literary scholars to debate whether Lewis's "A Vogue for Freedom" constitutes a new form. While I have heard chants and extemporaneous verbal performances to house music at balls and clubs, I am struck by the heavy layering of "traditional" Black American texts in this performance, which he/she calls "a vogue" (like "a blues"). One can hardly do it justice in prose description. Beginning with a mournful a capella of "Strange Fruit" delivered in perfect Billie Holiday phrasing and tones, a clip from the house music anthem "The Ha! Dance" interrupts. As if on the mic at a ball, Lewis intones, "NoJustusssssss, No Peace! No Racistass Po-leees!" The scat is resonant with jazz vocals, but distinct. No "Brrrrr. rrr.rrrr.rrr. Po-lice! . . . ra-tk k kat ta k kat ka Ooh!" There is no mistaking there is a fierce Black femme on the mic—carrying in the tradition, cadences, and timbre of legendary ball commentators, and this is as carefully and meticulously executed as the Billie Holiday piece. Lewis wants you to know who is speaking and in whose house you stand (shimmying). We have already been alerted by "Strange Fruit" that this is no carefree party. Quickly now: "No justice, Oooh! No justice, Oooh! . . . No just-tuss!" Imagine the children lining up to pummel the runway at a ball. "Fired up. We won't take it no more!" gives way to a melismatic performance of "We Shall Overcome." Grand march vogue beats play. The background singing voice is joined by a ball chant style: "Justice! Justice! Justice! Ooh!"

repeated and later drowned out by his beautiful tenor rendition of "Woke Up This Morning with My Mind Stayed on Freedom" and another chant, with more bass this time: "fuck the fucking police." Speaking for all the children who are bringing the energies and the grammars of the clubs and balls with them to the wide stage of polity, Lewis promises: "We ready. We comin' cha cha cha. We ready. We Coming, Ooh!" In another haunting rendition, he/she takes us deeper, to "This May Be the Last Time, I Don't Know." This he/she repeats with electronic high hats that sound like gunshots and a more subdued chant: "Black bodies.on.the.ground. Black. bodies.ontheground. Black.bodies.ontheground. . . . Mi.chael.Brown." Later, as if anticipating Cohen and with a similar frontal challenge to prospective queer allies, he/she sweetly sings, then we hear the ball chant frantically asking: "What side are you on? Ooh! Ooh! . . . What side are you on, my friend? Ooh!" It ends with more remixes of the spiritual/ freedom songs with new freedom chants performed as vogue ball chants, and verbal scat performances "Hands Up, Don't Shoot," interpolated with "We Who Believe in Freedom Cannot Rest." I wonder what Bernice Johnson Reagon would think of this, as I hear Sweet Honey in the Rock harmonies here. "Do you believe in freedom? Do you believe in Free?" It ends with a long list of "my brothers and sisters slain at the hands of police brutality and vigilantes" over a recording of an actual protest in which they chant to drums: "No justice no peace. . . . We're fed up! Won't take it no more." "A Vogue for Freedom" is not a mere cut-and-paste bricolage but rather a studied, expertly performed danceable dirge—a paean and a march—indeed, a vogue. It brings my mind to imagine what it must have been like the first times folks heard some queer sing a church song in a gin joint or rum shop—they share a rhizome, but we are used to the barriers between categories being strong enough to prevent the creeping cultivation of genius orchids and bamboo and lilies in gardens where we do not expect them to grow or where we have already planted other cultivars. No more—they are coming (cha cha cha), and we ought to get ready for the children assembling to pummel our politics.

Black/queer studies was literally created and necessitated by our dead and sick before us. We need not go as far back as enslavement to find the "stony road we trod" or "bitter chastening." Black gay men, for example, have indeed quite directly and fairly recently "come—treading our path through the blood" of our "slaughtered" brothers/lovers/AIDS dead—into academe, into executive positions in community-based organizations, into libraries, think tanks, publishing, and punditry.[41] The biggest new space in which we find ourselves—the HIV/AIDS industrial complex—is, of course, now in financial crisis like other speculative business concerns, from Wall Street to Queens Road in the Caymans, forcing the "Black gay" formulation to reconsider its relevance and pointing out the fact that Black gay men had not adequately examined the consequences of basing our project on "risk" and "pathology" rather than on more agency-rich formulations, which had been offered by Essex Hemphill, Joe Beam, Marlon Riggs, and the Black feminist lesbians from whom they drew inspiration and political education.

We (can) do better and must. The work of Black lesbian and gay artists from the late 1970s and early 1990s constitutes Black lesbians' and gay folks' "coming out" into the public sphere with a particular point of view and politics. Thanks to our poets (especially), essayists and singers and choreographers and DJs, novelists, and literary critics and performance scholars, segments of the Black LGBTQ and same-gender-loving community may no longer be, in Hortense Spillers's language, "word poor" and "beached"—unvoiced—on the shores of representation. A student of the intersectional political and intellectual work of Audre, Barbara Smith, Joe, and the Black feminist lesbians of the Combahee River Collective, Essex, for example, clarifies *the rub*. The articulation: the interpenetration of sex, sexuality, epistemology and ontology, race, and history, spirituality and political economy, which defined a Black gay and lesbian project. [42] He writes:

> For my so-called sins against nature and the race, I gain the burdensome knowledge of carnal secrets. . . . It often comforts me. At other moments it is sacred communion, causing me to moan and tremble and cuss as the Holy Ghost fucks me. It is a knowledge of fire and beauty that I will carry beyond the grave. When I sit in God's final judgment, I will wager this knowledge against my entrance into the Holy Kingdom. There was no other way for me to know the beauty of Earth except through the sexual love of men, men who were often more terrified than I. . . . Men emasculated in the complicity of not speaking out, rendered mute by the middle-class aspirations of a people trying hard to forget the shame and cruelties of slavery and ghettos.[43]

In the United States in the early 1980s, at the onset of the HIV/AIDS pandemic, Black same-gender-loving and gender nonconforming forms of making sex, literatures, and other expressive practices emerged, thereby pushing notions of erotic experience beyond heterosexual sex and reproduction.[44] For example, that Black lesbians announced that they (like to) fuck, and Black gay men, who were assumed to be fucking unconsciously and "unnaturally," added "now we think as we fuck" at what at the time was the height of the AIDS epidemic, constitutes a profound contribution to radical praxis.[45] This was a crucial moment in which it was clear that, as Phil Wilson, director of the Black AIDS Institute, commented, "they are going to let us die." Black lesbians, bisexuals, transgender folks, and gay men created community out of crisis—in Nepantla, in the life, *en el ambiente*—complex, troubled, and often riddled with *candela*. A number of projects—including, to name only a few extraordinary examples, Steven Fullwood's recovery of dusty boxes and old stories; Alexis Pauline Gumbs putting elders' wisdom in a mobile home and crisscrossing the country; Marvin K. White making tweets, statuses, and books out of ancestral wisdom; and Sally Thiam and the Caribbean Resource Network's recording and saving our histories so that they can be shared, analyzed, kept, and passed on rather than being passed on[46]— follow this agency-rich formulation which privileges the production and preservation of Black/queer narratives which reflect and indeed generate new ways of being.

A Return to the Classroom

My story came full circle in the same Morehouse College classroom in which I sat more than twenty years ago, as a now-retired sociologist scrawled "CONSEQUENCES OF HOMOSEXUALITY: ALIENATION FROM FAMILY, ALIENATION FROM COMMUNITY, HIV/AIDS" across the entire blackboard. In Spring 2013, my own class sat in John H. Wheeler Hall each week to discuss normativity, sexuality, gender, race, pleasure, and ethics from the perspectives of Black LGBTQ/SGL experiences, theory, and artistry. Though I physically traveled to that classroom only a few times during the semester, holding most sessions via videoconference from my faculty office at Yale, I realized how forcefully my own life as an engaged intellectual had been shaped by that early moment in the bad old days of imposed, nonprotective silence. Students—Marcus Lee and the beautiful bristers of Morehouse College Safe Space—invited me to teach a course that would examine the sorts of exclusions and new community formations that I had experienced as a Morehouse student and in the Atlanta community two decades prior. Some students were frustrated that we did not spend enough time on current images of Black queers in the media (one semester is hardly enough), but although such analyses abound in blog think pieces, our aim was not to explore Black queer exceptionals and "pathologicals," or Internet and television "ratchetness." Nor did we use our time to expose historical figures who were or are *in the life*. What is more interesting to me, and more critically instructive, is to pose questions like this one: What interests are served by the erasure, sanitization, or spectacularization of Black LGBTQ/SGL people and their sexual and gender practices? What is at stake in these projects, and for whom? Questions like these, in particular historic contexts, help us to approach Essex's "ass-splitting truth" in this extension of Joe's "cold-blooded" nights. This is what Black/queer pedagogy lays bare and builds upon. Among the range of final group projects that emerged from the course: a critical assessment of the general education requirements of Morehouse College, through a content analysis of syllabi and interviews with students; a report on media images of homosexuality in the Caribbean; an opinion survey of attitudes toward bisexuality on campus; and a brilliant genealogy of the political and intellectual presence of LGBTQ students on the Atlanta University Center campus, derived from archives and interviews. Thus we met our goal not only to rigorously engage in critical social and cultural theory and interdisciplinary intersectional scholarship and art but also to contribute to the already exciting, transformational "evidence of being" on campus.

> *like bread in our children's mouths*
> *so their dreams will not reflect*
> *the death of ours*
> *And, if we win!?*
> *There is no telling.*
> we seek—
> inward and outward
> at once before and after
> at home here, and there.
> Where it must always be, and could not be otherwise—
> *Beyond history,*
> for the *new and more possible meeting to come.*[47]

1. See Langston Hughes, "Mother to Son," in *Selected Poems of Langston Hughes* (London: Serpent's Tail, 1999).

2. See Audre Lorde, "Women Redefining Difference," in *Sister Outsider: Essays and Speeches* (Berkeley, CA: Crossing Press, 1984).

3. There is certainly a long tradition of this in Black/queer studies, which I will not rehearse here. For other work resonant with the impulse to see beyond single stories and to recognize moving through particular political, intellectual, and geographic spaces, see Carole Boyce Davies, "Beyond Unicentricity: Transcultural Black Presences," *Research in African Literatures* 30 (1999): 96–109.

4. While I understand that "assemblage" has gained currency as the standard translation for *agencement,* I want to resist the oversimplification of this translation here by retaining the original. See John Phillips, "Agencement/Assemblage," *Theory, Culture & Society* 23, nos. 2–3 (2006): 108–9.

5. E. Patrick Johnson, "Feeling the Spirit in the Dark: Expanding Notions of the Sacred in the African-American Gay Community," *Callaloo* 21, no. 2 (1998): 413.

6. From Audre Lorde's "A Litany for Survival," in *The Black Unicorn: Poems* (New York: Norton, 1978).

7. Gilles Deleuze and Félix Guattari, *A Thousand Plateaus: Capitalism and Schizophrenia,* trans. Brian Massumi (Minneapolis: University of Minnesota Press, 1987), 21.

8. E. Patrick Johnson, "From Black Quare Studies or Almost Everything I Know About Queer Studies I Learned from My Grandmother," *Callaloo* 23, no. 1 (2000): 120–21.

9. J. Lorand Matory, "The Homeward Ship: Analytic Tropes as Maps of and for African-Diaspora Cultural History," in *Transforming Ethnographic Knowledge,* eds. R. Hardin and K. M. Clarke (Madison: University of Wisconsin Press, 2012), 225.

10. Deleuze and Guattari, *A Thousand Plateaus,* 25.

11. Audre Lorde, "Age, Race, Class, and Sex," in *Sister Outsider,* 123.

12. M. Jacqui Alexander, *Pedagogies of Crossing: Meditations on Feminism, Sexual Politics, Memory, and the Sacred* (Durham, NC: Duke University Press, 2006), 269.

13. Here I borrow Frantz Fanon's language in his preface to *Black Skin/White Masks,* trans. Charles Lam Markmann (New York: Grove, [1952] 1967), 7.

14. Essex Hemphill, original introduction to *Brother to Brother: New Writings by Black Gay Men* (Washington, DC: Redbone Press, [1991] 2007), xxi.

15. Personal conversation with Marvin K. White, May 2013.

16. I hasten to observe that this is also a moment in which opportunistic criticism of the concept of intersectionality (distinct, of course, from fair critique of the concept) seems to be growing.

17. Mary Patillo used the term *unidisciplines* for what are usually referred to as "traditional disciplines" in her opening address, "Doctoral Black Studies at a Glance: Data on the 11 PhD Programs," at A Beautiful Struggle: Transformative Black Studies in Shifting Political Landscapes—A Summit of Doctoral Programs, Northwestern University Department of African American Studies, Evanston, Illinois, April 12, 2012.

18. Sharon Bridgforth, *Love Conjure/Blues* (Washington, DC: Red Bone, 2004), 9.

19. See Osmundo Pinho, "Race Fucker: Representações raciais na pornografia gay," *Cad. Pagu* 38 (January/June 2012); Vanessa Agard-Jones, "Le Jeu de Qui? Sexual Politics at Play in the French Caribbean," in *Sex and the Citizen: Interrogating the Caribbean*, ed. Faith Smith, 181–98 (Charlottesville: University of Virginia Press, 2011); Ana-Maurine Lara, "Of Unexplained Presences, Flying Ife Heads, Vampires, Sweat, Zombies, and Legbas: A Meditation on Black Queer Aesthetics," *GLQ: A Journal of Lesbian and Gay Studies* 18, nos. 2–3 (2012): 347–59; Lyndon K. Gill, "Chatting Back an Epidemic: Caribbean Gay Men, HIV/AIDS, and the Uses of Erotic Subjectivity," *GLQ: A Journal of Lesbian and Gay Studies* 18, nos. 2–3 (2012): 277–95; Alix Chapman, "The Punk Show: Queering Heritage in the Black Diaspora," *Cultural Dynamics* 26, no. 3 (2014): 327–45; Fatima El-Tayeb, *European Others: Queering Ethnicity in Postnational Europe* (Minneapolis: University of Minnesota Press, 2011); Rinaldo Walcott, "Outside in Black Studies: Reading from a Queer Place in the Diaspora," in *Black Queer Studies: A Critical Anthology*, eds. E. Patrick Johnson and Mae G. Henderson, 90–105 (Durham, NC: Duke University Press, 2005); Allen, *¡Venceremos? Erotics of Black Self-making in Cuba* (Durham, NC: Duke University Press, 2011).

20. Joseph Beam, ed., *In the Life* (Berkeley, CA: Crossing Press, 1984), 191; Essex Hemphill, ed., *Brother to Brother: New Writings by Black Gay Men* (Boston: Alyson Publications, 1991), iv.

21. See Lorde, "Litany for Survival."

22. See Armstead L. Robinson, Craig C. Foster, and Donald H. Ogilvie, eds., *Black Studies in the University: A Symposium* (New Haven, CT: Yale University Press, 1969).

23. See Joy James, *Transcending the Talented Tenth: Black Leaders and American Intellectuals* (London: Routledge, 1996); George Lipsitz, *The Possessive Investment in Whiteness: How White People Profit from Identity Politics* (Philadelphia: Temple University Press, 2006); Ann DuCille, "The Occult of True Black Womanhood: Critical Demeanor and Black Feminist Studies," *Signs: Journal of Women and Culture and Society* 19, no. 3 (1994): 591–629.

24. Combahee River Collective, "The Combahee River Collective Statement: Black Feminist Organizing in the Seventies and Eighties," in *Home Girls: A Black Feminist Anthology*, ed. Barbara Smith, 264–74 (New Brunswick, NJ: Rutgers University Press, 2000).

25. See Leo Bersani, "Is the Rectum a Grave?" *October* 43 (1987): 197–222; Lee Edelman, *No Future: Queer Theory and the Death Drive* (Durham, NC: Duke University Press, 2004); Janet Halley and Andrew Parker, *After Sex? On Writing since Queer Theory* (Durham, NC: Duke University Press, 2011); Michael Warner, *Fear of a Queer Planet: Queer Politics and Social Theory* (Minneapolis: University of Minnesota Press, 1993).

26. See, respectively, Jose Muñoz, *Cruising Utopia: The Then and There of Queer Futurity* (New York: New York University Press, 2009); Juana María Rodríguez, *Queer Latinidad: Identity Practices, Discursive Spaces* (New York: New York University Press, 2003); Gayatri Gopinath, *Impossible Desires: Queer Diasporas and South Asian Public Cultures* (Durham, NC: Duke University Press, 2005); Judith Halberstam, *The Queer Art of Failure* (Durham, NC: Duke University Press, 2011).

27. Joseph N. DeFilippis, Lisa Duggan, Kenyon Farrow, and Richard Kim, eds., "A New Queer Agenda," special issue, *Scholar and Feminist Online* 10, nos. 1–2 (Fall 2011/Spring 2012), accessed August 18, 2013, http://sfonline.barnard.edu/a-new-queer-agenda/#sthash.w4vNfiKs.dpuf.

28. Cathy J. Cohen, "What Is This Movement Doing to My Politics?" *Social Text* 61 (1999): 111–18.

29. Cathy J. Cohen, "Punks, Bulldaggers, and Welfare Queens: The Radical Potential of Queer Politics?" GLQ: *A Journal of Lesbian and Gay Studies* 3 (1997): 438. Emphasis mine.

30. Cathy J. Cohen, "Deviance as Resistance: A New Research Agenda for the Study of Black Politics," *Du Bois Review: Social Science Research on Race* 1, no. 1 (2004): 27–45.

31. Kenyon Farrow, afterword to "A New Queer Agenda," accessed January 23, 2015, http://sfonline.barnard.edu/a-new-queer-agenda/afterword-a-future-beyond-equality/.

32. Lisa Duggan and Richard Kim, preface to "A New Queer Agenda," accessed January 23, 2015, http://sfonline.barnard.edu/a-new-queer-agenda/preface/.

33. Cathy J. Cohen, "#Do Black Lives Matter? From Michael Brown to CeCe McDonald: On Black Death and LGBTQ Politics," December 2014, http://videostreaming.gc.cuny.edu/videos/video/2494/.

34. Smith, *Home Girls*, xxvii.

35. Roderick A. Ferguson, *Aberrations in Black: Toward a Queer of Color Critique* (Minneapolis: University of Minnesota Press, 2004), 110.

36. "Homespace" is my friendly amendment to bell hooks's "homeplace" (1991). See hooks, *Belonging: A Culture of Place* (New York: Routledge, 2009). I want to emphasize the fact that the *spaces* we create are not necessarily sited in a particular "place" but rather made or assembled through our interactions within it.

37. In gay African American Vernacular English (AAVE) parlance, the concept *conflama* is a conflation of "confusion" and "drama."

38. Lewis is known on SoundCloud as "fatfemme."

38. Paul Bass, "The 'Surge' Hits Church Street," *New Haven Independent*, November 14, 2014, accessed January 9, 2015, http://www.newhavenindependent.org/index .php/archives/entry/the_surge_hits_church_street/.

39. Jamal Terron Lewis (aka fatfemme), "A Vogue for Freedom," *SoundCloud*, accessed January 23, 2015, https://soundcloud.com/fatfemme/a-vogue-for-freedom.

40. From James Weldon Johnson and John Rosamond Johnson, "Lift Every Voice and Sing" (Black National Anthem). Poem written by Rosamond Johnson; first performed in 1899, in Jacksonville, Florida; set to music by James Weldon Johnson in 1900.

41. You will notice the absence of transgender and bisexual. This reflects the fact that the particularities of the "T" and "B" in LGBT had not been included until very recently.

42. Essex Hemphill, "Loyalty," in *Ceremonies* (New York: Plume, 1992), 63–64.

43. Activist Cleo Manago has advanced the "same gender loving" formulation in an effort to replace "gay" and "queer," which he maintains are "white names" (See "Black Manhood, Same Gender Love, and Civil Rights," September 7, 2009, https://www .youtube.com/watch?v=fbKxv_9_Hog). However, the brightly divided gender lines, lack of attention to lesbian and trans experiences, ahistoricism, and refusal to engage critical Black queer and Black LGBTQ formulations severely weaken this formulation. I use it here because of the resonance many find in this term, regardless of its faults. Let a thousand flowers bloom, all hands on deck, a polyamorous movement!

44. Essex Hemphill and Wayson Jones in *Tongues Untied*, DVD, directed by Marlon Riggs (San Francisco, CA: Frameline, 1989).

45. Schomburg Center, In the Life Archive (formerly known as Black Gay and Lesbian Archive); Mobile Homecoming Project; None on Record: Stories of Queer Africa; Sharing Tongues, respectively.

46. With respect and apologies, this rephrases lines (in italics) from Audre Lorde's "A Litany for Survival" and "Age, Race, Class, and Sex."

2

The Whiter the Bread, the Quicker You're Dead

Spectacular Absence and Post-Racialized Blackness in (White) Queer Theory

ALISON REED

☙

> *To be sensual, I think, is to respect and rejoice in the force of life, of life itself, and to be present in all that one does, from the effort of loving to the breaking of bread. It will be a great day for America, incidentally, when we begin to eat bread again, instead of the blasphemous and tasteless foam rubber that we have substituted for it.* —JAMES BALDWIN, *The Fire Next Time*

WHILE MANY CRITICS HAVE INTERPRETED James Baldwin's *The Fire Next Time* as liberal-integrationist or ultimately transcendent of racial politics altogether, part of the force of his argument lies in its incisive critique of whiteness as spiritually void, which he captures in the figure of white bread.[1] This "blasphemous and tasteless foam rubber" metonymically represents not only white supremacy as a sickness plaguing the nation but also Baldwin's theoretical meditation on how whiteness constructs itself against a fiction of blackness—without which its world shatters into abysmal meaninglessness. As he writes to his nephew: "Try to imagine how you would feel if you woke up one morning to find the sun shining and all the stars aflame. . . . Well, the black man has functioned in the white man's world as a fixed star, as an immovable pillar: and as he moves out of his place, heaven and earth are shaken to their foundations." Since whiteness defines itself by contrast, white Americans actively disinvesting in white supremacy would equal nothing short of reenvisioning their basis for identity. As an empty vessel of white fears, anxieties, and desires, overdetermined fantasies of blackness reflect the devastating effects of a society that cannot understand itself without symbolic figurations of so-called otherness. This violent project of identity formation, as Baldwin describes, must crumble before a new society can take shape—one based on freedom "close to love" and deeply politicized sensuality that dissolves hierarchy. Aware that sensuality may evoke "quivering dusky maidens or priapic black studs" in the U.S. popular imagination, Baldwin eschews stereotypes of thoroughly racialized embodiment, and the violence they authorize, for something "less fanciful." Shared histories of struggle testify to the pain and pleasure of living, an emotional complexity captured in the blues and jazz pulse of "ironic tenacity" from which white Americans recoil in its embedded sensuality.[2] Baldwin's concept of humble sensuality, the collective breaking of bread, provides nothing short of a vehicle for social transformation.

Taking seriously James Baldwin's aside on sensuality in *The Fire Next Time*, which critiques how whiteness depends on fetishizations of black sexuality to define itself through the metaphor of bland white bread, in this chapter I interrogate the uncritical use of racialized bodies as spectacular markers of queerness.[3] I am interested in how (white) queer theory as a discipline relies on spectacularized blackness to understand itself and, in so doing, racializes the term "injury" by collapsing the distinction between race and racism. Here I mean "injury" in the sense of both a physical wound and psychic harm. The popular conflation of race and racism produces what I call "spectacular absence," which locates an eerie evacuation of discussions of systemic racism in the everywhere-thereness of race in mainstream queer theory. By filtering the aesthetics of trauma through the racialized body, spectacular absence demonstrates the contradictory logics of representing people of color as both the victims of oppressive power structures and the heroes of their perceived overturning, which serves the political purpose of denying the persistence of racial injustices. Race as theoretical fetish satisfies an institutional need for multicultural representation and theoretical diversity, while perpetuating colorblind logics that foreclose possibilities for justice by denying the existence of white supremacy. Ultimately, I want to gesture toward alternative frames for sustained queer engagements with race, gender, and sexuality that address how racialized embodiment shapes and is shaped by interpersonal and institutional racism, refusing myths of a post-racial state.

Postwhite Injury: Shame on Me? Shame on You

Despite mounting evidence of homonormative complicity with and assimilation into the state, existent oppression along the lines of gender and sexuality fallaciously bolsters a victim narrative to displace white queer identity from the social and economic wages of whiteness. This disavowal of privilege produces white queers who performatively align themselves with a racialized "otherness." Recent successes of mainstream gay and lesbian organizing, marked by campaigns for so-called marriage equality, make all the more pressing the need for recuperating a sense of injured identity. As Chandan Reddy, Kenyon Farrow, and others have theorized, white queer politics hides white privilege behind legalistic analogies between race and sexuality, not to mention the violence of "Gay Is the New Black" mottos, predicated on the uncited co-opting of organizing strategies and language of the black freedom movement.[4] These insidious discursive strategies of disavowing privilege evade collective responsibility for addressing the ongoing unearned benefits of whiteness irrespective of class, gender, and sexuality. Neoliberal progress narratives easily let race slide into sexuality, as current demands for legal rights presume that the civil rights movement marked an end to racial injustice, making way for "colorblind" rhetorics that focus centrally on gender and sexuality. White gay and lesbian feelings of entitlement via their call for "gay and lesbian" to be added as an affirmative action category dangerously override a long history of racial injustices in the United States through a claim to marginalization along the lines of sexuality that erases the specific experiences of queer and trans people of color.[5] This disturbing move has a long history in white supremacy, and it points to the danger of single-issue identity politics, particularly in a historical moment that wields the language of antiracism to perpetuate global racial injustices. These uneven parallels between oppressions elide uneven relationships to privilege in order to idealize a fabricated and cohesive queer community. Scholars premise romantic notions of togetherness on the spectacular fetishization of the racialized body. I therefore argue that the entrenched whiteness of queer theory coincides with its positioning of people of color as markers of queer sexuality across this antidisciplinary, ever disciplining, discipline—providing another example of whiteness depending on subordination and exploitation to gain meaning, as it racializes sexuality to claim injury.

According to colorblind liberals, the "race problem" was put to rest after civil rights legislation; they erect monuments for figures like John F. Kennedy as benevolent saviors, while ignoring the fact that civil rights movements were led by people of color, many of whom were murdered as a result of their activism. Yet civil rights rhetoric lives on, as white people cast themselves as the past's heroes of civil rights and today's "victims" of affirmative action. Through discourses of "cultural pathology," "victim blaming," and spectacular white dissociation from individualized acts of racism divorced from their institutional context, colorblindness ideology charges conversations about race with irrelevance if not full-blown racism. In a society that disavows the existence of systemic forms of racism and celebrates "post-identity" politics in which all identity is constructed and thus supposedly equal, multiculturalism's safe containment of certain kinds of societally sanctioned difference allows it to coexist alongside colorblindness without being perceived as contradictory; when the nation pushes an agenda of diverse representation, equal opportunity, and cultural (rather than racial) "pathology," then race no longer *matters*.

Colorblindness operates in some queer theory through a dangerous swapping of terms, namely, a substitution of sustained conversations about systemic racism with race as such, particularly spectacular racialized embodiment. This disavowal turns on three related points:

1. From "Gay Is the New Black" to the original Netflix television series *Orange Is the New Black*, white queer sexuality gains mainstream traction through spectacular representations of blackness, cashing in on the Hollywoodization of trauma and vulnerability born out of white supremacy by locating those traumas in the past rather than as ongoing and systematic.
2. In the academy, sites of injury are spectacularly racialized and mobilized for theoretical study. I call the sterilization of trauma through processes of displacement and metaphorization "utopian trauma," a kind of colorblind melodrama that characterizes white liberalism's politics of spectacularized suffering. I use the term "utopian" because colorblind discourse imagines racism as

no longer existent in institutionalized form; if we already live in a utopian world without racism, then folks disavow their implication in its mechanisms and refuse to work toward its eradication. When queer theory deploys race but absents discussions of racism, it consolidates a racialized queerness as identity through the fetish of post-racialized blackness, sutured to trauma.

3. Contemporary scholars tend to conflate identity with oppression and thus see the former as something that must be overcome, ultimately reproducing colorblind logics while making way for the triumphant progress narratives of (neo)liberalism.

In *On Making Sense: Queer Race Narratives of Intelligibility*, Ernesto Martínez critiques what he calls "antirealist" stances that understand racialized personhood as only and necessarily a form of subjection.[6] The equation of identity with oppression fallaciously collapses the distinction between race and racism, neglecting that shared histories of struggle generate vital embodied forms of meaning-making. The colorblind formulation of race *as racism* fails to consider that historical traumas do not delimit the social meanings of race. However, if scholars take race on its own terms as completely distinct from racism, which is to say, mobilize race *as metaphor*, discussions of race can opt not to address institutional racism and thus risk reasserting liberal-individualist understandings of race at best or white supremacist fantasies at worst. In other words, if race and racism remain entirely separate from each other, race may be mobilized in colorblind ways to divorce discussions of structural racism from racialized embodiment. Using race as an analytic without sustained considerations of the way racial regimes operate makes metaphor of daily lived reality, ultimately reproducing hegemonic racial discourse while claiming participation in antiracist practice merely by evoking race. Claims to antiracism without seriously engaging the operation of power satisfy an institutional need, mirroring larger patterns of the incorporation of antiracist language into racially inequitable systems.

The instrumentalizing of race to illuminate queerness enables white mobility through fantasy projections of raced immobility—pointing to the seemingly paradoxical logic whereby discourses of colorblindness and racialized trauma meet in the sphere of the post-racialized body. We can here expand Robyn Wiegman's notion of *prewhite* injury, which explains the tendency of white people to disown their privilege by fabricating roots in a nonwhite identity, to what I call "postwhite injury" in a queer studies context. Wiegman discusses the white liberal tendency toward a kind of victimized whiteness born out of a class-based solidarity or historical patterns of immigration and racialization. This leads to fallacious claims to prewhite injury, in part motivated by affirmative action backlash, and set into motion by "the guise of an originary discursive blackness that simultaneously particularizes and dis-identifies with the political power of white skin." This "discursive blackness" is guilty of "participating in—indeed, actively forging—a counterwhiteness whose primary characteristic is its disaffiliation from white supremacist practices."[7] This strategic alignment of discursive blackness and deracinated whiteness reproduces white supremacy under the banner of progressivism.

Wiegman's articulation of claims to prewhite injury through discursive blackness operates powerfully in queer studies with a slightly altered timeline. Rather than returning to a past in which immigrants discriminated against on the basis of class or religion literally performed blackness in order to enter into the privileges of whiteness (recalling Al Jolson's infamous blackface performance in *The Jazz Singer*), white queer subjects perform "discursive blackness" in and through their entrance into queer sexual orientation or gender expression. This disavowal of privilege produces white queers who discursively align themselves with a racialized otherness fetishized as a counterhegemonic way of being in the world. Whiteness is deemed an apolitical, historically untethered anti-identity, while sites of injury, shame, debasement, and abjection appear through symbolic figurations of post-racialized blackness.

A U.S. culture of de facto segregation, which does not recognize itself as such, provides the conditions in which an illusory figuration of "otherness" can perpetuate itself even in supposedly radical fields of inquiry. Hiram Perez's critique of the 2003 Gay Shame Conference at the University of Michigan pinpoints this disturbing trend in queer studies. While Vaginal Davis and Mario Montez were present as performers, out of over forty invited participants, Perez was the only queer of color speaker in attendance. Thus, a "distressing racialized division of labor resulted at Gay Shame. White folks performed the intellectual labor while black and brown folks just plain performed, evidently constituting the spectacle of gay shame."[8] As Perez explains, the popular imagination links race and shame without explicitly addressing racism, silencing conversations about race with the pejorative charge of identity politics while simultaneously rethroning the white male subject as the implied "universal" term.

A Beautiful, Shameless Shame

The structural problem of turning toward race while evacuating conversations about racism encourages risky readings of recent scholarly production in queer theory. I examine Kathryn Bond Stockton's *Beautiful Bottom, Beautiful Shame: Where "Black" Meets "Queer"* not to individualize an institutional problem but to analyze how such pernicious readings get consolidated through discursive technologies. In so doing, I gesture toward other modes of scholarship that play to the possibilities of work like Stockton's without reproducing its pitfalls. All writing, most certainly including my own, risks rehearsing what it seeks to critique, for situated experiences and power imbalances make our research a minefield of cultural implications—producing assemblages and excesses of meaning often unintended. To open doors rather than close them, I read Stockton against a black queer studies text that generatively engages race, abjection, and trauma, offering other theoretical modalities. Despite the dangers of trauma as spectacle, much recent work in critical race and sexuality studies generatively examines the systematic traumas of racism through the lens of shame and abjection. Darieck Scott's *Extravagant Abjection: Blackness, Power, and Sexuality in the African American Literary Imagination* takes up black queerness through this lens while also looking to power and agency within these contested sites, refusing simple identification or correlation between blackness, queerness, and abjection. Against the racialized figure of absolute victimhood at the heart of spectacular absence, Scott's work offers a powerful antidote to the aestheticization of trauma—acknowledging the complex politics of interpellation, recognition, and loss.

Kathryn Bond Stockton's *Beautiful Bottom, Beautiful Shame* engages what she calls the "switchpoints" between blackness and queerness but, in so doing, reduces race to a literal wound on the skin, or to a sartorial layer. Thus Stockton's text exposes a number of larger theoretical trends: white queer theorists often divorce the material from the symbolic in such a way that white Continental philosophers theorize while critical race theorists produce other kinds of knowledges, further consigning black cultural production to the realm of representation *as replication* of existing social realities. Stockton's book, for example, unpacks a rich archive of African American novels, such as James Baldwin's *Giovanni's Room* and Toni Morrison's *Beloved*, with predominantly white theorists. While Baldwin's and Morrison's canonical theorizations of race might have produced a more generative analysis, this theoretical lens reproduces whiteness as an unmarked and universally applicable framework for interpretation. To make work "new," white queer scholars must often willfully ignore and thus fail to cite the critical race theorists with whom their work would be most productively engaged, defaulting to white Continental philosophers as a critical toolbox. Stockton curiously omits the interlocutors with which her text might be best positioned. She briefly cites and then dismisses bell hooks and Frantz Fanon, in addition to largely overlooking the thriving existence of black queer studies as a field, to move into an apparently innovative exchange of black and queer (distinct from black queer) abjections. While Darieck Scott's *Extravagant Abjection* also explores these intersections, he does so with foundations in African American literary and critical theory. He foregrounds social justice movements and histories as well as traumatic encounters with white supremacy. Stockton's book is absent of such context and even gestures toward the word *oppression* in quotation marks—an unexplained evocation and dismissal of institutionalized power in favor of "the melodramatic nature of the prejudice against blacks and queers."[9] Perhaps it is this ironic gesture toward racism that enables shame to shine in all its debasements.

Discursive and visual assaults abound in *Beautiful Bottom, Beautiful Shame*, forging newness through jarring juxtapositions—for example, the widely circulated photograph of Emmett Till's open-casket funeral wedged between whole pages devoted to Eldridge Cleaver and Norman Mailer, writers not by any stretch of the imagination sympathetic to black queer struggles. *Pulp Fiction*, *Fight Club*, and Robert Mapplethorpe sidle up to Stockton's take on black queerness. The cover of Stockton's book replicates this discursive violence by featuring J B Higgins's photograph *André*, which recalls Mapplethorpe's highly debated series, as a fetishized black man's body is poised in a fetal position with his face hidden from the camera. Scott's text features a more complex engagement with scopic regimes. His cover, Glenn Ligon's silkscreen portrait series *Figure*, brings together a nuanced imagistic repetition and layering of black abjection that engages the political act of looking as the site not just of interpellation but also of opposition and disidentification. I highlight these images not to speculate on the degree of decision and agency afforded the authors by each press in cover design (although it interests me that the identity investments of the artist chosen for each cover seem to closely align with those of the author) but to visually register the effects each text produces within its pages. The pitfalls of Stockton's work reflect a larger trend within queer theory of dangerously absenting racism from conversations about race.

In *Extravagant Abjection*, Scott also reads the figure of the black male bottom; however, his interest lies in the kinds of "counterintuitive power" found in seemingly powerless spaces of abjection.[10] It is not, as Stockton writes, the "wound of black skin" but the wounds inflicted by white supremacy that partially animate his claims.[11] In challenging work that proclaims the past as obstacle, Scott thinks through what generative potential might be found in "racialization-through-abjection as historical legacy, as ancestral experience."[12] Scott rereads Fanon against criticisms that suggest his work radically, even messianically, dismisses the past, arguing that for Fanon, history can be a vital resource. Stockton, in contrast, pathologizes memory by describing its "AIDS-like transmission."[13] In fact, the text drapes material realities in uneasy metaphors of AIDS, rape, mass incarceration, and slavery: for example, in her description of the "white man's slave narrative," the generic conventions of which she finds in Baldwin's novel *Giovanni's Room* and David Fincher's film *Fight Club*. Just in case this genre seems unclear or off-putting, she defines the white man's slave narrative as one "in which the labor-against-one's-will (one's slave labor) is mental labor and one is captive to something (or someone) in the prison of one's mind."[14] This definition risks reducing historical realities of slavery and mass incarceration to white spectacles of suffering.

Stockton's discussion of Quentin Tarantino's film *Pulp Fiction* casts as "strangely funny" the rape of Marsellus Wallace (Ving Rhames) by two white men before Butch (Bruce Willis) saves him.[15] Stockton admits this response to the scene of interracial rape and its subsequent lynching scene without weighing the historical script that animates such a ritual: the myth of the black male rapist/pure white woman, with its attendant castration rite. Tarantino's jumbled sensationalistic identity politics play and historical revisionism of white supremacist sexual violence condones a critical blind spot—an absenting of history—that enables Stockton's freedom to see the scene with fresh eyes and thus symbolically mobilize traumatic lived experiences of other people's social realities. Slavery's reduction to metaphor reappears later in the text as "slavery to the Ikea nest." What's more, race as clothing, or the "switchpoint between cloth and skin," rehearses multicultural paradigms of difference as additive.[16] Since race can be worn like a garment, the entire text cloaks material realities in postmodern play: depoliticizing the switchpoints between apparently white queerness and black bottomness. Institutional structures of racial capitalism slide into individualized sexual acts, as in the link drawn between the "stigma of people who live at the bottom of an economic scale" and "queer anality" (68).[17] Stockton's campy reading of race, then, which she terms "Dark Camp," adheres to Susan Sontag's controversial definition of camp as about surface and shame, with blackness illuminating the particular shames of white queerness.

Scott's work begins elsewhere. In tracing the psychosexual dimensions of racism via Fanon, he notes a taken-for-granted assumption of the field of black queer studies—race as sexualized, and sexuality as racialized. While Stockton claims to chart new territory by examining these switchpoints, Scott understands them as "relentless [and] repetitive." This "vertiginous doubly queer" positionality that Scott argues obsessively links queerness to the spectacular "imago of the black body" rests on the hypervisible, hyperbolic link between blackness and abjection in Eurocentric fantasy structures. Scott does not stop at how the white gaze fixes meaning on the epidermis, a colonialist projection of history and being that Fanon famously describes in "The Fact of Blackness." Instead, he theorizes the "interarticulated temporality" of death-in-life that refuses defeat.[18] Against a ubiquitous politics of hopelessness in a moment guided by a theoretical obsession with death, Scott looks to possibilities for decolonizing dominant knowledge formations. Rather than bolstering the imagination of a post-racial present, Scott finds Fanon's oft-cited and co-opted words—"I am not a prisoner of history"—to manifest new visions of collectivity born out of struggle.[19]

The Cult of Negation

In this essay I have argued that while the elision of considerations of black studies from (white) queer theory has been well documented, queer theory at the same time spectacularly represents racialized embodiment as a way into its stylized origin narrative of trauma. This fetishization of blackness produces its own logics of disavowal, reinforcing hegemonic understandings of race by articulating embodiment in post-racial terms. Whiteness, then, goes unacknowledged and unexamined, while uncritically reproducing multiculturalist logics that mainstream visibility can smooth over ongoing injustices, precisely by exploiting the hypervisibility of black bodies for a white queer politics of injury. As another example of the racialization of white queerness, I would like to compare how the HIV/AIDS epidemic is taken up by Stockton in *Beautiful Bottom, Beautiful*

Shame and by Lee Edelman in *No Future*, an exemplary text of what I shorthand as the cult of negation in queer theory, which takes as its motto "fuck the future" and embraces a politics of negativity that sees any vision of collectivity as sentimental fantasy.[20] Edelman's rejection of what he calls "reproductive futurism" locates queerness "as the place of the social order's death drive." Edelman's portmanteau, the *sinthomosexual*, replaces action and activism with the "act of repudiating the social."[21] While Stockton immediately sutures the black body to HIV/AIDS, stating that the AIDS crisis "bound black and gay communities, largely at the level of public language," discursively collapsing the distinct signifiers black and gay, Edelman's text, for all its focus on antirelationality and death, remains curiously silent on this historical juncture (mentioning AIDS only twice)—as silent as whiteness is absent from the way he positions his argument.[22]

In the space of a footnote, Edelman predicts and preempts the critiques scholars will lodge against him for his "apolitical formalism" as well as "bourgeois privilege," on which he has since rightly been called out.[23] Rather than recapitulate those important critiques of the unnamed white privilege shaping his arguments, what interests me here is that Edelman's rant against the promise of the future depends on whiteness as an unmarked, apolitical category. Whiteness hides as invisible and depoliticized, and so too does the historical context out of which his argument gains traction. Two traumas appear in their disappearance from the text, then: the HIV/AIDS epidemic, and whiteness as an identity defined through subjection and negation. The erasure of failed whiteness and loss at the heart of the project is individualized, instead of motivating collective responsibility for the broader networks in which Edelman articulates his distrust of the future: namely, the historical outbreak of the HIV/AIDS crisis and the medical industrial complex. Ultimately, Edelman's *No Future* enacts a politics of disavowal that erases the historical stage on which it was thought. This queer embrace of antirelationality over and against alternative epistemologies of collective social life mirrors larger theoretical moves across disciplinary boundaries. While Edelman wants us to "refuse the insistence of hope itself as affirmation," his conception of queerness as the undoing of identity negates both hope and history, ending in a bleak place where only the most privileged of queers would thrive: a place of absolute refusal of the social and the vital forms of collective knowledge found there. Edelman thus reads "access to a livable social form" as unquestioningly liberal, and all progress at its behest.[24]

As much as Edelman would like to see his project as not investing in the political stakes he finds futile, his disinvestment in the political is itself, of course, deeply political. These embraces of radical negativity foreclose taking seriously the fact that aggrieved communities strategically negotiate oppressive power structures without becoming trapped inside them; in the wake of daily traumas, possibilities exist not for self-annihilation but for imagining other ways to be. *No Future* cannot articulate trauma because that trauma has been spectacularly sutured to the blackness of which textual absence marks a disavowal of politics.

We need something more, not something that smells like teen angst but that smacks of utopia, something to rub against the grain of the cult of negation, which turns away from the social and embraces death as a supposedly radical form of rejection. Collective forms of annihilation morph into rhetorics of individual choice, as queers negate a politics of community through the decision to opt out of reproductive futurism. This move discards historical legacies and current manifestations of grassroots mobilizations for social change. However, the "utopian political aspirations and desires" of the black radical tradition put pressure on a privileged politics of negativity that disavows the historical traumas that enabled its articulation, reinforced by the institutionalized "post" that evokes competing narratives of moving beyond historical injustices and of feeling hopeless in the face of abstract accounts of power as totalizing—accounts critiqued by black feminist and black radical thinkers such as Patricia Hill Collins, Patricia Williams, and Cedric Robinson.[25] When queer theory sterilizes sites of injury by displacing material realities of trauma from their representation, lived experiences morph into post-racialized metaphors that preempt possibilities for justice.

Cosubject Seductions

To act is to be committed, and to be committed is to be in danger.
—JAMES BALDWIN, *The Fire Next Time*

The parenthetical whiteness that haunts mainstream queer theory must find other ways of punctuating its own traumatic disavowals, returning us to that "fixed star" of fabricated blackness illuminating the violence of white identity production. Baldwin suggests that the ongoing process of actively disinvesting in the privileges of whiteness in a white supremacist society requires looking to other models of subjectivity that do not require symbolic and material subjugations. If we listen closely rather than presuming to know, our research investments can tell us much about alternative ways of being in the world. Yet, as semioticians and cultural studies scholars, queer theorists often read the body as text and, in so doing, turn subject into object—making the "object" of analysis a product of ideology rather than a complex subject not wholly determined by but also determining the social order. At the same time, as Roderick Ferguson reminds us, the specific histories of queers of color produce a privileged optic on power, but we should be careful not to fetishize that positionality.[26] The spectacular absences of queer theory take that argument to its extreme, where fetishized blackness stands in for claims to white injury. We must move from object to subject lessons, refusing simplistic accounts of structural oppression that render identities wholly victimized and/or heroic; we must turn to archives that articulate more complex engagements with power.

Transformative potential for the politicized love Baldwin describes in *The Fire Next Time* has to be born out of grappling with legacies the past leaves on the present; these legacies are traumatic but also provide the raw material for active hope, a hope informed not by sleek political campaigns but by community-based practices of survival and resilience in the face of dire social conditions. No mere pipe dreams, the practice of self-introspection and love, the development of a critical social consciousness, and the eradication of heteropatriarchal white supremacy remain vital forms of collective mobilization and struggle. However, in the so-called post–civil rights era scholars often talk about utopian aspirations and social justice in the same way—as redundancies or as sentimental fantasies informed by naïve investments in change. Rather than perceiving the persistence of institutionalized inequity, denial of rights, mass incarceration, police murder, and other forms of state violence as signs of defeat, cultural workers continue to posit concrete visions of transformation. While activist-oriented scholarship risks performatively enacting rather than actively investing in justice,[27] queer theorists would do better not to abandon the work altogether but to ask: who are my interlocutors?

Supposed "objects" of research have always rejected their objectification. While Della Pollock warns that reformulating "the *subject and object of research as cosubjects* could mean that the pleasure of the fetishistic gaze is just doubled," I follow Pollock in advocating for an immersive performance ethnography in which the researcher's subjectivity becomes open to the transformative possibilities embedded in the creative process.[28] Let us shift from object lessons to what we might call *cosubject seductions*—seduction intentionally evoking both the dangers and pleasures of how our research can transform us and make necessary that we tell different stories about ourselves and each other in the process. Against the neoliberal rhetoric of newness, which licenses appropriation and disavowal, scholars, organizers, and radical pedagogues must be open to the porous and messy echoes of intellectual exchange. From community-based research to literary studies, the subjects who speak to us from the page, the stage, or the spaces in which we move do not need our ears as much as we need to practice the art of hearing. Let us take our cue from E. Patrick Johnson in restoring agency to the scene of performance, developing "queer epistemologies . . . from a writerly place called home."[29] Performance scholarship that theorizes the "reflective and reflexive nature of performance" as well as embodied writing as theory generates alternative ways of assembling our existence through language without purporting to transcend our own social location when we enter the wor(l)ds of our research.[30] As D. Soyini Madison writes in "That Was My Occupation: Oral Narrative, Performance, and Black Feminist Thought," listening closely to the way research subjects tell their own stories, theorize their own lives, and construct their own versions of reality challenges "the great imbalance of scholarly work that ignores black indigenous and intellectual traditions as critical and theoretical constructs that can guide and determine the analysis of texts and performances."[31] This is not to say a cosubject exchange will not involve mediated affect, performance, opacity, projection, and lost chains of signification, but it does suggest that if we really want to hear, we must listen to theorist/practitioners operating in contestation of master narratives of being and nation that evade histories and realities of racial injustice—constructing alternative archives that refuse to separate theory and literature, understanding literature *as theory*. Moving away from representational models of literature, texts actively make meaning and in so doing do not simply represent but transform social realities.

In refusing to separate oral history, performance, and literature from theory, scholars also need to reject the false binary between critical race theory and critical theory, which further reinforces the material/symbolic divide.[32] Challenging dominant forms of legibility, cosubject seductions draw from embodied identities and histories as vital forces for making meaning and forming coalition. Against the post-racialized suturing of queerness to shame, abjection, and death, we must extend the language for refusing to sever our greatest pains from our deepest pleasures. The pains of life forge new pathways for transformation by the kind of political love James Baldwin described half a century ago. As Toni Morrison cautions in *Playing in the Dark*: "The subject of the dream is the dreamer."[33] Not too queer to hope, I go in search of (spectacular absence's) shadows.

NOTES

James Baldwin, The Fire Next Time *(New York: Vintage, [1963] 1993).*

1. For (not unproblematic in their own right) complications of this misreading, see Henry Louis Gates Jr., "The Fire Last Time," *New Republic* 206, no. 22 (1992): 37–43; and Bill Lyne, "God's Black Revolutionary Mouth: James Baldwin's Black Radicalism," *Science and Society* 74, no. 1 (2010): 12–36. While Lyne reads one of Baldwin's most famous passages ("Do I really *want* to be integrated into a burning house?") as challenging the entrenched mainstream liberalism of his time with a black radical understanding of U.S. racial capitalism, he also argues that Baldwin "chooses colorblind love over racial solidarity with 'I love a few people and they love me and some of them are white, and isn't love more important than color?'" (26). Yet, since Baldwin's conception of love seeks to redistribute power through structural change predicated on social transformation, I would question the shaky foundations on which this claim of colorblind liberal humanism rests.

2. Baldwin, *Fire Next Time*, 9, 41, 43, 42.

3. For some examples of people of color being used to figure queerness, see the cases of Willie Horton, as Marlon Ross describes in "Beyond the Closet as Raceless Paradigm," in *Black Queer Studies: A Critical Anthology*, eds. E. Patrick Johnson and Mae G. Henderson (Durham, NC: Duke University Press, 2005); Vaginal Davis, Mario Montez, and Kiko, as Hiram Perez describes in "You Can Have My Brown Body and Eat It, Too!" in *What's Queer about Queer Studies Now?*, eds. David L. Eng, Judith Halberstam, and José Esteban Muñoz, special issue, *Social Text* 84–85 (2005): 171–92; and of Ed in Leslie Feinberg's *Stone Butch Blues*, as Siobhan Somerville describes in *Queering the Color Line: Race and the Invention of Homosexuality in American Culture* (Durham, NC: Duke University Press, 2000).

4. See Chandan Reddy, *Freedom with Violence* (Durham, NC: Duke University Press, 2011); and Kenyon Farrow, "Is Gay Marriage Anti-Black?" *KenyonFarrow.com*, March 5, 2004, accessed June 26, 2014, http://kenyonfarrow.com/2005/06/14/is-gay-marriage-anti-black/. See also Cathy Cohen's foundational essay, "Punks, Bulldaggers, and Welfare Queens: The Radical Potential of Queer Politics?" *GLQ: A Journal of Lesbian and Gay Studies* 3 (1997): 437–65.

5. For a summary of white claims to affirmative action along the lines of sexuality, see Ian Barnard's *Queer Race: Cultural Interventions in the Racial Politics of Queer Theory* (New York: Peter Lang, 2004).

6. Ernesto Javier Martínez, *On Making Sense: Queer Race Narratives of Intelligibility* (Stanford, CA: Stanford University Press, 2012), 8.

7. Robyn Wiegman, "Whiteness Studies and the Paradox of Particularity," *boundary* 2 26, no. 3 (1999): 123, 119.

8. Perez, "You Can Have My Brown Body," 172.

9. Kathryn Bond Stockton, *Beautiful Bottom, Beautiful Shame: Where "Black" Meets "Queer"* (Durham, NC: Duke University Press, 2006), 216.

10. Darieck Scott, *Extravagant Abjection: Blackness, Power, and Sexuality in the African American Literary Imagination* (New York: New York University Press, 2010), 9.

11. Stockton, *Beautiful Bottom, Beautiful Shame*, 214.

12. Scott, *Extravagant Abjection*, 6.

13. Stockton, *Beautiful Bottom, Beautiful Shame*, 5.

14. Stockton, *Beautiful Bottom, Beautiful Shame*, 153.

15. Stockton, *Beautiful Bottom, Beautiful Shame*, 114.

16. Stockton, *Beautiful Bottom, Beautiful Shame*, 220, 68. For more on the concept of "additive race," see Amanda Phillips and Alison Reed, "Additive Race: Colorblind Discourses of Realism in Performance Capture Technologies" in *Performance Art and Digital Media*, ed. Michael Nitsche, special issue, *Digital Creativity* 24, no. 1 (2013): 1–15.

17. Stockton, *Beautiful Bottom, Beautiful Shame*, 68.

18. Scott, *Extravagant Abjection*, 7, 8, 26.

19. Frantz Fanon, *Black Skin, White Masks*, trans. Charles Lam Markmann (New York: Grove, [1952] 1967), 229.

20. See Lee Edelman in the 2006 *PMLA* forum on the antirelational turn in queer theory: "Antagonism, Negativity, and the Subject of Queer Theory," *PMLA* 121, no. 3 (2006): 821–22.

21. Lee Edelman, *No Future: Queer Theory and the Death Drive* (Durham, NC: Duke University Press, 2004), 3, 101.

22. Stockton, *Beautiful Bottom, Beautiful Shame*, 73; Edelman mentions AIDS in *No Future* on pages 19 and 75.

23. Edelman, *No Future*, 157.

24. Edelman, *No Future*, 4, 104.

25. Fred Moten, *In the Break: The Aesthetics of the Black Radical Tradition* (Minneapolis: University of Minnesota Press, 2003).

26. As Roderick Ferguson explains, a "postnationalist American studies informed by women of color and queer of color social formations does not at all mean the idealization of the woman of color and queer of color subject" (*Aberrations in Black*, 143).

27. See Robyn Wiegman's *Object Lessons* (Durham, NC: Duke University Press, 2012), which critiques the way a politics of desiring justice animates disciplines such that scholarship becomes an end in and of itself. See also Sara Ahmed, "Declarations of Whiteness: The Non-Performativity of Anti-Racism," *borderlands* (e-journal) 3, no. 2 (2004): 1–59, on the "non-performativity" of white claims to antiracism.

28. Della Pollock, "Marking New Directions in Performance Ethnography," *Text and Performance Quarterly* 26, no. 4 (October 2006): 326.

29. E. Patrick Johnson, "Queer Epistemologies: Theorizing the Self from a Writerly Place Called Home," *Biography* 34, no. 3 (2011): 429.

30. Johnson, "Queer Epistemologies," 429. See also Della Pollock, "Performing Writing," in *The Ends of Performance*, eds. Peggy Phelan and Jill Lane, 73–103 (New York: New York University Press, 1998); and D. Soyini Madison, "Performing Theory/ Embodied Writing," *Text and Performance Quarterly* 19, no. 2 (April 1999): 107–24.

31. D. Soyini Madison, "That Was My Occupation: Oral Narrative, Performance, and Black Feminist Thought," in *Exceptional Spaces: Essays in Performance and History*, ed. Della Pollock, 319–42 (Chapel Hill: University of North Carolina Press, 1998), 322.

32. Deborah McDowell critiques the racialized divide between practice/theory— such that white women theorize, and black women practice, recapitulating the historical overembodiment of people of color and again "making theory a province shared between men"; see *"The Changing Same": Black Women's Literature, Criticism, and Theory* (Bloomington: Indiana University Press, 1995), 165. Ultimately, McDowell asserts that rather than claiming access to the realm of theory, an even better task "is to resist the theory/practice dichotomy, which is too broad, abbreviated, and compromised by hedging definitions to capture the range and diversity of contemporary critical projects, including the range and diversity of the contributions of black women to that discourse" (167).

33. Toni Morrison, *Playing in the Dark: Whiteness and the Literary Imagination* (Cambridge, MA: Harvard University Press, 1992), 17.

3

Troubling the Waters

Mobilizing a Trans* Analytic

KAI M. GREEN

&

IN 2012, I DECIDED TO TRANSITION from female to male with
the aid of hormones. This occurred after a year of field research for my
dissertation in South Central Los Angeles. Prior to my transition I was
well known as a black lesbian activist; thus, all of my relationships were
affected. Where did I belong now? As a black transgender man, I knew
that my gender troubled many black lesbian and gay community spaces. I
became less legible as a body fit for residence in black lesbian spaces. And
while I was never formally asked not to partake in black lesbian events, I
felt that my black transgender male presence disturbed certain members
of the community. For example, an organizer of an annual black lesbian
retreat that I had previously attended said that I could continue to attend
the retreat after having top surgery, as long as I did not take off my shirt.
Not having breasts was more of my *man* side, and that space was for
women who loved other *women*. I decided not to attend the retreat, believing that the organizer's policing of my body in that space was a missed
opportunity for this community to grow and be challenged. I was asked
to conform to a narrow notion of "lesbian" rather than have a community
respond to the varied ways a person might exceed the category altogether.

I open with my own personal story about my experience as a black trans man in a lesbian space as a jumping off point to think more seriously about the ways in which trans—as identity, trope, analytic—might be a productive way to trouble the waters of black sexual and gendered relations. More specifically, I want to explore trans as a productive site of possibility relative to black sexual identity politics and theories of black gender and sexuality—namely, black lesbian feminism and black queer studies.

The way my transgender body troubled black lesbian community is not necessarily *new*. Though they may have been unnamed, transgender people have historically always already been a part of the black gay and lesbian archive, but recognized only through what Ann Stoler calls complex "grids of intelligibility" that we may have yet to grasp because they, perhaps, went by some other name.[1] My project here, however, is not one of reclamation by which trans figures are rediscovered in the black queer archive and celebrated—as admirable as that project may be. Rather, I want to mine trans for its use value as a method or optic, one that, similar to queer, refuses temporal or spatial fixity. Moreover, I use it to articulate a unique relation between two or more identity categories where one marks the limits and excess of the other, simultaneously deconstructing and reconstructing or reimagining new possible ways of being and doing.

Trans as a way of naming and identifying transgender people became a part of the lesbian and gay lexicon formally in the late 1990s.[2] "Trans" is short for "transgender," an umbrella term that names a multitude of sexual and gendered identities, though it is most recognizable as a term that names a transgender man (FTM) or transgender woman (MTF). However, the *Merriam-Webster* dictionary provides the Latin origin of the term to mean "across, beyond, through, so as to change, from *trans* across, beyond."[3] And it is this latter definition that I would like to expand the definition from an identity category to a theoretical analytic. As such I find it useful to conjoin "trans" with another key term in transgender studies, the "asterisk," which when added to "trans," according to Avery Tompkins, may "open up *transgender* or *trans* to a greater range of meanings."[4] In this way, Trans* is an act of artfulness, an act of creation and possibility,[5] or, similar to Treva Ellison and my definition of "Tranifest," Trans* is the ability "to mobilize across the contradictions, divisions, and containment strategies produced by the state and other such large-scale organizations of power that work to limit our capacity to align ourselves across differences in ways that are necessary for social transformation."[6] Based on these definitions, I employ Trans* on multiple registers: as a decolonial demand; a question of how, when, and where one sees and knows; a reading practice that might help readers gain a reorientation to orientation. It is an analytic that has ontological, ideological, and epistemological ramifications. It is not perpetual alterity but perpetual presence. It makes different scales of movement or change legible. Trans* is the queer. Trans* is the colored.

I mobilize my capacious use of Trans* to also theorize the relationship between black, lesbian, and feminist in the term "black lesbian feminist." Feminism was not ever just about white women, though they became the representative subject for its politics. "Black lesbian" can be understood as a Trans* modifier of feminism. In the same way that black lesbians critiqued white feminism for creating a politics centered in whiteness that invisiblized black lesbian women, I use Trans* to critique black lesbian feminist politics, which at times disavows the presence of black trans subjects in order to present a coherent category, "black lesbian." I argue that "black lesbian" accommodates trans excess. A Trans* reading of black lesbian feminist texts illuminates those moments of fissure, contradiction, and coherence where the possibility of trans subjectivity troubles the coherence of "black lesbian."

For the remainder of this essay I stage a conversation between black lesbian feminism and transgender studies. Through a series of close readings of editorials by Alycee Lane that appeared in *Black Lace*, a black lesbian erotic magazine, I demonstrate how black lesbian as a Trans* modifier of feminism indexes the contradiction of (white) feminist exclusion of black women, at the same time as it forges a space for the expansion of the category "woman." Moving beyond the racial critique to one of gender, I use Trans* to rethink the category of "woman" beyond cisgender black women. While many scholars focus on the racial critique, I wish to highlight here the dynamic gender analysis that can be gleaned from black lesbian feminists. I am interested in the ways in which black feminists, by accounting for racial difference in their critique, opens its audience up to the multiple possibilities of gender within the category "woman." Through a Trans* reading of black lesbian feminist texts, I demonstrate how this opening of the category "woman" allows for a potential trans, as in transgender, subjectivity to be, sometimes named but often not.

FIG. 3.1. Image of bodybuilder from *Black Lace,* Issue 1, page 6. Courtesy of BLK Publishing Company, Inc.

How "Black Lesbian" Trans*s Feminism, or Can Women Have Dicks?

Black Lace, a black lesbian erotic magazine, was one of the many spin-off publications of *BLK Magazine,* a back gay and lesbian newsmagazine and publishing office. *Black Lace* printed its first issue in the spring of 1991, and a total of four issues were printed between 1991 and 1992. This publication included poetry, essays, erotic stories, art, and photographs. The representations of black women here were varied along the spectrum of masculinities and femininities. *Black Lace* is a material example of the ways in which black lesbians were moving and shaping their identities and challenging confining notions of gender binaries. Figure 3.1 shows a black woman flexing and holding a masculine pose. Muscles protruding, this woman is strong and athletic. Her gender non-conforming body is viewed as desirable in this magazine, though this woman in another realm might be demonized for her embrace of masculinity. *Black Lace* staged debates around the representation of black lesbian sexuality and gender.

Each issue of *Black Lace* included an introduction by editor Alycee J. Lane, who was then a graduate student in the Department of English at UCLA. Lane envisioned *Black Lace* as a safe space for black women to interrogate and express their desires and love for other black women. Every issue included a section of letters under the title, "Hot Lace Letters," which differed from usual letters to the editor because they contained sexual fantasies from black women. These scenarios included student-teacher role-play, steamy library scenes, and whatever readers were willing to come up with and share. All letters were published anonymously. Along with erotic fantasy, *Black Lace* also included advice columns that gave women sexual health information. This was especially important for black women, who in the late 1980s and early 1990s were not yet being addressed as an at-risk group for HIV/AIDS. *Black Lace* also featured socially current articles, such as "Oppression for Sale," which asked black lesbians to make themselves conscious of the companies that supported South African Apartheid and to boycott and write letters to those companies.

In the second issue of *Black Lace*, many of the "Hot Lace" letters were filled with women's fantasies of sex with dildos. Name Withheld from Norfolk, Virginia, wrote, "I'm glad to see that *Black Lace* is finally out! Reading the letters of the first issue has inspired me to set down one of my experiences.... Every woman has her fetishes and one of mine just happens to be that I love to be fucked in the ass. Fingers, vibrators, dildos, fists."[7] This column allowed women a safe space to share their sexual fantasies and build community while sharing explicit sexual encounters with other women. The erotic was accessed as a usable resource, and it freed black women from disciplining concepts of respectability and propriety.[8] However, everyone was not always in agreement; in this issue, two of the three letters included dildos in their fantasies, and all included fantasies of penetration. These letters were all listed under the title, "Dances with Dildos."

The dildo became a major site of antagonism in the magazine as it felt too phallocentric for some readers. One reader was disturbed by the images of dildos and black lesbians because they "played into stereotypes, particularly the one that claims lesbians want to be 'like men.'" This quotation highlights a major disagreement on the meaning of lesbianism and womanhood. Do lesbians have to be women? What kind of women? This is a discussion that has been had in women's and feminist studies as well.[9] This challenge is further articulated in the "Editor's Notes" in the first issue:

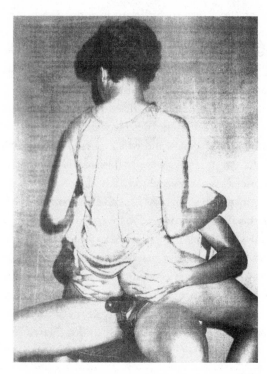

FIG. 3.2. Image of two people and dildo from *Black Lace,* Issue 3, page 7. Courtesy of BLK Publishing Company, Inc.

FINALLY! BLACK LACE AFTER TOO many late night and early morning conversations and political debates and asking should I? Or shouldn't I? And worrying about the devastating infinite measurements of political "correctness" and meditating on what it means, feels like to be an African American lesbian loving other African American lesbians, sex and multiple orgasms, knowing—do you hear me?—knowing that we have been and continue to be sexual animals to the Amerikan imagination, working our asses off to prove the perversion of that imagination all the while internalizing the frigid Victorian sensibility of no sex, I don't think about sex, I don't want sex, I don't even know what my own pussy looks like.[10]

Lane's opening to the magazine is forceful, directed to other black lesbians who love black lesbians. She is aware of the tropes, the controlling images of black deviancy that black people negotiate daily.[11] She notes here the ways in which that pressure, that knowing that you could easily slip into the same popular trope of the *perverse Amerikan imagination,* puts disciplinary pressure on the black body. The quest not to be that deviant body often produces an overinvestment in politics of respectability, a detachment from the body, so much so that you might not even know *what your own pussy looks like.* On the other hand, embracing one's sexuality might play into that *perverse imagination.* In many ways, this is what Audre Lorde names as the bind that prevents black women and black people from being able to access the erotic as usable resource.[12] Yet, for Lane, the response cannot be to censure what is thought of as pornography, because that, too, becomes another kind of oppression. She proclaims, "Let us celebrate. Let us share our fantasies frankly and honestly even brutally let's do the safe sex thing the dental dams the latex gloves let's laugh and love sex or lovemaking if that's what you call it to hell with what Amerika thinks to hell with what we've taught ourselves to think pledge allegiance to your entire black woman selves let us fuck suck eat screw scream our heads off loud enough for everyone to hear.[13]

Lane wants to take her power back and encourages readers to do the same by embracing different kinds of sex while questioning how black lesbian pleasure might look, feel, and be. Pleasure might be *brutal,* it might be *sex* or *lovemaking.* Black lesbian pleasure might take the shape of deviancy and pathology in the *Amerikan* imaginary. Indeed, in the Amerikan imaginary, black women have not had the privilege of easy access to the category "women"; too big, too tough, too strong, too black, too masculine, black women have always had a precarious relationship to the term. Woman has historically been theorized as a white possession or endowment. The distinction between sex and lovemaking is a response to Lorde's distinction between sensation and sensation with feeling.[14] For Lane, there is no judgment of either. There is, rather, a desire to make room for it all. Lane encourages the reader to let go of those binds and enjoy sex however you want it (as long as it is safe). In this way, I see Lane bringing a Trans* method or mode of being to her readers, she asks them to open themselves up to types of desire that might be demonized by the Amerikan imaginary, and instead of conforming to that fear, she encourages women to be bold and take risks. She asks that her readers free themselves from these controlling images, as such images work, with or without their self-discipline. Black lesbians were already viewed as excess to the category "black woman," just as black marked the limit of "woman," conceived in popular feminist (white) politics. So in many ways, the queer position of "black lesbian woman" functions as an opening up of the category "woman" in the first place. At once this gives new meaning to the category and unhinges it from biology so that the question of, "Can women have dicks?" might be answered in the affirmative. In this particular instance, *to have* means to acquire in prosthetic form, that is, the dildo. But this conversation illuminates a feminist discourse concerned with the confines of a gender binary that seeks to discipline a subject's actions based upon that subject's unchallenged placement within the category "woman." The "black lesbian as woman" is a direct challenge to the term's ability to articulate a coherent, stable, identifiable category of people. The question posed, "Can women have dicks?," then, is not just a question relevant to the *Black Lace* community but also a question continually asked in feminist spaces. Most notably, in the spring of 2015, the Michigan Womyn's Music Festival decided to answer the question in the negative and cancel a forty-year-old tradition instead of changing a policy that explicitly states that transgender women (who have not had bottom surgery) are unwelcome. Conversely, transgender men were welcomed in the space. What we can learn from these conflicts is that the gender category "woman" is a contested one. Others police who can and cannot belong to the category based upon biology and appropriate object choice. The question that *Black Lace* helps us understand is that despite women's ability to have dicks, those women in possession of dicks may not be included within the category of "woman," depending on who's determining the qualifications of inclusion. Thus, the magazine's discussion highlights the multiple ways that people make and remake the category "woman," illuminating both its capacious and foreclosing potential.

The Dildo as a Site of Trans* Intersection

Though readers pushed Lane to present "softer" and "gentler" images of women, Lane refused to abide. Instead, she responded by interrogating the dildo even more. In her essay following "Hot Lace Letters," she wrote, "What's race got to do with it?" In this piece, she decided to take a deeper look at the relationship of the dildo and race, especially as so many women evoked the object in their erotic stories. Because Lane often fantasized about dildos, she thought it would be a great idea to photograph one for the magazine. She had her own that was "six inches, rubbery, cheap, mauve," which she became self-conscious about when her friend told her she had race issues.[15] Her response to this friend was, "A dildo is a dildo, not a dick." She was satisfied with that response until it came time to find a photo suitable for the magazine. She visited a sex shop in search of a black dildo to photograph for the magazine. This shopping trip provoked the question, "What does it mean, exactly, when white hegemony extends to the production of dildos?"[16] The dildo was at once humanized, racialized, and "flesh" colored. Lane could not help but see how the black dildo's function as commodity in the sex store had ramifications in the lives of black cisgender men. This was a moment of Trans* reckoning.

She discovered bright-colored toys that were called "'psychedelic'" and "not human," though what she wanted was a brown dildo, that had a tone similar to her own. When she asked the owner where she might find one, he told her that they had sold out, and those are the ones that go the fastest. He pointed her toward a bin sitting on the floor. The bin was labeled, "Big Black Dick." The only ones available were "24 inches and thick as [her] arm." She could no longer think of dildos without thinking about their relationship not only to race but also to notions of humanity and monstrosity. The dildos that most resembled her flesh were mandingo-sized. She concluded: "The entire experience forced me to more critically examine how race permeates American culture. A sex toy easily becomes the location for racial terror and desire because sex itself is that location. We confront the violence of history and its consequences. We speak our allegiances according to the color we choose . . . what really needs to change is not so much the dildo, but constructions of race and the power behind these constructions. After all, what's race got to do with dildos?"[17]

Black lesbian sex toy shopping was not simply about a sex act; it was also political, entangled with capitalism and labor. The black or brown dildo was not just a dildo; it could not be detached from the black body ideologically, the cisgender black stereotyped mandingo figure. Lane confronts her relationship to sex toys and black men. The relationship is about black lesbian women's relationship to dildos, but also black lesbian women's relationship to cisgender black men. In her search to understand black women's sexuality, she encounters the stereotypes of black cisgender men, which not only affect black cisgender men but also black lesbians who are interested in finding toys that reflect their brown skin. Black women have always had to contend with their precarious relationship to the category of woman, as it has never been a category of feminine safety.[18] This is an example of how the signifier "black lesbian" Trans*s feminism as black women occupied this marginal space as individual black women when they tried to join feminist movements and realized that to be women they would have to, at least for the moment, forget about race and the oppression that they felt as black people in America.[19] *Black women* and *the black woman* become recognizable social and political categories by the very nature of their ideological persistence as pathological stereotype.[20]

Black feminist thought and praxis has traditionally entered the conversation of feminism by critiquing the limiting way that white feminism conceives of womanhood. Black women put pressure on the category "woman," pushing it to its conceptual limits relative to race, yet they circumscribe the same category relative to noncisgender bodies or nonheteronormative bodies who want to lay claim to the category. What is productive about black lesbian feminism, however, and especially how it manifests in *Black Lace,* is that it mobilizes the category "woman" to forge a politics of liberation that challenges a narrow heteropatriarchal conception of the term.

The erotic was not only a black feminist evocation to enact personal pleasure and liberate oneself sexually; for such black lesbians as Lane, this place of pleasure was being forged in a time of multiple crises. That material reality could not be escaped. Robin D. G. Kelley argues that in much of the scholarship on the working class, " play is seen as an escape from work," but when it comes to oppressed poor people of color, "the pursuit of leisure, pleasure and creative expression is itself labor."[21] Lane's analysis of the dildo allows for a better understanding of the relationship between work and play. For black lesbians, pleasure—finding, creating, and sustaining places of pleasure—is a battle against internalized and external heteronormativity and white supremacy. Lane argues that access to a liberated sexual self comes with a responsibility to do other kinds of work. She too makes a distinction between work and play. After encouraging women to fuck and screw, she goes on to say: "Then let's get off our backs, dammit, there's so much to do there's crack young black kids hating themselves poverty homelessness murdered black children black men black women George Bush Jesse Helms it's not enough to fuck not enough to search for the ultimate orgasm we have other lives to live other lives so wash your toys put your leather harness away kiss your lover(s) get up, I say, get up there's so much work to do, so much power in our erotic selves . . . Enjoy."[22]

The black feminist politics that Lane articulates and circulates is one that does not end with sex. The sex act itself is not going to bring about social transformation; there are multiple interlocking oppressions that Lane names: crack, poverty, and homelessness. Although Lane articulates these as struggles separate from sexual liberation, I argue that, with the placement of these social issues alongside an articulation of a desire for sexual liberation outside of deviancy or denial, the erotic is simultaneously work and pleasure, the erotic self does indeed exceed sex acts. The erotic self is not put away when a person *gets up* but is simply another place of erotic power. This inseparability of work and play is further inscribed in the text itself as the text rarely uses commas, periods, or grammatical markers to separate sentences or thoughts, demonstrating the messiness and complex dynamic of the erotic.

From the erotic knowledge comes a deeper knowing of self. What Lane learned and was able to articulate was the intimate relationship between the objectification of black men and the ways in which that has bearing upon black lesbian lives and living. Affirmation of this black erotic knowledge as a valuable resource challenges heteronormative valuations of knowledge production. Lane asks the reader to participate in an epistemological shift whereby we imagine the black lesbian outside of the paradigm of deviant, in need of discipline, or unseen.

When I interviewed Lane, I asked her about this debate, and she responded, saying, "I think some people were uncomfortable with the dildo stuff and were trying to get away from male representation blah blah blah. But you know, I wasn't willing to censor sex that way. This is how women are having sex with each other. You can have your critique, but this is my representation, and I am not gonna sit there and it may even be more radical than you are allowing it to be."[23] Lane challenged black lesbians to think seriously about representation, and she would not allow anyone's desires to be policed, even if there was a fear that somehow they would be thought to be identifying with men. Rather, she asked her readers to engage in understanding the multiple ways that they were women, lesbian, kinky, dildo wearing, free and unfree in the ways in which their race, indeed, their blackness could be potentially commodified and sold.

The Power and Limits of Name Changing

In 2011, I went home to visit my family and friends in the Bay Area. While having family dinner at a local diner, my rental car was broken into, and all my things were stolen: laptop, archival magazines that had been gifted to me, hard drives that contained back-up copies of interviews, credit cards, IDs, and checks. I felt violated. I felt out of control. But what I felt more than anything was a deep loss. As I cried and continued to have panic attacks and "breakdowns" over the next couple of days following the robbery, I realized I was crying from a place of pain and loss that was much deeper than my laptop or credit cards. I was crying and feeling loss of moments and pains I had never allowed myself to fully experience.

One evening during one of my "breakdowns," I spent a couple of hours looking at myself in the mirror. I longed to see and know myself, but it was difficult for me to do. I felt my face and body morphing before my eyes and beyond my control. I talked to myself. I told myself I was strong. I told myself I was beautiful even as I tried to make sense of the contorted vision I was presented with. I told myself that I would come back to myself, put myself back together, even though I felt that I was "losing" it. I realize that it is sometimes necessary to "lose" it. It is necessary to feel pain and loss, for it opens up space for something new. When I came back to myself, I was no longer "Kiana." I was "Kai." During those hours I spent with myself in the bathroom of the house I had grown up in, I watched myself change and come into new being. I began hearing a voice. It told me that my name was now Kai. I started repeating it, "Kai, Kai, Kai." Every time I said that name, I saw myself transform into a recognizable self in the mirror. Kai is the name the universe gave me, and it allowed me to see myself. From that moment on, I was Kai. Kai, a name that was Kiana taken apart and rearranged—I love them both.

Weeks later I looked up the meaning of the name Kai and found that it had multiple meanings in different places, but the ones that resonated with me most were the Japanese and Yoruba meanings. In Japanese, Kai may mean "big water," "ocean," "sea," or it may also mean "change." In Yoruba, it means "love." From this traumatic experience a new name was born. A new name marked a new iteration of self.

Name changing has been a tool used by transgender and genderqueer people, often divorcing ourselves from the gendered names we were given at birth. Not all transgender people change their names, but for those of us who do, it becomes a moment of self-reclamation and not simply gender self-determination but also self-determination whereby we challenge and disrupt the influence inheritance has on our present and future; it is no longer pre- or overdetermined by biology or blood. Giving oneself a new name is not unique to the transgender experience. Many oppressed communities and individuals have articulated the importance of name changing as a political act. The change of name enables the possibility of a new articulation of self, a self that is detached from the name that was bestowed upon the subject by parents or through other kinds of inheritances, such as slavery. This aim to break away from a given name is what Audre Lorde might also call an act of poetry, "for it is through poetry that we give names to those ideas which are—until the poem—nameless and formless, about to be birthed, but already felt."[24] Articulation of self through naming is an essential component of a black feminist ethic, whether it be to name oneself or to name a group of people, black women, whose unique positionalities were not accounted for in dominant feminist movements that uphold a white cisgender female body as the representative subject. Black women were caught in a matrix whereby they were rendered invisible, because "women" implied "white" and "black" conjured "male."[25]

Renaming has a black feminist genealogy. In Toni Cade Bambara's interview, "How She Came by Her Name," she discusses the importance of renaming herself as an act of self-empowerment, a practice with a long history that she traces through black women writers. She writes: "Toni Cade Bambara—the minute I said it I immediately inhabited it, felt very at home in the world. This was my name. It is not so unusual for an artist, a writer, to name themselves; they are forever constructing themselves, are forever inventing themselves. That's the nature of that spiritual practice. Maya Angelou changed her name. Toni Morrison definitely changes her name—Chloe Wofford?!! Audre Lorde changed the spelling of her first and last names."[26] There is great potential for empowerment in naming oneself, but the act of naming or renaming has its limitations. What happens when you rename yourself and those around you refuse to call you by that new name? A new name does not always mark a fundamental shift in being or the conditions that help to produce said being. A new name can trouble history because it changes the index. As people change names, it requires that we know all names if we want to locate them in the archive. In a similar way, as groups like "black lesbian feminist" separate themselves or assert themselves as cohesive category, they become a category separate from but still fundamentally connected to that which they came to critique, "feminist." So Kai is a transgender man, but Kai is also all of the experiences that created and made manifest Kiana, though she is no longer the representative of my current manifestation of self. Tracing and understanding these transformation processes is important because it helps us understand and validate that which was already present, yet unnamed.

I move to another editorial piece by Alycee Lane that highlights the tension between naming as empowerment and naming as surface change.

FIG. 3.3. Image of word collage from *Black Lace,* Issue 4, page 26. Courtesy of BLK Publishing Company, Inc.

In the fourth and final issue of *Black Lace* she wrote an article entitled, "Queerness and Other Identities." The article was first given as a talk at the 1991 Creating Change Conference. This was a time when "queer" was a term being mobilized and emerging in academic discourse, prompted by radical HIV/AIDS activists who articulated a radical intersectional politic. The term "queer" troubled lesbian and gay studies, as it asked the field to account for more than nonnormative sexualities. Queer named compulsory heterosexuality, a result of nuanced interlocking webs of power that relied on patriarchy and a rigid gender binary.

The image that accompanies this article lists a multitude of identity categories that people may use to self-identify or may be identified as whether they want to be or not.[27] People use these identity categories to reclaim power over their image. For example, Lane discusses the use of the term "nigga" or "nigger" and how it can be "counterhegemonic"; at the same time, "niggers in the context of hateful lyrics or any other context are not affirmed, empowered niggers but niggers you lynch on the streets ... Blacks. African Americans."[28] There are many ways to name a black person

(nigger, black, negro), and some of those names are put to use to demonize a whole group of people. What Lane shows us is that those very
same names can be repurposed to call forth subversive reinvention. Lane
argues that those names that they, black lesbian women, call themselves
are limited if they do not change the state-sanctioned violence that black
people are subjected to. To name oneself is powerful but limited if others
do not affirm that name or value it. Lane concludes: "And with all these
words to confuse and disorient me, I still have to worry, finally, about the
frequency with which my names—empowered or not—are recited over
LAPD airwaves, each and everyday of my life."[29]

Naming can be a powerful act, but the names that we use to call ourselves into community might be the same names used to keep us captive
or the same names used by our captors to demonize and pathologize. If
this is the case, then we should not be so concerned with the empowerment of giving oneself a new name, a new category, fixed and coherent.
We should instead be invested and committed to making space where the
ability to constantly change one's name, the power to constantly transform,
and shift is an option. I am more interested in holding onto the potential of possible name changes than the actual *new* name itself, because
it is this potential to be made anew and undone perpetually that marks
ongoing transformation. The new name marks both a beginning and an
ending, but these are not fixed or always clear either. The moment I became Kai was also a moment of becoming a different iteration of Kiana.
I am not suggesting an end to new identities through naming but that
it might be useful for us to pause on the ways in which we are always
already in the presence of absence at every new iteration of self or selves.
No one has said it better than Marlon Riggs when he asserted that black
both is and it ain't.[30] A Trans* method asks that we not be so invested
in what follows black is or black ain't but rather that we be attuned to
the ways in which black is made present or not, when, where, how, why,
and, most important, in relation to what. A Trans* method requires that
we be more attuned to difference rather than sameness, understanding
and declaring that our sameness will not protect us. We must move to
those uncomfortable places of contradiction and conflict, and in those
moments we will develop a more critical and nuanced analysis of the
conditions under which we are required to live, named and unnamed. A
Trans* method show us how people become representable as things, categories, and names because it shows us the excess as a perpetual challenge
to containment.

Conclusion

We must listen for the fullness embedded in the silences and gaps, the moments of existence before the name or the category came to do its work upon the body. We must be more attuned to the present absences which calls for a Trans* method. One of the ways in which black queer studies scholars have challenged us to engage black sexuality and gender is through simultaneous black and queer acts of (re)membering. Black queer studies staged this work in the gap and in the silence of queer studies and black studies, which articulated themselves as mutually exclusive. Black queer studies helped us call out the missing, the ones who are with us, but neglected. A Trans* method further names the work of charting the present absences in multiple sites of intersection by demanding a moment of critical presence. A Trans* method is a tool that helps us embark on the work of listening, understanding, and reading as both intellectual and political practices. It allows us to see certain things that might not normally be seen. It also enables us to understand how that seeing is being shaped.

As the T in LGBTQI becomes more apparent in popular culture, it is important that we still hold fast to a Trans* analytic, knowing that representation is not enough. We know that it is not enough, for just as Laverne Cox and Janet Mock have become the popular beautiful women of color representing the transgender movement, there have been countless other unnamed (and named, but names we are not familiar with) transgender women and men who have been harassed, violated, and murdered in the streets. At the heart of black feminist praxis is a push to make the lives of disappeared black women matter.[31] In order to make that argument, black feminists showed us how the category of woman failed to account for the unique experience of black women. This critique both challenged and clung to the category itself. I consider the identities that have not yet come to cohere as nameable but are ever present with us. How do we carry those not only as simple additions to an ever-growing acronym, LGBTQI, but instead hold them up as future Trans* operations that will come to do work and further open us up to new possibilities? This is the charge of a black queer studies *for now*, and by now I mean in this current historical moment, but I also use "for now" to imply the temporariness of this method as one that is unfixed so that we might always be open and ready for a name changing considering what is necessary for now is not necessary for always.

NOTES

1. Ann Laura Stoler, "Colonial Archives and the Arts of Governance," *Archival Science* 2, nos. 1–2 (March 1, 2002): 91, doi:10.1007/BF02435632. I interviewed Archbishop Carl Bean, founder of Unity Fellowship Church and cofounder of the Minority AIDS Project. In our interview he describes himself as transgender, always feeling kinship with his trans sisters. He stated that even though most would not accept his trans proclamation, he still held on to it. He did not change his pronouns or medically transition, which makes his trans illegible to many who might not have the tools to read or know his trans presence that exists under the moniker of "gay cisgender male." Carl Bean, interview by Kai M. Green, February 11, 2013.

2. Stephen Whittle, "Forward," in *The Transgender Studies Reader* (New York: Routledge, 2006), xi.

3. "Trans-: on or to the other side of: across or beyond," accessed April 8, 2015, http://www.merriam-webster.com/dictionary/trans-.

4. Avery Tompkins, "Asterisk," *TSQ: Transgender Studies Quarterly* 1, nos. 1–2 (May 1, 2014): 26–27, doi:10.1215/23289252–2399497.

5. Trystan Cotten, *Transgender Migrations: The Bodies, Borders, and Politics of Transition* (New York: Routledge, 2012), 103.

6. Kai M. Green and Treva Ellison, "Tranifest," *TSQ: Transgender Studies Quarterly* 1, nos. 1–2 (May 1, 2014): 222, doi:10.1215/23289252–2400082.

7. See "Dances with Dildos: Hot Lace Letters," *Black Lace*, Summer 1991.

8. Audre Lorde, "Uses of the Erotic: The Erotic as Power," in *Sister Outsider: Essays and Speeches* (Berkeley, CA: Crossing Press, 1984), 53–60.

9. Alycee J. Lane, "What's Race Got to Do with It?," *Black Lace*, Summer 1991.

10. Lane, "What's Race Got to Do with It?," 3.

11. Patricia Hill Collins, *Black Feminist Thought: Knowledge, Consciousness, and the Politics of Empowerment*, rev. 10th anniversary ed. (New York: Routledge, 2000).

12. Lorde, "Uses of the Erotic."

13. Lane, "What's Race Got to Do with It?," 3.

14. Lorde, "Uses of the Erotic."

15. Lane, "What's Race Got to Do with It?," 21.

16. Lane, "What's Race Got to Do with It?"

17. Lane, "What's Race Got to Do with It?"

18. Gloria T. Hull, *All the Women Are White, All the Blacks Are Men, but Some of Us Are Brave: Black Women's Studies* (New York: Feminist Press, 1982); Robyn Wiegman, *American Anatomies: Theorizing Race and Gender* (Durham, NC: Duke University Press, 1995); Jacob Hale, "Are Lesbians Women?," *Hypatia* 11, no. 2 (May 1, 1996): 94–121, doi:10.1111/j.1527–2001.1996.tb00666.x; Collins, *Black Feminist Thought*; Katherine

McKittrick, *Demonic Grounds: Black Women and the Cartographies of Struggle* (Minneapolis: University of Minnesota Press, 2006); Barbara Smith, ed., *Home Girls: A Black Feminist Anthology* (New Brunswick, NJ: Rutgers University Press, 2000).

19. Anita Cornwell, a black lesbian, joined the Radical Lesbians in 1971 and started writing for a mostly white lesbian feminists' journal, *The Ladder*. She was hopeful about coalition building but was disturbed at a conference when a Black Panther was shot and that murder seemed not to have relevance in the white lesbian feminist world. By 1974 she had changed her tone of hopefulness in that she realized more and more that to be a lesbian feminist she would need to forget her blackness and that would mean death for her. This is just one example of what many black women were experiencing in the women's movement (http://sitemaker.umich.edu/lesbian.history /lesbian_feminism, accessed March 15, 2012).

20. Black feminists such as Patricia Hill Collins, Toni Cade Bambara, and bell hooks have examined the role of the masculinized and/or emasculating black female tropes—from Mammy to Sapphire to Hoochie Mama—in the U.S. imaginary.

21. Robin D. G. Kelley, *Yo' Mama's Disfunktional! Fighting the Culture Wars in Urban America* (Boston: Beacon Press, 1997), 45.

22. Lane, "What's Race Got to Do with It?," 3.

23. Alycee J. Lane, interview by Kai M. Green, May 24, 2011.

24. Audre Lorde, "Poetry Is Not a Luxury," in *Sister Outsider*, 36.

25. Hull, *All the Women Are White*.

26. Toni Cade Bambara, "How She Came by Her Name," in *Deep Sightings and Rescue Missions: Fiction, Essays, and Conversations* (New York: Vintage, 1999), 206.

27. A similar move was made by Facebook in 2014. See Aimee Lee Ball, "Facebook Customizes Gender with 50 Different Choices," *New York Times*, April 4, 2014, accessed April 14, 2014, http://www.nytimes.com/2014/04/06/fashion/facebook -customizes-gender-with-50-different-choices.html.

28. Alycee Lane, "Queerness and 'Other' Identities," *Black Lace*, 1992, 26.

29. Lane, "Queerness and 'Other' Identities," 27.

30. Marlon Riggs, *Black Is . . . Black Ain't* (DOCURAMA, 2009).

31. Kimberly Springer, *Living for the Revolution: Black Feminist Organizations, 1968–1980* (Durham, NC: Duke University Press, 2005).

4

Gender Trouble in *Triton*

C. RILEY SNORTON

SET IN 2II2, Samuel R. Delany's *Triton* (1976) is an amalgamation of concepts and characters that gives rise to a series of reflections on the possibilities and limitations of logic, science, identity, space, and life. As Kathy Acker suggests in the foreword to the 1996 edition, *Triton* opens up conversations, "not only about identity, desire, and gender, but also about democracy, liberalism, and otherness. And perhaps, more than anything, a conversation about societies that presume the possibilities of absolute knowledge."[1] Having two subtitles—"An Ambiguous Heterotopia" and "Some Informal Remarks toward the Modular Calculus, Part One"—it is a curious work of fiction. While the second subtitle is an erudite description of the reigning episteme (and techne) in *Triton*'s lifeworlds, the first subtitle positions the novel as in dialogue with Ursula K. Le Guin's *The Dispossessed: An Ambiguous Utopia* (1974) and signals the novel's inclusion within the genre of postmodern (science) fiction. After all, it is Michel Foucault who coins "heterotopia" to describe the juxtaposition of several spaces in one place and the relationship of those spaces to time ("heterochronies") and meaning.[2] However, and as Delany pointed out in an interview about the novel, *Triton* is also interested in medical definitions of the term: "The removal of one part or organ from the body and affixing it at another place in or on the body. That's called a heterotopia. A skin graft is a heterotopia. But so is a sex change."[3]

Delany's coupling of heterotopia's multiple meanings is a keen narrative intervention that illuminates the term's cultural and political significance for theories of identity.[4] As such, this essay places Delany's novel in dialogue with contemporary debates in black, feminist, and trans scholarship to examine the utilities of heterotopias for making sense of racial and gender difference. As my close reading of the novel bears out, heterotopias are not necessarily liberatory spaces, just as plurality and difference are not "good" in and of themselves. Thus gender's troubles on Triton in the twenty-second century and some of the troubles with gender currently are not that gender is unable to proliferate but that the techniques for normativizing gender so often shape one's phenomenological experience of it. In this sense, both Delany's novel and Judith Butler's oft-cited passage on drag in *Gender Trouble* (1990) suffer from similar forms of mischaracterization, which equate gender electivity and performativity with freedom from (gender) identity.[5]

The frequency with which both works have been misread underscores critical investments in what Roderick Ferguson has described as the academic "malignancies of recognition" and reminds us of Lauren Berlant's notion of "cruel optimism," which often accompanies narratives of institutional belonging.[6] In what follows, I attend to the synchronicities of time, space, and meaning that give rise to a significant subplot, which has largely gone unremarked in the critical literature on *Triton*: the relationship between the novel's protagonist, Bron Hellstrom, a blonde, blue-eyed transwoman, and her friend and later love interest, Sam, a transracial (white to black) transman. At times, their story provides an account of how certain contemporary arrangements of knowledge portend a future ordering of things. But Bron and Sam's ambiguous relationship also opens up different pathways for reading the significance of identity on Triton (and here on Earth), as their interactions highlight the conjunctures and fissures between assimilation and inclusion, philosophy and fiction, biopolitics and necropolitics, change and transformation.

An Ambiguous Love Plot

In *A Sense of Wonder: Samuel R. Delany, Race, Identity, and Difference*, Jeffrey Tucker describes Delany's Triton as "an ideal society, but not one characterized by unity, totality, or singularity, but by the enormous multiplicity of subject positions available to be occupied." Tucker argues that while social identities are not devoid of meaning, they are categories embraced through affiliation as opposed to those hegemonically imposed: "On Triton, gender—as well as race and sexuality—can be changed as routinely and with as little fuss as we might change a hairstyle."[7] That sex changes are common on Triton, and society divides humanity into "forty or fifty sexes, falling loosely into nine categories,"[8] furthers Tucker's claim, when he suggests that "it is the kind of multitudinous blossoming of identities to which Judith Butler's critique [in *Gender Trouble*] aspires, 'a radical proliferation of gender' that will 'displace . . . gender norms.'"[9]

However, Triton's so-called paradise is premised on another Foucauldian concept: disciplinary power, a set of techniques, which "produces new forms of agency through individuation and multiplication."[10] The quantification and categorization of gender and sexuality on Triton already heralds the proliferation of gendered possibilities as not displacing but regimenting and sedimenting gender (norms). On Triton, characters also exercise other forms of "control" over their bodies, electing to desire particular types of people and undergoing rejuvenating procedures to guard against any effects of aging. In other words, Triton's government— referred to as the "computer hegemony"—provides self-regulation under a veneer of freedom through choice. Its dispensation toward radical libertarianism is intimately linked with the onset of an intergalactic war to maintain the possibility of multiple ways of life.

Yet critics often make sense of the novel's narrator, protagonist, and antihero, Bron Hellstrom, as an insensible figure in Triton's political and cultural landscape. Robert Elliot Fox, for example, suggests, "Coming from a world with a rhetorical but actually illusory freedom [here Fox is referring to Hellstrom's birthplace of Mars], Bron is sadly unprepared to deal with implications of a more concrete and demanding freedom."[11] And even though Andrew Butler rightly suggests that prejudice still exists within Triton's heterotopia, he does so by citing Hellstrom's (frequently internal) monologues, which display sexism, transphobia, homophobia, and racism, as "more the fault of the individual citizen than a reaction to societal inequalities."[12]

When readers first encounter Sam, a fellow resident in Bron's same-sex, nonspecified sexual preference co-op, they are treated to a host of Hellstrom's prejudices, as the novel pays close attention to Sam's stature, filtered through Bron's envious gaze: "From the balcony, Sam leered hugely, jovially, and blackly over the rail. . . . Sam came down the narrow, iron steps, slapping the bannister with a broad black hand. It rang across the room. . . . He had a large, magnificent body which he always wore (rather pretentiously, Bron thought) naked. . . . He came over to stand at the table's edge and with black fists on narrow, black hips, gazed down over the arrayed pieces. Bron hated Sam."[13] As the narrative delves further into Bron's thoughts on Sam in this encounter, readers come to understand Bron's numerous (failed) attempts to make sense of Sam—and his success. As Bron ponders over a series of incidents regarding Sam, Bron determines that "Sam was not so average," "had an amazing mind," and concludes: "He was just a good-looking, friendly intelligent guy doing his bit as some overworked salesman/consultant." Bron's conclusion is false. Sam is a high-ranking diplomat for the Outer Satellites: "Far from being 'oppressed' by the system, Sam had about as much power as a person could have, in anything short of an elected position. Indeed, he had a good deal more power than any number of elected officials."[14] Sam's position of power also draws readers into the realities of the intergalactic war that acts as a backdrop to Bron's banal life.

Sam, however, is just one instance of a recurrent narrative formulation, in which cross-gendered figures act as the face of the state. For example, on Triton (as well as on Mars) police officers are gendered irrespective of their sex. The phenomenon of cross-gendering that accompanies figurations of power seems to bespeak the novel's implicit question-cum-critique about the relationship between gender and power. Thus far from trans characters acting as subversive figures within the narrative, they appear as instruments of the state and instrumentalizations of power, emblematic of power's ability to diversify and proliferate. Judith Butler makes a similar point in her response to particular readings of *Gender Trouble:*

> The bad reading goes something like this: I can get up in the morning, look in my closet, and decide which gender I want to be today. I can take out a piece of clothing and change my gender, stylize it, and then that evening I can change it again and be something radically other, so that what you get is something like the commodification of gender, and the understanding of taking on a gender as a kind of consumerism . . . [treating] gender deliberately, as if it's an object out there, when my whole point was that the very formation of subjects, the very formation of persons, *presupposes* gender in a certain way—that gender is not to be chosen and that "performativity" is not radical choice and it's not voluntarism. . . . Performativity has to do with repetition, very often the repetition of oppressive and painful gender norms . . . This is not freedom, but a question of how to work the trap that one is inevitably in.[15]

Triton's gender electivity and transition represents a variation on the inevitable "trap" of gender. Indeed, the proliferation of identities (and the process by which characters come to inhabit them) on Triton takes place within the context of increasing technologically determined biocentrism, where bodies are shaped into categories-cum-cartographies of (human) life, as determined by socially agreed-on and scientifically mapped genetic routes.

And, yet, even as trans figures are elevated socially and politically, Bron's reactions to Sam remind us that transphobia remains a compelling framework with which to understand gender in all its various forms. Having taken a trip with Sam to Earth on a research and diplomatic mission, Bron learns of Sam's transgender and transracial history:

> "Before I came to Triton, I was a rather unhappy, sallow-faced blonde, blue-eyed (and terribly myopic) waitress at Lux on Iapetus, with a penchant for other sallow, blonde, blue-eyed waitresses, who, as far as the young and immature me could make out then, were all just gaga over the six-foot-plus Wallunda and Katanga emigrants who had absolutely infested the neighborhood; I have this very high, very useless IQ and was working in a very uninspiring grease trough . . ."
>
> Bron Tried not to look shocked. . . . Bron suddenly didn't feel like talking any more, unsure why. But Sam, apparently comfortable with Bron's moody silences, settled back in his (her? No, "his." That's what the public channels suggested at any rate) seat and looked out the window.[16]

Bron's use of "his" to mark Sam's difference in this moment recurs in Bron's thinking throughout the novel—often referring to Sam as a "he-she." However, the appearance of "his" in scare quotes here is simultaneously a marker of Bron's transphobic discomfort and a signal to how gendered forms of address are mediated (and imposed) by "public channels." In this sense, one might regard Bron's internal ruminations as a kind of paranoia, "an unintended consequence" of a set of social and political imperatives that would include political correctness, such as John L. Jackson has argued in *Racial Paranoia*.[17]

Sam's explanation is also (admittedly) paranoid, demonstrated in the ways his account works to distance himself from the "young and immature" waitress with the "very useless IQ." His contemptuous description of the black "emigrants" that "absolutely infested" Lux on Iapetus is syntactically peculiar as readers are left unsure whether these are thoughts occasioned by an earlier "immaturity" or antiblack beliefs maintained in the present. This ambiguity is perhaps amplified by the inclusion of Katanga, a "real" place folded into dialogue. Indicative of the narrative's relationship to the contemporary political climate of the novel's inception, the "Congo Crisis"—sometimes referred to as the "Katanga Crisis"—was an ongoing political issue throughout the early to mid-1960s.[18]

The simultaneity of Sam's racial and gender transition ensures that analogy and disanalogy are insufficient for assessing the cultural and political implications of the character's transformation. As Cressida Heyes remarks in her response to Janice Raymond's (failed) disanalogy between transracial and transgender politics, seriously considering both forms of transition "require[s] more than an assertion that the former exists while the latter does not, when this is itself arguable."[19] Heyes argues that race's "ambivalent relationship to dichotomy" is markedly different from typical conceptions of gender, such that "while the politics of race often does operate to reduce racial conflict to 'black versus white,' especially in U.S. contexts, dominant racial taxonomies all admit of several racial groups. Thus it is less clear what a transracial would cross between; there is more than one permutation."[20] While I agree with Heyes on the necessity of distinguishing between racial and sexual formations and with her subsequent conclusion that (dis)analogies in these instances only serve to code transsexuality as white, I would suggest—and *Triton* seems to bear out—that hybrid models of identity do not undo the telos of transition narratives.[21] In fact, my reading of *Triton* implores us to consider how hybridity and multiplicity are generated effects of (disciplinary) power. The lessons of *Triton* are that transitions are always already imbued with hierarchies of social value and the exponentialization of choice is not equivalent with the democratization of human life. As the final scene between Sam and Bron makes clear, this is an affective and political concern.

Sometime after Bron's transition, she finds Sam again. While their relationship might be understood through the lens of gender rivalry, this last scene marks a shift for the novel's protagonist. After expressing her desire to join Sam as one of his wives and following his rather blunt refusal, Bron muses:

> At one point there had been something she had thought she could *do* better than other women—because she had *been a man*.... So she had become a woman to do it. But the *doing*, as she once suspected and now knew, was preeminently a matter of *being*; and *being* had turned out to be, more and more, specifically a matter of not *doing*.... What was she

trying to do? Bron asked herself. And found the question as clearing as Sam's name a minute before. It had to do with saving the race . . . no, something to do with saving or protecting . . . men? But she was a woman. Then why . . . ? She stopped that thought as well. Not her thoughts, but her actions were pursuing some logical or metalogical concatenation to its end. To try and ask, much less answer, any one of those question would pollute, destroy, shatter it into a lattice of contradictions that would crumble on expression. She knew that what she wanted was true and real and right by the act of wanting. Even if the wanting was all—[22]

This passage is the narrative crystallization of heterotopia's ambiguities, conjoining the term's Foucauldian and medical conceptualizations. It takes the form of Foucault's argument that heterotopias "make it impossible to name this and that . . . because they destroy 'syntax' in advance, and not only the syntax with which we construct sentences but also the less apparent syntax which causes words and things (next to and also opposite one another) to 'hold together.'"[23] Bron's meditation on her desire (to transition, to desire) and her subsequent confrontation with the limits of sensibility portend the novel's (first?) conclusion: an utterly quiet scene in which Bron is overtaken by a silent terror as she contends with the idea that certainty (of choice, of identity, of desire) would never come.

As Delany explains, Bron is a case study, a figure whom the reader is "not supposed to identify" but rather look at "from the outside."[24] Thus readers are instructed to "look at the specific texture of the character's everyday-world" and begin asking, "[What] might produce such a life-texture?"[25] In seeming response to the questions Delany poses, Edward K. Chan argues that "we are meant to understand the social fabric of *Triton* as a field of unlimited subject positions and infinite choice," such that readers encounter "the shock of what we imagine as social difference."[26] Yet Chan also rightly points out that the preponderance of typologies and surfaces throughout the narrative contribute to "'stricter' categories that deal with social difference" to elucidate the novel's emphasis on the circulation of markers of social difference as they are situated in an imaginary future."[27]

Bron, however, is unlike other transsexuals—or heterotopias—on Triton; her transition is motivated by a desire not to be another gender (or a compliance with an identification or identity model of sex change) but to find a way to be the woman who could mate with the type of man she imagined she was. And, ultimately, as the final scene with Sam demonstrates, Bron is only contented by the fact of wanting at all. Whether one accepts Bron's rationale or reads it symptomatically, as an action taken to cope with the consequences of war, her decision to transition pivots on the interrelationship of heterotopia and biopower. After all, modular calculus—as a system of rationales that can predict and encompass all human behavior—and the types of procedures that make sexual reassignment relatively effortless for the inhabitants of Triton are emblematic of the kinds of biotechnologies that optimize the lives of some, even as they sanction the deaths of others. Bron's heterotopic identity emphasizes how difference is not only present but also facilitated and proliferated in the future world of Triton. Bron's sex change is an action that is imaginable to the protagonist only in so much as it offers a distinctive node for her to see herself within the teleology of man.

As Roderick Ferguson has written, parallel logics were employed in women's and ethnic movements (and their academic institutionalization): "The U.S. ethnic and women's movements represent powerful confrontations with and evaluations of the figure of Western man as well as attempts to replace him with other characters, characters that represented the real existence and viability of other idioms and histories." For Ferguson, these movements represented a new era of biopower, in which subjects (and disciplines) are constituted by particularity and difference.[28] Sylvia Wynter made a similar point when she argued that black studies mistook the map for the territory by focusing on psychic revaluations of blackness ("Black is beautiful," etc.) rather than attending to how blackness unravels the teleology of man.[29] Yet *Triton* also implores us to consider how multiplicity and electivity are compatible with modes of domination, as it narrates the myriad ways commodification-cum-classification are valued techniques in the normativization and management of identity.

On Heterotopias, Trans Politics, and the Myth of Inclusion

According to an interview with Delany, the novel was written, in part, to explore the epistemological significance of political struggle and social movements. As Delany remarked, "Basically it arose out of some social ideas": "What I start from is the fictive element, considered in terms of a series of questions. What would you like the *effects* of the government to be? What would you like the world to look like as you walk down the street? What unpleasant things could you tolerate in that world? What others do you simply not want to be there at all?"[30] The political context of the novel's publication, where municipalities around the world were forced *again* to contend with changing political landscapes, as new and differently visible groups of people were demanding freedom from repression and violence and full entrance into the category of "citizen" and "human," situates the importance of *Triton* as a meditation and signification on the relationships between the seemingly exponential proliferation of (contested and acceptable forms of) difference and rapidly changing political strategies for containment.[31] (And, as Roderick Ferguson argues in *The Reorder of Things*, the U.S. academy was a laboratory for employing and refining such techniques.[32])

Moreover, as Delany maintained in the same interview, the novel grapples with the dichotomy between the "bricoleur"—one who makes use of any material to address a problem at hand—and the "engineer." As Delany relates, "The engineer doesn't feel she's started to work . . . until she's got an overarching principle to apply to the solution of the problem, which she then implements as carefully and accurately as possible by precise technical means, moving in to take care of finer and finer problematic details—until hopefully, principle wholly absorbs problem."[33] One might read the politics of the novel's publication as offering the counterpoint in this dialectic between bricoleur and engineer, but as *Triton* makes clear, the shared "problem" for both approaches to governance is "identity."

On Triton, difference is encoded into the structure of governance. Characters are socially encouraged and technologically empowered to select identities that suit them at any particular moment: political dispositions, religious practices, and all imaginable forms of social difference are categorized and accepted (within given parameters). The calculability of difference commingles with its unthinking affirmations to act as a tactic for containment, management, and the political reincorporation of different identities. Thus *Triton* affirms recent scholarship that attends to various normativizing strategies that subtend identity and performativity.[34] But Delany's work also explicates a critically important (and overlooked) dimension of the use of heterotopia in the interdisciplines. A heterotopia is not a postmodern twist on a utopia. Rather, and as Foucault explained, "[its] role is to create a space of illusion that exposes every *real* space, all the sites inside of which *human life is partitioned*, as still more illusory. . . . Or else, on the contrary . . . to create a space that is *other*, another real space, as perfect, as meticulous, as well arranged as ours is messy, ill constructed, and jumbled."[35]

And here we might think of Achille Mbembe's work on vertical sovereignty and the crucial relation between the "good life" and the lives (subject to colonial and neocolonial rule) that must be sacrificed toward that ideal.[36] This is to say that chief among heterotopia's "radical inclusivities" is its capacity to accommodate biopolitical and necropolitical modes of governance, holding them together within the same political framework and making *space* for both to exist in seeming noncontradiction. As scholars of black gender and sexuality, we might consider refraining from celebrations of multiplicity, as if difference, itself, indexes social progress or transformation. Lest we pave the road to Triton's beautiful nightmare, we must attend to the politics of race, gender, and sexuality without the pretense that working on such issues places us any closer to a radical ideal. These politics are always *ambiguous*, and those things that are offered up as liberatory are illusory (akin to Foucault's formulation of heterotopias as spaces of illusion). What Delany writes in his (second) conclusion on the ambiguity of freedom on Triton is a powerful warning to us now:

> Our society in the Satellites extends to its Earth and Mars emigrants, at the same time it extends instruction on how to conform, the materials with which to destroy themselves both psychologically and physically—all under the same label: Freedom. To the extent they will not conform to our ways, there is a subtle swing: the materials of instruction are pulled further away and the materials of destruction are pushed correspondingly closer. Since the ways of instruction and the ways of destruction are . . . only subtly and secretly tied by language, we have simply, here . . . yet another way for the rest of us to remain oblivious to other people's pain.[37]

NOTES

1. Kathy Acker, "On Delany the Magician: A Foreword," in Samuel R. Delany, *Trouble on Triton: An Ambiguous Heterotopia* (Middletown, CT: Wesleyan University Press, 1996), xii.

2. The term first appears in Michel Foucault's *The Order of Things: An Archaeology of the Human Sciences* (New York: Random House, 1970) and finds additional elaboration in a lecture presented and later translated and printed as "Of Other Spaces," trans. Jay Miskowiec, *Diacritics* 16, no. 1 (1986): 22–27.

3. Samuel R. Delany, "On *Triton* and Other Matters: An Interview with Samuel R.

Delany," *Science Fiction Studies* 17, no. 3 (1990), accessed May 31, 2013, http://www
.depauw.edu/sfs/interviews/delany52interview.htm.

4. Elsewhere I have written on the significance of Delany's *Triton* for delimiting
the boundaries of black studies. See "On Black Studies: An Ambiguous Heterotopia,"
Black Scholar 44, no. 2 (2014): 29–36.

5. Butler responds to "the bad reading" of *Gender Trouble* (New York: Routledge,
1990) in "The Body You Want: Liz Kotz interviews Judith Butler," *Artforum* 31, no. 3
(1992): 82–89.

6. Roderick A. Ferguson, *The Reorder of Things: The University and Its Pedagogies of
Minority Difference* (Minneapolis: University of Minnesota Press, 2012), 14; and Lauren Berlant, *Cruel Optimism* (Durham, NC: Duke University Press, 2011).

7. Tucker draws extensively on Tom Moylan's *Demand the Impossible* (1986),
which argues that *Triton* exercises "the practices of imagining a radical other to what
is" and theorizes heterotopia as the "post-capitalist, post-modern, post-Enlightenment,
post-industrial society as utopia was to capitalist, bourgeois society." Jeffrey A. Tucker,
A Sense of Wonder: Samuel R. Delany, Race, Identity, and Difference (Middleton, CT: Wesleyan University Press, 2004), 42–44.

8. Delany, *Trouble on Triton*, 117.

9. Tucker, *Sense of Wonder*, 42–44.

10. Ferguson, *Reorder of Things*, 31.

11. Robert Elliot Fox, "The Politics of Desire in Delany's *Triton* and *Tides of Lust*,"
in *Ash of Stars: On the Writing of Samuel R. Delany*, ed. James Sallis (Jackson: University Press of Mississippi, 1996), 45.

12. Andrew W. Butler, *Solar Flares: Science Fiction in the 1970s* (Liverpool: Liverpool
University Press, 2012), 156.

13. Delany, *Trouble on Triton*, 25.

14. Delany, *Trouble on Triton*, 26.

15. "The Body You Want."

16. Delany, *Trouble on Triton*, 126–27.

17. John L. Jackson Jr., *Racial Paranoia: The Unintended Consequences of Political
Correctness* (New York: Basic Civitas, 2008).

18. From 1960 to 1963, Katanga seceded from the First Republic of the Congo as
its own state. It is currently a province of the Democratic Republic of the Congo.

19. Cressida J. Heyes, "Feminist Solidarity after Queer Theory: The Case of Transgender," *Signs* 28, no. 4 (2003): 1103.

20. Heyes, "Feminist Solidarity after Queer Theory," 1103.

21. Heyes is not suggesting that conceptions of race are not in any way related to
popular conceptions of gender: "The category of 'race' carries with it a (racist) biological
baggage that gives related meaning to medical interventions: race, in one (misguided)

part of the popular imagination, is a natural category that adheres to bodies rather than history; thus changing one's body can change one's race (or the perception of one's race—the same thing, or not, depending how you think). However, a (differently racist) discourse understands race as a superficial aspect of identity: 'we're all the same underneath.' If we are, in some sense, 'all the same' (where 'same' is coded 'white'), then 'transracialism' makes no sense. This latter humanist position has more of a grip on our thinking about race, I would argue, than it does in the case of gender" ("Feminist Solidarity after Queer Theory," 1103).

22. Delany, *Trouble on Triton*, 262–63.

23. Michel Foucault, *The Order of Things: An Archaeology of the Human Sciences* (New York: Random House, 1973), xviii, quoted in Delany, *Trouble on Triton*, 292.

24. Delany, "On *Triton* and Other Matters."

25. Samuel R. Delany, *Shorter Views: Queer Thoughts & the Politics of the Paraliterary* (Middletown, CT: Wesleyan University Press, 2000), 329.

26. Edward K. Chan, "(Vulgar) Identity Politics in Outer Space: Delany's 'Triton' and the Heterotopian Narrative," *Journal of Narrative Theory* 31, no. 2 (2001): 191.

27. Chan, "(Vulgar) Identity Politics," 181–82.

28. Ferguson, *Reorder of Things*, 31, 33–34.

29. Sylvia Wynter, "On How We Mistook the Map for the Territory, and Re-imprisoned Ourselves in Our Unbearable Wrongness of Being, of *Desêtre*: Black Studies toward the Human Project," in *A Companion to African-American Studies,* eds. Lewis R. Gordon and Jane Anna Gordon (New York: Blackwell Publishing, 2006), 107–18.

30. Delany, "On *Triton* and Other Matters."

31. The novel's republication in 1996 comes at what is considered the height of neoliberalism.

32. Ferguson, *Reorder of Things.*

33. Delany, "On *Triton* and Other Matters."

34. See, for example, Ferguson, *The Reorder of Things*; Susan Stryker, "Cross Dressing for Empire" (lecture presented at Northwestern University, February 2012); Jin Haritaworn and C. Riley Snorton, "Trans Necropolitics: A Transnational Reflection on Violence, Death, and the Trans of Color Afterlife," in *Transgender Studies Reader,* eds. Susan Stryker and Aren Aizura, 2nd ed. (New York: Routledge, 2013), 66–75.

35. Foucault, "Of Other Spaces," 27. Emphasis added.

36. Achille Mbembe, "Necropolitics," *Public Culture* 15, no. 1 (2003): 11–40.

37. Delany, *Trouble on Triton*, 302–3.

5

Reggaetón's Crossings

Black Aesthetics, Latina Nightlife, and Queer Choreography

RAMÓN H. RIVERA-SERVERA

☕

IN A JULY IO, 2013, EDITORIAL PUBLISHED in *Claridad*, the pro-independence weekly newspaper in Puerto Rico, social psychologist and scholar Angie Vazquez lamented the "regressive movements" of a contemporary culture where women assumed the passive role in *perreo*, the best-known choreographic arrangement in reggaetón social dance. Reggaetón is a hybrid hip hop musical subgenre grounded in Jamaican dance hall.[1] Its dance style is similarly explicit in its mimicking of the sexual act and equally grounded in an Afro-Caribbean choreographic repertoire that invests in rhythmic isolation of the hips and articulation of the buttocks. In the perreo choreographies that concern Vazquez, the dancers are arranged along hierarchically gendered lines. In the most basic version of this dance, women position themselves with their backs to their male partners as in a back grind or a freak but bend over fully, sometimes touching the floor with their hands, to flaunt their buttocks in a back-and-forth rocking hip isolation against their co-performer's groin area. Explicitly imitative of doggy-style sex, perreo has been at the center of much controversy for the past decade, including the infamous 2002 campaign to legislate against its public performance in Puerto Rico by then senator Velda González.[2]

For Vazquez, perreo models "hardcore, fetishistic, voyeuristic and de-personalized" sexual relations and gendered socialization. She identifies in this choreographed display a history of sexual violence that goes as far back as the rape of slave women by their overseers. It is precisely the weight of this foundational history of slavery that "assaults her mind" and fuels the dangerous play that perreo choreography supposedly enacts. This contemporary but "regressive movement" is also seen as a challenge to the progressive narrative of feminist political and cultural achievement on the island. As she states: "From the old feminism and its struggles we have arrived at a butt culture; a hedonist philosophy that subjugates woman, treating her, and letting herself be treated, as a dog."[3]

I take Vazquez's worries about a *nalga-cultura* or butt-culture turn in Puerto Rico seriously. I recognize and sympathize with her concern for reggaetón's gendered violence. Reggaetón as a musical culture has indeed maintained an aggressively *machista* attitude toward women as sexual objects. However, in this essay I am invested in identifying feminist and queer uses of reggaetón. That is, I want to work against the grain of the prevalent and all too deterministic criticism of this musical culture to identify the ways in which women, including queer women, have gained tactical forms of agency and pleasure from within reggaetón's normative heteropatriarchy. My concern is not with the few female reggaetón artists who have gained recognition both in popular and academic circles as offering a potentially feminist front to the industry. Instead, I focus on the women who move to reggaetón's beat but are not slave to its rhythm, those who navigate the crowded dance floors of this now mainstream musical force.[4] In doing so, I look at the ways in which the black aesthetics of reggaetón and the sexually charged and, yes, gendered imbalances of this musical culture are played with seriously in Latina feminist and queer cultural practice.

In what follows, I look at reggaetón choreography as presented in Latina social dance settings to explore how perreo may be done otherwise to feminist and queer ends. I discuss *Gran Perreton* (2005), a short video documenting a perreo dance marathon organized by visual artist Carolina Caycedo and an example from my ongoing ethnographic fieldwork into Latina queer social dance since the mid-1990s to model a grounds-up approach to this genre that centers the microagencies of dancerly acts.[5] I contend that these examples offer critical engagements with reggaetón that are as aware of the genre's potentials, politics, and pleasures as they are of its shortcomings and pitfalls. Throughout, I argue that much of the generative force behind feminist and queer iterations of reggaetón is to be found in a serious engagement with the black aesthetics, and potentially the politics, of the genre.

On the Blackness of Reggaetón and Queer Latinidad

Central to my intervention is an insistence in the recognition of the blackness of *latinidad*, especially in Puerto Rican and queer contexts.[6] I hope the issues raised in this short essay will serve as an invitation to scholars to continue the expansion of the ethnic and geographic specificity of the intellectual and political project of black queer studies to Latina/o and Latin American contexts and communities. The visionary models advanced in Third World feminism since the early 1980s and queers of color critique since the 1990s are key to this enterprise.[7] But in addition to the comparative and coalitional models that seek to bring black and Latina/o experience together, we also need to more substantively recognize the very fact of blackness—as historical materiality, aesthetic and political imaginary, and contemporary identitarian coordinate—in Latina/o life. The growing field of Afro-Latina/o studies and the now-established focus on gender in the study of the African Diaspora in Latin America bode well for the future trajectories of this much-needed conversation.[8] Queer perspectives are unfortunately still marginal to, though certainly emergent, in these discussions.[9]

Reggaetón's multidirectional and still expanding social geography yields a complex map that interanimates black, Latina/o, feminist, and queer cultural politics as the genre, grounded in an Afro-Latina/o experience and aesthetics, engages African American figurations of hip hop music and styling and circulates along the same global hip hop routes to pop culture communities worldwide. That is, the blackness of reggaetón is always already intertwined with U.S. and hip hop global modalities of blackness and, in turn, influences these realms. To engage this cultural platform from an LGBTQ vantage point is not just to queer latinidad but to queer blackness writ large.

Reggaetón, Puerto Rico's early twenty-first-century popular music export to the world, has been credited with enabling the extension of the 1999 Latin music explosion in the United States well into the first decade of this century.[10] A musical hybrid that draws from African American and Latin American hip hop, Jamaican dance hall, Panamanian ragga, and other Afro-Latin American musical genres such as salsa, merengue, bachata, batucada, and more, this subgenre of global hip hop has been variously understood as not authentically black or as excessively working-class black.[11] Attacks to the hip hop legitimacy of the genre have pointed to its commercial success and production values, its break from U.S. old-school genre-specific codes and conventions (for example, singing MCs), and its latinidad (interpreted as not-black) as deviations or bastardizations of what is erroneously narrated as an exclusively U.S. African American cultural form.[12] Conversely, a large number of the early dismissals of the genre by Puerto Rican critics characterized reggaetón as a U.S. import and pitted it against more "autochthonous" national music such as salsa or bomba.

The vast majority of the critical engagements with the debates over reggaetón have focused on the question of performed ethnic, racial, national, or genre authenticity and, in some instances, working-class politics.[13] Unfortunately, much of the scholarship to date has assumed the logics of ethnicity, race, and class to operate along a heteropatriarchal axis. Latino masculinity has been the main currency of this debate, even when launching feminist critiques of the genre. I take a queer turn into the blackness of reggaetón by pursuing how Latinas access choreographic repertoires open to gender and sexual play. In this formulation, the black aesthetics of reggaetón offer performance modalities that enable alternative and pleasurable feminist and queer exchanges in and through dance. If, as E. Patrick Johnson has observed, "the dialectic formulated through the process of gender and sexual performativity demonstrates the incoherence of black heterosexuality," then this incoherence is productively mined in the performance contexts that I turn to where dancing within a black aesthetic queers the assumed coherence of racial as much as gender and sexual coordinates.[14] Blackness is here both identity and aesthetic, assumed and appropriated in ways that render the entanglements of race, class, gender, and sexuality in a complexly choreographed dance that is as pleasurable as it is dangerous.

In looking at the creative maneuvers of women who delve into reggaetón aesthetics in assertively feminist and queer ways, I offer a particularly Latina/o and queer engagement with J. Jack Halberstam's challenge to U.S. feminists' conservative investment in a politics of reproduction focused on securing white middle-class traditions and ideals of good or proper living. Halberstam states, "What if we actually started to notice the ways in which race and sexuality have become hopelessly entangled with notions of the normal and the perverse, so that we could see the ways in which the white family hides its secrets behind thick layers of presumed normativity, while black families in particular but also Latino and Muslim families are regularly cast as excessive or intolerant, traditional and behind the times? The 'what if' is fun and hopeful but it is also serious and penetrating and might just bring us to new ideas about old topics."[15] What if instead of lamenting a turn to nalga-cultura in Puerto Rican popular culture as regressive we were to pursue its pleasures and potentials?[16] What if we were to understand this turn as a challenge to the teleology of white middle-class Puerto Rican feminism and its emphasis on respectability and mainstreaming? What if the perreo dynamics were to be taken seriously as a working-class black feminist and queer politics?

Choreographing Complexity: Cats and Dogs, or How the Booty Rules the Dance Floor

Vazquez's objections to perreo, a repetition of more than a decade-old argument, relies on the presumed debased position of women dancers who assume sexually submissive positions in the execution of reggaetón dance. This argumentative premise supposes that women have no agency in the choreographic arrangements and execution of perreo. Furthermore, it concludes that this act of submission of the rear end constitutes a backward move in the feminist politics of mainstream ascendancy and respectability in Puerto Rico. However, a closer look at the practices of perreo in reggaetón nightlife offers a more complex picture of what in fact is at play on the dance floor.

A performance event and documentary short by visual artist Carolina Caycedo offer a good first example of how reggaetón may present more multidirectional agentive possibilities for dancers.[17] In 2004, Caycedo held a reggaetón dance-off at Don Raúl's Bar and Restaurant, a popular weekend hangout spot on the northwestern coastal municipality of Rincón, Puerto Rico. The promotional materials announced the Gran Perretón, as the event was named, as a dance competition. Participants registered in the contest as couples and stood to win a romantic dinner and overnight stay at a beachfront hotel.

Pictured at the center of the promotional ad was a sunglasses-clad heterosexual couple assuming the iconic perreo pose: his groin against her buttocks, right arm raised at the shoulder and bent at the elbow to flex his bicep in a display of male bravado. His counterpart, knees bent and torso leaned forward, turns her head behind her right shoulder toward her partner as if to confirm the success of her submission. She is encouraged by the comics-style sound effect text, strategically placed around her head, exclaiming, "Hasta abajo!" ("All the way down!") and "Tra-Tra!," reggaetón's most recognizable rhythmic vocalization.

Is it really submission of the female dancer we are invited to look at in this scene? Is it the reduction of woman to bitch that so concerns Vazquez about perreo that we witness in this flashy advertisement? The couple is, in fact, surrounded by no fewer than twenty digitally collaged images of dogs of various breeds, one pair in the midst of mating, suggesting, perhaps, that the analogy so feared by the critic is indeed unraveling before us in this visual display of reggaetón machismo in its most literally sexual and dogged, pun intended, way. However, a more careful look that accounts for the "creativity and resistance" advertised as the criteria for evaluation in this event, written in bold letters at the bottom right corner of the ad, might suggest alternate routes to our interpretation. This may be further enhanced by yet another visual clue in this very content-busy ad. The woman at the center of the ad holds in her hand leashes that radiate outward from her position as the central figure of the image. Attached to the leashes are a large number, though not all, of the dogs surrounding her. That is, despite what Vazquez might read as the woman's degrading self-positioning as a dog, she is the one potentially mastering the pack.

The fifteen-minute documentary video of this more than five-hour collective durational performance—competition started at 10:00 p.m. and concluded at 3:00 a.m., but dancing continued until dawn—further invites the possibility of creativity and resistance by women who perform perreo. The video opens in silence with the colorful image of the promotional ad described above, camera zooming into a close-up of the groin to buttocks contact area (which includes the hands of the female dancer holding the blue-rope dog leashes). The close-up cuts to a black screen followed by a view of Raúl's Bar in black-and-white footage along with a now-audible reggaetón chorus and the encouraging exclamations of the DJ/host. This establishing shot pulls back slightly to focus on a couple dancing in the foreground and then quickly (in five seconds) transitions to a four-way split screen featuring four different perspectives and groups of dancers on the same dance floor. The result is a dizzying frenzy of moving bodies, made more fragmentary by the effects of the strobe light, in a difficult-to-generalize choreographic collage. Yes, there are discernible couples engaged in traditional perreo dancing, but the feel is more collective, almost atmospheric at this point in the video.

The sense of the dance crowd, the pack, if we are to extend the visual pun of the advertisement, is further enhanced by the sequences of participatory sing-alongs when the sound is lowered and the club patrons collectively perform the muted lyrics. The breakdown here is explicit in its gender binary. "Cómo dice corillo?" (How does it go my crew?), exclaims the DJ, inviting all to venture into this playful fill-in-the-blank game to Don Omar's 2003 hit single "Dale Don Dale," featuring vocals by Puerto Rican reggaetón singer Glory, best known as La Gata Gangster (The Gangster Cat).[18] The men fill in for the chorus to Don Omar's lyrics: "Dale Don dale / Pa' que se muevan las yales / Pa' activar los anormales." Here men call on the MC to get going, to fire up the dance floor so the women get moving and the "freaks" get activated. The women respond by filling in Glory's part in collective moans, "Ay papi!" and "Dale papi / Que estoy suelta como gabete!"[19] From here on, the video cuts rapidly from song fragment to song fragment in the evening's sequence, extending reggaetón's bestiary from the dog that characterizes perreo dancing to "cats in heat" and "cats in need of therapy" that further literalize perreo's sexually explicit referents.[20]

Granted, the sexual flirtations performed above are beyond innuendo. They fuel the rather expected heteropatriarchal charge of the event, even in anthropomorphically offensive ways. But the choreographic dynamics they animate, as documented in Caycedo's video, cannot be simply characterized as a scene of female submission. Choreographically, it is the women who dominate the film. As couples are called into the final portions of the competition, it is the women's skilled movements and manipulation of their partners, who display a much more limited range of dance ability, that become the primary feature of Caycedo's documentary.

The women are, to say the least, acrobatic in their feats. They contract their buttocks to the music's rhythm while lowering their bodies to the ground. They top their men who lay almost horizontally as they gyrate their hips in commanding fashion. They adjust, push, shove, and direct their partners on the dance floor as the men, in turn, attempt to keep up by matching movement shapes and rhythms dictated by their *gatas* or *perras* (cats or dogs) and awkwardly attempting to resume their mimicking of the manly, top-fucking roles that characterize their choreography. At one point, one of the women uses another man, sitting by the edge of the dance floor, as a prop to support herself while she moves. Meanwhile, her partner dances behind her oblivious to the fact that they have become a trio. The narrative of the dance may feature men spanking ass and thrusting their groins onto bent-over women, but the qualitative execution of movement clearly showcases, and I would argue favors, the women's agency as skilled dancers and choreographers.

This "new feminism," as it is announced in Caycedo's artist statement, focuses on the ways "women take advantage of their sexual attraction, beauty and body language to achieve their goals."[21] This proposition, that women consciously mobilize their corporeality as a feminist strategy, resonates with feminist performance scholar Rebecca Schneider's understanding of the potentially "explosive literality" of the body in performance.[22] In Schneider's study, it is precisely the tactile, literal presence of the body that challenges age-old traditions of women's bodies as simply objects to be looked at. Granted, Schneider is working from within an art historical tradition, but it is also the tactility of bodies dancing on the reggaetón dance floor that most successfully emerges as an intervention in Caycedo's film. From the collective constitution of the *corillo*, or crew, as collective motion/action to the choreographic ingenuity of women in perreo dance, it is the visual that becomes easily overwhelmed as perreo agency turns objects of scopophilic fascination into tactically and tactile moving subjects. Furthermore, the fact that men are called into performance, as choppily ill-executed as their dancing might be, means that they are prevented from assuming an exclusively voyeuristic position in the club. They are as much in motion and on display as the women in this dynamic. But it is the women who advance the dance repertoires of this social scene.

Popular music scholar Raquel Rivera concurs with the agency to be found in these sexually explicit displays of perreo dancing as framed in Caycedo's artist statement. However, she objects to what she sees as an overall lack of recognition of reggaetón's heteropatriarchal historical and contemporary contexts. Rivera explains,

> I sympathize with Caycedo's impulse to defend and celebrate *perreo* from its detractors. However, rather than eliding the issue of sexual explicitness or the male supremacist context within which *perreo* takes place, as Caycedo does in her statement, I think we push along the debate much further if we just confront the issue head on. Yes. *Perreo* is

more sexually explicit than tango and flamenco. So? The level of sexism of a certain cultural expression is not in direct correlation with sexual explicitness. Yes. *Perreo* is a space rife with sexism. Just like every other realm in our sexist society.[23]

I agree with Rivera's concerns, but as I have argued above, I find the strength of the women represented in Caycedo's film to be born not of a naïve ignorance of the embodied economies at play in the dance floor but of a masterful navigation of a terrain overwhelmingly built to disadvantage them for their own tactical benefit. This is not an easy argument for Caycedo to advance, and perhaps it is best articulated in the film than in her artist's statement. The gender dynamics of the genre are nothing but appallingly skewed, but attending to choreographic strategies of the women, their creativity and resistance, allows us to identify microlevel realms of practice that make reggaetón's nightlife not only bearable but also pleasurable for many of the women involved.

It is important to return to the question of blackness here. For, as I state at the opening of this essay, the musical and dance culture of reggaetón is grounded in a black aesthetics tradition. Considering the historical politico-economic marginalization and stigmatization of blackness, especially working-class blackness, by many Puerto Rican elites, women's sexually assertive and explicit showcasing of reggaetón bodies in articulate black motion may also represent an intervention into the politics of elite propriety where many feminist political programs on the island seem trapped. I do not think this is the motivation behind Vazquez's objections to perreo, but it is a risk performed by her dismissal. I see an ethnographic investment in the microagencies of women who participate in reggaetón as a much-needed response to the comfortable middle-class and often aspirationally white logics of "educated" political actors.[24] Here I am in agreement with Deborah Thomas, Beth-Sarah Wright, and Donna P. Hope, who see in the sexual explicitness of dance hall performers in Jamaica the cultural agency of black working-class women framed by a political economy of colonization, slavery, and postcolonial nation-building that demanded heteronormative conceptions of black masculinity and femininity and rigorous controls of black female sexuality.[25]

The strategies performed by the women on the reggaetón dance floor model the concept of "citizenship from below" that Mimi Sheller has developed to understand the queer ways in which subaltern actors figure out routes into agency that may at times, in large part owing to the contextual unevenness of the politico-economic terrain, lead to the repetition of hegemonic forms of social and cultural arrangements. This does not mean that we ought to discard women who dance reggaetón because of the genre's overwhelming emphasis of male dominance. In fact, we ought to document and understand the ways in which women labor to gain a sense of freedom within these contexts. As Sheller explains, "The historian of freedom who seeks traces of subaltern agency must also look beneath conventional definitions of political agency and of citizenship and seek out the unexcavated field of embodied (material and spiritual) practices through which people exercise and envision freedom."[26] Sheller advances the concept of "erotic agency" to catalogue the realm of activity in Caribbean social and cultural arrangements where subaltern subjects not only claim their sexual freedom but engage in a political effort that "works our bodies toward an expansive engagement with life, implying a more holistic locus for citizenship that reaches far beyond the state and its strictures of erotic subjugation in exchange for recognition as a citizen."[27] In moving their behinds in expertly choreographed sequences and commanding their partner's co-performance on the dance floor, the women of reggaetón documented in Caycedo's film find their erotic agency in and through black performance.

Lesbian Erotics and Reggaetón's Racialized Queerness

The complex choreographic economies of reggaetón dance, rendered full of feminist potential in Caycedo's video documentation, are further textured in queer social dance environments where different approaches to sexual and gender identity and performance intersect with and trouble the dominant scripts of reggaetón heteropatriarchy. If the women in Caycedo's film found "erotic agency" along heterosexual lines of activity, the women at the queer dance establishments where I have been conducting fieldwork over the past fifteen years found in reggaetón a genre of cultural practice full of queer possibilities.[28]

At Club Karamba, a Phoenix, Arizona, Latina/o queer establishment frequented largely by Mexican American queer Latinos and their Anglo admirers, reggaetón entered the scene around 2005. At the time the genre was widely distributed and characterized via radio airwaves and media in the Phoenix metro area and throughout the nation as the second coming of the 1999 Latin music explosion that catapulted the careers of Ricky Martin, Shakira, Jennifer Lopez, and others into international fame. While the 1999 explosion brought Latin "spice" to mainstream U.S. pop music, reggaetón's vibe was decidedly of a darker hue. I have discussed elsewhere how reggaetón music was incorporated into the primarily Mexican and Mexican American focus of the Latina/o queer nightlife in Phoenix because its novelty as mainstream pop culture at a time when Latinas/os in pre-economic-crisis Arizona were flirting with the fantasies of mainstream ascendancy. In these contexts, the black aesthetics of Puerto Rican performance invited other Latinas/os for whom reggaetón was sufficiently familiar but not intimately known to perform their queer sexualities through racialized scripts.[29] In this sense, Caribbean black aesthetics enabled erotic agency in Latina/o communities less frequently identified as black.

During their smoking break at the outdoor patio, Dulce and Andrea, a Mexican American femme lesbian couple then in their midtwenties, spoke rather candidly about their perception of reggaetón as black. Dulce commented that for her "reggaetón is just like black hip hop but in Spanish. I dance it just the same." Andrea intervened, "I think black but I don't think hip hop black. I dance mostly like a merengue or salsa but with little steps. My arms I guess do salsa and my feet just do the littlest steps." Observing their dancing together corroborates both of their characterizations as general patterns. Dulce tends to assume a masculine hip hop swagger, feet slightly parted and parallel to shoulders, torso slightly slanted backward, arms extended up and to the sides and around Andrea. She mostly takes simple side-to-side steps with an upper torso bouncing contraction. Andrea, on the other hand, assumed a Latin social dance position, as in salsa or danzón, and though she matched Dulce's modest step sequence side to side, she fully articulated her arms, sometimes resting an arm on her partner's shoulder or raising it above their heads, delicately wiggling fingers in complete independence from the music's rhythm. Instead, her rhythm was marked by her articulation of the hips side to side in the merengue choreography she called attention to in our patio discussion.

However, Dulce and Andrea's choreography changes significantly when Daddy Yankee's reggaetón anthem "Gasolina," featuring Glory's sexually titillating come-ons, is spun by the DJ. Almost instantaneously, they assume a perreo position, with Dulce continuing to play a masculine hip hop swagger, although both of them present femme gender choices, and Andrea turns around and begins to back up into her partner. I took the marked difference with which they approach their dancing to this song as a sign of Daddy Yankee's popularity still less than a year after the release of his third album, *Barrio Fino*, in 2004. However, in a follow-up interview with the couple a few weeks later, Dulce and Andrea jointly and effusively swooned over Glory as Andrea stated, "Esa negra es bella! (That black woman is gorgeous!) I mean, damn! Forget Daddy Yankee, we'll take her home anytime!" When I asked further if it was Glory's performance in the track that prompted the shift in their choreography, Andrea responded, "Of course! She is our girl! She is in all the backups. Even if it is not her, we imagine it to be her. That white boy has nothing on her. She is *prieta* [dark] like us. Para ella hay que *perrear* (For her we have to do the perreo dance)." Hearing Andrea refer to Daddy Yankee as a white boy is not necessarily a dismissal of his identity as a Latino as much as it is an acknowledgment of Glory's more visible black difference. That such a difference is marked as desirable, her prieta light-skin blackness as a match to Dulce and Andrea's dark brownness, demonstrates the ways in which racial and sexual desire are interlinked in Latina lesbian choreographies. In this particular instance, Glory, an Afro-Puerto Rican reggaetón performer whose role as a back-up singer is assumed to be secondary to Daddy Yankee's act, emerges as the protagonist in the dance floor performances of Mexican American lesbian fans. The secondary or minor text is here transformed into the primary one, positioning Glory's blackness as central to the dancers' declared connection and love for Daddy Yankee's "Gasolina" song.

I want to turn to another example from Karamba where the racial erotics of reggaetón fuel affirmative performances of race. Alma, an Afro-Mexicana femme lesbian immigrant from the coastal region of Tabasco, who arrived in Phoenix in 2002 and worked at a Mexican supermarket in South Phoenix, once mentioned to me that reggaetón's arrival had finally given her the upper hand with her light-skinned butch girlfriend from Jalisco. She explained:

> Always when we went out. I mean always. It was she who led on the dancing. Mostly cause it was her music, and she was familiar so she was bossy when dancing. But when reggaetón came in, she was clueless! I mean clueless! Like she was used to moving her hips side to side maybe, but how in the world was she going to do the perrito dance? So, I started leading. I mean, not like I was the man, she still plays that, but I had to tell her what to do, how to move. Basically I was now bossing her around. And she got good!

Alma's story about finding an opportunity in reggaetón's blackness to assert her own Afro-Mexican heritage through performance also helped her gain some agency with her more dominant butch girlfriend. Her negotiation was not a challenge to her butch/femme arrangements—in fact, she took great pride in the gendered nature of their relationship—but a tactical negotiation, a microagency, within the established parameters of her social situation. Most important, dancing reggaetón with her clueless girlfriend provided her an opportunity to mark her racial difference from a position of strength within an ethnonational social scene where blackness remains largely absented from the public purchase of Mexican and Mexican American ideas about *mestizaje*.[30]

What Dulce and Andrea and Alma and her girlfriend (whom I never met during my fieldwork) demonstrate with their particular experiences and approaches to reggaetón dancing are the ways in which the heteropatriarchal scripts of reggaetón are easily destabilized in the queer practices of Latina lesbian dancers. They enter the space of the club with their own desires for an erotic agency not afraid of playing with gender but also secured in its queer difference from the mainstream cultural text. That the blackness of reggaetón also enabled the particular erotic charge of each of their routines furthers the reach of reggaetón's potential as a performance aesthetic loaded with complicated and oftentimes oppressive race, gender, and sexual ideologies, to recall Johnson's dialectic above, but ultimately vulnerable to queer choreographies.

Reggaetoneras to the Dance Floor, Please!

It would be a mistake to suggest that the simple act of performing a skillful perreo routine constitutes an exclusively resistant act. As I have explained throughout this essay, neither the presumed heterosexual women in Caycedo's video nor the queer women at Club Karamba engage reggaetón without encountering its gendered and homophobic violence, negotiating its racial politics relative to Puerto Rican as well as U.S. Latino ethnoracial hierarchies and histories and participating in a dance that is charged with potential pleasures as much as pains. As Tracy Sharpley Whiting concludes in her landmark study into the role of young women in hip hop from the video vixen to the stripper to the groupie, "hip hop is an obvious landmine of contradictions."[31]

But I believe in the significant and much-needed role feminist and queer critique can play in an engagement with hip hop that is attendant to its politico-economic and representational disadvantaging of black women and queers but that also unearths quotidian microagencies, perhaps less charged with the transformational force of movement politics but significant, even necessary, for the daily survival of a multitude born into the hip hop generation. How these politics unravel in the context of reggaetón and its circulation among Latina/o communities, in Puerto Rico and the United States, where blackness has been historically undervalued but enthusiastically consumed, renders the queer politics of reggaetón even more explosive.

Vazquez's dismissal of reggaetón as a downward descent into a nalga-cultura represents too limited an assessment of the gender and queer politics of the genre. Nalga-cultura has long been at the center of Puerto Rican public life. Before the advent of reggaetón, the buttocks assumed a central role in the national fascination with popular Puerto Rican performers such as Iris Chacón, who flaunted her buttocks on national television as a guest on David Letterman's *Late Night Show* in the 1980s, and Jennifer Lopez, whose rear end catapulted into international fame during the Latin explosion in the late 1990s and has figured prominently in close-up shots in the majority of her film appearances.[32]

In light of that history, the distinction between the female star or the "video ho" as given to be looked-at objects of a national heteropatriachal spectatorial community is perhaps what is most spectacularly undone in the social dance practices unraveling in the Rincón, Puerto Rico, beach bar or the Phoenix, Arizona, Latina/o queer dance club. In both these locations, the focus of the action is on bodies in motion queerly articulating a performance script rooted in homophobic and sexist violence. Nonetheless these performances master the skills of a black aesthetic that elevates the status of the butt in perreo, and Latina/o culture more broadly, from the presumed passivity of bottoming in anal sex or the symbolic stand-in for racist stereotype and female submissions, into the skillful performance of agency. This agency is limited, compromised even, but persistent. In her move to install a politics of feminist respectability, Vazquez overlooks black choreography as feminist queer intervention. Understanding reggaetón's queer potential requires a descent from the heady politics of an armchair feminism into the nitty-gritty of a grinding hip or a contracting behind where an embodiment of black aesthetics playfully intimates a risky but potential rerouting of hip hop's libidinal economy in specifically, pleasurable Latina/o queer ways.

1. Angie Vazquez, "El giro a la nalga-cultura," *Claridad* (San Juan, Puerto Rico), July 10, 2013, accessed July 11, 2013, http://www.claridadpuertorico.com/content.html ?news=D82BE672B54606465703E7236680878D.

2. For an account of some of early debates that fueled the conversation around reggaetón, see Raquel Rivera, "Policing Morality, *Mano Dura Stylee*: The Case of Underground Rap and Reggae in the Mid-1990s," in *Reggaeton*, eds. Raquel Rivera, Wayne Marshall, and Deborah Pacini Hernandez (Durham, NC: Duke University Press, 2009), 111–34.

3. Vazquez, "El giro a la nalga-cultura."

4. For important and nuanced feminist discussions of reggaetón's leading female exponent, Ivy Queen, see Jillián M. Vázquez, "*En mi imperio*': Competing Discourses of Agency in Ivy Queen's Reggaetón," *Centro Journal* 17, no. 2 (2006): 61–81; and Alexandra T. Vazquez, "Salon Philosophers: Ivy Queen and Surprise Guests Take Reggaetón Aside," in Rivera, Marshall, and Pacini Hernandez, *Reggaeton*, 300–311.

5. I am aware of the different forms of evidence presented by an art video that documents a performance event and ethnographic observations and interviews obtained from my own witnessing of performance. My argument rests on the live choreographies of dancers in club settings, those documented in Caycedo's video, and those I encountered in fieldwork. Different arguments could be made about reggaetón music videos where choreographic agency is much more under the control of industry standards and expectations or about amateur uptakes of the reggaetón music video aesthetic in social media platforms such as Facebook and YouTube, where dancers may assume authorship for their dancing.

6. By *latinidad* I mean "the ethnic and panethnic imaginaries, identities, and affects that emerge from the increased intersection of multiple Latina/o communities." See Ramón Rivera-Servera, *Performing Queer Latinidad: Dance, Sexuality, Politics* (Ann Arbor: University of Michigan Press, 2012), 22.

7. Foundational figures to Third World feminism are the works of Chandra Talpede Mohanty, Audre Lorde, Cherríe Moraga, and Gloria Anzaldúa. For queer of color criticism, see the works of Roderick Ferguson, José Estaban Muñoz, and E. Patrick Johnson.

8. Especially laudable is Miriam Jiménez Román and Juan Flores, eds., *The Afro-Latin@ Reader: History and Culture in the United States* (Durham, NC: Duke University Press, 2012).

9. Some key contributions to feminist and queer studies of blackness in Latin America include Jafari Sinclair Allen, *¡Venceremos?: The Erotics of Black Self-making*

in Cuba (Durham, NC: Duke University Press, 2011); Omise'eke Natasha Tinsley, *Thiefing Sugar: Eroticism between Women in Caribbean Literature* (Durham, NC: Duke University Press, 2010); and Donna M. Goldstein, *Laughter Out of Place: Race, Class, Violence, and Sexuality in a Rio Shantytown* (Berkeley: University of California Press, 2003).

10. I discuss the 1999 Latin explosion and its 1980s precursors in *Performing Queer Latinidad*. See especially the section "Latin Explosions, Pink Dollars, and Conservative Pushback," 10–16.

11. I discuss the debates around the ethnoracial authenticity of reggaetón in "Musical Trans(actions): Intersections in Reggaetón," *Trans: Revista Transcultural de Música* 13 (2009), http://www.sibetrans.com/trans/a62/musical-transactions-intersections-in -reggaeton.

12. See Raquel Z. Rivera, "Between Blackness and Latinidad in the Hip Hop Zone," in *A Companion to Latino Studies*, eds. Juan Flores and Renato Rosaldo (Oxford: Blackwell Publishing, 2007), 351–62.

13. See Rivera, Marshall, and Pacini Hernandez, *Reggaeton*, for a broad sample of this scholarship.

14. E. Patrick Johnson, *Appropriating Blackness: Performance and the Politics of Authenticity* (Durham, NC: Duke University Press, 2003), 74.

15. J. Jack Halberstam, *Gaga Feminism: Sex, Gender, and the End of Normal* (Boston: Beacon Press, 2012), 8.

16. In 1999 Joan Morgan published an important articulation of her experience as a "hip-hop feminist." In advancing this position she moves away from black-and-white clear-cut choices over specific MCs or political programs in favor of the "subtle, intriguing shades of gray" where "contrary voices meet." See Morgan, *When Chickenheads Come Home to Roost: My Life as a Hip-Hop Feminist* (New York: Simon and Schuster, 1999), 62.

17. Caycedo was born in London, of Colombian descent, and was raised in Colombia before moving to Puerto Rico as an adult.

18. For a critical discussion of Glory's work, see Félix Jiménez, "(W)rapped in Foil: Glory at Twelve Words a Minute," in Rivera, Marshall, and Hernández, *Reggaeton*, 229–51.

19. The men's lyrics translate as "C'mon on Don, c'mon / So the chicks get on moving / So we activate the freaks." The women's response is "C'mon papi / Cause I'm as loose as a shoelace!" Translation by the author.

20. Women as cats in heat are referenced in Don Omar's "Dale," which is included in his album *The Last Don* (2003). Women are characterized as cats in need of therapy in Wissin and Yandel's "La Gitana," which is also featured in Caycedo's video.

21. Carolina Caycedo, "Artist Statement," cited in Raquel Rivera, "Perreo and Power: Explicit Sexuality in Reggaetón" (unpublished paper presented at the Latin American Studies Association Annual Conference, Rio de Janeiro, June 2009).

22. Rebecca Schneider, *The Explicit Body in Performance* (London: Routledge, 1997), 2.

23. Rivera, "Perreo and Power," 4.

24. In her presentation at the Latin American Studies Association Annual Conference (see note 21), Raquel Rivera also calls for an ethnographic look into these practices. Citing José A. Laguarta Ramírez and Nahomi Galindo Malavé's critique of the feminist dismissal of reggaetón as coming from middle-class academics, Rivera invites us to attend to the racial implications of this division. I see both issues as critical to understanding reggaetón's agency, in this essay and in my work at large. See my *Performing Queer Latinidad* for an extended discussion of reggaetón racial and class politics in inter-Latina/o contexts.

25. Donna P. Hope, *Inna di Dancehall: Popular Culture and the Politics of Identity in Jamaica* (Kingston: University of West Indies Press, 2006); Beth-Sarah Wright, "Speaking the Unspeakable: Politics of the Vagina in Dancehall Docu-videos," *Discourses in Dance* 2, no. 2 (2004): 45–59; Deborah Thomas, *Exceptional Violence: Embodied Citizenship in Transnational Jamaica* (Durham, NC: Duke University Press, 2011).

26. Mimi Sheller, *Citizenship from Below: Erotic Agency and Caribbean Freedom* (New York: New York University Press, 2012), 6.

27. Sheller, *Citizenship from Below*, 279.

28. This section developed out of ethnographic research conducted at Latina/o queer nightlife establishments in Phoenix, Arizona, from 2004 to 2007 with subsequent check-in visits in 2008 and 2009. Most interviewees were recruited at the site. Interviews were conducted at or near the club premises. Informants have been assigned substitute names to protect their privacy.

29. See my "Dancing Reggaetón with Cowboy Boots: Frictive Encounters in Queer Latinidad," in *Performing Queer Latinidad*, 168–203.

30. *Mestizaje* is a term that refers to racial amalgamation, especially between European and indigenous populations, since the beginning of colonization in the Americas. It became entangled with nationalist ideologies in many Latin American states and other political and cultural forces, intent in uniting diverse populations at the advent of the postcolony. In the United States, it has continued to greatly influence the racial imaginaries of Latinas/os, especially Mexican Americans. Blackness, although included in many versions of mestizaje across the Americas, is generally de-emphasized to uphold the European/native dyad as foundational. For important recent discussions of mestizaje, see Alicia Arrizón, *Queering Mestizaje: Transculturation and Performance* (Ann Arbor: University of Michigan Press, 2006); and Rafael Pérez-Torres, *Mestizaje: Critical Uses in Chicano Culture* (Minneapolis: University of Minnesota Press, 2006).

31. Tracy Sharpley Whiting, *Pimps Up, Hos Down: Hip Hop's Hold on Young Black Women* (New York: New York University Press, 2007), 149.

32. See Frances Negrón-Muntaner, "Jennifer's Butt," *Aztlán: A Journal of Chicano Studies* 22, no. 2 (1997): 181–94; and Mary Beltrán, "The Hollywood Latina Body as Site of Social Struggle: Media Constructions of Stardom and Jennifer Lopez's 'Crossover Butt,'" *Quarterly Review of Film and Video* 19, no. 1 (2002): 71–86.

6

I Represent Freedom

Diaspora and the Meta-Queerness of Dub Theater

LYNDON K. GILL

☟

BLACK LESBIAN POLITICAL SCIENTIST and recent foremother of black queer theory, Cathy Cohen, has for nearly a decade and a half challenged queer theorists and activists to pursue the kind of radically queer politics that refuses to blindly set itself against all heterosexuals:

> I envision a politics where one's relation to power, and not some homogenized identity, is privileged in determining one's political comrades. I am talking about a politics where the nonnormative and marginal positions of punks, bulldaggers, and welfare queens, for example are the basis for progressive transformative coalition work. Thus, if any truly radical potential is to be found in the idea of queerness and the practice of queer politics, it would seem to be located in its ability to create a space in opposition to dominant norms, a space where transformational political work can begin.[1]

For Cohen, "punks" and "bulldaggers"—both race-specific, often derogatory references to gay and lesbians, respectively, within certain African American communities—must make common cause with so-called welfare queens or largely heterosexual black single mothers presumed in the warped U.S. American popular imagination to be living like royalty on public assistance.[2] She insists that queerness as a coalitional politics can bring about progressive transformation to the extent that it takes seriously the theoretical and political mandate of queerness as a norm-opposing strategy. What might it mean to marry this political strategy to performance art practice in an African diasporic context? In this black queer marriage of politics and performance, what else might *queer* mean in addition to lesbian, gay, bisexual and transgender (LGBT)-identified? Jamaican Canadian playwright and performance artist d'bi.young ani-tafrika gestures toward these outer limits of queer meaning. Through the prism of her life and work, young offers a challenge that reaches beyond the recognition of queer life and artistry in Jamaica's cultural archipelago. Instead, young—a disciple of Jamaican expressive arts—invites us to expand the boundaries of queer recognition by following Cohen's lead and returning us, instructively and perhaps reluctantly, to its radical root.

It is no secret that d'bi.young identifies openly and quite courageously as queer.[3] But if this "black, queer, african, jamaican, canadian, caribbean mother" never hesitates to profess her queerness, she nonetheless aligns herself with a particular species of queer:[4]

> Me nah inna nobody band camp. Me no wear t-shirt. Me nah have to advertise so. I represent freedom. If me want deh wit [have a romantic relationship with] a tranny, me deh wit a tranny . . . me deh wit everybody. Me have a track record [her laugh is sweet and spicy]. Me want identify as androgynous. Me believe in freedom. Me in solidarity [with lesbians, gays, bisexuals], but don't put me in any box. Me identify as "queer." I like how it sounds and me like how it spells. It allows me to be like a fish.[5]

Insistent upon swimming the fluid range of queer identifications, young refuses a queerness confined by static categories of sexual orientation alone—especially if these are based on parochial presumptions about sex/gender transparency and stability.[6] Although aligned with LGBT communities—as a result of both her sexual and political desires, but especially because of her aggressive gender nonconformity—young is determined to hold "queer" to its word, in other words, to live it as an opportunity to embrace deviance as a liberatory category, a category that is not fixed but flexible enough to accommodate various modes of existence that the "normal" attempts to sequester as marginal.[7] In this respect, young returns us to the founding impulse of queer theory while echoing more recent scholarship especially by queer feminist of color theorists who insist that not all members of LGBT communities are identically queered, and in fact, many of these ostensibly marginal bodies enjoy the privileges of racist, sexist, and xenophobic norms.[8]

This particular engagement with d'bi.young foregrounds one of her most emotionally and psychically disorienting plays. Part of a theatrical trilogy that I will discuss shortly, benu is a one-woman production that documents the trials of a black, immigrant, new single mother as she suffers the after effects of both systemic medical negligence and forced split-family migration. A queer composite of monologue, spoken word poetry, and the barest modern dance gesticulation, this is most certainly a genre-bending play. An original piece commissioned by Montreal's Théâtre La Chapelle, benu underwent various workshop productions before its premier as part of the theater's 2009–10 season.[9] And yet, one of the most vital elements of d'bi.young's process is the insistence that each of her plays—from first scripting to its premier and beyond—remains a living, breathing, evolving work. Each play matures perpetually under the guidance of both the artist's itinerant imagination and the insightful suggestions of her audiences in various places. In a 2010 interview, young had this to say about resisting the finality of her work: "[Following a conventional Euro-American theater model,] you work and you create and you do process and you end up with a product that is unchanging, with an aim to end up with a perfect product that is unmanipulatable, that is untouchable, and that exists in some sort of make-believe, pristine place of perfection. I'm not really concerned with that. My work is always evolving. So, whether we call it a world premiere, whether we call it a workshop, it's always a work in process to me."[10] This perpetual malleability challenges certain conventional norms of theatrical method in favor of a (black) feminist methodology that emphasizes, among other things, collectivity and keen attention to process as vital for creativity.[11] This methodological orientation is part of the queerness of young's plays. But what if a Cohen-inspired queer posture—a norm-contesting politics that equally governs the creative arts—provides the definitive criteria by which a life, a work, a process counts as queer? Surely, there must still be honest, well-founded resistance to a queerness ostensibly divorced from lesbian, gay, bisexual, or transgender identities, experiences, or communities. How can benu be so queer if the play itself is devoid of a single LGBT character?[12]

It is in approaching this uncomfortable question that we begin to approach d'bi.young's usefulness to the necessarily uneasy—though hardly new—tension within the conceptualization of black queerness. Does aligning ourselves with the philosophical spirit and rebellious fortitude of progressive deviants make us queer regardless of nonnormative desire or sex/gender "transgressions"?[13] Certainly these registers of queerness are not mutually exclusive, but since Cohen's important intervention, how attentive have we been to the types of black queerness that foreground an antinormative posture in an effort to resist "queer" as a handy replacement for increasingly unwieldy umbrella acronyms?[14] What if the play's queerness closely resembles the queerness of its playwright? Perhaps we begin to grasp the queer potential of the play once we can recognize that *benu* mirrors d'bi.young's own commitment to contesting any fetishization of the "normal" across various categories. And yet, even though young inhabits the play literally (as its sole actor playing various roles) and figuratively (as its mother/author), does black queer recognition still demand an explicitly recognizable LGBT character in the play itself? Can we recognize as queer a play in which that character does not appear? Is this absence of same-sex desire or gender nonconformity (beyond young's own cross-gender performance) a troubling shortcoming of this play in particular and the entire *sankofa trilogy* in general?

Dub: A Queer Sound Legacy

Allow me to approach the question of *benu*'s queerness from an even wider perspective to properly contextualize d'bi.young and her artistry within the lineage of a rebelliously queer—even if its progenitors may not have conceived of it as such—Jamaican performance genre. Let us begin with *dub*. More than a mere music genre, dub describes an aural aesthetic and archive birthed in late 1960s Jamaica and based on a surreal manipulation of sound technologies.[15] Dub innovators such as Osbourne "King Tubby" Ruddock, Lee "Scratch" Perry, and Errol "ET" Thomas gifted a new postmodern sound to their newly postcolonial nation through deconstructing sound itself. These quick-eared engineers stripped songs down to their base elements and playfully remixed those destabilized fragments, but only after submerging the sound in reverberation and *riddim* (a pared-down sound that would by the early 1990s evolve into its own Jamaican-inflected British music genre, *drum'n'bass*). The result is a highly technical and technologically mediated mash-up that ethnomusicologist Michael Veal has poetically baptized a "language of fragmented song forms and reverberating soundscapes."[16]

This new sound paradigm derived its name "dub" from the very technology through which it was originally mediated. Dubplates—the acetate discs used to test recordings before creating the master disc from which vinyl records would be pressed—were the first copy (or doubling and hence "dub" for short) of a recording.[17] Although these dubplates had a much more limited lifespan than vinyl records, they were the principal technology that reggae music creation and promotion collectives (synecdochically referred to as "sound systems") used to create novel remixes with which to compete in music competitions (*sound clashes*) against rival sound systems. This is doubling with a difference; the original sound is copied *in a way* to produce a completely reconfigured sound that nonetheless echoes—sometimes quite literally—with snatches and phrases of the original. The ephemerality of this unique dub mix grooved into the dubplate offered an exclusive privilege that only enhanced the excitement of these clashes for the community of listeners able to experience the limited fifty or so plays of a record. Dub's competitive impulse and the limits of its initial recording technology made for a genre obsession with and sustained by innovation. However, few of dub's original innovators might have anticipated that the application of its sound aesthetics to the very first instrument—the human voice—would result in a new genre of performance poetry.

According to the Jamaican literary scholar and poet Mervyn Morris, the term "dub poetry" was actually prefigured in a 1976 article by Jamaica-born, British dub poetry founding figure Linton Kwesi Johnson, who used the metaphor of dub music to define what he called *dub-lyricism* among reggae DJs who frequently talked over the tracks they played: "The 'dub-lyricist' is the dj turned poet. He intones his lyrics rather than sings them. Dub-lyricism is a new form of (oral) music-poetry, wherein the lyricist overdubs rhythmic phrases onto the rhythm background of a popular song."[18] And yet, nearly simultaneously, another of dub poetry's founding figures Orlando "Oku Nagba Ozala Onuora" Wong was actively popularizing the term "dub poetry" across the pond in Jamaica, where the first dub poets had been emerging throughout the second half of the 1970s.[19] At a public discussion at the Jamaica School of Drama on January 17, 1986, Onuora offered this oft-quoted definition of dub poetry: "It's dubbing out the little penta-metre [pentameter] and the little highfalutin business [a mimicked English colonial ostentatiousness] and dubbing in the rootsical, yard, basic rhythm that I-and-I know [a local Jamaican, Rasta-inflected sound consciousness]. Using language, using the body. It also means to dub out the '-isms' and schisms [discriminatory ideologies and practices] and to dub in consciousness into the people-dem head. That's dub poetry."[20] A politically conscious (determinedly anticolonial in this instance), norm-contesting (and thus in a sense radically queer) gauntlet had been thrown down in Jamaican expressive culture.

By the late 1970s and early 1980s, the Jamaica School of Drama (now the School of Drama in the Edna Manley College of Visual and Performing Arts) had become a grassroots conservatoire for dub poetry, indirectly cultivating the generations of poets who have had the deepest influence on the very character of the genre. Formed in 1979 beneath the branches of the now-mythic lignum vitae (from the Latin for "wood of life") tree on the drama school's grounds and cohered by the echoing credo "Word! Sound! Power!," the *Poets in Unity* group was the pulsing heart of the dub poetry movement in Jamaica and produced many of the legendary figures in the poetic genre, including Michael "Mikey" Smith, Jean "Binta" Breeze, and Anita Stewart.[21] How appropriate that such a resolutely Jamaican artistic movement should blossom beneath this dense-wood, medicinal tree from which grows Jamaica's national flower. These midwives of dub poetry ushered into the world an art form that has perhaps been most artfully defined by critical theory and social justice scholar G. A. Elmer Griffin in his review of Christian Habekost's *Verbal Riddim: the Politics and Aesthetics of African-Caribbean Dub Poetry*: "Dub poetry is a highly developed, politically charged rhythmic art form which merges local musical folk idioms (initially reggae) with political commentary and analysis. It combines values of poetry, the properties of voice as instrument, and the power of the vernacular, spoken in the context of political resistance and identity assertion. It places itself subtly and elusively between political speech, dramatic recitation, and song."[22] The sound legacy of this polymorphous interstitiality, undergirded with a rebellious politics, attunes us to the larger queerness of dub poetics—a border challenging queerness on the move.

Making Dub Epic: Dub Dramaturgy and the *sankofa trilogy*

In the northern reaches of North America, directly influenced by the work and encouragement of Onuora, the first generation of Canadian dub poets—matriarch among them Lillian Allen—were not only expanding the geographic reach of this genre-bending and highly politicized dub poetics but also transforming the very nature of its political orientation. Numerous scholars taken with dub poetry—most recent and incisive among them the literary theorist and black diaspora scholar Phanuel Antwi—have noted how aggressively it has been remixed with woman of color feminism in the Canadian context.[23] The Jamaican-born and primarily Toronto-based founding mothers of Canadian dub poetry include not only Allen but also other near mythic figures such as Afua Cooper, ahdri zhina mandiela, and again Anita Stewart (now living in Canada). It is this literal and figurative dub poetry lineage that performance artist d'bi.young inherits directly from Stewart, her mother. As an adolescent, young would follow in her mother's footsteps, undergoing initial performance baptism in youth programs at the Jamaica School of Drama and the School of Dance (now also part of Manley College). And in 1993, young would continue on the path her mother had walked by joining Stewart in Canada. It is in Canada's particularly feminist-of-color-influenced dub poetry landscape that d'bi.young—unabashedly black, queer, and feminist—first makes a significant name for herself.

Under her mother's guidance and profoundly influenced by the particularly theatrical and dance-driven "choreopoetry" of playwright, director, and dancer mandiela, d'bi.young levies a challenge in and through dub as a bridge between poetry and theater. young dutifully and consistently credits Stewart with having gestured toward this performative innovation at least two decades earlier. In a summoning that has become mythic, young cites the visionary legacy of her mother's drama school thesis *Dubbin' Theatre: Dub Poetry as Theatre Form* as a treasured inheritance.[24] First and foremost a storyteller baptized in the tradition of dub poetics, young herself has been pushing the performative limits of dub aesthetics for over a decade. Inspired by her mother's work and mandiela's working of the form she christens *dub theater*, young mounts her first play in 2001: *yagayah: two.womben.black.griots*. d'bi.young not only cowrites this play about friendship and loss shared between two Jamaican women but also performs in it alongside performance artist and theater studies scholar Naila "Keleta Mae" Belvett.[25] And since this first play, young has written and performed in ten additional works. She has also published two collections of poetry, *art on black* and *rivers . . . and other blackness . . . between us*.[26] However, these accomplishments pale in comparison with her most precious creations, her sons Moon and Phoenix, born in 2004 and 2008, respectively.[27] The fact that d'bi.young is both a conscientious dub dramatist and a dedicated queer mother has revealed a perhaps unsurprising synchronicity between mothering (as actuality and as metaphor) and crafting narrative.[28] It is no coincidence that the very first storytellers many of us encounter are the women who bring us into the world and/or guide us early through it. Telling stories is an epistemological art form that not only has the power to explain the world to us but also provides an opportunity to nurture a deep concern for that world and each other. From cradle to grave, we thrive on stories gathered and shared.

Premiering in 2003 at New York City's Hip-Hop Theater Festival, the Dora Mavor Moore Award–winning play *blood.claat* is only the beginning of the story.[29] It is with the addition of *benu* and then *word!sound!powah!* (which premiered at the Toronto Fringe Festival in 2010) that young's story comes to a kind of unresolved completion as a dub theater epic.[30] If the idea for a dub theater trilogy had been indirectly planted in d'bi. young's imagination from the age of seven or eight when she first saw the 1957 film *The Three Faces of Eve,* based on Corbett Thigpen and Hervey Cleckley's psychiatric study of a woman suffering from dissociative identity disorder (commonly referred to as "multiple personality disorder" and often confused with schizophrenia), the idea would not begin to bear fruit until a year after the birth of her first child. young has weaned the plays of the *sankofa trilogy*—she at one time flirted with titling the series *The Three Faces of mudgu sankofa*—right alongside her sons, so it should come as little surprise that motherhood is one of the governing tropes of the epic.[31] But motherhood here is symbolic of a more abstract intergenerational (perhaps even cross-temporal) conscientiousness that insists on the vital importance of the past for crafting a desirable future.

Undoubtedly influenced by a period spent living in Ghana (where the Akan are predominantly found), d'bi.young names the trilogy as well as the family whose lineage it follows for the Akan language word *sankofa,* which loosely translates into the English phrase "return for it." Represented by two Asante (an Akan people) Adinkra symbols—one a bird with its head turned backward reaching for an object on its back, and the other a more abstract rendering of the bird that resembles a heart—the sankofa principle indirectly gestures toward an intergenerational/cross-temporal love impulse.[32] Enticing us to look back as a way to move forward, the *sankofa trilogy* is principally concerned with the unfolding of lineage, the cycles of life, and the forcefulness of legacy.

It is instructive, then, that d'bi.young begins with blood. In fact, "blood"—the dub poem, which appears on young's debut full-length album *wombanifesto*, played after performances of *blood.claat*—closes a symbolic circle.³³ "Blood" may end the play, but the poem—written as both homage and woman-centered rejoinder to Linton Kwesi Johnson's classic 1975 dub poems "Five Nights of Bleeding" and "Dread Beat and Blood"—initiated the play's creation. While Johnson's poems document unrest among black peoples in the urban enclaves of 1970s England, young's poem documents systemic quotidian violence against women's bodies globally and calls for the reevaluation of the miracle of menstruation by recasting the blood cloth (any cloth used to absorb menstrual fluid and the source of the sullying Jamaican curse word *bloodclaat*) as a tie that binds women together, a ritual object, a saturated spiritual talisman. *blood. claat* introduces fifteen-year-old mudgu sankofa, a direct descendant of Jamaican National Hero Queen Nanny of the Maroons—an Asante woman born in the late seventeenth century. *benu* continues the story through the physical and psychic trials of twenty-eight-year-old sekesu sankofa, mudgu's sole daughter. And *word!sound!powah!* completes the trinity with the resilient protest poetics of twenty-year-old benu sankofa, sekesu's only daughter.³⁴

A shared bloodline (a sanguine metaphor for descent) certainly links these women in the narrative of the play, but it is in d'bi.young's nearly eerie embodiment of all three women (as well as all the other characters in all three plays) that their unity becomes unavoidable, sutured through young's selfsame body, her selfsame blood, her selfsame self. The tremendous acting challenge of shifting seamlessly between multiple roles onstage is part of a new performance genre young has dubbed *biomyth monodrama*, which is simultaneously an artful refiguring of multiple personality disorder and a playful mingling of (auto)biography and mythography. Inspired by Caribbean American lesbian feminist poet and theorist Audre Lorde's usage of the term "biomythography" in the title of her autobiographical experiment *Zami: A New Spelling of My Name—A Biomythography*, young embraces the potential of this new Lordean literary genre, a genre that Lorde biographer Alexis De Veaux pithily characterizes as an artful "blending of truth, mythmaking, and social history."³⁵ Through conscientiously alchemizing the life experiences of her mother, her own biography, the birth of dub poetry, ancient Egyptian and Dahomey mythology, Yoruba cosmology, Jamaican folklore, and the transcendent wonder of nature, d'bi.young creates an inspired landscape that holds together history and ancestry, the tangible and the metaphysical.

A Black Queer Horizon: *benu* and the Challenge of Looking Askance

The queer middle child of d'bi.young's *sankofa trilogy*, it is hardly surprising that *benu* proves the most challenging of the sister plays. Physically, emotionally and psychically disorienting in performance—for audience and actor alike—*benu* demands one's full emotive and imaginative attention. A shape-shifting composite of performance genres, the play is about the trials of mudgu sankofa's daughter, sekesu—only just born at the end of *blood.claat*—now a twenty-eight-year-old new mother herself. Perhaps the fact that sekesu shares her name with the legendary younger sister of Queen Nanny of the Maroons foreshadows the rocky row she has to hoe. As the story is told, the mythic Sekesu spends a lifetime risking life and limb running toward freedom in the bosom of Jamaica's mountainous interior but meets her maker shackled still in the merciless grip of slavery. In the legend, Sekesu's child, Mudgu, escapes the plantation with the help of a bit of poison and claims her place as part of a rebellious royal lineage. What might it mean then for mudgu sankofa—herself named for this deadly herbalist who finally achieves her mother's dream—to baptize her daughter with the name of the mythic mother who dies displaced, abandoned, and longing? This eerie inversion is a discomforting premonition. sekesu sankofa is marked for turmoil.

It is telling that although sekesu is the principal character of the play—her mother does appear in abstracted poetic interludes, but these are distanced figuratively and literally from the action of the central story line—*benu* is named for sekesu's daughter, who is born in the very first scene of the play and remains an infant throughout its unfolding. benu—the child—symbolically displaces her mother. A diasporic daughter left with her newborn girl-child to eke out an existence on the frigid brow of North America, sekesu is far from the land of her birth, far from her birthmother (an aching resentment overwhelms even the mention of her), and far from the only mother she has known (her grandmother, whom the cold has forced back to Jamaica). But this play is as much about the parallels between the alienating circumstances and impossible choices haunting the lives of three generations of sankofa women as it is about the cruelty of institutional structures that determine the limited range of choices. And it is these structures that are summarily called into question by the time baby benu—a fourth-generation sankofa woman—is able to raise her voice in protest. But for now, benu is a baby still, and her mother—like her mother before her and her mother before her—is forced to choose. d'bi.young lives with these hard choices—as a daughter and as a mother—and with the difficult feelings they stir, the embarrassing though all too common feelings that we force so many mothers to hide. If, as young readily admits, she struggled through a tumultuous postpartum depression to complete a stageable script for *blood.claat*, then she actively embraced *benu* as an opportunity to struggle *with* postpartum depression—five years after the birth of her first son and one year after the birth of her second—as an emotional synecdoche for all the swallowed feelings and the *un*natural distance that can open treacherously between mother and child.[36]

Too Light and Grace for This Place: On Diaspora and Queer Transcendence

Though ostensibly heterosexual and gender norm conforming, sekesu might be read as a kind of queer character by virtue of her existence outside "state-sanctioned, normalized White (and in this instance, 'properly national' or rightfully Canadian), middle- and upper-class, male heterosexuality."[37] young lays bare the complexity of sekesu's battle with self and society—an unnerving challenge that pushes from the outside in as forcefully as it pushes from the inside out—and asks us to recognize our responsibility to and personal accountability for her (and thus, each other) even despite the seemingly autonomous systems that we all have a hand in sustaining.[38] sekesu's struggle is also the African diaspora's struggle. She is haunted by a physical, emotional, and psychic instability that results from a hastily administered epidural during childbirth, an inefficient, overcrowded medical system, and a generations-deep resentment about being "abandoned" by a mother forced to travel abroad to make a better life for her. These ghosts are not hers alone. young's play pushes us to align ourselves with those "whose everyday life decisions challenge, or at least counter, the basic normative assumptions of a society intent on protecting structural and social inequalities under the guise of some normal and natural order to life."[39] In a society where the norm is unjust, unequal, unfair, and unethical, an antinormative orientation insists on revealing the unnaturalness of the "natural" order. This kind of queer identification is the foundation for a radical politics that highlights the tragedies of our current existence and encourages us to conceive of other ways of being. d'bi.young uses sekesu's heartbreaking story to highlight the horrifying effects of various norms on her so as to encourage a queer kind of norm suspicion among her audience members.

And though this norm-questioning posture may not be directly linked to same-sex desire or gender nonconformity per se, what if young's play is attempting to foster a larger queer orientation of the general public? This political orientation has the potential to benefit all of us who stand presumably outside the perverse charmed circle of "the normal." Where does the confidence to claim this antinormative solidarity come from in a world that stigmatizes various kinds of queerness? Perhaps young is showing us that it comes from a determined hope in the potential for—physical *and* metaphorical—redemption, renewal, rebirth. And, in fact, she nests optimism about these changes of heart, mind, and form within the trunk of the play itself. The cosmogonic *myth of the benu bird*, which parallels the play's principal narrative, introduces the sacred firebird of ancient Egypt—an early antecedent of the Grecian phoenix. This Ben(n)u bird not only lends its name to the play itself (and the child born in its opening scene) but also provides the play's principal metaphor for the difficult glory of new beginnings.[40]

A tale told by a "bird-womban"—whose name transposes the firebird and the womb as sacred symbols of new life—young's myth not only threads sekesu's story but also provides a link between the four generations in the sankofa lineage. A mythic composite of all four sankofa women, this character embodies these women's connection to each other through the womb. This flesh and feathers instantiation of the Akan principle quite literally keeps the past in plain sight on this family's journey toward the future—a not-so-subtle allegory for the African Diaspora itself. And the blind faith that an infant with a warrior lineage holds promise for the future—even if her mother falls to ashes—is a subtle reassurance *benu* offers in its final disorienting moments. Lost to visions of her past that might be an awakened second sight or epidural-induced delusions, sekesu is convicted of gross negligence in the play's final scene for abandoning her infant at home while seeking emergency medical attention—for these seeming mental disturbances—in an overcrowded Toronto hospital.[41] Exposing the heartlessness of split-family migration/return induced by transnational capitalism and the institutional neglect of working-class black immigrant single mothers even in *the* presumed public service provision Shangri-La of North America (Oh, Canada), *benu's* final scene also proves disorienting and reassuring for attempting to align a principally Canadian audience with sekesu over and against the state.

No longer simply a monstrous mother who has absentmindedly abandoned her child, sekesu is re-presented in young's telling as a new mother struggling to do the best she can for her daughter and herself under monstrous circumstances. This reorientation is a kind of queer turn, radical because it asks us to indict the state—as proxy for a perverse status quo—in the very moment that the state criminalizes sekesu. And it is in light of this political reorientation that *benu* becomes recognizable as a kind of queer play in a Cohenian sense. In addition, young's play also challenges us to wed Cathy Cohen's broadened perspective on the radical potential of (black) queer theorizing/politics with cultural studies scholar Rinaldo Walcott's articulation of black (queer) diaspora theory.[42]

One of the most prominent recent forefathers of the black queer diaspora concept, Walcott encourages us to pull Cohen beyond the United States to consider the wider world of black queer potential to upset or at least interrupt various normative logics throughout the African Diaspora. This is a diaspora that Walcott reminds us is no stranger to norm-challenging queerness: "As we know, the diaspora by its very nature, its circumstances, is queer. What do I mean by this? I mean that the territories and perambulations of diaspora circuits, identifications, and desires are queer in their making and their expressions."[43] So, if the African Diaspora itself is a queer phenomenon in large part for resisting the normative logic of nationalist affinities and identities in favor of transnational affinities and identities, then it makes sense that an itinerant black queer diaspora-minded artist like d'bi.young—she has lived in, worked across, and connected arts practitioners between more than a dozen countries in the last decade—offers a queer kind of challenge through this decidedly diasporic play.[44]

Undoubtedly, not all diasporic subjects recognize, share, or encourage these transnational affinities. In fact, *benu*'s vision of diaspora proves far more troubling than comforting, and through this disturbance, young provides an unsettling glimpse at the insecurities, anxieties, and vulnerabilities of diaspora.[45] This middle play in the trilogy insists that diasporic disorientation is as much a part of the material and affective inheritance of black communities globally as the deep reserve of cultural and emotional strength. However, outside of a whole host of conventional and convenient racial, gendered, and nationalist norms, black diasporic subjects are primed for a certain kind of reorienting queer consciousness. But what might this diasporic disorientation mean for black LGBT subjects in diaspora? Our queer orientation is of still another sort that may often but not necessarily always find affinity with a radically antinormative posture. Perhaps d'bi.young and the *sankofa trilogy* could serve as a bridge between queerness as an embrace of gender nonconformity/same-sex desire and queerness as a radical norm-challenging politics.

What if this self-described queer artist is using her family of plays to experiment with what queerness might mean in a meta-identificatory sense, resisting the convenience of identity labels in favor of more fluid principles and more concrete politics? What might it mean for black queer artists to attempt queer work that does not squarely face same-sex desire or gender nonconformity as focal points? If we can recognize d'bi.young's trilogy and especially its troublesome middle play as experiments in rebellious queer representation, might they serve as a pointed response to work by nonqueer artists that focuses intently on normalizing LGBT experiences to the detriment of a larger radical queer politics? Black queer diasporic artists like d'bi.young, who are adamant about undermining the seduction of heterosexual/gender norm-conforming privilege but still determined to play loosely with *all* solidifying identity constraints and the representational expectations weighing upon them and their work, may in fact be part of a black queer avant-garde that is as discomforting as it is innovative.[46] But this is precisely what queerness in its most theoretically expansive sense was meant to do—make us uncomfortable enough to accept a new normal and eventually wean us off of normality altogether. Why should black queer artists want anything different for us in a moment when black queerness as a simple, often apolitical umbrella reference for black LGBT life and work is getting increasingly institutionalized, packaged, and commodified for mass consumption? Expansive and defiant despite the absence of explicit LGBT characters, d'bi.young's *sankofa trilogy* in general—and *benu* as a peculiar experiment in particular—represents the queerest kind of black queer play, a troublesome intracommunal challenge to the comforts of diasporic black queer intelligibility.

NOTES

I offer my deepest gratitude first to E. Patrick Johnson for inviting me to be a part of this historic follow-up text to the path-breaking Black Queer Studies *anthology. It is an honor to be included among the black queer avant-garde. My anonymous reviewers deserve high praise for their encouragement, precision, and patience. And for their efficiency, generosity, and grace, I offer my most heartfelt thanks to Anita Stewart, Wisaal Abrahams, Phanuel Antwi and, of course, the incomparable d'bi.young anitafrika.*

1. Cathy J. Cohen, "Punks, Bulldaggers, and Welfare Queens: the Radical Potential of Queer Politics?" in *Black Queer Studies: a Critical Anthology*, eds. E. Patrick Johnson and Mae G. Henderson (Durham: Duke University Press, 2005), 22.

2. An unintentional double entendre in Cohen's use of "punk" draws together an (African) American vernacular reference to particularly feeble gay men and a global movement cohered around a confrontational music genre. For a precise engagement with this terminological crossroads, see Tavia Nyong'o, "Punk'd Theory," *Social Text* 23, nos. 3–4 (2005): 19–34; and a subsequent special issue of *Social Text* edited by Jayna Brown, Patrick Deer, and Tavia Nyong'o, "Punk and Its Afterlives," *Social Text* 32, no. 3 (2013).

3. Chris Dupuis's November 3, 2011, cover story, "Straddling the World: d'bi.young Craves New Spaces," in *Xtra!*, one of Canada's most widely circulated gay and lesbian free newsprint magazines, was perhaps one of the loudest testaments to young's bold embrace of *and* by LGBT communities. The article's accompanying nude profile portrait of young eccentrically adorned with animal horns and an abundance of necklaces, bracelets, and waist beads speaks to the kind of provocative queerness with which she aligns herself.

4. Holly Luhning, "Accountability, Integrity, and *benu*: An Interview with d'bi. young," *Alt.theatre Magazine* 8 (September 2010): 11.

5. d'bi.young, interview with the author, July 24, 2011. I owe special gratitude to Christopher A. Walker for his assistance with translating the nuance of Jamaican Creole English.

6. Reading a magical double entendre in the "spells" queerness casts on d'bi.young, Canadian black diaspora scholar Phanuel Antwi encourages attention to the sound seduction of *queer* as an incantation that works on young even as she works through it like an obeah woman (Antwi, conversation with the author, March 26, 2016).

7. See Cathy Cohen's incisive essay "Deviance as Resistance: A New Research Agenda for the Study of Black Politics," *The Du Bois Review* 1, no. 1 (2004): 27–45, for a critique of the "normal" as a priority of black politics, thus deepening and extending the argument she famously makes in "Punks, Bulldaggers, and Welfare Queens."

8. On the early academic articulation of queer theory, see, for a start, Sedgwick, *Epistemology of the Closet* (Berkeley: University of California Press, 1990); Michael Warner, *Fear of a Queer Planet* (Minneapolis: University of Minnesota Press, 1993); and Warner, *The Trouble with Normal* (New York: Free Press, 1999). For a critical challenge to and expansion of queer theory by queer feminists of color, see, for a start, M. Jacqui Alexander, *Pedagogies of Crossing: Meditations on Feminism, Sexual Politics, Memory, and the Sacred* (Durham, NC: Duke University Press, 2005); and Jasbir Puar, *Terrorist Assemblages: Homonationalism in Queer Times* (Durham, NC: Duke University Press, 2007).

9. Founded in 1990, Théâtre La Chapelle has long been a catalyst for Canadian avant-garde performance art that combines contemporary theater, modern dance, and experimental music; see www.lachapelle.org. This provenance explains in part *benu*'s revelrous genre bending, an undoubtedly encouraged d'bi.young trademark.

10. Luhning, "Accountability, Integrity, and *benu*," 16.

11. This communal process-oriented art practice is precisely the "collective creation attentive to continuous incompletion" that Phanuel Antwi lyrically identifies as constitutive of black life in the Americas—as represented through the dub music genre—in his essay "Dub Poetry as a Black Atlantic Body-Archive," *Small Axe* 19, no 3 48 (2015): 66.

12. Certainly, *benu* is distinct from young's 2004 play *androgyne*, an uneasy lesbian love story about lifelong friends coming to terms with their attraction to each other and the internalized homophobia that threatens to keep them apart. Across migration and memory, shifting back and forth between Jamaica and Canada, the troubled lovers of this earlier play render it perhaps more easily recognizable as queer.

13. Nadia Ellis's *Territories of the Soul: Queered Belonging in the Black Diaspora* (Durham, NC: Duke University Press, 2015) takes up this question with a particularly historically minded aplomb and poetic precision. Ellis insists definitively that queer (diasporic) potentiality not be confined to landscapes of same-sex desire or gender deviancy.

14. Reassuringly, Cathy Cohen is quite clear early on that she does not mean to erase the historically specific relationship between "queer" as a stigmatized category and same-sex desire or gender nonconformity. She is careful not to equate the relationship between "marginal" heterosexuals and all LGBT folks, recognizing that heterosexuality even for those outside of every other norm still comes with its privileges. This further emphasizes her point that not all queers stand on equal footing. See Cohen, "Punks, Bulldaggers and Welfare Queens," 43–44.

15. Antwi, "Dub Poetry," 65.

16. Michael Veal, *Dub: Soundscapes and Shattered Songs in Jamaican Reggae* (Middletown, CT: Wesleyan University Press, 2007), 2.

17. Toop, *Oceans of Sound: Aether Talk, Ambient Sound, and Imaginary Worlds* (London: Serpent's Tail, 2001).

18. Originally cited in Mervyn Morris, "Dub Poetry?," *Caribbean Quarterly* 43, no. 4 (1997): 1.

19. Habekost, *Verbal Riddim: the Politics and Aesthetics of African-Caribbean Dub Poetry* (Amsterdam: Rodopi, 1993), 15–22.

20. Cited in Morris, "Dub Poetry?," 3; also cited in Carolyn Cooper, *Sound Clash: Jamaican Dancehall Culture at Large* (New York: Palgrave Macmillan, 2004), 289–99.

21. Habekost, *Verbal Riddim*, 23. Perhaps the most notable exception to this cadre of drama school dub poets is the troublesome figure of Allan "Mutabaruka" Hope, who continues to add breath to the genre in Jamaica and internationally.

22. G. A. Elmer Griffin, "Word Bullets." Review of *Verbal Riddim: The Politics and Aesthetics of African-Caribbean Dub Poetry*, by Christian Habekost." *Transition* 66 (1995): 60.

23. Antwi, "Dub Poetry," 75–80.

24. Habekost, *Verbal Riddim*, 34–35.

25. d'bi.young, conversation with the author, October 10, 2015. While *yagayah* is the first play she publishes, the very first play young writes—also in 2001—is *Selfine Loathing* about a young woman negotiating self-love.

26. d'bi.young, *art on black* (Toronto: Women's Press, 2006); and *rivers . . . and other blackness . . . between us: (dub) poems of love* (Toronto: Women's Press, 2007). It is important to note that undergirding much of young's work both on and off stage is a philosophical and methodological ethos she has built around eight core principles. These mnemonic SORPLUSI principles are self-knowledge, orality, rhythm, political content/context, language, urgency, sacredness, and integrity. Partially inherited—young insists—from Anita Stewart's early theorizing about the character, political potential, and theatrical aspirations of dub poetry, young has spent over a decade expanding and developing these principles. Vital for fostering what young frequently refers to as an "ecosystem of responsibility and accountability" that we all share, the eight SORPLUSI principles provide a guiding frame not only for a lively creative practice but also for a creative *living* practice.

27. Also in 2008, young founded the *anitafrika dub theatre* (its name an homage to her mother and Mama Africa) in Toronto. As one of its principal projects, this theater company hosted a free artist-in-residency program that combined theater-based arts training and holistic wellness practices. And in 2011, based on the model of the residency program, young founded the YEMOYA Pan-Afrikan Performing Arts Institute (www.yemoya.org) while residing with her sons in Cape Town, South Africa. Named for the Yoruba goddess of motherhood and oceanic journeys, this now transnational institute hosts working retreats for artists through its Watah School initiative, which though rooted in Toronto still branches into the world (www.thewatahtheatre.org).

28. For one of the most gorgeously thorough treatments of black queer diasporic motherhood as literal social phenomenon *and* as metaphor for social engagement, please see Alexis Pauline Gumbs, "We Can Learn to Mother Ourselves: The Queer Survival of Black Feminism, 1968–1996" (PhD diss., Duke University, 2010).

29. d'bi.young, *blood.claat* (Toronto: Playwrights Canada Press, 2005).

30. The title *word!sound!powah!* intentionally echoes the Poets in Unity credo as a tribute to the now legendary relationship between dub poetry and Jamaica's preeminent drama students. Six years subsequent to the premier of *word!sound!powah!*, young begins a new spirited epic. Eagerly anticipated, the *Orisha Trilogy* debuts—appropriately—with the 2016 premier of the play *Eshu Crossing the Middle Passage.*

31. d'bi.young, *sankofa: blood.claat, benu, word!sound!powah!* (Toronto: Playwrights Canada Press, 2013).

32. The loose translation of "sankofa" and this reading of the heart/love symbolism in its more abstract rendering owe much to a series of ongoing transnational conversations with Phanuel Antwi.

33. d'bi.young, *Wombanifesto* (Havana: Studio Havana Cuba, 2010).

34. For a more detailed engagement with the narrative of and staging instructions for each of the plays in the trilogy, please see the compilation text of young's *sankofa* (2013) that not only provides the complete scripts but also includes critical essays that introduce the trilogy and each of its component plays.

35. Audre Lorde, *Zami: A New Spelling of My Name* (Watertown: Persephone, 1982; and Alexis De Veaux, *Warrior Poet: A Biography of Audre Lorde* (New York: W.W. Norton, 2004), 412.

36. d'bi.young, *blood.claat*, 8.

37. The title of this section comes from an ominously prophetic line in *benu* that mudgu sankofa recites in a poetic interlude: "Our beings are too light and grace for this place" (cited from an unpaginated early draft of the play that d'bi.young provided to the author). Cohen, "Deviance as Resistance: A New Research Agenda for the Study of Black Politics," *Du Bois Review: Social Science Research on Race* 1, no. 1 (2004): 29.

38. Luhning, "Accountability, Integrity, and *benu*, 12.

39. Cohen, "Deviance as Resistance," 33.

40. It is probably no coincidence that young names her son "Phoenix." The naming of her second-born and of the second sibling of the *sankofa trilogy* after reborn firebirds reflect indirectly on young's own metaphorical resurrection—as mother and artist—from the ashes of postpartum depression.

41. d'bi.young, *benu* (unpublished performance script, 2009), 45.

42. Rinaldo Walcott, "Outside in Black Studies: Reading from a Queer Place in the Diaspora," in *Black Queer Studies*, eds. E. Patrick Johnson and Mae G. Henderson (Durham, NC: Duke University Press, 2005), 90–105; Walcott, "Somewhere Out There: The New Black Queer Theory," in *Blackness and Sexualities*, eds. Michelle Wright and Antje Schuhmann (Berlin: Verlag, 2007), 29–40.

43. Walcott, "Outside in Black Studies," 97.

44. Chris Dupuis, "Straddling the World," in *Xtra!* (November 3, 2011): 17.

45. For a contestable testament to the antisocial anxieties and unfulfillable longings of the black diaspora as a particularly aligned queering of the concept, again see Ellis's *Territories of the Soul*, 2–6.

46. This expectation-defiant, representationally rebellious black queer creativity of course brings to mind James Baldwin's *Giovanni's Room*, a text in which the metapresence of blackness aligns precisely with the metapresence of queerness in young's trilogy. See Baldwin, *Giovanni's Room* (New York: Dial Press, 1956).

7

To Transcender Transgender

Choreographies of Gender Fluidity in the
Performances of MilDred Gerestant

OMISE'EKE NATASHA TINSLEY

Prologue

LET ME TAKE YOU BACK. When I arrived on the west bank of the
Mississippi River in August 2005, everything in my life was midsum-
mer, bright, and new. I had just moved to Minneapolis for a new job at
a new university, was living in a newly painted apartment by a lake I ran
around every new morning, wore new white clothes and answered to a
new, seven-day-old name, Iyawo Yemoja Sango, the name of a newly initiated priest in the Ifa (African Diaspora) tradition. So who was surprised
that even though I had not finished my first book I was suddenly inspired to
research a new, second project? An analysis of twenty-first-century Caribbean fiction by queer writers, this dream project delved into historical
novels that imagined complex genders and sexualities through the metaphor of maritime travel. The project seemed bright and shiny as beaches,
and I rushed into it headlong, in a weekend penning an article I thought
would become the introduction to my next book.

But the longer I sat with this book, the more choked, the more stagnant it became. The directions I followed and answers I found seemed too easy, too pat—and while this apparently pleased funders and tenure committees, it left me uneasy. So I went back to texts I had gathered for my project, looking for what unexpected things they might have to say about Caribbean lesbian, gay, transgender, and queer experience that I was still missing. I quickly found my answer: *nothing*. This was because the vocabulary I'd been using to describe these authors, the descriptors they used for their own identities—queer, lesbian, transgender—appeared nowhere in their work. No characters, no narrators, no one in the novels used these words. Instead they talked about many kinds of desires, caresses, loves, bodies, and more. And over and over again, they talked about something that was such a big part of my life but that I never expected to find in most queer fiction: spirituality, Afro-Caribbean religions. Not one of these authors wrote about "queers," but almost everyone wrote about lwa—that is, about the spirit forces of the Haitian religion Vodou.

And why wouldn't they? In its cosmology as well as its community formation, Vodou is radically inclusive of creative genders and sexualities. Practitioners work to communicate with sacred energies called lwa—forces of nature including the ocean (Agwe), land (Azaka), metals (Ogu)—to achieve personal harmony and fulfill their life purposes. Dealing with forces of nature, many of these lwa model and mentor the divinity of gender and sexual complexity: Danbala, the simultaneously male and female rainbow serpent; Gede, the hypersexual lwa of death and sex; and Nana Buruku, the androgynous moon-sun, all inspire and protect creative genders and sexualities. But I was fascinated by the recurrence of one figure, who multiplied herself in these texts as if in a hall of mirrors: the beautiful femme queen, bull dyke, weeping willow, dagger mistress Ezili. Ezili is the name given to a pantheon of lwa who represent divine forces of love, sexuality, prosperity, pleasure, maternity, creativity, and fertility. She is also the force who protects *madivin* and *masisi,* that is, female and male gender- and sexually variant Haitians.[1] And Ezili, I was coming to see—Ezili, not queer politics, not gender theory—was the prism through which so many contemporary Caribbean authors were projecting their vision of creative genders and sexualities. Finally, five summers later and into a winter, I was coming to see.

That winter, discarding plans carefully laid out in grant applications, I decided that I wanted to write a book that would be a reflection on same-sex desire, Caribbeanness, femininity, money, housing, friendship, and more; I wanted to write a book about Ezili. My loving, unfinished meditation on Ezili would open space to consider how, as Karen McCarthy Brown writes of the pantheon, "these female spirits are both mirrors and maps" for gender and sexually complex African Diaspora subjects.[2] And it would reflect on Ezili as spirit, yes, but also on Ezili as archive. That is, I wanted to evoke the corpus of stories, memories, and songs about Ezili as an expansive gathering of the history of gender and sexually variant people of African descent.[3] I would not be looking to cast light on the (somewhat familiar) argument that this archive shows how spirituality allows gender and sexually complex people particular kinds of "self-expression," sympathetic as I am to such claims. My choice to follow the lwa instead would explore how a variety of engagements with Ezili—songs, stories, spirit possessions, dream interpretations, prayer flags, paintings, speculative fiction, films, dance, poetry, novels—perform black feminist intellectual work: the work of *theorizing Afro-Atlantic genders*. This is the kind of theorizing Barbara Christian asked us to take seriously when she reminded scholars that "people of color have always theorized . . . And I am inclined to say that our theorizing . . . is often in narrative forms, in the stories we create, in riddles and in proverbs, in the play with language, since dynamic rather than fixed ideas seem more to our liking."[4] In reflecting on Ezili's theorizing, then, I look to situate a discussion of Afro-Atlantic gender and sexual complexity not primarily through queer studies but within a lineage of black feminisms: a lineage that pushes me to ask what it would sound like if scholars were to speak of Ezili the way we often speak, say, of Judith Butler—if we gave the rich corpus of texts engaging this lwa a similar explanatory power in understanding gender.

Ezili's faces prominently mark work by queer Caribbean writers and performers, including novelists Nalo Hopkinson and Ana Lara, poets Assotto Saint and Lenelle Moïse, and filmmakers Anne Lescot and Laurence Magloire. Unable to do justice to even a fraction of these individuals here, though, in this essay I focus on the Vodou-inspired performances of Haitian American artist MilDred Gerestant. I discovered MilDred's work long ago, when I was a hopeful, stud-struck graduate student. In the 1990s, MilDred shot to fame in New York's drag king scene, dressing, dancing, and dragging as a smooth mackdaddy who played with and subverted stereotypes of African American masculinity. But in coming to my meditations on Ezili, I have been gifted with the chance to rediscover this artist's work. Dazzlingly, mesmerizingly, MilDred's recent performance has moved her musical citations from hip hop to Haitian Vodou: "Dance-HaitianGender" and "I Transcender" draw on Afro-Caribbean ritual, and particularly on Haitian lwa Danbala, Baron Samedi, and Ezili, to choreograph culturally specific imaginations of gender fluidity. Her performances integrate masculine and feminine variations of these lwa in order to creatively embody the limits to Global North vocabularies of "transgender," suggesting an alternative in *transcender*—that is, in engagement with the submerged epistemology of Afro-Caribbean religions. And as she does, she acts out how black and Caribbean bodies choreograph the meaning of gender in many historically specific, beautifully outrageous, creatively human ways. This is MilDred's work, this is Ezili's work, and for the next few pages I will try to make it mine too: so please follow me in my short scholarly performance as I attempt to find words to dance with MilDred's lwa, to mirror Ezili's rhythms.

Scene One

Welcome, welcome back: this is the East Village, New York, 1999. A longtime crowd favorite, drag king Dréd glides onstage at Club Casanova amid hollers and cheers, peering at the audience from behind her silver-rimmed shades. Mildred "Dréd" Gerestant proclaims herself a "multi-spirited, Haitian-American, gender-illusioning, black, shaved, different, God/dess, anti-oppression, open, non-traditional, self-expressed, blessed, gender bending, drag-kinging, fluid, ancestor supported and after all that—non-labelling woMan" whose drag star shot heavenward when she was crowned 1996 Drag King of Manhattan at the fabulously chocolate, largely black and Latina HerShe Bar.[5] She quickly went on to become one the few black performers to cross over into largely white drag king counterculture blossoming in the city in the mid-1990s, parading her smooth, 1970s-inspired act five or six nights a week. Tonight—working it black funk-style—she emerges with her back to the audience, then confidently turns to slick back the hood of her old-school black track jacket and pump her ringed, braceleted arms and fingers forward to the beat of the Sugarhill Gang. As the rap progresses, she strips off her black suit to reveal another suit of silky black men's pajamas, then—deftly as the ladies' man Dréd is—unbuttons her Hugh Hefner pajamas to unleash a red bikini, black patent miniskirt, and bulging, well-packed red jock, revelations punctuated by a distinctly masculine, jutting chin nod. The audience coos and shouts in appreciation of the attitude, the package, the king.

"I like all kinds of music; I'm versatile in a lot of things," Dréd tells interviewers Sarah Chinn and Kris Kranklin. "But one thing definitely is that I like the traditional old funky disco. I've always liked classics like 'Disco Inferno,' 'Shaft,' 'Superfly.' . . . I saw some of those movies when I was a kid, and when I was older, I was like 'Gee, I wish I lived in that era.' In a way now, when I dress up, I'm living, you know, in my own way, in that era."[6] In her lucid analysis of Dréd's soul/funk drag king act, Jana Evans Braziel argues that the artist's performance of the hit songs and singers she loved as a child at once offers audiences a homage and a parody: a homage to black men she admires, and a parody of the overwhelmingly white audience's stereotypes of mackdaddy and superfly. "It is, I argue, the cultural gaze of the audience that Dréd parodies, and not the black male performers that the performance artist appropriates," she writes. "Dréd's king performances parody racist and racialized sociocultural constructions of black masculinity and the circulation of stereotypes in the American cultural imaginary."[7] But even while executing this complex dance around mackdaddy-ness, the gender possibilities of Dréd's performance stumble when she tries to entice her audience into taking in her bra and her jock, her skirt, and her beard at the same time. The final striptease reveals the softness of breasts without necessarily softening her act into femmeness in her audience's eyes: the confident nod of her chin, the set of her eyebrows, the squaring of her shoulders all continue to register more Shaft than Foxy Brown, and the crowd cheers more loudly at her crotch grab than her cleavage reveal.

But what lesbian does not love a big black dildo, and didn't Foxy Brown (or Pam Grier) end up as the straight sister on the *L Word*? Or, in other words: while the mackdaddy, the stud, and the aggressive have been widely eroticized in (white) lesbian communities, the lingeried, lipsticked black femme has all too often been treated as a tenuous apparition, barely visible. Dréd herself, for example, appeared on an episode of the *Maury Povich Show* dedicated to drag; rather than kinging, here she dressed as a drag queen. During the show she was one of the performers who removed her wig (a classic drag queen flourish) to "reveal" the self under the clothes. When confronted with her shaved head, the audience took this as proof that Dréd must be male; that is, they were quite vocally willing to accept only markers of white femininity—for example, long hair—as evidence of womanness. Queer audiences are not necessarily more adept at reading black femmeness, either. Bajan/Canadian femme TJ Bryan relates an incident when she came to a poetry slam dressed in heels, red lipstick, and skintight black dress, only to be written up in an article in "the city's queer community rag" accompanied by a picture of her face grafted onto the body of a black male boxer. While this picture ostensibly extolled her champion-worthy performance, Bryan offered another interpretation. "We, Black femmes, can often be masculin(ized)—automatically viewed, treated, and cruised as butches," she writes thoughtfully. "And even if we are seen as Femmes, we can still be devalued or just plain not perceived as Femme(inine) in any sense but the sexual—not just in the larger world, but also inside of queer/Black/'colored' communities of supposed resistance."[8]

This persistent masculinization of black lesbians continues a long, violent history of colonial fictions that categorized black women as inherently, irretrievably masculine—that insisted that black gender differentiation is minimal and a mark of "primitive" societies lacking the sophistication necessary to produce refined queens (in addition to virile chiefs). Writing on sexologists' dissection of black female bodies in the nineteenth century and what this means for the construction of black lesbian genders, Matt Richardson forcefully puts forth: "The Black becomes the aporia between sex and gender such that the two never meet in any fashion that would satisfy the dictates of normative heterosexuality."[9] Dréd's insistence on developing creative, pliable language around her queer gender—*fluid, non-labelling, woMan, womb-man*—should not be interpreted only as a matter of personal self-expression, then. No, even as it acts in fun, it enacts the importance of expressing a black femmeness, curviness, bejeweled-ness, open-thighed-ness that never has to be erased: oh, *no*, girl—*not even while working your daddy mack.*

The question, though, following her around New York at the turn of the millennium: how to get her (largely white) queer audiences to *see* that, to see the African diasporic gender dance that she's choreographing? Black trans performer Storme Webber, in conversation with Dréd in the film *Venus Boyz*, offers: "I feel like we're very much in the tradition, too: because in African societies . . . there were always cross dressers, and there were always people who played both roles, both gender roles, a lot of times they were the people who were the spiritual people, who were the medicine people, who were the healers."[10] So, how could Dréd make visible that she performs *in the tradition*—in a black tradition of finding healing in expressing multiple genders?

Scene Two

Bonswa: this is Haiti's 10th Department, New York Diaspora, 1998. The landmark exhibition *The Sacred Arts of Vodou* is electrifying the American Museum of Natural History, and an outburst of Haitian dance surrounds the event. While Jean Léon Destiné's dance company and the Ibo Dancers give talks at the exhibit, the Alvin Ailey revival of Geoffrey Holder's Vodou-inspired dance drama *The Prodigal Prince* draws audiences intrigued by sacred arts encountered in the museum. Unlike drag king shows, Haitian dance concerts are a well-known phenomenon in Manhattan. The 1970s wave of Haitian migrants included a number of dancers and choreographers, and in the 1980s, when La Troupe Makandal began staging Vodou ritual as concert dance, other companies followed suit. The explicit goal of such performances was to render Vodou more respectable in diaspora, and while considerations of gender and sexuality have never been excised from these performances of respectability, both are enacted as intensely, unerringly cis- and hetero. *The Prodigal Prince*, for example, climaxes in stylized sex between the female lead—Ezili herself—and the titular prince, a character based on renowned painter Hector Hyppolite. Celia Weiss Bambara describes their love scene thusly: "Each bends his/her knees and begins to circle his/her hips while facing each other. They circle their hips and then throw their pelvises forward."[11] Unlike descriptions of drag kings, the split pronoun "his/her" here indicates not that each performer combines masculine and feminine gender expressions but that dancers of "opposite" sexes meet to charge the show with heterosexuality. And, indeed, enacting gender contrast becomes part of representing Haiti's "dignity" onstage, of visualizing conformity to imperial epistemologies that read gender differentiation as proof of "civilization." Though its title might allow for it, *The Prodigal Prince* is *not* a drag king show.

In this same city, these same years, MilDred—transitioning from her drag king repertoire to new kinds of performance art—is piecing together a very different picture of Vodou dance. Kirsty MacDonald's short film about her work, "Blending the Female and Male through MilDred," contains a long scene in which MilDred—clad in a man's black button-down shirt and suede blazer, offset by heavy hoop earrings and black lipstick—stands on a New York street and speaks into the camera about her relationship to Vodou. She starts with a formulation not unlike La Troupe Makandal's: "It's interesting because in Haiti there's a lot of Voodoo, Vodou—and it's gotten a bad name as black magic. I don't believe that Vodou is black magic; I don't practice it but I've read about it and seen videos on it. And what it is is a rich ... umm ... experience of the *divine*, you know, of the ancestors, following and appreciating the spirits that guide and protect you." But then she continues more queerly:

> And I've seen some videos where people practicing rituals, in Vodou rituals, like, they would be possessed by another spirit, but sometimes that spirit would be the opposite gender. So if a man, for instance, was possessed by a female lwa (they call it), or spirit, he would take on the characteristics of that spirit and dress up like her and move like her. And there are women who have been possessed by male spirits, and they would take on the mannerisms of umm, those male spirits. And that's how I felt about my show, when I would be Dréd: that this male energy was so intense that I would be taken over sometimes by the spirit, but in a safe way.[12]

MilDred's deceptively simple discussion of Vodou gives words—and her own radiant style—to a submerged epistemology of gender variance that recasts dominant white and North American queer understandings, say, of butch-femme. She smiles and puts forth that all people have the possibility to be simultaneously man and woman, Shaft and Foxy Brown, packing and lacy, not because gender is constructed, or performative, or any other queer theoretical word but because they are surrounded by male and female spirits at the same time and may temporarily *become* these spirits at any time. She goes on to give her listeners a literally and figuratively Creole formulation of queer gender as she intones with the cadence of a prose poem: "Nou *tout* gen tou le de andedan nou: *We all have both in us. Se yon benediksyon Bondye ba nou. It's a blessing that God has given us.*"[13] This moment literalizes the work MilDred looks to take on in her art: the work of translating to her fellow New Yorkers a Kreyòl understanding of gender in which gason (man) and fanm (woman) expressions refuse binarization, and all aspects of mwen (the self) can be loved and embraced vigorously. Kreyòl is her first language, MilDred also tells viewers in this scene. And—so unlike relentlessly gendered French—this is a language in which nouns, adjectives, and pronouns are never gender inflected, with one third-person singular pronoun, *li*, to communicate she/he and his/her without the divisive backslash. This gender undividedness, too, is what MilDred's performance looks to translate.

Her bilingual poem here also calls out the gender (and other) queerness inherent in Vodou's understanding of benediksyon—blessing—that is, the intimacy between human and divine. If everyone has both male and female lwa guiding them, protecting them, moving their bodies, spirits, and thoughts, then doesn't everyone at some time—depending on which lwa comes into their body and when—have the potential to consider themselves gender "fluid," as MilDred calls herself? *The Prodigal Prince's* climactic scene between Ezili Freda and Hippolyte is based on a dream recounted by the painter, in which Freda appeared and gracefully guided him to become an artist by gifting him with visions of the humans and lwa he was to paint. But what if, rather than interpreting this as a dream in which Freda seduces Hippolyte, we visualize it as a moment when Hippolyte becomes Freda: when he begins to see with her eyes, paint with her hands, bring her into the world through his own body? What if the man fully realizes himself only by listening to the woman in him? And what if he danced in such a way that the audience could see him transition to "his/her," simultaneously a male-bodied person and an archfeminine lwa? Maybe this would be just what it takes to transition from endlessly looped performances of the black gender stereotypes that we all know and cannot escape into *something else*—into the kind of gender expression Rinaldo Walcott heralds as "modes of self-fashioning that allow for a reconstruction of black manhood from the place of incoherence and femininity which might be best exemplified, or at least typified, in recent representations of and by black trans-cultures."[14]

The possibility of *this* kind of gender choreography is what Dréd's new-millennial performance art—a series of pieces that combine Haitian dance, music, and original poetry—explores. As she puts it in her description of "I Transcender": this work "is a mix of dance, poetry and music experiencing the spiritual dance expressions of the fabulous Haitian God/desses: sexy Danbala, cross dressing Baron [sic] Samedi and beautiful Erzulie."[15] In dancing gods and goddesses into god/desses, MilDred does for Danbala, Bawon Samedi, and Ezili something similar to what her drag act did for Shaft and Superfly. She at once pays homage to the characters she portrays and troubles the gaze of audiences who come with black-and-white, predefined notions of these characters' pleasures and dangers. Yes, she challenges both North American–centric understandings of genderqueerness and the heterocentric gaze of those who come to watch Haitian dance with the expectation that certain roles are for male-bodied dancers and others for female-bodied and that boy will always meet girl—somewhere other than in the movement of a single performer. Dressing Bawon Samedi in a skirt and Ezili in a beard, she reflects queerness into Ezili's mirror and beckons to her audience *to look differently*.

Scene Three

March 11, 2010: at the WOW Cafe Theatre in New York's East Village, three one-wo/man shows premiere to a sold-out house. "Get three new shows for the price of one each night! Come Experience MilDred's NEW Show: 'I Transcender: The Gender Expression of Haitian Gods and Goddesses,' choreographed by the fabulous and talented Sokhna Heathyre Mabin. Tantra Zawadi presents 'Soldier Blues,' an exploration through word, music, and movement of the battlefield of the soul and heart. And also introducing a new performance by Sokhna Heathyre Mabin!"[16] Mil-Dred is the star act. Costumed in flowing white robes, she begins her performance dancing the lwa she calls "the sexy Danbala," a serpentine spirit whom one priest describes as "a bisexual entity containing both the male and the female . . . a unified force of sexuality."[17] Stage lights dim, bringing into further relief the candles on the altar that stands at the back of her set, and MilDred transitions into her dance as Bawon Sanmdi, lwa of death and rebirth.

Now, for those audience members who have been seeing her drag for years, the next costume offers a surprise: who knew they had been seeing her perform Bawon for over a decade? Dréd often paraded her mack-daddy smoothness in black suits topped with shades and a black hat or hood, including one particularly memorable and jaunty top hat. This is Sanmdi's signature costume reappropriated, macked out: his top hat, sunglasses, and black frock coat in diaspora. When Sanmdi came dressed in Dréd's drag, the artist's embodiment of this lwa was all about performing black (female) masculinity. But tonight MilDred recostumes and regenders this Bawon. Still shielded behind black shades, she unbuttons her jacket to reveal the contours of breasts; she replaces black pants with a swirling skirt and men's shoes with heels and dances in full energy recolored by a red light. Sanmdi, and MilDred, have danced their way from baron to baron/baroness, from drag king to drag king/queen.

Now, this costume change evokes another variation of Bawon Sanmdi's dress: he sometimes pairs his frock coat with a raffia skirt. In a radio interview with Victoria Gaither, MilDred says: "Through my research I'm finding out some amazing things about these god/desses. For example, one of the goddesses and gods that I'm going to be portraying, on stage through dance, ritual, poetry, and music, is Bawon Sanmdi, and he, he's the lwa of the dead, and he's also lwa of sex and resurrection. . . . But also, interestingly enough, he's . . . depicted as a figure who crosses traditional gender boundaries through cross-dressing or expressing bisexuality."[18] The Sanmdi she reads about in a raffia skirt, along with the Sanmdi she portrays in cloth skirt and platforms, performs culturally specific choreographies of the *masisi* (sissy) as well as the *gwo nèg* (big man)—or, in MilDred's case, of movements where the masisi meets the gwo nèg. Elizabeth McAlister writes of the Gede, the pantheon of death spirits headed by Bawon: "The ultimate destabilizers, Gede mediate yet disrupt dichotomies ... Androgynous yet vulgar, they perform an ambiguous gender scheme where both femininity and masculinity are parodied and ridiculed."[19] While Gede and Bawon are phallic spirits who love to sing about their big dicks, McAlister underscores their simultaneous "effeminacy" and specifically links them to transfemininity as she claims: "Very like drag queens in the United States, the Gede are brilliant social critics of gender."[20] They are also, she suggests, the lwa most closely associated with slavery, arriving at ceremonies with memories of enslavement that they pass on to practitioners. And Bawon's gender satire and re-memory of slavery seem intimately related: dancing and brandishing a cane that is at once a switch and a dildo, he comes to deconstruct all those violently binary oppositions invoked to justify slavery: master/slave, rich/poor, mind/body, spirit/sex, gendered/ungendered, queen-making/unqueenly.

But MilDred's "transcender" Bawon is not exactly the spirit that McAlister describes. Oh, no—it takes just one look to see how this performer not only self-consciously queers Sanmdi but also diasporizes his/her style. Her jacket is not a frock coat but a blazer reminiscent of Richard Roundtree's John Shaft; his skirt is not raffia but the kind of cotton boho chic skirt Beyoncé has been wearing in her turn to 1970s styles. And how many black drag kings perform as Shaft or black drag queens as Beyoncé? MilDred's distinctly African North American styling of Sanmdi suggests that when her audiences witness black trans/gender performance, they may look for models not (only) in white kinging and queening but in African diaspora performance traditions—in transcender as well as in transgender. And then a more sustained gaze at MilDred's dance reveals another diasporic twist to her version of Sanmdi. Instead of straight-up gender satire, MilDred performs transcendering as a supplement to—and comment on—the dips and sways of normative black genders.

Look closely at her from the waist up, first, and see that there's a hint of the *her* in *his* dress. The choker that accessorizes Sanmdi's blazer expresses what Dréd's drag collaborator Shon calls *smoothness*: an expression of black queer man(ish)ness which produces itself through loving relationship to women and womanness, "showing men and women how women should be treated" by honoring the woman within the man as well as the woman beside the man.[21] The smoothness MilDred brings to her blazer tonight asks: Butches, brothers, studs, why not share a necklace with your woman? Why not share a string of connections with your woman? But look down now, and you'll see something more dramatic. Her peasant skirt and platforms flare out to make the fanm *literally* beneath the gason, the high heels beneath the blazer, and as she dances, it is her woman "half" that literally holds up the man, that at once stabilizes the entirety of Sanmdi's incoherent gender just enough so s/he does not fall over, and shakes it up to keep it continually moving, dancing, transcendering. This gender mixing isn't the striptease, the surprising finale, as it was in her drag; no, it's the whole dance. Now make no mistake, the heels she dances in are an important addition to Sanmdi's costume. While a skirted Haitian Sanmdi might dance barefoot, MilDred comes out more than well heeled, masterfully balanced in Foxy Brown–height shoes that visualize black femme-ininity's ability to rise. Describing learning to love feet that she never felt were pretty enough, MilDred writes that she came to understand them as "powerful roots to our Haitian culture–our Haitian ancestors."[22] And oh, the ancestors—the funny ones, the sissy ones, the ones who insisted on being womanish when everyone told them they couldn't—they are riding high on those shoes tonight.

Scene Four

Lanmou mwen, vini, an nou danse; lanmou mwen, you're here, *you came back.* As MilDred's Bawon Sanmdi exits the stage, the final character of her Haitian god/dess performance emerges: the beautiful, endlessly desirable, divinely insatiable Ezili. Metres Ezili, we know that you have arrived when Sanmdi raises a hand mirror to his/her face, slowly, lovingly removes his/her hat and beard, paints *her* lips in tantalizingly kissable black lipstick, and changes into a flowing top that matches her newly flowing, feminine dance. *Full moon on my back, I do not lack,* MilDred's Ezili tells us. Now, this lovely moment may usher in a new surprise for MilDred's faithful audience members: how were they to know that they had also been watching Ezili for years? At the end of her drag act, Dréd peered into just this kind of hand mirror to remove her beard—then, to her audience's delight, reached into her well-packed jock to reveal the apple lodged inside, raising it to her mouth and taking a loud, tempting bite. But where this drag finale was focused on the apple, humorously rescripting the biblical story of Eve, "I Transcender" focuses on the power of the mirror and its link to another understanding of the relationship between femininity and divinity. Both apple and mirror are symbols of Ezili, who, when she arrives in ceremony, is immediately handed a mirror to gaze into and "dream of perfection," as Sallie Ann Glassman puts it.[23]

When MilDred transitions from Sanmdi to Freda, she begins the final act of her show with a dance that seems, at first glance, to have moved beyond her act's earlier embrace of gender incoherence to end up luxuriating in the girly, womanly lace and roses that Metres Freda can command. But if you look closely into Ezili's mirror here, another, more complicated reflection emerges. Mildred's mirror-framed debearding and lipsticking is an act that makes visible what femme activists have begun to call "ftoF," or female to femme transition. Meaning, as femme writer and filmmaker Elizabeth Stark says, that—like male to female transitions—females' coming into queer femininity is neither natural nor default but an intentionally orchestrated process: "My sexuality and desires, my sensibility and my gender expression are all going against the grain of the expected female. In fact, becoming a femme in a world that insists on a certain femininity . . . without taking on that enforced femininity is a delicate, powerful move; a transition indeed, that is underinvestigated and overlooked."[24] But MilDred, of course, is not rescripting what this white femme experiences as "enforced femininity." No, she is movingly, seductively, powerfully embodying a kind of luxurious, champagne-kissed, sugar-coated womanness that, as a queer black female, she was never supposed to claim—let alone dance and be applauded for.

Stark also celebrates femme-ininity in terms that mirror MilDred's act more closely. "Femmes," she says, "know how to fail and succeed at femininity at the same time. We use our flaws, our fat, our hairiness, our loud mouths, our oversized brains and our excessive accessorizing to celebrate ourselves and those we love."[25] MilDred's transition to Freda does not fail and succeed at femininity at the same time, though, so much as it embodies and disidentifies with Freda at the same time. Her movement into this character both echoes and refuses Alfred Métraux's striking description of Ezili Freda's arrival in his classic *Voodoo in Haiti*: "At last, in the full glory of her seductiveness, with hair unbound to make her look like a long haired half-caste, Ezili makes her entrance. . . . She walks slowly, swinging her hips," and demands to be clothed in pink and white.[26] But while MilDred's Freda enters slowly, swinging her hips, and while she, too, uncovers her head, she refuses to become this long-haired, fair-cheeked mulatta. Instead, she bares the glory of her perfectly shaved head and, rouging her lips, bypasses Freda's signature pink in favor of a rich black. Yes, these choices in self-aestheticizing consciously blacken Freda when black is "supposed" to be neither beautiful nor Ezili-like. For part of Mil-Dred's difficulty in performing the fanm in her, she clearly states, comes from the necessity of transitioning her own internalized standards for ideal womanhood from blonde-loving to Afro-positive. "Growing up," she writes, "I was constantly teased for the same things I once hated about myself, but now through the power of self-transformation and self-love, love about myself. 'Tar baby' becomes beautiful dark cocoa skin; nappy hair becomes perfectly shaped shaved head; four eyes . . . a mystical clairvoyance through almond shaped eyes."[27] In other words, white viewers are not the only New Yorkers in need of unlearning that blackness and femininity are discordant, and when MilDred blackens Freda, she publicly performs an act of *emancipation from mental slavery*. An nou danse, my cocoa-skinned Freda, dance for Haiti tonight!

And just as much as MilDred's hair and makeup beautify blackness, they queer Ezili-ness too. This is absolutely not *The Prodigal Prince's* Ezili. She dons no headdress here, nor does she drape herself in Madonna blue. Instead, this Freda's well-lit, perfectly shaped shaved head looks "visibly queer," as black femme Marla Stewart puts it.[28] And her black lipstick—the only makeup she wears, notice—reflects the queer Afro-punk subculture rocking Brooklyn in the 2010s. If you met Ezili Freda at a black lesbian club in Brooklyn in 2010, now, *this* is what she would look like; *this* is how she would dance with the femmes, butches, and aggressives who, starstruck, cannot help but approach her.

Outro

MilDred's performance concludes with Ezili, and so mine will as well. Ending today, I want to tell a story that is not so much a conclusion as it is an anecdote I could just as well have opened with. As I meditated on MilDred and her queering of Haitian diaspora to write this essay, I found myself returning again and again to a night in Aux Cayes during my first trip to Haiti in 1998. Again and again, I replayed an unlit, outdoor conversation with novelist Edwidge Danticat, when I asked her about the existence of a space for people like me and my lovers—femmes, butches, dykes, queers—in Haiti. "Oh, no," she gently and generously told me.

"No. If you are looking for *those* women, you are looking in the wrong place and the wrong way." "No," she smiled and laughed for a moment. Where I needed to go was *to a Vodou ceremony*. Dancing "I Transcender," MilDred is bringing the Vodou ceremony to us, challenging us to rethink black and Caribbean gender. And, most simply, I am asking that we show up and listen to what MilDred and Sanmdi and Ezili have to say and to accept their challenge to North American queer and transgender studies.

NOTES

1. Several spelling variations of this spirit's name are common in English, including Erzulie, Erzuli, and Ezili. For consistency, I have opted to use "Ezili"—the most common spelling in Kreyòl—throughout.

2. Karen McCarthy Brown, *Mama Lola: A Vodou Priestess in Brooklyn* (Berkeley: University of California Press, 1991), 221.

3. Lisa Ze Winters citing Brent Hayes Edwards in "Specter, Spectacle and the Imaginative Space: Unfixing the Tragic Mulatta" (PhD diss., University of California, Berkeley, 2005), 23.

4. Barbara Christian, "The Race for Theory," in *Making Face, Making Soul: Haciendo Caras*, ed. Gloria Anzaldúa (San Francisco: Aunt Lute Press, 1990), 336.

5. Cited in Ifalade TaShia Asanti, ed., *Tapestries of Faith: Black SGLBT Stories of Faith, Love, and Family* (Long Beach, CA: Glover Lane Press, 2011), 34.

6. Sarah Chinn and Kris Franklin, "King of the Hill: Changing the Face of Drag—An Interview with Dred," in *Butch/Femme: Inside Lesbian Gender*, eds. Sally R. Munt and Cherry Smyth (London: Continuum, 1998), 152.

7. Jana Evans Braziel, *Artists, Performers, and Black Masculinity in the Haitian Diaspora* (Bloomington: Indiana University Press, 2008), 122.

8. TJ Bryan, "You've Got to Have Ballz to Walk in These Shoes," in *Brazen Femme: Queering Femininity*, eds. Chloë Brushwood Rose and Anna Camilleri (Vancouver: Arsenal Pulp Press, 2003), 147.

9. Matt Richardson, personal communication, September 2011.

10. Gabriel Baur, *Venuz Boyz* (Onix Films, 1998).

11. Celia Weiss Bambara, "Did You Say Banda? Geoffrey Holder and How Stories Circulate," *Journal of Haitian Studies* 17, no. 1 (Spring 2011): 184.

12. Kirsty MacDonald, *Assume Nothing: MilDred Gerestant*, October 31, 2010, accessed July 24, 2013, http://www.youtube.com/watch?v=pWAg3DsEnaA.

13. MacDonald, *Assume Nothing*.

14. Rinaldo Walcott, "Reconstructing Manhood; or, The Drag of Black Masculinity," *Small Axe* 13, no. 1 (March 2009): 77.

15. Music-by-Yoko and King Tut, "A Night of Three Goddesses: 'Powerful Women,'" June 28, 2010, accessed July 24, 2013, http://www.nypl.org/events/programs /2010/06/28/night-three-goddesses-powerful-women.

16. Music-by-Yoko and King Tut, "A Night of Three Goddesses."

17. Randy P. Conner and David Hatfield Sparks, *Queering Creole Spiritual Traditions: Lesbian, Gay, Bisexual, and Transgender Participation in African-Inspired Traditions in the Americas* (New York: Routledge, 2004): 57.

18. MilDred Gerestant, with Victoria Gaither, "A Night of Three Goddesses," March 7, 2010, accessed July 24, 2013, www.blogtalkradio.com/ . . . /a-night-of-3 -goddesses-featuring-actress-mildred-gerestant.

19. Elizabeth McAlister, "Love, Sex, and Gender Embodied: The Spirits of Haitian Vodou," in *Love, Sex, and Gender in the World Religions*, eds. Joseph Runzo and Nancy M. Martin (Oxford: One World, 2000), 138.

20. McAlister, "Love, Sex, and Gender Embodied," 139.

21. Judith "Jack" Halberstam and Del LaGrace Volcano, "Class, Race, and Masculinity: The Superfly, the Mackdaddy, and the Rapper," in *The Drag King Book* (London: Serpent's Tail, 1999), 142.

22. MilDred Gerestant, "Who Am I—D.R.E.D—Daring Reality Every Day." Accessed April 17, 2016. Archived at http://womenwritersinbloompoetrysalon.blogspot .com/p/poetry-garden-archives.html.

23. Sallie Ann Glassman, *Vodou Visions: An Encounter with Divine Mystery* (New York: Villard Books, 2000), 25.

24. Elizabeth Stark quoted in Jacob Anderson-Minshall, "Is Femme a Gender Identity?" *Bay Times,* July 20, 2006, accessed July 24, 2013, http://www.sfbaytimes.com /?sec=article&article_id=5213.

25. Anderson-Minshall, "Is Femme a Gender Identity?"

26. Alfred Métraux, *Voodoo in Haiti* (New York: Pantheon, 1989), 113.

27. "The Early Years: MilDred Gerestant Closet Interview with StyleLikeU," *Stylelikeu,* March 21, 2011, accessed July 24, 2013, http://stylelikeu.com/closets/mildred -gerestant/#ad-image-0.

28. Marla Stewart cited in Ulrike Dahl, *Femmes of Power* (London: Serpent's Tail, 2009), 105.

8

Toward a Hemispheric Analysis of Black Lesbian Feminist Activism and Hip Hop Feminism

Artist Perspectives from Cuba and Brazil

TANYA L. SAUNDERS

☺

I AM A BLACK, QUEER, GENDER-NONCONFORMING WOMAN from Baltimore, Maryland, who went to Cuba at the age of 20. I was interested in understanding the global hegemony of Cuba as an ideological counterbalance to U.S. American capitalist and imperialist discourses. Four years later, I met Las Krudas CUBENSI, in Havana, Cuba. I remember entering La Madriguera, an alternative arts space in Havana, and seeing two black women (Wanda and Odaymara Cuesta) pass by. Our eyes met, we paused, and then we slowly continued walking while looking at each other. And then, nearly in sync, we stopped and started chatting, I do not remember who decided to start inquiring about the other first. Aesthetically, the three of us were marked by black queer aesthetics: dashikis, Afros, dreadlocks, timberlands, sagging jeans. When we started to chat, we realized that a lot of people had told us about each other. Eleven years later, in 2013, I received a call from Las Krudas; they were invited to Brazil by Brazilian black feminist activists to participate in the 2013 AfroLatinidades: Afro-American, Afro-Latina, Afro-Caribbean Festival in Brasilia

FIG. 8.1 Left to right: Olivia Prendes, Lú AfroBreak, Odaymara Cuesta, Tiely Queen, and the author at the LadyFest Music Festival, São Paulo, Brazil, August 2013. Photo courtesy of Las Krudas.

(http://afrolatinas.com.br/), and this expanded into their Brazil tour; I went on the tour as their manager.

Figure 8.1 pictures Las Krudas CUBENSI, Lú AfroBreak, and Tiely Queen and was taken in São Paulo at the LadyFest Music Festival during their 2013 tour. The artists were each familiar with each other's work via word of mouth (for example, Tiely learned of Krudas from Mexican activists) and via their own searches online for other women in hip hop. Figure 8.2 shows me, Krudas CUBENSI, and, behind Olivia Prendes, Brazilian researcher Giselle dos Anjos Santos, who went to Cuba to study Cuban black feminism. The group is composed of hip hop feminist activists, Anarcafeminist activists (the organizers of LadyFest), and lesbian activists (the organizers of the Women's March, which drew nearly ten thousand women to a concert featuring Las Krudas CUBENSI in Praça Roosevelt [Plaza Roosevelt] in São Paulo). The Brazilian activists and researchers were drawn to Cuba and to Las Krudas for similar reasons to mine: Cuba represents an ideological counterweight to rampant U.S. American capitalism, imperialism, racism, and sexism.

FIG. 8.2. São Paulo, Brazil, 2013. Photo courtesy of Tanya L. Saunders.

This essay is a comparative study of the three members (Odaymara Cuesta, Odalys [Wanda] Cuesta, and Olivia Prendes) of the group Krudas CUBENSI (Havana, Cuba), Tiely Queen (São Paulo, Brazil), and Lú AfroBreak (São Paulo, Brazil). Through focusing on the artists' personal encounters with socially conscious hip hop movements, I examine why these women were moved to become artivists (artists whose artistic production is their activism), who decided to dedicate their lives to hip hop feminism and LGBT activism. With its hemispheric approach to black identity politics, this essay seeks to bring attention to an understudied phenomenon: the transnational, queer Afro-diasporic, black feminist encounters and exchanges occurring across national borders, specifically those occurring via hip hop activism. Greater attention should be given to the emergence of transnational black lesbian feminist and black queer activism within hip hop as a key element of global hip hop activism, as well as contemporary transnational black feminist and black queer activism. To this end, this essay documents the presence of global hip hop feminists, specifically black-identified, queer Afro-descendant women, who are in conversation with each other through hip hop, thereby rupturing the commonly accepted wisdom of the "invisibility" of women and "homosexual" artists within global hip hop—a discourse that threatens to effect that which it claims simply to describe.

I focus specifically on black feminist politics, in which activists encourage the embracing of one's blackness and one's African cultural heritage. This is a profoundly radical idea in a hemisphere where day-to-day racial politics depends on the outright rejection or the downplaying of that which is "African." Moreover, countries such as Brazil and Cuba are *culturally* Afro-descendant nations. As such, I highlight a major contradiction that exists within these countries and the West broadly: the African roots of Western culture and Western modernity are often silenced and/or downplayed (depending on the country) as a means of reproducing (and legitimating through silences) the Eurocentrism of Western modernity and Western coloniality. One effect of the myopic view of Eurocentric notions of "art" is that it limits our understanding of the various ways in which artistic and aesthetic interventions function as political discourse, forms of social deliberation, subject formation, and political activism in the West.

The women discussed in this essay are all out lesbians who variously identify as black and/or Afro-descendant. They are a part of a larger transnational network of artists, activists, and intellectuals who are participating in antiracist, hip hop feminist and LGBT activism through hip hop. Hip hop feminism is a form of black feminism. In Cuba and Brazil, contemporary black LGBT activism and black feminist discourse emerged from hip hop feminism or at the very least is in conversation with it. Data were drawn from participant observation and interviews with twenty hip hop artists as well as ten state officials, scholars, and producers associated with Cuba's Underground Hip-Hop Movement (CUHHM) in Havana, Cuba (1998–2013), conducted as part of a larger semilongitudinal study. The data also includes participant observation and interviews with a total of ten hip hop artists from São Paulo, Brazil (2008–13).[1]

Artivist Art Worlds and the Black Public Sphere

Hip hop has become a significant countercultural space in which a sector of the global hip hop community—composed of artists, activists, and collectives—has used music, art, and performance to level antiracist critiques.[2] These criticisms range from arguing for a more inclusive society and a more inclusive form of capitalism to outright anticapitalist and anticolonial discourses that offer more radical critiques of contemporary Western society. For those who self-identify as being part of the socially conscious and critical sector of global hip hop, the genre functions as a culturally based social movement, linking a transnational network of artists, scholars, and activists. In short, within the larger global hip hop community, there is a sector for whom hip hop functions as a tool for political deliberation and critique. Within this community, lesbian feminist hip hop performers have emerged as respected community leaders and cultural workers who challenge the consciousness of their fellow citizens.

One thing that distinguishes global hip hop social movements from the global hip hop music scene more generally is that the former constitute an activist "art world" in the sense defined by sociologist Howard S. Becker.[3] As an activist art world, hip hop movements comprise people who are invested in their art, in entertaining and/or educating for the purposes of effecting social change, and in disseminating their work to a local and global audience. While some self-identify as activists within hip hop, there are others who are connected aesthetically to the political activism of hip hop solely through their identification with hip hop culture.

Some scholars engage hip hop as a black public sphere: a space where those of African descent, who have often been excluded from the bourgeois public sphere of previous generations, including black lesbians, can organize to challenge social exclusion and racial and sexual violence.[4] When we consider hip hop as a diasporic music culture in an American (regionally speaking) context, the term "hip hop nation" has particular resonance among socially conscious or "underground" hip hop fans.[5] The global reach of the "hip hop nation," as an identity politics and politicized transnational public sphere, can be found in the manifestos of hip hop collectives throughout the world and in the lyrics of global hip hop artists who proclaim to work for social change.

Theorizing Hip Hop Feminisms and Hemispheric Afro-diasporic Feminisms

In this essay, I offer a regionally situated definition of hip hop feminism that draws on the work of Aisha Durham and Gwendolyn D. Pough. Pough defines hip hop feminism as "a worldview ... an epistemology grounded in the experiences of communities of color under advanced capitalism, [and] a cultural site for rearticulating identity and sexual politics."[6] Durham similarly argues that hip hop feminism is "a socio-cultural, intellectual and political movement grounded in . . . situated knowledge . . . [which] recognize[s] culture as a pivotal site for politi-cal intervention to challenge, resist and mobilize collectives to dismantle systems of exploitation" rooted in the legacies of colonialism; hip hop has become central to a new generation of black feminist critique.[7]

Black feminist epistemologies have hardly developed in isolation; in the case of late twentieth-century black feminist praxis, transnational anticolonial and revolutionary nationalist struggles had a profound ef-fect on second-wave, black feminist leftists within the United States. Black feminist leftists in the United States were significantly influenced by transnational struggles against heteropatriarchy that were also a part of revolutionary nationalist and transnationalist struggles for liberation, as were black feminists in Cuba and Brazil.[8] Additionally, the queer of color critique has always been a part of radical black feminist activ-ism, especially in black internationalist feminism, as black women have been aware of the ways in which questions of race, heteronormativity, nation, and colonialism/imperialism are mutually reinforcing axes of power that have had a profound effect on black women's lives.[9] It is in this way that the queer of color critique, emerging from black feminism, is not reflective of ideas that emerged as a result of U.S. American exceptionalism but are ideas and discourses that emerged in relation to transnational discussions concerning black liberation in which U.S. American leftist black feminists took part. These transnational conver-sations also included critiques of the relationship between hegemonic notions of blackness and the heteropatriarchy embedded in nationalist struggles.

Hip hop feminists have also addressed the relationship between black-ness and heteropatriarchy embedded in hegemonic, transnational, socially conscious hip hop discourse and activism. Given the privileging of only a male-gendered and (hetero)sexualized black body in hip hop, simply being a woman who enters into hip hop makes an intervention into its linguistic and cultural imaginary a queer act.[10] It is in this way that the emergence of feminist space or women-centered space within hip hop communities marks an opening into black queer space and, as such, opens the door for various forms of black queer subjects who were assigned female at birth to represent themselves. Black lesbian feminists are also key actors in global hip hop feminist movements.

FIG. 8.3. Left to right: Odaymara Cuesta and Olivia Prendes, July 30, 2013, at Balaio Café in Brasilia, Brazil. Photo courtesy of Tanya L. Saunders.

A Brief Overview of the Artists' Contexts

Odaymara Cuesta and her partner, Olivia Prendes, compose the Cuban underground hip hop group Las Krudas CUBENSI. Odalys Cuesta, Odaymara's sister, also frequently performed with the group until about 2008. Las Krudas CUBENSI was founded in Havana, Cuba, in the late 1990s but left the country in 2006 to participate in global feminist movements, especially hip hop feminist and LGBT movements.[11] This essay seeks to contextualize its diasporic work in Cuba, where it began, as a means of highlighting the way in which diasporic praxis is not premised upon physical travel.

From about 1965 to 1998, the post-1959 Cuban state declared that it had solved Cuba's social problems resulting from culturally entrenched racism, sexism, and class inequality. Cuba clearly made advances in health, reproductive health, education, and quality of life. In the 1990s the Cuban state began to publicly recognize the "errors of the Revolution," which included state-sanctioned homophobia and the state's nearly forty-year silence on the social persistence of racism and sexism. This, as state officials have now begun to recognize, has permitted new forms of racism and sexism and the intensification of unaddressed forms of race- and gender-based social inequality to emerge at the material level after Cuba was forced to liberalize its economy in the 1990s. Cuba's investment in its cultural programs has resulted in a dynamic cultural sphere that functions as a nascent civil society.[12] The members of Las Krudas CUBENSI are key figures in one of the arts-based social movements within the politicized cultural sphere. Much of the state's contemporary discussion of these issues can be directly linked to the activism of Cuban artivists. In Cuba, Las Krudas utilized the socially critical space provided by the CUHHM to address the intersectional oppression and social isolation of black lesbians in Cuba, with an eye toward addressing the issues facing black women and lesbians throughout the Americas.

In 2013, I interviewed Jorge Enrique, the editor in chief of the Cuban hip hop magazine *Movemiento*. He reflected on the invisibility of black women in Cuban society and the role that Cuban hip hop feminists made to bringing visibility to Cuban lesbians:

JORGE: Therefore, the power absorbed those two big issues. The women rappers and male rappers began to engage the Cuban society, they began to push these two big issues up, and up it went. Basically, CENESEX must thank the rap movement in Cuba, like many other institutions that now say . . .

TANYA: Sorry. Why CENESEX?

JORGE: I give the example of CENESEX because the first people who came out on a public stage about their homosexuality were the women rappers, absolutely no one else, even when they were emblematic figures of Cuban culture, like the late Sara González, who was openly lesbian. . . . I repeat here, except for the lesbian female rappers, nobody before them had touched the subject. I can assure you.

TANYA: The history of Cuba?

JORGE: Yes, of Cuba let's see, let's see, let's see, . . . the History of Cuba . . . well, it was Sara González, Tanya, Albita Rodríguez. Here I can mention a million lesbian artists, but those that we knew were lesbians, it was because somehow we were in that circle . . . but publicly, as in a social discussion, never. In fact, in Cuba gay expressions were always visible in terms of the male. I began to think, Jorge, is there machismo within the gay community? That's fucked up! But it's real, because in a way it was more natural to see a gay man, people would say: hey, look at that [faggot], but when you talk about a lesbian, that is something that has more resistance.[13]

In the longer interview, Jorge argues that it was the women MCs (masters of ceremony) who brought the issue of gender inequality (economic and cultural) and homosexuality back into the public sphere, and did it with an attention to racial inequality. I have noted elsewhere that lesbians in Cuba are perceived as disgusting and unfeminine and face higher rates of negative perceptions among the general population than do bisexual and gay men.[14] The name of the group itself, Las Krudas CUBENSI—translated as "the crude ones," the "crude women," and even as "the crude feminine subjects," who are also "Cuban"? "Yes!" (CUBEN-SI)—reflects a critique of and a challenge to the resistance and the disgust that arises with the mere mention of "lesbian," something that is also viewed as "foreign" and "un-Cuban." Cuban women MCs took an intersectional approach to understanding their own inequality and, as a result, touched upon several issues that affected nearly everyone in Cuban society. Black feminism of the CUHHM marks the emergence of post–Special Period *Cuban* feminism despite the elimination of independent political groups after 1959.

Tiely Queen is a solo MC, producer, and actress based in São Paulo, Brazil. Tiely started performing in the early 1990s as part of a popular São Paulo–based hip hop group called Fator Ético. She initiated the NGO Hip Hop Mulher in 2008 as a way to connect a diverse group of female hip hop artists and cultural participants throughout Brazil. Tiely Queen participates in LGBTT (lesbian, gay, bisexual, transvestite, and transsexual) and feminist activism. In her early years as an MC, she did not incorporate these themes into her music and performances. When she decided to focus more on her career as a producer—a decision that is interlinked with her development of a feminist and lesbian identity—Tiely integrated support for LGBTT artists and political discourses into her work. Lú AfroBreak is an LGBTT and feminist activist and a b-girl in the AfroBreak Crew, based in Diadema, São Paulo. Lú works as the coordinator and educator at the Rede Cultural Beija-Flor, a nonprofit organization that works to find alternative solutions to empower street kids. Both are committed and known for their work with youth locally and nationally, with much of their work based in São Paulo's impoverished suburban communities.

Tiely and Lú also live in a country that has a long history of black feminist activism and black feminist institutions. For example, black women activists have been at the center of contemporary housing and land rights movements across Brazil.[15] In Brazil, the major tension that exists between white feminists and black feminists is that in a country that claims to be raceless, and therefore absent of racism, white feminists are disinterested in race and explicitly refuse to address the issue.[16] Meanwhile, black feminists struggle with the sexism of the male-dominated black social movements and the culturally entrenched racism of larger Brazilian society. In recent decades, Brazil began to grapple with the country's culturally entrenched forms of racism and racial inequality, which led to the state supporting organizations such as Geledés (the Black Women's Institute). In the 1990s, Geledés began working directly with and mobilizing women hip hop artists, holding educational events and symposia for hip hoppers. Artists such as Tiely and Lú were among the young black artists who attended events organized by black feminist organizations such as Geledés.

Las Krudas CUBENSI and Cuban Hip Hop

Known for its work in Cuba's critical arts scene as the founders and members of the world-renowned group Tropazancos, a stilt-walking group that often performs in the city center in Havana, Las Krudas CUBENSI was asked by Cuba's International Underground Hip Hop Festival's organizers to perform at the 1998 festival. After this experience, Las Krudas CUBENSI decided to pursue activism within the CUHHM because members saw it as a community that lent itself to the creative energies of Cuban youth of African descent, a global platform where Cuban youth could finally have a voice. A number of works have been published that examine the significant political and social impact of Las Krudas's LGBT artivism in Cuba.[17] Together, these works show that Krudas CUBENSI's intervention in the CUHHM has also been an intervention into the pre-existing black feminist discourses of the movement, which inadvertently reinforced heteronormativity through its focus on heterosexuality as a definitive aspect of black femininity.

From the moment Krudas CUBENSI began performing at hip hop shows, they were bothered by the lack of women onstage, which resulted in a lack of diversity among representations of femininity within Cuban hip hop. Olivia Prendes says the following about how Krudas CUBENSI hoped to contribute to the presence of women in hip hop: "[In] 2000 and 2001 was the first real appearance that we had with music produced by Pablo Herrera and by us as well with lyrics that we felt were necessary. Feminist, pro-lesbian and pro-woman, in order to show the hip hop community that there exists another group of women who are not like

FIG. 8.4. LesQueens performing at the Lesbian March, São Paulo, 2014. Photo courtesy of Preta Pretina.

the ones they normally see onstage, where many of them accompany their husbands, many of them singing choruses for the MCs."[18]

Krudas CUBENSI felt that the critical artistic and intellectual space of hip hop was one in which they could make a feminist intervention vis-à-vis hegemonic discourses surrounding women. They decided to first focus on feminist discourses, arguing for women's autonomy, self-esteem building, and a self-identity developed independent of men instead of in relation to men. Also, as Jorge notes above and as I discuss elsewhere, there exists a public discourse concerning male homosexuality, largely because of male privilege.[19] However, a lesbian was something that people could not fathom. In a 2006 event organized at the Rhizome Anarchist Collective in Austin, Texas, a public discussion that happened just weeks after Krudas CUBENSI arrived in Cuba, Odalys spoke about the themes they discuss in their music and Las Krudas's arts-based activism:

There are people expressing themselves and dotting the "i's" in Cuba, that is, Krudas, who are doing their activism, and their way of being [and living is] through their art, their way of fighting, of combating that which is bad, to rip up the bad herbs and plant the good herbs. It's like transforming that which is bad, the stress, the negative of society from our point of view in art, and in thought. . . . To sew light takes time, and it's not because for me there is a message [that is] new, because there are women who have been talking for a long time about the inequality of rights, but for me this seems to be a more dense message because it talks about race, it talks about sexuality, class, internationality . . . our community, as a result, receives us in a strong way, and [has done so] so consistently that at some point we believed and became determined to release it to the world, to the planet.[20]

Here Wanda talks about the diversity of themes that Las Krudas addressed in their work in Cuba between 1998 and 2006, which included race, gender, sexuality, class, global inequality, and environmental rights. As such, Krudas's message was an influential one: they connected numerous social themes and discussed multiple forms of social oppression and, most important, showed how they are all interconnected. This allowed Krudas to develop a large and diverse audience both in Cuba and abroad. While in Cuba, Krudas CUBENSI were also contacted by international hip hop festivals, feminist music festivals, LGBT music festivals, and many other groups representing various genres of youth music cultures and arts-based social movements who listened to socially conscious hip hop and heard about Krudas CUBENSI via word of mouth. However, the group was often denied permission to leave Cuba for various reasons ranging from questions concerning their "message" to the difficulty of navigating Cuba's cultural bureaucracy as independent artists. When they finally had an opportunity to travel abroad, they decided to live primarily outside of Cuba, where they could better access international networks, but still continue to participate indirectly in the movement at home. This decision eventually lead to their 2013 Brazilian tour, where they finally had an opportunity to meet two fans who are also black feminist lesbians working for social change through hip hop.

Tiely Queen and Lú AfroBreak: Hip Hop Activism in Brazil

Tiely Queen and Lú AfroBreak identify with the transformative nature of hip hop, personally and as a tool for social change. It was for this reason that, like Krudas CUBENSI, they were attracted to the genre. In a 2012 interview, I asked Tiely why she entered into hip hop:

I liked the challenge that it poses.... For this reason I liked it ... it was only later ... much much later that I began to realize that there did not exist anything [within hip hop] that talks about lesbians, for example. So I felt more of the challenge, and I wanted to consume more you know? And at this point it was the beat, it was the beat you know? It elevates you and it's something that you have, something that you feel in the blues, in jazz, you know that movement, those nuances, that beat, all of those things frenetic and strong ... you know that it is something that is transformative, for this reason it feeds me, and for this reason it interests me and I identify with it, it's in the subjective camp, the question of music and the other is the visual identification as well. And the way of dressing, the way of talking.... I think it's beautiful I identified with it, like being a lesbian woman.[21]

Tiely explains that she was drawn to the aesthetic of hip hop, the style of dress, and its transformative nature. Tiely, like Krudas CUBENSI, comes from a theater and literature background. She is a trained artist. She was drawn to music because of its ability to move people. She enjoyed how the beats of the music caused her to feel and think differently, and the lyrics challenged her. She was particularly attracted to the hip hop lifestyle, which she felt would have significant aesthetic implications for her artistic production. Before Tiely began to self-identify as a feminist and engage feminist theory, she developed her feminist consciousness through her everyday experiences in her local socially critical hip hop community. Her initial interest in hip hop, she notes, had nothing to do with her being lesbian. In fact, she identified as neither a lesbian nor as a feminist when she first began participating in hip hop. Even after becoming actively involved in the LGBTT social movement and Brazil's independent hip hop scene, she does not self-identify as an activist but as an artist participating in activism. When I asked Tiely about the development of her feminist and lesbian identity, she explained that as she learned more and more about the events and symposia organized and advertised by hip hop artists, she decided to take advantage of the events to educate herself. And it was through this process that she became exposed to feminism and eventually began to develop a black feminist identity and, later, a black lesbian identity. Like Krudas CUBENSI and Lú AfroBreak, Tiely was moved to intervene in the local hip hop movement because she was frustrated with the invisibility of women and the exceptionally small number of women who were central figures on stage—this is the challenge she

FIG. 8.5. Lú AfroBreak dancing during the performance of LesQueens, Brazil's first black lesbian (now black queer) feminist hip hop group, at the Lesbian March, São Paulo, 2014. Photo courtesy by Preta Pretina.

spoke of—the challenge of feeling that she needed to make an intervention into whose experiences are represented in hip hop.

Lú AfroBreak, on the other hand, takes a different perspective. Lú entered the hip hop scene as a break-dancer in 2003. She also was struck by the absence of women in the movement, particularly in the area of break dancing, and decided that she could best contribute to hip hop by becoming a b-girl. Lú, like Krudas CUBENSI, identifies as an activist. She also identifies as a militant within hip hop, which in a Cuban context translates into being "super underground"; she is an independent artist who is so critical of capitalism that she flirts with being explicitly anticapitalist. While Tiely's activism is a complement to her work as an artist, for Lú, her art is a vehicle for her activism. For her, hip hop is revolution. It is consciousness. And anyone who believes that there should be or could be a relationship between the market—specifically the music industry—and

FIG. 8.6. Tiely performing with LesQueens at the Lesbian March, São Paulo, 2014. Photo courtesy of Preta Pretina.

hip hop is someone who, according to Lú, has become commercialized; they have ceased to be relevant to the grassroots, underground, activist vision of hip hop, even if they are commercial artists with a socially conscious message (a perspective that is quite common in underground hip hop in Brazil and in much of the world). Lú argues that being a militant in hip hop is not just about disagreeing with hegemonic ideas but also about doing work that strives at all times to improve the future of coming generations. From her perspective, helping future generations to have access to culture and education is a form of social service, especially for peripheral communities.

Lú, like Tiely, developed her black feminist and black lesbian feminist identity through participating in her local hip hop movement, which exposed her to other social movements; she encountered LGBTT movements through participating in black feminist events, which exposed her to Anarcafeminist activists who are also involved in the activist art world.

Thus, in addition to trying to improve the situation of both her community and black people, as she says, she also runs workshops and programs to create space for the training and support of b-girls and works to bring hip hop culture to LGBTT spaces and those associated with Anarcapunk scenes.

Conclusion

In 2008, at a concert at BAAD!, the Bronx Academy of the Arts and Dance, a young, black, queer-identified woman approached Las Krudas. While they were talking to the other artists at the event who were from various parts of the Americas, I struck up a conversation with the young woman. Come to find out, she was from Baltimore as well. She heard about Las Krudas from some friends and decided to go to Cuba to see them perform. She showed me her forearm; the lyrics of Las Krudas's song "Eres Bella" (You Are Beautiful) were tattooed onto her forearm. She commented that she did not have a chance to talk to them in Cuba after their concert, but when she found out that they were going to be in the Bronx, she traveled to see them. She was excited that she had an opportunity to show them personally how much they impacted her.

A lot has happened over the artivists' careers. Las Krudas CUBENSI is now composed of two members, and the three original members live outside the United States. They have traveled throughout Latin America, the United States, and Canada and are on their way to Europe. Krudas CUBENSI has actively been engaged in queer social movements, as well as transnational hip hop movements. In the case of Tiely and the two remaining members of Las Krudas CUBENSI, their lesbian feminist identities have also changed over time—these three artists no longer identify as female. They still identify as black feminists, but they are also more male-identified, with one of the artists being in the process of transitioning, while the other two are rethinking their relationship to their gender identities.

These artivists are even making an intervention into language politics, forgoing the use of "o" in words to represent the universal subject—for example, *ser humanos* (human beings), where "o" is both masculine and the default universal ending in Spanish and Portuguese words, as well as "@," which is one language intervention that is currently popular. The "@" looks like "o" (masculine) and "a" (feminine) together. Instead, the artivists are using "x," which challenges the male/female binary in their languages and also rejects the masculine "o" as the universal gender for "humans." The usage of "x" in zines, blogs, Facebook pages, and other forms of print media is becoming popular among queer and LGBT artists and activists. Las Krudas CUBENSI, for example, is now writing their name as KRUDXS CUBENSI. I give these examples to highlight the ways in which the transnational and the regional dimensions of how black queer identity politics are challenged, changed, rearticulated, reproduced, and (re)defined—much of it occurring rapidly over the last ten years. I want to draw attention to the significant role that people assigned female at birth continue to play in transnational black queer politics.

The transnational dimension of black queerness is such an understudied area of research that as the years go by, as activists' politics change and as societies change in the Americas, academic scholarship is missing an important opportunity to write into history, to analyze, to theorize, and to just simply understand the regional and global reach of contemporary black queer politics. Largely absent is documentation and analysis of the ways in which black gender, sexual politics, and identities are being redefined in international contexts, including the U.S. American context.

NOTES

1. A 2011–12 Fulbright Scholar Award to Brazil also facilitated part of my data collection in São Paulo.

2. Tricia Rose, *Black Noise: Rap Music and Black Culture in Contemporary America* (Middletown, CT: Wesleyan University Press, 1994); Halifu Osumare, *The Africanist Aesthetic in Global Hip-Hop: Power Moves* (New York: Palgrave Macmillan, 2008).

3. Howard Becker, *Art Worlds* (Berkeley: University of California Press, 2008).

4. Tricia Rose, *Black Noise: Rap Music and Black Culture in Contemporary America* (Middletown, CT: Wesleyan University Press, 1994); Black Public Sphere Collective, *The Black Public Sphere: A Public Culture Book* (Chicago: University of Chicago Press, 1995); Mark Anthony Neal, *What the Music Said: Black Popular Music and Black Public Culture* (New York: Routledge, 1998); Osumare, *Africanist Aesthetic in Global Hip-Hop*.

5. Marcyliena Morgan and Dionne Bennett, "Hip Hop and the Global Imprint of a Black Cultural Form," *Daedalus, the Journal of the American Academy of Arts and Sciences* 2 (Spring 2011): 177.

6. Gwendolyn D. Pough, "An Introduction of Sorts for Hip-Hop Feminism," in *Home Girls Make Some Noise!: Hip-Hop Feminism Anthology*, eds. Gwendolyn D. Pough, Elaine Richardson, Aisha Durham, and Rachel Raimist (New York: Parker Publishing, 2007), vii. Also see Himanee Gupta-Carlson, "Planet B-Girl: Community Building and Feminism in Hip-Hop," *New Political Science* 32, no. 4 (2010): 515–29; and Ana Sobral, "Unlikely MCs," *European Journal of English Studies* 16, no. 3 (2012): 259–71.

7. Aisha Durham, "Using [Living Hip-Hop Hop] Feminism: Redefining an Answer (to) Rap," in *Home Girls, Make Some Noise!*, 306; Gwendolyn D. Pough, *Check It while I Wreck It: Black Womanhood, Hip-Hop Culture, and the Public Sphere* (Boston: Northeastern University Press, 2004); Rose, *Black Noise*; Adreanna Clay, *The Hip-Hop Generation Fights Back: Youth Activism and Post–Civil Rights Politics* (New York: New York University Press, 2012).

8. Cheryl Higashida, *Black Internationalist Feminism: Women Writers of the Black Left, 1945–1995* (Urbana-Champaign: University of Illinois Press, 2013); Sujatha Fernandes, *Cuba Represent!: Cuban Arts, State Power, and the Making of New Revolutionary Cultures* (Durham, NC: Duke University Press, 2006); Ronnie Armstead, "Las Krudas, Spatial Practice, and the Performance of Diaspora," *Meridians* 8, no. 1 (2008): 130–43.

9. Combahee River Collective, "The Combahee River Collective Statement: Black Feminist Organizing in the Seventies and Eighties," In *Home Girls: A Black Feminist Anthology*, ed. Barbara Smith, 264–74 (New Brunswick, NJ: Rutgers University Press, 2000).

10. Nikki Lane, "Black Women Queering the Mic: Missy Elliott Disturbing the Boundaries of Racialized Sexuality and Gender," *Journal of Homosexuality* 58, nos. 6–7 (2011): 775–92.

11. For those interested in Las Krudas's immigration experience and the move from Cuba to the Cuban Diaspora, see Celiany Rivera's documentary *Reina de mi Misma, Queen of Myself: Las Krudas d'Cuba* (DVD, 2010).

12. Martín Sevillano and Ana Belén, *Sociedad civil y arte en Cuba: Cuento y artes plásticas en el cambio de siglo (1980–2000)* (Madrid: Editorial verbum, 2010).

13. Jorge Enrique, interview with the author, Havana, Cuba, 2013. CENESEX is the Cuban National Center for Sex Education.

14. Tanya Saunders, *Cuban Underground Hip Hop: Black Thoughts, Black Revolution, Black Modernity* (Austin: University of Texas, 2015).

15. Keisha-Khan Y. Perry, *Black Women against the Land Grab: The Fight for Racial Justice in Brazil* (Minneapolis: University of Minnesota Press, 2013).

16. Derek Pardue, *Brazilian Hip Hoppers Speak from the Margins: We's on Tape* (New York: Palgrave Macmillan, 2011).

17. Jafari S. Allen, *¡Venceremos?: The Erotics of Black Self-making in Cuba* (Durham, NC: Duke University Press, 2011); Armstead, "Las Krudas"; C. Rivera-Velázquez, "Brincando bordes, Cuestionando el Poder: Cuban Las Krudas' Migration Experience and Their Rearticulation of Sacred Kinships and Hip Hop Feminism," *Letras Femeninas* 34, no. 1 (2008): 97–123; Rivera-Velázquez, dir., *Queen of Myself: Las Krudas d' Cuba* (Tortuga Productions in association with Krudas CUBENSI, 2010); Tanya Saunders, "Black Lesbians and Racial Identity in Contemporary Cuba," Black Women, Gender

and Families 4, no. 1 (Spring 2010): 9–36; Saunders, "Grupo OREMI: Black Lesbians and the Struggle for Safe Social Space in Havana," *Souls: A Critical Journal of Black Politics, Culture and Society* 11, no. 2 (2009): 167–85; Saunders, "La Lucha Mujerista: Krudas CUBENSI and Black Feminist Sexual Politics in Cuba," *Caribbean Review of Gender Studies* 3 (2009): 1–20; Saunders, *Cuban Underground Hip Hop*; Fernandes, *Cuba Represent!*

18. Olivia Prendes, interview with the author, Havana, Cuba, 2006.

19. See Saunders, "Grupo OREMI," "La Lucha Mujerista," and *Cuban Underground Hip Hop*.

20. Author's transcription from event.

21. Tiely Queen, interview with the author, São Paulo, Brazil, 2012.

9

The Body Beautiful

Black Drag, American Cinema, and
Heteroperpetually Ever After

LA MARR JURELLE BRUCE

$\ominus$

Larger than life is just the right size. —NOXEEMA JACKSON

PERCHED BEFORE A VANITY IN A DIMLY LIT ROOM, a lean, bare-faced, bare-chested, middle-age white male presses play on a cassette deck. Music will set the mood as he prepares to dress. Before long, that bare, beige face will wear scarlet lipstick, heavy foundation, a swath of artificial lashes, and an expression of serene satisfaction flanked by chandelier earrings and curls of auburn hair that unfurl from a bouffant wig. Before long, that bare chest will ease into a padded black corset and royal purple evening gown with billowing cape to match. His most prominent accessory, though, is the demure nicety inflecting his every gesture.

This first figure is visually upstaged by a second vanity-sitter, more pertinent for our purposes. Bare-chested—but covered with make-up from first sight and never bare-faced before our eyes—a muscular, thirty-something, dark-skinned black male transforms in a boudoir of his own. He tweezes arched eyebrows above impossibly long and gilded eyelashes (not so much false as fantastic), beats foundation into high brown cheekbones with a gargantuan powder puff, fastens to his head a copper-colored wig whose straight locks fall just past his brawny shoulders, applies brown butt pads, carefully tightens a candy-cherry-red corset, and slips on matching patent-leather pumps. He completes his ensemble with a leopard-print gown and orange faux-fur boa, but not before he kicks up his stockinged legs and squeals ecstatic laughter. His satisfaction is more boisterous and effusive than that of his leaner, paler counterpart. Compared to that white figure—who will function as visual and ideological standard-bearer of the ensuing plot—this black figure is larger, louder, gaudier, and posited as the locus of black corporeal excess merged with queer excess.

All the while, opening credits flash across the screen and the voices of hip hop feminists Cheryl "Salt" James and Sandra "Pepa" Denton, along with singer-songwriter Bernadette Cooper, emanate from that cassette player:[1]

> I'm up and coming, I am a child (am a child)
> I'm legendary, hey, I'm free and wild (free and wild)
> My cha-cha pumps [. . .], I've got them on [. . .]
> And I work the runway (left-right-left-right-left), baby, all night
>   long
> I am the only one (the only one) there is no other,
> I am mother,
> I am body beautiful.
> I am grand (grand diva), I am the queen (queen bee)
> A masquerade (who am I?), I'm fantasy (you're a fantasy)
> I am the house (the whole mansion) of elegance
> Featuring, I am body beautiful (body beautiful).[2]

Salt-N-Pepa performs a house-meets-hip-hop anthem of self-adulation. Each woman basks in her "body beautiful"—or, more accurate, as "body beautiful"—relishing her femme self in sync with the queens at their vanities. So begins the 1995 American drag queen, road-trip, buddy comedy *To Wong Foo, Thanks for Everything! Julie Newmar* and its opening theme, "I Am the Body Beautiful."[3]

The song abounds with drag queen fundamentals and queer idioms: the significance of "legendary" status, the practice of "working the runway," the primacy of queer "mother"-ing, the conferral of "queen" and "diva" titles, the merits of "masquerade," and the efficacy of "fantasy."[4] So, too, do African American–rooted idiomatic and stylistic elements infuse the tune: its house and hip hop modalities; Pepa's vernacular proclamations, later in the song, that "I gets down with my bad self" and "it's all good"; and the perennial presence of call-and-response (a sort of dialogic repetition-with-revision) throughout.[5] This latter feature is especially prominent in the passage above. "Grand" is repeated and revised into "grand diva," the call of "queen" elicits the response "queen bee," and "house" is upgraded into "the whole mansion." Phrases retain something of their original content but are riffed, amplified, and beautified with repetition, qualities common in both black and queer performance milieus. In short, this scene showcases drag queens channeling black women musicians who themselves are channeling black queer drag and ballroom legends who are in turn channeling glamorous women. This series of citations forms a chain—a fancy necklace that loops full circle, as it were—of appropriative and innovative black, feminine, queer performance.

Even as I take pleasure in the film's opening, with its glorious body-positive ethos, I approach *To Wong Foo* with caution. After all, it is the product of a frequently Eurocentric, antiblack, homophobic, and hetero-sexist, Hollywood industrial complex. What labor, I wonder, does such an industry demand of "the body beautiful"? As she "work[s] the run-way" and her hips ricochet "left-right-left-right-left," I imagine the "work" she might perform for the Left, for the Right, and for the moderate Center, too.

To Wong Foo debuted amid a wave of mid-1990s pop culture Americana prominently featuring black drag queens.[6] In this essay, "drag queen" will denote a person assigned male at birth (whether eventually self-identified as cisgender man, transgender woman, or otherwise) who performs styl-ized spectacles of femininity for the enjoyment of audiences. In partic-ular, I fix my gaze upon three films in this zeitgeist: Beeban Kidron's *To Wong Foo*, with Wesley Snipes as black drag diva "Noxeema Jackson"; Baz Luhrman's extravagant Shakespeare adaptation, *Romeo + Juliet* (1996), co-starring Harold Perrineau as a black "Mercutio" who per-forms in drag; and Clint Eastwood's darkly comedic Southern Gothic murder mystery, *Midnight in the Garden of Good and Evil* (1997), featur-ing real-life drag performer and "preoperative transsexual" woman Lady Chablis, playing a dramatized version of herself.[7] Released in 1995, 1996, and 1997 respectively, at the height of Clinton-era multiculturalist and LGBT-"friendly" neoliberalism, each movie depicts a black and queer(ish) drag persona in a predominantly white and heterosexual setting. Sig-nificantly, these characters are drag performers within the logics of the film worlds they inhabit—distinct from, say, Flip Wilson's "Geraldine" or Tyler Perry's "Madea," who are not posited as drag queens, but rather as stereotypically domineering black women.[8]

In the essay "Walk-on Parts and Speaking Subjects: Screen Representations of Black Gay Men," Phillip Brian Harper notes that "social categories that seem essentially to exemplify the condition of marginality have in fact long been key components of the cultural 'mainstream,' insofar as they have served to define and delimit the recognized center of the social structure."[9] Harper proposes a representational dialectic: "Marginal" figures stand in stark contrast to "mainstream" subjects, highlighting and reifying the demarcation between periphery and "recognized center." Members of the cultural majority shore up their solidarity—and become more cohesive and coherent to their own selves—in collective contradistinction to that marginalized Other.

In the films I explore, three black drag queens (one "gay man," one man of ambiguous sexuality and homoerotic propensity, and one "preoperative transsexual" woman) do more than "define and delimit the recognized center." My central claim is that these black bodies beautiful are recruited as sidekicks, bodyguards, matchmakers, mammies, and martyrs on behalf of that center. In fact, they are conscripted to serve a hegemony that I label "heteroperpetuity."[10] The heteroperpetual encompasses a range of political imperatives, legal mandates, social arrangements, as well as cultural practices and productions mobilized to perpetuate heteronormative dominion, which is overwhelmingly white and bourgeois in the United States. Heteroperpetuity works to convince us that (white and middle class) heteronorms are desirable, natural, essential, and eternal. All the while, it produces material structures and conditions to sustain those heteronorms.

Like Lee Edelman's influential formulation of "reproductive futurism," my theory of heteroperpetuity exposes the exclusionary futures and narrow visions of happily-ever-after engendered by heteronormativity. Unlike Edelman's notion, heteroperpetuity is attuned to the significance of race in structuring those exclusionary futures and is not fixated on the hegemonic icon of the (presumptively white and sacrosanct) "Child." There is another "child"—the black, queer, imperiled "child" featured in the Salt-N-Pepa lyrics—who clamors for my attention. Besides, I refuse to throw out the baby with the heteronormative bathwater.[11]

The heteroperpetual infuses cultural artifacts ranging from life insurance policies to Dick-and-Jane picture books to political campaign ads.

And yet, nowhere in American culture is heteroperpetuity more vividly illustrated and effectively mass-circulated than in the cineplex. To expose the insidiousness of this regime, I highlight its hegemony over black drag queen characters whose spectacular queerness and blackness would seem, at first blush, antagonistic to the heteroperpetual. That fact is that these films stage black queer misbehavior and orchestrate black queer advances—both sexual and ideological—in order to ritually manage and subordinate those advances. It bears emphasis, however, that these rituals of subordination sometimes fail, and these queens sometimes defy the heteroperpetual systems that employ them.

In American mainstream cinema, the quintessential representation of heteroperpetuity is also the most ubiquitous of film clichés: a young, straight, white couple strolls or marches into the sunset together to presumably marry, procreate, inherit the earth, and live happily, heteroperpetually ever after. In the pages that follow, I ponder what happens when black drag queens join the procession.

Noxeema's Revenge

To Wong Foo is a queer-inflected variation on a common Hollywood formula: the tale of citified fish out of water who become stranded in a backwoods locale, endure initial culture clash, get to know and come to love a group of small-town bumpkins, receive their love in return, dramatically intervene in those bumpkins' lives, and learn unexpected life lessons in the process.[12] In *To Wong Foo*, the "fish" are three queer cosmopolitan New York drag divas driving cross-country to Los Angeles to compete in a national drag competition.[13] When their glamorous convertible breaks down midtrip, Noxeema Jackson, Vida Boheme (Patrick Swayze), and Chi-Chi Rodriguez (John Leguizamo) find themselves marooned in a landlocked town named Snydersville. Notably, they are a multicultural coterie: Vida is Caucasian American, Noxeema is African American, and Chi-Chi is Latino American (ostensibly mestizo). As if to compensate for its Asian American absence, the movie's title references "Wong Foo," an ostensibly Asian or Asian American person who has earned thanks from screen icon Julie Newmar.

All three protagonists conceal their drag queen identities from the locals and pose as cisgender, urbane "career girls." With the exception of the opening shots that precede Vida's makeup application, all three continuously inhabit "womanly" personae. We never see the three out of womenswear and makeup, never learn their legal names, never glimpse a photograph of any in conventional men's clothing. Despite this round-the-clock residence in femininity, Vida, Chi-Chi, and Noxeema do not identify as transwomen. Early in the film, Noxeema sketches a taxonomy of three forms of gender transgression: "When a straight man puts on a dress and gets his sexual kicks, he is a transvestite. When a man [sic] is a woman trapped in a man's body and has a little operation, he [sic] is a transsexual. When a gay man has way too much fashion sense for one gender, he is a drag queen."[14] According to Noxeema, these three queens are gender-transgressive gay men—not straight men dressing in women's clothing, not transwomen, not preoperative transsexuals. Still, the three refer to themselves with feminine pronouns; I will follow suit and henceforth refer to each as "she" and "her."

Stranded in Snydersville, each queen quickly settles in and commences some heteroperpetual task. Although Noxeema is my primary concern, I want to briefly ponder her drag sisters and their labors. First, there is Vida Boheme, the lead protagonist of the film. Soon after arriving in town, Vida assists an abused local wife and mother named Carol Ann (Stockard Channing) by rescuing her from a beating at the hands of her husband and inspiring her to break free from his dominion. With Vida's encouragement, Carol Ann transforms from a cowering, homely housewife often wearing a muumuu into to a willful and independent woman. In a climactic scene toward the film's end, she becomes something of an honorary drag queen, donning a red gown with floral lace and veil that might have been plucked from Vida's closet.

Vida's anointed task is to intervene in a physically and emotionally abusive heterosexual marriage. In one poignant scene, she uses male-bodied physical strength to pummel the abuser and her expertise in "career girl" femininity to counsel Carol Ann toward independent womanhood. Notably, then, it is a combination of "manly" brawn and "womanly" know-how that equips Vida to help Carol Ann. Owing to this drag queen intervention, Carol Ann is better suited for righteous romance—not with her abusive husband, but with some nobler man. This is Vida's heteroperpetual contribution.

Carol Ann later reveals that she knew Vida's secret all along and that she nevertheless embraces her friend: "I don't think of you as a man and I don't think of you as a woman. I think of you as an angel." Intended as high praise, Carol Ann's words efface the fact of Vida's transgressive male femininity. Vida is no angel. Rather, Vida is a gay man, made of flesh and blood and bone, who provisionally performs womanhood while stranded in a small town. Carol Ann would rather picture her friend as genderless and harmless, with wings instead of testes. While there are radical genderqueer subjectivities that claim the status of neither man nor woman, Carol Ann's designation seems to serve a far more conservative aim.[15] She interpellates Vida as something of a new-age eunuch: not fully "man," not nearly "woman," utterly sterile (nonreproductive, desexed, scoured of erotic energy), and almost holy.

Next among *To Wong Foo*'s three queens is Chi-Chi Rodriguez. To have Noxeema tell it, Chi-Chi is initially an impetuous "little Latin boy in a dress," lacking the grace required for queendom. In the meantime, Chi-Chi must settle for drag "princess" status, tentatively conferred on her by Vida and Noxeema at the start of the film. While in Snydersville, Chi-Chi meets Bobby Ray (Jason London)—a young, handsome bumpkin who knows nothing of Chi-Chi's maleness.

Bobby Ray is smitten with Chi-Chi and gleefully courts her. Initially, Chi-Chi welcomes his advances, unconcerned with what might happen if Bobby Ray discovers her sex. Reprimanded by Vida and Noxeema, Chi-Chi ends the courtship before it is consummated and without confessing her secret. To heterosexist audiences, fearful of queer seduction, this denouement brings relief: Chi-Chi never ensnares a heterosexual man, and Bobby Ray never engages in homosex. Instead, the "little Latin boy in a dress" bows out graciously so that an adolescent girl named Bobby Lee—Carol Ann's daughter, who seems as guileless as her male counterpart—may pursue the young hunk. Chi-Chi even coaches Bobby Lee in the art of feminine allure.

Within *To Wong Foo*'s heteroperpetual project, Chi-Chi transforms from a queer provocateur, threatening to thwart heteroperpetuity, into an innocuous matchmaker and style guru who cheers on a young, straight, white couple.[16] The union of Bobby Ray and Bobby Lee is the exemplary heteroperpetual event of *To Wong Foo*, with the young couple seemingly earmarked for "happily ever after." Chi-Chi's concession is so commendable that it earns the respect of Vida and Noxeema; the two finally award her drag "queen" status. Heteroperpetual service is the decisive feat in Chi-Chi's bildungsroman.

Chi-Chi also avoids an ostensibly riskier revelation of her male anatomy. Midway through the film, a posse of grimy local hoodlums corner Chi-Chi in a secluded knoll at the edge of town, inching nearer with menacing grins and predatory looks. The scene anticipates sexual assault, perhaps gang rape. Such misogynistic violence would likely be compounded with homophobic and transphobic violence if Chi-Chi's assailants were to discover her sex. Thankfully, these atrocious scenarios are avoided when Bobby Ray suddenly drives up in a pickup truck and calls out to Chi-Chi. With astonishing levity, she skips off to the young man she calls her "knight in shining pickup truck" and escapes uninjured. Committed to comedy, the film does not take seriously the awful violence these men might have perpetrated. They accost Chi-Chi with the brazen impunity of those who do not fear retribution—and they nearly go unchecked, but for Noxeema. My primary concern in *To Wong Foo*, Noxeema Jackson is an outspoken and unapologetic black drag diva whose no-nonsense pragmatism checks Chi-Chi's naïveté and balances Vida's idealism.[17]

Though Noxeema's intervention is not explicitly mounted to avenge Chi-Chi, it nevertheless achieves that end. After those same men make lewd gestures and hurl catcalls at a group of mostly middle-aged local women on the street, Noxeema springs into action. She determines that the catcallers have offended the sensibilities of Snydersville's honorable ladies and must be taught respect. Noxeema approaches Tommy, the group's ringleader, and the following exchange takes place:

NOXEEMA: What's all this noise?
TOMMY: Oh, baby. You are a *whole* lotta woman. I know what you need.
NOXEEMA: I hardly think that you're the man to give it to me. [...] I think you should apologize to me. And I also think you should apologize to those ladies over there.
TOMMY: I ain't apologizing to no ladies, no way.
NOXEEMA: Just as I expected. Do you like my nails? [Noxeema shows Tommy her nails and then, in one deft swoop, grabs him by the balls. Noxeema leads him, as though he is on a tight leash, across the road to the ladies.]
NOXEEMA: Well, Tommy, this is Miss Vida, and Miss Clara, and this is Miss Katina, and Miss Myrna, Miss Loretta, and of course Miss little Bobby Lee. Now, Tommy, when you encounter such gorgeous ladies, the correct way to greet them is to say, "Good Afternoon, ladies." Can you say that, Tommy? [Noxeema tightens grip on Tommy's testicles.]
TOMMY: [groans and strains.] Good afternoon, ladies!

Noxeema serves heteroperpetuity by policing and enforcing its codes of propriety. The same men who preyed upon Chi-Chi now stand timid and slack-jawed before her black girlfriend. How is it that a group of

FIG. 9.1. Noxeema Jackson (Wesley Snipes), teaches a young man etiquette in *To Wong Foo, Thanks for Everything! Julie Newmar* (dir. Beeban Kidron, United States, 1995).

goons stand overpowered and outmanned by a solitary black "woman"?[18] The answer bulges from Noxeema's form-fitting top. She is, as Tommy puts it, "a whole lotta woman" and more. Noxeema's massive biceps, shoulders, and chest spill from her tops and dresses.[19] Within a visual matrix that Frantz Fanon would call "negrophobic," the black body is imagined to be always already excessive and unwieldy: a grotesque dark mass threatening to overflow. Whereas Noxeema embraces excess for dramatic aesthetics and self-making, negrophobia posits such excess as a symptom of black abjection. In the case of male blackness, that imagined excess condenses into the icon of the big black dick. Fanon suggests that, upon encountering a black man, a negrophobe imagines that "[the black man] *is* a penis."[20] Within a negrophobic imaginary, Snipes-as-Noxeema might be read as a hulking "penis": pressing against the drag that barely contains it, nearly splitting the seams, always threatening to burst forth and penetrate whiteness. Of course, this threat never materializes in the film. The drag holds.[21]

Even if the townsfolk do not perceive Noxeema's biological maleness, prevailing Sapphire stereotypes posit black ciswomen as patently unfeminine and, in fact, masculine and domineering in their own right.[22] Indeed, tropes of "masculine" black womanhood and "hypermasculine" black manhood merge in antiblack racist fantasies that paint all blacks as overaggressive, violent, ferocious beings. (That feral masculinity should not be confused with the patriarchal manhood often posited as the exclusive prerogative of white men.) Hortense Spillers suggests that black women and men in the West are categorically "ungendered," always already incommensurate with and alienated from Western gender binaries. As a result, Spillers remarks, "'Sapphire' enacts her 'Old Man' in drag, just as her 'Old Man' becomes 'Sapphire' in outrageous caricature. . . . In other words, in the historic outline of dominance, the respective subject-positions of [black American] 'female' and 'male' adhere to no symbolic integrity."[23] Within that historical outline, Noxeema would resemble "Sapphire enact[ing] her 'Old Man' in drag," *even if she were a ciswoman*.

In order to punish Tommy, Noxeema performs an act of violence that is often feminized in film and inflicted by women and children confronted by adult male assailants: she attacks his testicles.[24] However, she does not simply administer a swift, defensive kick to his balls and then run off. Instead, she grabs his testicles, she squeezes them, twists them, leads him by them, slowly feeds him words to speak to the affronted women, and seems to relish the process. Thus, the film both feminizes and sexually aggressivizes Noxeema's revenge. If we read this assault as an act of sadistic erotic indulgence, it is the most fully realized sexual deed depicted in *To Wong Foo*. This testicular assault also functions as a figurative castration, rendering its victim both emasculated and symbolically impotent. Noxeema invokes negrophobic terror of (big-dicked) black manhood and (ball-busting) black womanhood as menace to white male sexual self-esteem.[25]

Vis-à-vis the symbolic impotency and implied degeneracy of these young men, the figurative castration of their ringleader, and the postreproductive ages of most of the women insulted, Noxeema's intervention concerns a patently marginal and nonreproductive site of heterosexual encounter. This caveat is important, because it differentiates Noxeema's heteroperpetual service from Vida's and Chi-Chi's. Vida intervenes in a heteronormative (i.e., middle-class, reproductive, home-owning, and invidiously patriarchal) marriage, and Chi-Chi helps prime a doting pair of young heterosexuals for "happily ever after." Noxeema, on the other hand, is stationed on the street, away from the reproductive, heteronormative home and hearth, outdoors and apart from its exemplary couples. While Noxeema's streetwise blackness equips her to intimidate young roughnecks, it also makes her potentially threatening to that home and hearth. That is to say, even as she polices those men on behalf of white heteronormativity, the film's narrative polices and sequesters Noxeema to protect heteronormativity.[26] If those thugs' (misogynistic) threat is checked by Noxeema's intervention, Noxeema's (phobogenically black) threat is checked by plot structure and narrative intervention.

Noxeema's other valiant deed while in the town involves an elderly widow named Clara (Alice Drummond). Clara seems to be suspended in a semicatatonic daze and refuses to actively acknowledge or speak to anyone. When Noxeema tells Clara about her dreams of movie stardom, the drag queen ends up delivering a speech so moving that it inspires the widow to finally speak. Noxeema's speech is rife with metacinematic irony. She decries "the white Hollywood machine," the very industry that brings her to life, explaining that "my plan is that while in Hollywood I will be approached by an eminent producer, at the Ivy, no doubt, to star in the lush film version of the Life of Ms. Dorothy Dandridge. Yes, that noble blacktress who never played domestic help. And then whose career was crushed by the white Hollywood machine." Like Dorothy Dandridge, Noxeema Jackson never technically performs "domestic help." She never works in the home and hearth of heteroperpetual domesticity, but she is occasionally employed as glamorous groundskeeper in its public squares.

A Drag Queen Saved My Life

A long, far cry from landlocked Syndersville, Baz Luhrman's *Romeo + Juliet* is set in "Verona Beach," a fictional coastal town rendered to resemble contemporary southern California.[27] In keeping with the "SoCal" motif, Romeo (Leonardo DiCaprio) and his Montague peers are portrayed as "surfer" types who frolic on beaches, wear tropical-patterned shirts, don sun- and dye-bleached hair, and perform boyish bravado. Racially, they appear to belong to the category of WASPy whiteness.

In contrast, the Capulets are posited as (white) ethnic Italians and racially mestizo. The white ethnicization of the Capulets is achieved through the dramatic Italianness of the Capulet patriarch (Paul Sorvino). He speaks with a thick Italian accent, and in the decisive fete scene where Romeo meets Juliet, he performs an operatic aria while dressed in a sequined Romanesque toga.[28] Though the senior Capulet's Italianness differentiates him from the WASP type, he remains safely in the precinct of late-twentieth-century whiteness. Meanwhile, Tybalt Capulet (nephew of the Capulet patriarch and cousin to Juliet) and his kinsman Abra are played by light-skinned, ostensibly mestizo-Latino actors John Leguizamo and Vincent Laresca.[29] Inasmuch as Latinidad is commonly read as a "racial" category in the United States—though it is more accurately a multiracial ethnic formation—Tybalt is coded as both ethnic and racial Other.[30] Tybalt and his Capulet cohort dress in slick red and black getups, don elaborate holsters, handle firearms like experts, and battle with the aplomb of seasoned gangsters. Within prevailing pop cinema stereotypes, the Capulet men alternately resemble menacing (Italian) mobsters and (Latino) gangbangers. Notably, Juliet Capulet is played by Claire Danes, a blonde-haired, fair-skinned, self-declared WASP and popular ingénue in the 1990s.[31] Juliet exhibits none of the ethnoracial otherness of her kin, and thus the pairing of Romeo and Juliet bears no visual trace of interraciality.

In a film full of eccentric characters, Romeo's friend Mercutio outdoes them all. My primary interest in *Romeo + Juliet*, Mercutio makes his entrance wrapped tight in a white sequined miniskirt, with matching white sequined halter top, on silver platform pumps, and beneath a platinum blonde Marilyn Monroe wig whose loose curls flutter in the wind on a beach where the Montague boys have gathered. All the while, he sports a goatee, brandishes a very muscular body, wears tacky clothing, and evinces a campy "low drag" aesthetic rather than glamorous, "high drag" effect. What's more, he is a dark-skinned black man. Either his blackness or his gender-transgressive performance would mark Mercutio anomalous in the film. Intent on presenting Mercutio as an overdetermined Other, the film fashions him both black and drag queen.

Though the dialogue in *Romeo + Juliet* remains mostly faithful to Shakespeare's script, Luhrman incorporates several musical numbers to illuminate characters and propel the narrative. Music is especially important to Mercutio, who enters accompanied by Kym Mazelle's cover of Candi Staton's disco tune "Young Hearts, Run Free."[32] Mercutio prances across the beach to announce to his Montague friends that he has gained them access to the Capulet ball. He hands Romeo a tiny pill with a red heart and arrow inscribed into it, perhaps the amphetamine drug "ecstasy," to rile Romeo's senses and ease his worry over his failing romance with Rosaline. Amid their revelry, Mercutio mounts an old stage on the beach and lifts his skirt to gleefully bare his black behind while dancing to "Young Hearts, Run Free." While Romeo is the story's central protagonist, it is Mercutio who leads the pack. Dressed in drag, he is nevertheless, and all the more, the alpha male of the crew. Judged according to stereotypical gender codes—which link masculinity with aggression and femininity with wigs and skirts—Mercutio is simultaneously more "masculine" and more "feminine" than his Montague companions.

As they ride to the ball in a red convertible, fireworks ablaze behind them, the Montagues raise guns in the air, and Mercutio lip-syncs his theme song (see Figure 9.2). In this sequence, as the Montagues' gun-toting bravado is juxtaposed with Mercutio's lip-syncing bravado, as Romeo's stainless steel pistol and Mercutio's sequined halter top glint side by side, the two men seem like two sides of the same shiny coin of farcical and melodramatic masculinity. And yet, even as Mercutio's presence undermines the Montagues' macho posturing, he is also a crucial catalyst for that macho. He is Romeo's best friend, hype man, enabler, drug supplier, and motivational speaker, encouraging the Montagues in their macho exploits. In short, Mercutio is the exclamation point that amplifies the Montague machismo and the interrogation mark that throws it into question.

The next scene begins with Mercutio performing in drag at the Capulet costume ball. Now decked in a white sequined miniskirt, white garters, a white sequined cape, a white sequined choker, elbow-length white satin gloves, and a gleaming white Afro wig, he lip-syncs his leitmotif once again. Surrounded by a throng of olive-skinned, dark-haired men dressed in magenta sequined vests, Mercutio mouths:

> Young hearts, run free
> Never be hung up
> Hung up like my man and me
> Mmmm, my man and me
> Oh, young hearts
> To yourself be true
> Don't be no fool, when
> Love really don't love you

Although the song's title and its festive disco-meets-salsa orchestration may seem to condone carefree and careless love, the lyrics actually caution young lovers to "never get hung up" and admonishes them, "Don't be no fools." Similar counsel comes from Friar Lawrence as he officiates the wedding of Juliet and Romeo and pronounces these fateful words: "love moderately; long love doth so."[33] Mercutio's "free" love and Friar Lawrence's "moderate" love both entail pragmatism and circumspection. In this scene, black drag performance is the extravagant technology for dispensing crucial but unheeded advice. Romeo and Juliet, two "young

FIG. 9.2. Mercutio (Harold Perrineau) on his way to the Capulet ball in *Romeo + Juliet* (dir. Baz Luhrman, United States, 1996).

hearts," tragically do become "hung up": entangled in a matrix of confusion, sorrow, and doom.

The cinematography of the drag scene simulates the visual and kinesthetic sensation of Romeo's drug-induced high. The sequence is fast-forwarded so that performers and spectators seem to scramble about in a blur of Dionysian dazzle and flesh while Mercutio's song crescendos to a blaring climax and Juliet's father bursts into a fever-pitched aria. And then, abruptly, the song and sequence end. The film cuts to a quiet scene of Romeo in a bathroom, dunking his head in a sink of water, descending from his high, newly sober, and ready to encounter his fate. His Juliet.

At this critical juncture in the film, a delirious high is replaced by pensive sobriety; the kinetic disco tune is superseded by a slow love ballad entitled "Kissing You"; actor Harold Perrineau, whose own voice does not sing "Young Hearts, Run Free," is supplanted by Des'ree, the in-film performer and real-life recording artist whose actual voice croons "Kissing You"; Mercutio's spectacular gender-transgressive performance in a racy white miniskirt with garters and a bra top is deposed by a ciswoman's gender-normative performance in a modest white cocktail gown. Within the film's heteroperpetual logic, wild (queer) partying winds down as the screen readies for the serious business of falling in (heteronormative) love. That is, queerness recedes and heteronormativity takes center stage. These transitions and contrapositions paint the black drag queen as foil whose purported excess and unruliness, by sheer contrast, normalizes the white heterosexual love with which it is juxtaposed. Mercutio's performance works to "define and delimit the recognized center."

Mercutio's sexuality was the object of speculation well before *Romeo + Juliet*'s queered iteration of the character. A number of postmodernist theater scholars have conjectured about Mercutio's protohomosexuality and the possibility of his repressed—or simply unconfessed—romantic love for Romeo.[34] These queer readings emphasize Mercutio's coded language. In the scene that will culminate in Mercutio's death, the following exchange takes place between Mercutio and Tybalt:

TYBALT: . . . Gentlemen, good den: a word with one of you.

MERCUTIO: And but one word with one of us? couple it with something; make it a word and a blow.

TYBALT: You shall find me apt enough to that, sir, and you will give me occasion.

MERCUTIO: Could you not take some occasion without giving?[35]

If Shakespeare's text equivocates same-sex desire, Perrineau's performance brings queerness to the fore—or the backside, as it were. No longer in drag in this scene, Luhrman's Mercutio is dressed in black slacks and an unbuttoned white shirt, baring his glistening dark-brown chest. When Mercutio proclaims "make it a word and a blow," Perrineau delivers the line with a bawdy laugh and flourish that seems to emphasize the contemporary American double entendre of the signifier "blow." Mercutio's implicit suggestion becomes "make it a word and a blow [job]." In case the blow job reference is lost on the audience, when Mercutio subsequently asks, "Could you not take some occasion without giving?" he accentuates these lines by turning his back to Tybalt, lifting up his shirt, and poking out his buttocks. Thus accompanied, his words invoke anal sex. The implicit question becomes, "Could you not take some [ass] without giving [some ass]?" Mercutio seems to be a proponent of anal-penetrative versatility between men.

Mercutio's love for Romeo, romantic or not, moves him to risk his own life for his friend. When Tybalt attempts to stab Romeo, Mercutio uses his own body to shield his friend and is mortally wounded in the process. In casting Mercutio as a black man, *Romeo + Juliet* rehearses the common filmic and literary trope of the black buddy who sacrifices himself to protect his beloved white friend.[36] The black buddy's body serves as proxy for the white body in incidents of intense violence and suffering—a sort of tragic interracial stunt-double. The sacrifice of the black body ensures the survival of the white body.[37] For Romeo, however, that survival is ephemeral. Mistaking Juliet for dead, Romeo eventually commits suicide by swallowing a vial of poison. When Juliet discovers her dead husband, she kills herself with Romeo's gun. In the seconds before his own death, Mercutio exclaims, "A plague o' both your houses!" prophesizing and perhaps provoking the tragic fates of Romeo and Juliet.[38] Mercutio's final words rebuke the heteropatriarchal warfare and heterosexual drama that precipitate his death, yielding a sort of oblique critique of heteroperpetuity.

The "star cross'd lovers" do not walk into the sunset and into the materiality of heteroperpetuity, but they accomplish heteroperpetual ascent all the same.[39] No matter that Romeo Montague and Juliet Capulet are dead; no matter that their "houses" are rebuked and plagued: the grand myth of "Romeo and Juliet" remains virile, exalted, immortal, endlessly reproduced, and endlessly reproductive. Their physical deaths do nothing to diminish their metaphysical afterlives as one of the West's most iconic heterosexual couples, as its reigning epitome of romantic love. And so it is: In Baz Luhrman's *Romeo + Juliet*, the death of a black drag queen helps launch a young white couple into eternity, toward a million sunsets and more. Mercutio is cast as martyr for the cult of white heteroperpetuity, a queer black sacrificial bull on one of its grandest altars. Defiantly, though, he rails against the heteroperpetual with his last breath.

The Empress and the Mammy

The Montague masquerade just barely outdoes the opulent plantation parties portrayed in Clint Eastwood's *Midnight in the Garden of Good and Evil*. Inspired by John Berendt's bestselling nonfiction book of the same name, the movie *Midnight* is a semifictionalized Southern Gothic murder mystery and dark comedy set amid the aristocratic enclaves of Savannah, Georgia, in the 1980s. Baroque mansions and lavish soirees are backdrops as the film both celebrates and satirizes the eccentric decadence of the high society it depicts. A wealthy gay socialite, Jim Williams (Kevin Spacey), has killed his young vagabond lover, Billy Hanson (Jude Law). Though Jim claims he acted in self-defense, he stands trial accused of murder. Meanwhile, a young New York City–based journalist and author named John Kelso (John Cusack)—coincidentally in the city to report on one of Jim's parties—lingers in Savannah, eager to cover the sensational trial.

In the original book, and in the factual events upon which it is based, Berendt is a self-avowed gay man. The film straightens Berendt into the character John Kelso, fashioning a heterosexual hero more palatable to a heteronormative audience. However, another real-life Savannah denizen remains queer in adaptation. Lady Chablis, also known as the "Grand Empress of Savannah," is a real-life "preoperative transsexual" black woman and local drag performer who plays herself in *Midnight*.[40] Chablis steals the show as a coquettish southern belle who relishes both genteel manners and raunchy mischief.

While performing her cabaret act in a Savannah nightclub, Chablis singles out a middle-age white couple "necking" in the audience:

"Is this your boyfriend? Your husband?"

"Husband."

"What does Mr. Man do for a living?"

"He's a doctor."

"He's a doctor? Girl, you better grow you some nails honey 'cause if he's a gynecologist he is mine. . . . I'm gonna take him away from you . . . [To the doctor:] You wanna give me a physical? *I have nothing to hide.*"

In this scene, Chablis playfully threatens to tear asunder a white, bourgeois husband and wife. Of course, these words are delivered in a cabaret act and framed as comical banter. Chablis appears to pose no serious threat to their heteroperpetual prospects; she is framed as farcical foil who elicits mock anxiety—or at most a very mild anxiety—in the couple. Their white, heterosexual, bourgeois union remains intact, its boundaries consolidated, its structure "defined and delimited" in the face of a black drag queen who stands so clearly outside of it. Unlike Noxeema Jackson or Mercutio, Chablis does not manifest overt tropes of black male hypermasculinity. However, she does still comically traffic in stereotypes of aggressive and masculinized black womanhood.

After the married doctor rebuffs her, Chablis turns her attention to John. Because Chablis was acquainted with both Jim and Billy, John has been pursuing her in his investigation of the murder and trial. In Chablis's dressing room after the performance, when John asks her how she's doing, she replies, "I'm fine honey. Still hiding my candy. You want me to unwrap it for you?" Much like her cabaret quip that she has "nothing to hide," Chablis's "candy" comment alludes to the fact of her penis. It is an open secret, articulated through innuendoes and double entendres used for revelation or obfuscation, depending on who is listening and when. Rather than fully conceal her trans identity in order to "pass" as a ciswoman or else categorically announce her trans identity, she ornately reveals and then conceals it, relishing every moment, as though playing a game of peek-a-boo. It bears mentioning that, in a virulently transphobic society, such play entails great risk.

John knows about Chablis's "candy," but there are other objects of Chablis's affections who do not know. In the scene where Chablis offers to unwrap her candy, she also describes a tall, blonde mechanic "boyfriend" of hers who knows nothing of her male anatomy. From this scant description, we may infer that he is working-class and white, and that he practices heterosexual desire. To a transphobic sensibility, Chablis likely registers as a cunning imposter preying on a hapless, cis-oriented heterosexual. However, the film works to defuse such anxiety by keeping the relationship utterly remote and immaterial; the mechanic is only mentioned once, hardly described, and never portrayed on screen. He ultimately amounts to a fleeting nonpresence. Like *To Wong Foo*, *Midnight* incites and then allays anxieties around queer advances.

In a later scene, Chablis flirts with another man who seems to believe that she is a ciswoman. Donning an ultratight sequined gown, Chablis sashays uninvited into an African American cotillion ball. She sits seductively on the lap of a young black man and asks him whether he has ever been arrested. When he responds that he was once arrested for "disturbing the peace," Chablis snaps back, "I've got a piece you can disturb." Chablis plays peek-a-boo with this ostensibly straight young man: She evokes her penis in a pun that is likely lost on him; she metaphorically pulls it out, confident that he will not see.

Surrounded by Savannah's black elite—amid an ornate pageant of bourgeois respectability intended to arrange couplings that will heteroperpetuate a desired pedigree—Chablis makes mischief. She coaxes the young man onto the dance floor, dances provocatively with him, and finally bends over in front of him and presses her behind against his crotch as guests gawk with shock or amusement. John panics, cuts in, leads her away from the young man, and calmly cautions her to "behave yourself." Once again, *Midnight* stages queer advances and then curbs them to placate the transphobic discomfort they may incite. Chablis will eventually "behave," but not before she makes a bit more trouble.

In a courtroom scene that follows the cotillion, the Grand Empress dramatically misbehaves again. As star witness for Jim's defense, Chablis is expected to characterize the dead young hustler as volatile and violent, thus corroborating Jim's claim of self-defense. Ahead of her testimony, however, Chablis announces to John that "those folks think they're using the doll, but the doll's using them right back. I'm gonna use that courtroom as my coming out party." True to form, Chablis makes another scene: She recasts the courtroom as stage, takes the stand like a glamorous starlet, and recites her testimony as though it were a monologue in a one-woman show.

In the course of her testimony, Chablis reveals her trans identity and scandalizes the courtroom audience. Considering that Savannah is depicted in the film as a tight-knit and gossip-prone community, it is curious that folks are so surprised by Chablis's revelation and by Jim's disclosure of his homosexuality. Although the film portrays Savannah as an utterly eccentric world—where a man walks an invisible dog, an elderly woman carries an antique loaded revolver in her bra, a miniature horse leashed like a dog is fed hard liquor, and another man keeps live flying bees tethered to him with string while threatening to poison Savannah's water supply—the town is remarkably conservative in the face of explicit queerness.

Conservatism characterizes the town's racial politics, too.[41] Alongside Chablis, a second figure of black womanhood looms in the *Midnight* milieu and reveals a great deal about Savannah's racial order: the figure of the black maid. She is peripheral and yet central, constantly dispensed and utterly indispensable, always near and yet distant amid those lavish parties. Black maids move about in monochrome uniforms, cooking meals, setting tables, escorting white socialites, rarely speaking, and uncannily conjuring the "afterlife of slavery" in late-twentieth-century Georgia.[42]

A third figure of marginalized black womanhood is also instrumental to *Midnight*'s storyline. Among the shrubbery and headstones in the Garden of Good and Evil—a graveyard in Savannah for which the film is named—a hoodoo practitioner named Minerva (Irma P. Hall) performs rites to alternately satiate and instigate the dead.[43] In fact, Minerva is critical to the film's denouement. The trial culminates in Jim's acquittal, but it is soon after revealed that Jim did maliciously murder Billy. The film implies that Billy's ghost, mediated through Minerva, exacts revenge on Williams by causing him to die of an ostensible heart attack at the precise site of Billy's death. Remarkably, then, three figures of marginalized black womanhood—a drag queen, a quiet cohort of maids, and a hoodoo priestess—are perched at the edges of the film's social milieu; they function to "define and delimit" its center, and are decisive in *Midnight*'s Savannah.

With the trial concluded and otherworldly vengeance achieved, the film draws to its heteroperpetual close. Beguiled by Savannah, John decides to remain in town indefinitely, lease an apartment, and court a Savannah local named Mandy (Alison Eastwood). In the film's final scene, John and Mandy exit John's new apartment and begin to stroll down a Savannah street. There they encounter Lady Chablis walking Uga, the University of Georgia bulldog mascot. She announces, "Now you know you two ain't going nowhere without a chaperone" and reveals that she has prepared the couple a batch of her famous "kickin' chicken." Chablis joins the couple, basket of chicken in hand, and the trio ambles through a picturesque park nearby (see Figure 9.3). The resulting tableau manifests that heteroperpetual cliché of the straight white couple proceeding into happily ever after—with the noteworthy addition of a bodacious black drag queen.[44]

Although the label of "mammy" is too loosely bandied about in pop culture punditry, there is much in this scene to invite such a charge: Chablis has relinquished her lust for John and instead treats him with maternal affection. She issues innocuous sass; she prepares to cook some chicken; and she moves through a backdrop of stately Georgia mansions and plantations where Southern white wealth thrives alongside black service. On these registers, she resembles the icon of mammy—though her slender frame and hidden "candy" complicate such a reading.[45]

The specter of mammy flickers elsewhere in *Midnight*. Describing Savannah to a business associate who is back in New York City, John proclaims, "This place is fantastic. It's like *Gone with the Wind* on mescaline. . . . They walk imaginary pets . . . on a fucking leash here . . . and they're all heavily armed and drunk. New York is boring." (In *Midnight*, mescaline may function much like ecstasy did in *Romeo+Juliet*: as a psychotropic substance that might make black drag more palatable to white, heterosexual male subjects like Romeo Montague and John Kelso.) *Gone with the Wind* features the most iconic mammy figure in the history of American cinema, named only "Mammy," for which Hattie McDaniel earned the first Oscar awarded to an African American. John recognizes the lingering resemblance between the Georgia of old and contemporary Georgia, and the film sketches that likeness through this final image of Chablis. I do not mean to deny Chablis's agency (and I will return to the issue of her agency at length) but rather to emphasize how heteroperpetual logics and projects interpellate defiant bodies beautiful. Even a bodacious black preoperative transsexual drag queen can be urged to "behave" and chaperone a young white couple through a Savannah park in the afternoon, after *Midnight*, toward heteroperpetually ever after.

FIG. 9.3. Lady Chablis "chaperones" John Keslo (John Cusack) and Mandy Nicholls (Alison Eastwood) as they stroll toward heteroperpetually ever after in the final scene of *Midnight in the Garden of Good and Evil* (dir. Clint Eastwood, United States, 1997).

Coda: Redressing the Body Beautiful

To Wong Foo, *Romeo + Juliet*, and *Midnight in the Garden of Good and Evil* manifest an American mainstream craving for black queer spectacle—an instance of what black feminist theorist bell hooks would call "eating the Other"—in the 1990s.[46] If the documentary film *Paris Is Burning* and Madonna's "Vogue" song and video, both mass-released in 1990, whetted an American appetite for black drag and black gender-transgressive performances; if RuPaul's 1993 "Supermodel" single and album fed that hunger; if Dennis Rodman's low-drag publicity stunts in 1997 were cheap snacks, then *To Wong Foo*, *Romeo + Juliet*, and *Midnight in the Garden of Good and Evil* were easy-bake, mid-decade meals to satiate a popular cultural desire to "eat the [black drag] Other."

Remarkably, this craving for the spectacle of black drag has been usurped by a postmillennial feeding frenzy on the specter of the black "down low"—another transgression of heteronorms that captivates mainstream America and is primarily associated with black men. These shifting cultural appetites parallel and reflect shifting cultural fixations in the mid-nineties and postmillennial periods. In the 1990s, under regimes of transnational trade, American commercial interests gleefully recruited, conscripted, and exploited national Others as manual laborers. These drag queen films evince a corresponding recruitment of racial and sexual Others as heteroperpetual laborers. Both drag queens and, say, Mexican migrant workers, were Others traditionally subjected to violence and expulsion from the U.S. body politic—but in mid-1990s America, both groups were provisionally desirable for incorporation into neoliberal and imperial projects. In *To Wong Foo*, *Romeo + Juliet*, and *Midnight*, drag queens are brought into something of a hegemonic, heteroperpetual trade agreement that stipulates that queens will be tolerated—even celebrated—as long as they perform heteroperpetual service and ultimately respect negrophobic, homophobic, and transphobic codes of conduct.

Our current cultural fixation on the "down low" parallels and analogizes the cultural sentiment of the domestic War on Terror. In a post-9/11 United States—marked by heightened surveillance and paranoia about stealthy enemy combatants—the fear of down-low men in the heteronormative bed parallels the fear of terrorist "sleeper" cells in the American homeland. One wonders whether Barack Obama's ascendancy, the jubilation that overtook liberal constituencies, and the hope of a progressive cultural turn sparked or stoked in Viacom producers an enthusiasm for RuPaul's "Drag Race" television series. The show premiered just thirteen days after Obama's first inauguration.[47]

This essay opened with a ceremony of dressing the body beautiful and closes with a meditation on redressing that body beautiful. I want briefly to ponder the progressive and subversive resonances of these black drag portrayals. My hope is to offer an optimistic interpretation, akin to what Eve Sedgwick labels a "reparative reading."[48] Though their bodies beautiful work in heteroperpetual service, we cannot write off these drag queen characters as only helpmeets of the status quo. In fact, all three issue critiques of the heteroperpetual, however ambiguous or inchoate. Noxeema calls out "the white Hollywood machine," ironically signaling awareness of institutionalized white supremacy in American cinema. Mercutio's "plague" malediction rebukes the heteronormative romance and warfare that engender his death. Finally, there is Lady Chablis, whose peek-a-boo praxis and commitment to "using them right back" warrant special attention.

The only off-screen and "real-life" drag queen among this essay's protagonists, Lady Chablis has her own website, PlanetChablis.com. Featured in a Q&A section of the site is the question, "Is She a Drag Queen?" Chablis's succinct response is, "If you bitches pay me to be one I am!"[49] Chablis announces to visitors that she will strategically and contingently accept the title "drag queen," but only inasmuch as it benefits her materially. It would seem that when the title no longer profits her, she will reserve the right to dismiss it. The fact that a queen is hired or conscripted for heteroperpetual work does not obliterate her agency or entirely eclipse her subjectivity. Perhaps such service is part-time work. Once that filmic Chablis is done chaperoning; once her "kickin' chicken" is served; once that sun, into which white straight couples walk toward heteroperpetuity, has set: maybe, then, in an extrafilmic domain, after the credits, later in the day, perhaps under moonlight, Chablis's subjectivity and agency are utterly unhired and unbossed.[50] Recall Chablis's words before her courtroom scene: "Those folks think they're using the doll, but the doll's using them right back." Perhaps these words reverberate outward to the film's director, producers, and further, still, to the audience consuming her image: *I'm using you right back.* Notwithstanding her heteroperpetual work, Chablis has used Hollywood and Savannah to achieve wealth, influence, joy, and an extraordinary platform for queer self-making.

At the close of *To Wong Foo*, Noxeema declares that "larger than life is just the right size," articulating a preference for exorbitance that is perennial in high-drag performance. Perhaps larger than the cineplex screen is just the right size, too. Perhaps these black queens will quit their heteroperpetual service, commiserate with other queer people, congregate with other black folks. After all, that infinite space beyond the purview of the film is not the exclusive domain of the straight, white "Child" of straight, white couples. Perhaps our heroines-in-drag merely detour into heteronormative domains as they march, or "work the runway" in "cha-cha pumps" toward sunsets, full moons, and happily-ever-afters of their own. Perhaps they will reciprocally love, have sex, (re)constitute queer familial systems, "mother" queer children, fashion queer futures, and star in love stories and revolutionary dramas that may never screen at a theater near you.[51]

NOTES

This essay originated ten years ago as a paper in Joanne Meyerowitz's "Research in the History of Sexuality" graduate seminar at Yale University. I am grateful to Joanne and also to Terri Francis, Kara Keeling, and Marlon Ross for their generous and generative feedback on earlier versions. Thanks also to L. Lamar Wilson for encouraging me to submit to the anthology and to Isaiah Wooden for his meticulous eye as I prepared these pages for publication.

1. For a poignant discussion of Salt-N-Pepa's feminist hip hop, see Tricia Rose, "Never Trust a Big Butt and a Smile," in *That's the Joint! The Hip Hop Studies Reader*, ed. Mark Anthony Neal (New York: Routledge, 2004).

2. Salt-N-Pepa, "I Am the Body Beautiful," *To Wong Foo, Thanks For Everything! Julie Newmar: Music from the Motion Picture* (MCA, 1995). Although Salt-N-Pepa are credited on the soundtrack and perform the version on the soundtrack CD, the version performed in the film is vocalized differently and more prominently features Bernadette Cooper.

3. *To Wong Foo, Thanks for Everything! Julie Newmar*, dir. Beeban Kidron (Universal City: Universal Pictures, 1995), DVD.

4. Black gay ballroom culture is a complex site of innovative and appropriative performance, in which communities of predominately queer, urban, African American and Latino American people form familial communities called "houses" and participate in contests of dance, charisma, sex appeal, mimicry, fashion, and artifice called "balls." For further information, see Marlon Bailey, *Butch Queens Up in Pumps: Gender, Performance, and Ballroom Culture in Detroit* (Ann Arbor: University of Michigan Press, 2013).

5. The term "repetition with revision" was notably forwarded by Henry Louis Gates Jr. in his theory of African American literature. See Henry Louis Gates Jr., *The Signifying Monkey: A Theory of African-American Literary Criticism* (New York: Oxford University Press, 1988). Performance scholars and theorists have usefully applied "repetition with revision" to Afrodiasporic performance and to performance more generally. See, for example, Margaret Drewal, "The State of Research on Performance in Africa," *African Studies Review* 34, no. 3 (December 1991): 41; Harry Elam Jr., "Signifyin(g) on African-American Theatre: 'The Colored Museum' by George Wolfe," *Theatre Journal* 44, no. 3 (October 1992); Joseph Roach, *Cities of the Dead: Circum-Atlantic Performance* (New York: Columbia University Press, 1996), 29.

6. Among these cultural productions are Jennie Livingston's 1990 documentary film, *Paris Is Burning*; Dennis Rodman's low-drag publicity stunts; and the rise of RuPaul, America's most famous drag queen.

Concerning *Paris Is Burning*, which portrays black queer ballroom culture and highlights the drag repertoire within it, see Judith Butler, "Gender Is Burning: Questions of Appropriation and Subversion," in *Bodies that Matter: On the Discursive Limits of "Sex"* (New York: Routledge, 1993), 81–98; Phillip Brian Harper, "'The Subversive Edge': *Paris Is Burning*, Social Critique, and the Limits of Subjective Agency," *Diacritics* 24, nos. 2/3 (Summer–Autumn 1994): 90–103; and bell hooks, "Is Paris Burning?," in *Reel to Real: Race, Sex, and Class at the Movies* (New York: Routledge, 1996). Granting the importance of the film and the scholarship it inspired, I turn to a cadre of films that garnered far less scholarly attention but yielded far greater box office receipts. Unburdened by documentary or "high" culture aspirations, these films baldly cater to heteronormative fears and fantasies within America's cultural mainstream.

7. John Berendt, introduction to *Hiding My Candy: The Autobiography of the Grand Empress of Savannah*, by The Lady Chablis with Theodore Bouloukos (New York: Pocket Books, 1996).

8. Jamie Foxx's "Wanda," Martin Lawrence's "Sheneneh," and Eddie Murphy's "Rasputia" are other prominent examples of cross-gender comedic personae of African American actor-comedians. Though these characters are not drag queens, per se, queer potentiality still attaches to them for at least two reasons. First, the trope of the masculine black woman is an always already queered trope, especially if we heed Hortense Spiller's insistence that blacks in America have an unstable, vexed, incommensurable relationship to Western gender normativity. Second, the spectacle of gender-disruptive performance always already has a queer potentiality. Even when performers are avowedly straight, playing for heteronormative audiences, and catering to homophobic, sexist, and misogynist cultural appetites, the mere image of a man in elaborate drag contains queer resonance within it.

9. Phillip Brian Harper, "Walk-on Parts and Speaking Subjects: Screen Representations of Black Gay Men," *Callaloo* 18, no. 2 (1995): 390.

10. The term "heteroperpetuity" contains the word "perpetuity," a standard terminology within corporate contracts governing reproduction of musical, literary, photographic, and motion picture media. The term is used to designate infinite duration of a given license or copyright. Thus constructed, my neologism draws attention to the role of corporate capitalism in structuring—and *super*structuring, as it were—American cinema and the heteronormative, Eurocentric, and bourgeois ideologies it propagates.

11. In *No Future: Queer Theory and the Death Drive* (Durham, NC: Duke University Press, 2004), Lee Edelman asserts that "[the] Child remains . . . the fantasmatic beneficiary of every political intervention" and further that "queerness names the side of those not 'fighting for the children,' the side outside the consensus by which all politics confirms the absolute value of reproductive futurism." Proposing a "queer oppositionality," he declares that "the queer comes to figure the bar to every realization of futurity, the resistance, internal to the social, to every social structure or form" (4). Edelman suggests that *every* futurity is irredeemably complicit with heteronormative dominion and that *all* children are subsumed within his figure of the hegemonic "Child." He fails to differentiate between the white, normative, sacrosanct "Child" enshrined within white heteronormative dominion and the many children who are not only excluded from the auspices of the "Child" but are systematically denigrated and imperiled by that same regime of the "Child."

Responding to Edelman's claim that "the future is kid's stuff," performance theorist José Esteban Muñoz offers this crucial corrective: "In the same way all queers are not the stealth-universal-white-gay-man invoked in queer anti-relational formulations, all children are not the privileged white babies to whom contemporary society caters." He further writes, "The future is only the stuff of some kids. Racialized kids, queer kids, are not the sovereign princes of futurity." See Esteban Muñoz, "Cruising the Toilet: LeRoi Jones/Amiri Baraka, Radical Black Traditions, and Queer Futurity," *GLQ: A Journal of Lesbian and Gay Studies* 13, no. 2 (2007): 363–64.

12. Of course, that fish-out-of-water motif manifests in the casting of Wesley Snipes and Patrick Swayze—famous as übermacho action heroes and hetero heartthrobs—in roles as drag queens. This offbeat casting was perhaps the film's greatest comedic draw.

13. Trophies at the New York semifinal competition are doled out by a black queen, "Rachel Tensions," played by real-life famed drag performer RuPaul Charles. RuPaul's cameo in the film, and his character's bestowal of praise upon the film's protagonists, may imply the real-life performer's blessing and authoritative endorsement of *To Wong Foo*.

14. Notably, Noxeema misgenders the male-to-female postoperative transsexual as "he."

15. Concerning genderqueer identities and subjectivities, see Joan Nestle, Clare Howell, and Riki Wilchins, eds., *GenderQueer: Voices from Beyond the Sexual Binary* (Los Angeles: Alyson, 2002); and Kate Bornstein, *Gender Outlaw: On Men, Women and the Rest of Us* (New York: Routledge, 1994).

16. The figure of the desexed gay style guru reached its apex with the hit makeover show *Queer Eye for the Straight Guy*, which aired on Bravo TV and NBC from 2003 to 2007. See Jennifer Arellano, "'Queer Eye' 10 Years Later: The Fab Five's 'Make-Better' Legacy," *Entertainment Weekly*, October 20, 2013, accessed January 19, 2015, http://insidetv.ew.com/2013/10/20/queer-eye-10-years-later-the-fab-fives-make -better-legacy/.

17. Before they arrive in Snydersville, Vida, Chi-Chi, and Noxeema make a pit stop at a hotel where they are presumed to be guests at a women's club convention. Among the convention activities is a women's basketball tournament in which Noxeema decides to compete. As he slam dunks over the heads of female basketball players, Snipes seems to cite his iconic role in the interracial basketball buddy comedy *White Men Can't Jump* and manifests one of the most prominent figures in American iconography of black manhood: the superior basketball player.

Although Patrick Swayze enjoyed similar status as Hollywood macho man and heartthrob, his Vida is so meticulously buttoned up, her reserve so thoroughly maintained, that the actor's offscreen leading-manhood is far more effectively constrained and withheld. Conversely, both actor Snipes's and Noxeema's manhoods seem to burst the seams that cloak them.

18. These disparate responses are attributable, in part, to context. The incident with Chi-Chi seems to have taken place at the secluded edge of town, whereas the confrontation with Noxeema occurs in the town square; perhaps the watchful eyes of the townsfolk deters these predators. However, this explanation does not account for the complex web of social relations and stereotypic filmic tropes manifested in these two episodes.

19. For another take on the prominence of Wesley Snipes's muscles in *To Wong Foo*, see Cindy Fuchs, "Arms and the Man: Wesley Snipes' Biceps and the Uneasiness at the Heart of Wong Foo," *Philadelphia City Paper*, September 7, 1995, http://citypaper .net/articles/090795/article026.shtml.

20. Frantz Fanon, *Black Skin, White Masks*, trans. Richard Philcox (New York: Grove Press, 2008): 147.

21. See Fanon, *Black Skin, White Masks*; Maurice O. Wallace, *Constructing the Black Masculine: Identity and Ideality in African American Men's Literature and Culture, 1775–1995* (Durham, NC: Duke University Press, 1992); Arthur Flannigan Saint-Aubin, "Testeria: The Dis-ease of Black Men in White Supremacist, Patriarchal Culture," *Callaloo* 17, no. 4 (Autumn 1994): 1054–73.

22. For an especially egregious example of the masculinization of black womanhood within racist antiblack epistemology, see Satoshi Kanazawa, "Why Are Black Women Less Physically Attractive Than Other Women?," *PsychologyToday.com*, May 15, 2011. (Due to controversy, the original article and hyperlink have been removed.)

23. Hortense J. Spillers, "Mama's Baby, Papa's Maybe: An American Grammar Book," *Diacritics* 17, no. 2 (1987): 66, 68.

24. Even the little orphan Annie kicks her captor in the balls. See *Annie*, dir. John Huston (Culver City, CA: Columbia Pictures, 1982), DVD.

25. See Fanon, *Black Skin, White Masks*, especially chap. 6, "The Black Man and Psychopathology."

26. Worth noting is a scantly developed subplot of interracial romance between townsfolk. Jimmy Joe (a black man who is ostensibly the only Snydersville resident of color, played by Mike Hodge) and Beatrice (a white local played Blythe Danner) harbor a mutual but suppressed attraction. For much of the film, the two are exceedingly apprehensive around each other, but in the atmosphere of increased tolerance that the queens bring to town, Beatrice and Jimmy Joe are finally emboldened to express attraction to one another.

The film portrays him as soft spoken, courteous, and hardworking (he runs a quaint restaurant) in a setting where the most visible men include an abusive husband, a bigoted sheriff, a group of sexual predators, and various "poor white trash" types. The film endorses their interracial romance (the presence of a bashful interracial couple suits the film's avowedly liberal, multicultural sensibility), but only after it reveals Jimmy Joe to be emphatically and categorically respectable. It is as though the film must assure its audience of the benevolence of Jimmy Joe before blessing the interracial union.

27. *Romeo + Juliet* was filmed in the San Francisco Bay as well as Mexico City and Veracruz.

28. Although Italianness was once excluded from normative whiteness in America, since the 1930s it has been largely incorporated into whiteness and endowed the legal and social benefits of white privilege. See, for example, Matthew Jacobson, *Whiteness of a Different Color: European Immigrants and the Alchemy of Race* (Cambridge, MA: Harvard University Press, 1999).

29. Although Abram is a Montague in Shakespeare's original script, Luhrman's "Abra" is a member of the house of Capulet.

30. The white/Latino binary and battle here recalls the 1961 film *West Side Story*, which, of course, is itself a loose interpretation of *Romeo and Juliet*. Significantly, Italians and light-skinned Latinos are often mutually subsumed within fetishistic fantasies of swarthy, hot-blooded "Latinness." Within pop cinema iconographies, the Capulets alternately resemble menacing (Italian) mobsters and (Latino) gangbangers.

31. "Claire Danes: Teen Angst," *Movieline.com*. December 1, 1995, accessed December 2014, http://movieline.com/1995/12/01/teen-angst/.

32. Kym Myzelle, "Young Hearts, Run Free," *William Shakespeare's Romeo + Juliet: Music from the Motion Picture* (Capitol Records, 1996).

33. William Shakespeare, *Romeo and Juliet* (New York: Washington Square Press, 1992): 2.6.14.

34. See Joseph A. Porter, *Shakespeare's Mercutio: His History and Drama* (Chapel Hill: University of North Carolina Press, 1988), 143–63; Fred Wharton, review of *Shakespeare's Mercutio: His History and Drama* by Joseph A. Porter, *South Atlantic Review* 56, no. 1 (January 1991), 103–5; Carla Freccero, "Romeo and Juliet Love Death," in *Shakesqueer: A Queer Companion to the Complete Works of Shakespeare*, ed. Madhavi Menon (Durham, NC: Duke University Press, 2011); Paul Hammond, *Love between Men in English Literature* (New York: Palgrave McMillan, 1996), 59.

35. Shakespeare, *Romeo and Juliet*, 3.1.39–45.

36. For more information on the interracial buddy genre, see Ed Guerrero, *Framing Blackness: The African American Image in Film* (Philadelphia: Temple University Press, 1993). Concerning sacrificial black buddies in particular, see Jennifer Gillian, "No One Knows You're Black! 'Six Degrees of Separation' and the Buddy Formula," *Cinema Journal* 40, no. 3 (Spring 2001): 47–68.

37. Regarding the objectification of black bodies and black pain to uphold white comfort and pleasure, see Deborah Walker King, *African Americans and the Culture of Pain* (Charlottesville: University of Virginia Press, 2008).

38. Shakespeare, *Romeo and Juliet*, 3.1.91.

39. Shakespeare, *Romeo and Juliet*, Prologue.6.

40. See Lady Chablis, with Theodore Bouloukos, *Hiding My Candy: The Autobiography of the Grand Empress of Savannah* (New York: Pocket Books, 1996).

41. Jim and other wealthy Savannahians are concerned with preserving and enshrining old Southern architecture and artifacts, suggesting a nostalgic attachment to the Old South. Of course, architecture and artifacts weren't the only "objects" populating the pre-Civil War plantation: *black human chattel* did, too. Any nostalgia for Old Southern "things" must reckon with this history.

42. Saidiya Hartman forwards the notion of "the afterlife of slavery" in her influential monograph *Lose Your Mother: A Journey along the Atlantic Slave Route* (New York: Farrar, Straus, and Giroux, 2007). Hartman writes, "If slavery persists as an issue in the political life of black America, it is not because of an antiquarian obsession with bygone days or the burden of a too-long memory, but because black lives are still imperiled and devalued by a racial calculus and a political arithmetic that were entrenched centuries ago. This is the afterlife of slavery—skewed life chances, limited access to health and education, premature death, incarceration, and impoverishment" (6).

I do not mean to imply that maid service is always already abject or should be viewed as seamlessly continuous with chattel slavery. Rather, I mean simply to highlight the persistence of black servitude alongside white wealth in *Midnight*'s Savannah, a persistence unaddressed in the film's plot and unremarked on by its characters. Though these women may live fulfilling lives, the film depicts them only as domestic servants.

43. For a poignant discussion of Hollywood misrepresentation and sensationalization of African-derived cosmologies and spiritual practices, see Barbara Browning, *Infectious Rhythm: Metaphors of Contagion and the Spread of African Culture* (New York: Routledge, 1998).

44. Lady Chablis is not the only figure who walks alongside the young couple in this final tableau. While Chablis walks Uga on the couple's right, another black figure appears on their left—an elderly man named Mr. Glover, one of Savannah's eccentric characters, who is walking a nonexistent dog. Twenty years earlier, when Mr. Glover's former employer passed away, his will stipulated that the dog-walker should continue to be paid to perform his duty. The dog died a few years after its owner, but the now-elderly Mr. Glover continues to walk a leash in order to continue receiving pay. Indeed, an elder black servant in the American South is relegated to performing an absurd task for what likely amounts to meager earnings. By positioning Lady Cha-

blis to literally mirror a servant performing a ludicrous errand—she is his visual and conceptual counterpart, as they both flank the couple and both walk "dogs"—the film subtly posits Chablis as co-servant and as absurd.

45. Concerning the latter-day incarnations of "mammy," see, for example, Jo-Ann Morgan, "Mammy the Huckster: Selling the Old South for the New Century," *American Art* 9, no. 1 (Spring 1995): 86–109. See also bell hooks's discussion of the mammy archetype in *Ain't I a Woman: Black Women and Feminism* (Boston: South End Press, 1981); and Patricia Hill Collins's examination of "mammy" as "controlling image" in *Black Feminist Thought: Knowledge, Consciousness, and the Politics of Empowerment* (2nd ed.; New York: Routledge, 2000).

46. bell hooks, *Black Looks: Race and Representation* (Boston: South End Press, 1999), 21–40.

47. A recent example of the enduring appeal of the black drag queen motif: *Kinky Boots*—a 2013 Broadway musical based on a 2005 British film comedy—is the story of Charlie, a white, bourgeois shoe factory owner whose business is on the verge of bankruptcy. He joins forces with a black drag queen named Lola to revive his business, recasting it as a "kinky boot" factory catering to drag queens and fetishists. In addition to saving Charlie's business, Lola helps save Charlie's love life and self-esteem. At the 2013 Tony Awards, the show won for best musical, and Billy Porter, as Lola, won for best actor.

48. Eve Kosofsky Sedgwick, "Paranoid Reading and Reparative Reading, or, You're So Paranoid, You Probably Think This Essay Is about You," in *Touching Feeling: Affect, Pedagogy, Performativity* (Durham, NC: Duke University Press, 2003): 123–52.

49. "The Lady Chablis," accessed December 2014, http://www.planetchablis.com/.

50. Shirley Chisholm famously used "Unbought and Unbossed" as a campaign slogan for her successful bid for Congress. She also used the slogan as title for her 1970 autobiography, *Unbought and Unbossed* (New York: Houghton Mifflin, 1970).

51. Concerning queer futures and futurity, see José Esteban Muñoz's gorgeous *Cruising Utopia: The Then and There of Queer Futurity* (New York: New York University Press, 2009).

10

Black Sissy Masculinity and the Politics of Dis-respectability

KORTNEY ZIEGLER

GLADYS BENTLEY WAS A PIONEER. A critical but often overlooked figure of the Harlem Renaissance, Bentley troubled gender roles onstage and off with a unique ease that recognized her agency as a black queer woman while revealing the pernicious stereotypes that has characterized black women as hypersexual, unattractive, aggressive, and immoral. During her performances, she openly sang about anal sex and other forms of sexual deviancy while dressed in a flawless white tuxedo and top hat. At a time when gender presentation was heavily policed at the hands of anti-cross-dressing laws of New York, Bentley risked imprisonment for her on- and offstage kinky transmasculine performances. At the same time, Bentley risked another type of "law" infringement to a burgeoning black middle class that performed "respectable" representations of gender roles, which concealed one's sexual practices in an effort to promote racial uplift.[1]

In this essay, I demonstrate how Bentley's drag performances suggest a type of queer kinky politics that both adheres to and challenges dominant constructions of black female sexuality through the concept of sissy play—a type of BDSM role-play under the cross-dressing rubric where a male pleasurably embodies hyperfeminine attributes in order to offset his masculinity. Though Bentley did not identify as male, I apply this sub-

FIG. 10.1. Page from article "I Am a Woman Again," showing Bentley in her tuxedos. *Ebony*, August 1952.

set of cross-dressing play to interpret her work with the idea that black women have always been perceived as embodying "masculine" qualities due to discourses of white racism that have positioned them as aggressive, dominant, overbearing, sexually promiscuous while at the same time sexually undesirable. Read in this way, sissy imagery can make clear how the symbolic appropriation of feminized masculinities by black women, can work to transform dominant notions of black sexuality and gender.

Sissy Male, Sissy Maid

Gladys Bentley was born in Philadelphia to a Trinidadian father, George, and an African American mother, Mary. As Bentley matured her parents threatened her with institutionalization because of her strong fascination with boys' clothing, eventually provoking her to escape to the perceived safe haven of a 1920s queer Harlem.

While in Harlem, Bentley's queer identity flourished as rapidly as did her career, due to her being able to wear her preferred choice of male clothing and capitalizing on it. She became one of the top performers in Harlem's black blues scene, which thrived on white patrons who sought out explicit representations of black queer sexuality that a performer such as Bentley offered. Eventually, however, her nightclub presence, like most black queer Renaissance figures, began to fade with the start of the Great

Depression. Struggling to maintain her act, she moved to the West Coast and began to perform in San Francisco nightclubs, such as the legendary gay cabaret club Mona's, still donning her signature tuxedo, but this time backed by a chorus of white men in drag.

As the country took a turn toward McCarthyism, Bentley began to publicly disavow her lesbian identity and embraced heterosexuality. To accompany her new image, Bentley published a brief autobiography titled "I Am a Woman Again" in the August 1952 volume of *Ebony* magazine. In it she describes how she had banished her lesbian past and had done so with the help of falling in love with a man and the use of estrogen hormone therapy:

> I had bitterly fought with all my heart, mind and body, the love and tenderness, the true devotion of a man who loved me usefully and whose love I could return the awakening within me of the womanliness I had tried to suppress. Today I am a woman again through the miracle which took place not only in my mind and heart—when I found a man I could love and who could love me—but also in my body—when the magic of modern medicine made it possible for me to have treatment which helped change my life completely.[2]

Bentley asserts that these two elements—male companionship and female hormones—helped to bring her from the depths of the "sex underground" and that now she is "a woman again." Peppered throughout the article are images of Bentley, in full female drag, that America was not used to. (See Figure 10.2.) She is shown in a set of photographs performing domestic chores such as washing the dishes, tasting food for her husband, newspaper columnist J. T. Gibson, and making the bed that they both assumedly sleep in together. Underneath, the caption reads: "Miss Bentley enjoys the domestic role that she shunned for years. She lives in [a] modest, tastefully-appointed home directly in the rear of the home she purchased for her mother."[3] The next photograph depicts her holding up a chain of pearls to her face while staring at herself in the mirror, suggesting that her newfound femme identity is not haphazard; rather, it is one that is carefully crafted and well thought out.

In "A Spectacle in Color," author Eric Garber reads Bentley's autobiography as part of her larger act of assimilation as outside societal pressures and financial hardships eventually forced Bentley to conform. He writes that "out of desperate fear for her own survival (particularly with an aging mother to support) Gladys Bentley started wearing dresses, and

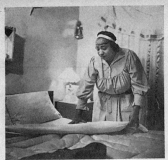

Turning back cover of bed. Miss Bentley prepares to make homecoming husband comfortable. Singer has authored numbers for Mills Brothers and for comedian Timmie Rogers, as well as dance routine for Peg Leg Bates.

Taste-testing dinner she has prepared for husband J. T. Cipion, Miss Bentley enjoys domestic role which she shunned for years. She lives in modest, tastefully-appointed home directly in rear of similar home she purchased for her mother.

I AM A WOMAN AGAIN *Continued*

son—until the miracle happened and I became a woman again.

The miracle came about when I discovered and accepted the one glorious thing which, for so many years, I had bitterly fought with all my heart, mind and body; the love and tenderness, the true devotion of a man who loved me unselfishly and whose love I could return: the awakening within me of the womanliness I had tried to suppress.

Today I am a woman again through the miracle which took place not only in my mind and heart—when I found a man I could love and who could love me—but also in my body—when the magic of modern medicine made it possible for me to have treatment which helped change my life completely. I am happily married and living a normal existence. But no matter how happy I am, I am still haunted by the sex underworld in which I once lived. I want to help others who are trapped in its dark recesses by telling my story.

Makes Mark In Show Business

BEFORE THE MIRACLE happened, I had made my mark in show business. At the age of 16 I left my home in Philadelphia and went to New York. I was lucky enough to get an audition in the office of a Broadway agent. Delighted with the rhythm and torchy numbers I did, he arranged for me to cut eight record sides. I received my first professional wages, a check for $400. I was very excited.

My records had a gratifying success, but I soon found out that one could not just sit around proudly and rest on one's laurels as a new recording artist. I began going to bars late at night, sitting in for entertainers when they were on their rest periods and picking up tips. One night, in Connie's Inn, a little club near the old Lafayette Theater, I met a friend who told me that the Mad House on 133rd Street needed a pianist right away. Their pianist had gone to Europe with *Blackbirds*.

"But they want a boy," my friend said.

"There's no better time for them to start using a girl," I replied.

At the Mad House, the boss was reluctant to give me a chance. I finally convinced him. My hands fairly flew over the keys. When I had finished my first number, the burst of applause was terrific. One of the white customers walked over, handed me a five dollar bill and said:

"Please play something else. We don't care what it is. Just play. You're terrific."

The boss came over. "Play as long as you like," he said. "When you're finished, come to my office."

I continued for two hours, then went to hear my fate. I was offered $35 a week and began work right on the spot.

For the customers of the club, one of the unique things about my act was the way I dressed. I wore immaculate white full dress shirts with stiff collars, small bow ties and skirts, oxfords, short Eton jackets and hair cut straight back.

The club where I was working was flourishing in the era of the Black Renaissance, that lush period in Negro art, literature and show business. Cultural-minded whites like Heywood Broun and Carl Van Vechten were sponsoring Negro artists. One night Mr. Van Vechten came to the club and that was the beginning of patronage by top-drawer society folk from downtown.

My $35 salary went to $125 a week and, what with tips from generous patrons, I did very well indeed. The club was renamed "Barbara's Exclusive Club" after my stage name—Barbara "Bobbie" Minton.

From Harlem I went to Park Avenue. There I appeared in tailor-made clothes, top hat and tails, with a cane to match each costume, stiff-bosomed shirt, wing collar tie and matching shoes. I had two black outfits, one maroon and a tan, grey and white. The elaborate mid-Manhattan club where I appeared had a 75-foot silver and onyx bar and mirrors everywhere. I was an immediate success. Soon I was living on Park Avenue in a $500-a-month apartment. I had servants and a beautiful car. The club where I worked overflowed with celebrities and big star names nightly. I played for many affairs for New York's merry mayor, Jimmy Walker.

After Park Avenue came a string of successful engagements in the best white clubs all over the country, including Cleveland, Pittsburgh and Chicago. Next came Hollywood and an engagement in a small, intimate and beautiful San Bernardino club. The whole Hollywood colony turned out to see and hear me. Mary Astor frequented the club. So did Arthur Treacher, Cesar Romero, Bruce Cabot, Hugh Herbert, Cary Grant, Johnny Weissmuller, George Burns, Gracie Allen, George Raft, Barbara Stanwyck, Robert Taylor, Alice Brady, Lawrence Tibbett and Ruth Chatterton.

This is a glimpse into the wonderfully-exciting career which was mine over the years. Although today there is not as much sensational publicity surrounding me, I am still a star, still enjoying success as a featured name in clubs and releasing records.

FIG. 10.2. Page from article "I Am a Woman Again," showing Bentley making a bed and cooking dinner. *Ebony*, August 1952.

sanitizing her [nightclub] act."[4] While it might be true that Bentley's shifting identity helped keep her relevant in the entertainment business, I deviate from Garber and follow James Wilson, who does not completely eschew the implied queerness of Bentley's heterosexual performance. In his more recent *Bulldaggers, Pansies, and Chocolate Babies: Performance, Race, and Sexuality in the Harlem Renaissance*, Wilson centralizes the notion of gender as subversive performance to point out that Bentley's autobiography, like her musical career, reflects her genuine knack for making clear the performative aspects of her "straight" identity. He writes: "Yet rather than completely concealing her former self within the new characterization, Bentley occasionally offers privileged, unmistakable glimpses of the performer within the role, presenting the impossibility of locating the 'real' Gladys Bentley and affirming the impossible task of finding the truth behind the portrayal."[5]

In the case of the photographs, although it is correct to assume that Bentley's performance of femininity was coached for the camera by the *Ebony* photographic and editorial staff, Wilson's perspective affords her with representational agency, as evidenced through the ways in which she takes control of the photographic gaze by referencing her queer "past." The article does function as an implicit proponent of black female domesticity—a central tenant of strong black woman ideology—but it is also about the queer implications embedded within the images. Following Wilson, I too offer Bentley agency by reading the photographs as representative of sissy male imagery that queers the heteronormative portrait of black female domesticity they attempt to paint.

According to Efrat Tseëlon, a sissy is a male who receives pleasure "by being put in women's clothing or underwear, and/or being forced to serve as a ladies maid" by performing domestic duties. Coached by a dominant figure into performing the right feminine comportment, the goal of a sissy is to replicate femininity with the belief that submission through domestic servitude is the "ultimate example of femininity." This includes "limp wrist, feet together, stooping instead of bending, [and] sitting with legs crossed at the knees." All "gesturing must be feminine in nature and responses must elude to the sissies knowledge of their position in life."[6]

Though sissies are trained to be submissive, the irony involved in the sissy scenarios, Tseëlon writes, is that "the cross-dressing boy-girl ultimately triumphs, since underneath his frilly apron, there is the unmistakable sign of manhood."[7] In the case of Bentley, her manhood is not located between her legs (even though she claimed to have an abnormal clitoris, implying a somewhat male anatomy); rather, her manhood is represented by her black masculine queer past. To unravel the sissy connotations embedded in the article, I turn to Roland Barthes and his work on revealing the hidden meanings coded in photographic messages.

In his essay "The Photographic Message," Roland Barthes argues that the "photograph is not only perceived, received, it is read, [and] connected more or less consciously by the public that consumes it to a traditional stock of signs." Barthes further explores this notion in *Camera Lucida* (1981), as he asserts that all images hold a dual capacity, through what he defines as the punctum—the details of a photograph that "prick" the viewer in an attempt to make the image sensible to them. With this attention to specific detail, an emotional attachment to that specific aesthetic representation is produced, and as Barthes states about his own responses to photography, the presence of the punctum "changes my reading, that I am looking at a new photograph, marked in my eyes with a higher value . . . this 'detail' is the punctum."[8] Barthes insists further that the punctum of the photograph is something that is both already there and an addition to the image. It is a specific detail that provokes the imagination to interrogate and disrupt cultural and historical meaning.

The converse to punctum, "studium," is defined as the intentionality of the photograph based on the intent of its producer. Barthes writes, "To recognize the studium is inevitably to encounter the photograph's intentions, to enter into harmony with them, to approve or disapprove of them, but always to understand them, to argue within myself, for culture (from which studium derived) is a contract arrived at between creators and consumers."[9] The studium works through notions of pleasure and presents facts (that is, dates, locales, historical figures); the punctum destabilizes the studium.

Barthes's concept of the punctum and studium is useful in understanding the queer possibilities embedded within Bentley's ostensibly heteronormative representation. While the intentions of the photographer, editors, and caption writers of her biography might have constructed the message(s) of the image to present her in a heteronormative manner, the reader can interpret its queer punctum in a number of ways.

In the headlining image to her essay, Bentley is shown sitting down draped in a shapeless white housedress while holding an oversized scrapbook that profiles her drag performance history. (See Figure 10.3.) Instead of her usual top hat, she wears a feminine bow that hangs down the right side of her face. Her look is coy, as her eyes focus toward the direction

Looking over scrapbook, Gladys Bentley reviews fabulous night club career. Now a West Coast resident, one-time male impersonator has written 400 songs in last five years, says she will publish no-holds-barred book about her life. Miss Bentley wrote such tunes as *Gladys Isn't Gratis Any More.*

FIG. 10.3. Page from article "I Am a Woman Again," showing Bentley holding her scrapbook. *Ebony*, August 1952.

of the camera but slightly off and up to the right side of the frame. She smiles shyly as she holds the scrapbook like an infant: her right hand cradles the back while her left hand, in the shape of a fist, sits right underneath the portrait of her in a black top hat and bow tie. Unlike the live Bentley, however, it is the portrait of her in drag in the scrapbook that is controlling the gaze of the image as its center location in the frame positions it as "looking" directly at the camera.

Presumably, as this image sits on top of the article, it is meant to serve as the primary representation of Bentley's new heterosexuality through its size and content. For one, the dress and headwrap that she is wearing captures the reader's attention, as their whiteness stands out against the black background in which she is photographed. This stark contrast in color draws readers to this distinct symbol of femininity, forcing them to associate her identity with the appropriate clothing that a woman should wear and prohibit the "mistake" of interpreting her body as male. Furthermore, the decision to place Bentley in white alludes to Victorian notions of sexual purity as white dresses, in the context of heterosexual marriage, have historically symbolized respectable female innocence and virginity. Additionally, as baptism in the Christian tradition has historically relied on its practitioners to wear white as a symbol of forgiveness, the photographer, by placing Bentley in this particular dress, intends (the studium of the image) to present her as one who actively holds a desire to be forgiven for her deviant sexual past and therefore affords her a new and acceptable sexual identity based on Christian-inspired conservative values.[10]

The scrapbook is also important to note, as it also participates in the construction of Bentley as appropriately feminine and heterosexual. For one, the photograph of her in drag both literally and physically serves as a direct contrast to the woman who is holding it. Its position offset but parallel to Bentley's face mimics a mirror reflection, insinuating that the image is indeed her, while its smaller size suggests that the performance of masculinity it represents is inauthentic or untrue. Additionally, the presence of the second strikingly similar if not the same image of Bentley on the opposite page in the book is not as opaque as its centered counterpart and seems to be almost translucent on the page. Whether it is a possible result of bad lighting or Bentley's failure to adequately care for her archives that produced the faded image, its visibility works to further signify the demarcation between her old and new identities by metaphorically standing in as a representation of her faded past.

The contents of this image, then, help to present a portrait of a woman who seemingly enjoys her participation in heteronormative gender performances. Therefore, the photograph participates in the narrative of strength by painting Bentley as a survivor of her misguided sexual past. Moreover, as notions of black female strength include domesticating black womanhood, the choice of clothing and submissive facial expressions she emotes serve to underscore Bentley's housewife identity. Like the rest of the photographs in the article, however, this image is haunted by her openly queer past through implicit references to a feminized masculinity.

In particular, the multiple images of Bentley in the photograph draw on what Meyers defines as "the woman-with-mirror-motif"—a popular way in which women draw on mirror iconography to "subvert the hegemony of misogyny," through its versatile symbolism. If, as Michelle Wallace notes, that ideals of strong black womanhood are based on misogynist modes of thinking that position black women as emasculating matriarchs, the use of mirror imagery in this instance functions as a challenge to this idea.[11] Bentley's masculine drag self-reflected against her strong black woman domestic persona conceptually implies the duality of her identity and presents them as being permanently connected and innately influenced by each other. Ultimately, this presents Bentley as neither truly female nor male; rather, it marks her as a gender chameleon whose true identity encompasses both. In this way, we can interpret the live Bentley as a feminized version of her masculine self—or as a sissy male in female clothing.

Dominatrix Lady English asserts that a BDSM sissy male knows "that however [he] may try, he will never be equal to that power and eloquence the superior woman holds. He dresses as he does, not as an attempt to be a woman, or even pose as one, but rather to honor her by denying his masculinity through humility."[12] Read in this manner, the representation of Bentley takes on new eroticized meanings by denying the desexualized aspects of the matriarch image, which is enshrined in notions of black domesticity.

For instance, though the white dress references puritanical ideas of virginity, thus implying a nonsexual identity, understood within the economy of sissy male aesthetics, the dress ironically affords her sexual agency and desirability. Claudia Varrin reminds us that a primary goal of sissies in BDSM scenarios is to replicate femininity in a manner that will render their performances as sexually attractive. Thus sissies adopt white clothing in an effort to eroticize their masculinity, as the color white is associated with softness, vulnerability, submissiveness, but, ultimately, sensuality.[13] In this sense, Bentley's white dress makes her desexualized and assumed "emasculating" black femininity more attractive and less threatening by implying that a sensual and erotic-natured woman exists underneath her outward symbol of domesticity.

The meaning implied by the gaze of the live Bentley is also transformed when approached under the lens of sissy masculinity. Her slight look away from the image and the gaze of the spectator indexes an element of sissy play where sissies perform their feminized masculinity by submitting to the domination of "real" males. Of course, the drag Bentley is not a "real" male; however, in the context of an article that attempts to contain her masculinity within the realm of domesticated strong black woman ideology and label her drag masculinity as deviant and proof of a "curable illness," the drag image then represents the "real" man that Bentley could never be. Though effeminate, Bentley's drag self is the dominant male to which her performance of domesticity submits. A gesture that points to the ways in which black masculinity and femininity is always already perceived as queer, Bentley's submissive sissy gaze also makes clear how certain performances of black womanhood are shaped by queer inflections of masculinity.

Along with her live body, the location of the three drag faces in the frame presented as being aligned in an offset row conjures up references to staged family portraiture wherein "notions of normative bourgeois familial formations [are] represented" through an explicit adherence to gender roles.[14] For example, as Richard Brilliant notes, the history of presenting the nuclear family through photography has cultivated a "long-standing portrait tradition of representing the family as a cohesive group, led by a dominant male."[15] In these types of photographs, it is the patriarch who takes on the focal point of the portrait, usually sitting down as his family surrounds him. As the center of attention, he controls the gaze, implying his control over the family. In the imagined family portrait of Bentley, it is her drag image that stands in as the figure of authority in her symbolic family. Positioned in the center of the text with eyes glaring directly toward the photographer's lens, the image forces spectators to acknowledge it and recognize its masculinity as important and powerful. At the same time, like the doting wife imagery that exists in traditional family portraiture, real-life Bentley is accordingly portrayed as an equally supportive partner suggested through the placement of her hand on top of the image, implying a connection of intimacy between her and the representation of masculinity the image sets forth.

What is particularly subversive about this symbol of patriarchy is the queer incarnation of black masculinity it promotes. As mentioned above, within the context of the article, drag Bentley is unintentionally positioned as a "real" man at the same time her "real" female sex prohibits an authentic masculinity. Understood in this way, the symbol of patriarchal authority that controls the photographic gaze of the family portrait is ultimately rendered as a failed version of (black) masculinity due to its effeminate nature. Bentley's position as "wife" to the sissified masculine version of herself, however, alludes to the heteronormative institution of marriage, which theoretically marks male/female domestic couplings as socially and legally legitimate. As such, the sissified patriarch and masculine wife together present a legitimized figuration of the respectable black nuclear family—albeit a queer one.

If we are to read Bentley's feminine drag as an embodiment of a sissy masculinity that foregrounds submission as sexual agency, then the photographs in the article of her performing domestic chores further emphasize this position, particularly through the representation of sissy maid aesthetics.[16] On her website dedicated to the training of sissy maids, dominatrix Lady English defines them as "simply submissive men who dress in feminine attire (normally a frilly maid uniform) and do domestic service for a Mistress. Sometimes their attire is as simple as wearing panties, bra and an apron, but most of the time they are dressed ultra feminine with petticoat and ruffle.... It's not just about the clothes they wear. A sissy maid will endure a great deal of training to be feminized and learn their job. In addition to training they also work very hard to please their Mistress." Most important, a sissy maid's submission "to domestic work isn't a reflection of an attitude that a woman should be relegated to keeping a house either." Rather, the sissy maid "cleans house because it is a service to [their dominant] and a means to unseat the masculine image of always being the head of a household." To be a sissy maid is to celebrate and eroticize domestic servitude.[17]

A key element of Lady English's definition of sissy maid role-play that serves as a site of subversive masculinity that this chapter explores is the idea of associating domestic duties with pleasure. For black women who have always occupied the role of the domestic, their subservient duties have never been associated with pleasure, except that of the mythological mammy figure whose pleasure derives from serving whites. Patricia Hill Collins defines the role of the mammy as follows: "The first controlling image applied to African American women is that of the mammy—the faithful, obedient domestic servant. Created to justify the economic exploitation of house slaves and sustained to explain black women's long-standing restriction to domestic service, the mammy image represents the normative yardstick used to evaluate all black women's behavior." Pictured as a large, black, jolly, and obedient woman, the physical attributes of the mammy as desexualized and unattractive servant, "mollifie[d] racial anxieties by rendering a physiological black presence acceptable to white-inflected beauty culture."[18] In effect, it is the physicality of her body and her willingness to defend, nurture, protect, and console white families over her own that position the mammy figure as emblematic of the impossible strength embedded in the strong black woman archetype.

Barbara Omolade points out that strong black woman ideology has forced blacks to take on the role of the mammy through a process of what she defines as "mammification"—a self-inflicted belief that pressures them to assume mammy-type roles of servitude and submission to whites. Speaking to the black female presence in the professional realm, Omolade's perspective of the "new mammy" figure, however, is connected

to the myth of the black matriarch, as "her assertive demeanor identifies her with the mammy."[19] Essentially, both figures are denied access to
femininity and sexual agency as they equally fail to commit to gendered
ideals of true womanhood: while the mammy is nurturing and caring,
she is inadvertently depicted as asexual. Conversely, the black matriarch
lacks nurturing qualities due to her aggressive nature and is therefore de-
eroticized and perceived as not being sexually desirable.

It is safe to assume that, throughout her very public life, Bentley was
forced to navigate the restraints of self-imposed mammification given that
her fan base comprised mainly white audiences who sought out primitive
images of blackness, as well as the role of black matriarch owing to her
newfound heteronormative relationship. The images of her performing
domestic chores in the *Ebony* article demonstrate an engagement with
mammy iconography, primarily symbolized through the choice of wide
shots that emphasize her physicality and domestic abilities by highlighting
her body size. However, if we interpret the photographs as Bentley's enact-
ment of sissy maid aesthetics, the mammy iconography it promotes may
be inflected as potentially erotic and sexualized through the articulation
of pleasure received by performing such roles "she slammed for years."[20]

For example, Bentley harps on the happiness she achieved from the
expected domestic roles of heterosexual marriage, as it allowed her to be
perceived as a "true" woman: "Even though our marriage did not last, I will
always have a special feeling for Don because it was his loving tenderness
which turned me back toward the path of normalcy." The accruement of
normalcy by capitulating to gender roles "brought me happiness during our
marriage [and] the joy of knowing that, after all, I was as much a woman
as any other woman in the world."[21] The photographs of Bentley that accompany her multiple statements of happiness throughout ironically work
against this, as they present an expressionless-faced wife washing dishes
and making the bed—signaling a detachment or unhappiness with the
overdetermined roles. They also signify on the innate domestic qualities of
black womanhood, as her actions seem programmed, almost robotic.

Bentley's words of happiness do indeed reflect her willingness to participate in domestic servitude as a path to accurately embody authentic
womanhood. According to Melissa Daniels and Rene Carter, a primary
aspect of sissy maid role-play is the notion of *forced feminization*:

> In this storyline there is a dominant person (either male or female)
> who "forces" a male into assuming a submissive and overtly feminine

role. The submissive male is often portrayed as *unwilling* and *reluctant*. What makes this fantasy difficult to understand is that the submissive male (while pretending to be reluctant) actually WANTS this treatment. Their protests and demands for the treatment to stop are often surface deep, while their arousal and deepest fantasies crave the fantasy to continue with even more intensity. . . . By allowing someone else to play the "villain" and to MAKE the fantasy happen, the guilt that the submissive male feels can be relieved and they can enjoy the concept of acting and feeling feminine.[22]

In following Daniels and Carter, I articulate Bentley's mannerisms and gestures through the concept of forced feminization. In this case, the villains who impose the humiliating domestic roles onto Bentley are the invisible mammy and matriarch symbols the photographs signify on. Their symbolic power underscores Bentley's implied innate masculinity and renders her attempted femme-domestic persona as pure theatricality. The blank facial expressions, then, no longer come to connote dread and unhappiness; instead, they imply a masochistic pleasure received in this instance of aesthetic mammification. Furthermore, because this masochistic pleasure feeds on the knowledge of "the submissive male to accept that they have to behave, look and perform as a submissive female," without the presence of visible embarrassment, Daniels and Carter note that "the entire fantasy may not be arousing for them at all and can easily let them remember the guilt and disdain they feel for the fantasy they have while aroused."[23] Approached in this way, the stern faces exhibited by Bentley disturb the studium by inferring a delightful shame in the cultivation of her domestic identity. Unlike the mammy or matriarch who has been "stripped of the palliative feminine veneer" associated with domestic work, Bentley's sissy maid reinscribes the black mammy figure with erotic pleasure.[24]

Bentley's Sissy Blues

The human voice is a powerful tool that, because of its status as both part of the body and outside it, maintains an important role within the linked space between gender transgression and desire. In particular, as the octave of the voice helps to mark one's body as male or female, the manipulation of it through groans, grunts, shrieks, or yells can challenge perceptions of masculinity and femininity and thereby influence erotic identification. Francesca Royster explores the notion of the voice as an important physical site of erotic possibility. In *Sounding Like a No-No: Queer Sounds and Eccentric Acts in the Post-Soul Era*, she writes that "the throat is an erotic space that can both encode and undercut gender. It is the site of performative expression where desire becomes manifest—where desire is transformed into communication. . . . Throats are part of the erotic act, commanding, whispering, [and] swallowing."[25]

Although Royster articulates amorphous vocality that is applicable to all bodies, in *The Power of Black Music*, Samuel A. Floyd explores the concept of black vocality and locates its origin within the transatlantic slave trade. Floyd argues that the particular vocal rhythms and patterns of the black voice stem from a conscious attempt to retain African performance practices in the new world. He locates the ring shout—a religious ritual that provided enslaved blacks with pleasurable physical entertainment through song and dance—as the locus of black vocality. It was within these circles where "call-and-response figures and polyphony [is made visible] with hand-clapping and the 'smiting of breasts' serving as substitutes for drum playing . . . all rising in piercing and staccato intensity to finally reach a climax."[26] Furthermore, as enslaved blacks were denied the ability to speak their own languages, the vocal gestures of crying or shouting represented the syncretism of European language with African identity. It is these cultural legacies that, Floyd asserts, have come to be retained and embraced by postbellum blacks.

The discography of Bentley follows in the vast tradition of African American music, as her dramatic vocal style fluctuates between falsetto and alto pitches that collectively reflect the tensions of this cultural history, while her grunts, moans, and growls—sounds that are generally associated with sexual pleasure—provide a deeper context in which to interpret her "black voice" as a complex expression of black queer sexuality. In particular, her vocal manipulations follow in line with other black female blues singers who referenced black queer possibilities by calling attention to the subject of the effeminate black man in what is defined as "sissy blues"—an unofficial subset of the blues genre in which explicit references to male homosexuality and the effeminate masculinity of lesbians are interrogated by black women.[27] For example, Ma Rainey's "Sissy Blues" (1926) presents the fears and anxieties some black woman have toward the sissy male stealing their partners; "Prove It On Me" (1928) demonstrates the ways in which black women themselves embody sissy masculinity to assert their own sexual and gender identity. Furthermore, in the context of physicality, black female blues singers are perceived as having voices similar to their male counterparts and bodies that exude "a strong physical" presence.[28] All of this added to notions of black female strength to which sissy blues alludes.

Keeping in line with the idea of sissy imagery as reflective of a man's attempt at honoring womanhood by reinscribing his masculinity with submissive feminine qualities, I associate Bentley's vocal manipulations of her perceived innate masculinity as a black female blues singer as representative of this erotic power exchange. I follow Easton and Hardy's assertion that BDSM vocatives form the basis of sissy power relationships wherein the context and cadence of particular terms of address work to reinforce the user's subject status.[29] Thus, transformational agency emerges since the vocatives deployed by the sissy "speakers in dominant and submissive relationships must modify the predominant social frameworks" in order for the sissy's performance of femininity to succeed in the BDSM fantasy.[30] As I demonstrate in my analysis of "How Much Can I Stand," Bentley enacts this transformational agency by constructing a space of black female critique of gender roles through sissy vocatives that fluctuate between the gendered power relationship of masculinity and femininity. Ultimately, this vocal play underscores the perceived subordinate status of black woman in order to lend erotic power to the strong black woman figure by embedding queer possibilities.

In her essay titled "Sapphonics," Elizabeth Wood explores the work of lesbian opera singer Ethel Smyth to argue that the female voice can signal toward a type of transvestism that embodies the voice of sexual dissonance, "that, like the gaze, can bespeak an odd, unnatural desire." She continues: "I call this voice Sapphonic for its resonance in sonic space as lesbian difference and desire. Its sound is characteristically powerful and problematic, defiant and defective. Its flexible negotiation and integration of an exceptional range of registers crosses boundaries among different voice types and their representations to challenge polarities of both gender and sexuality as these are socially—and vocally—constructed.[31] Wood states that Smyth's sapphonic voice openly declared her lesbian identity through the metaphor of fugue and fugal counterpoint, where the fugue represents constructions of identity while the counterpoint indexes the restraints of the fugal bond.

In the simplest of terms, a fugue is an imitative counterpoint where one element of the song is initiated, then repeated either in the same pitch or transposed. Accordingly, two or more individual voices are constructed, although they are intended to represent one unique voice. The history of African American music has cultivated the polyvocality of the fugue, with genres such as funk, hip hop, gospel, and jazz containing elements of vocal repetition and syncopated beats. Blues, in particular, is the most representative of this concept as its chord structure is designed to represent and reflect the sadness of the human voice and vice versa.

Bentley's use of the fugue can be heard on all the albums she recorded with Okeh Records during her streak of popularity in 1920s America, with songs such as "How Long, How Long Blues," "Worried Blues," and "Moanful Wailin' Blues" all containing a multiplicity of her sometimes abstract voices. In one of her most famous songs, "How Much Can I Stand," recorded in 1928, Bentley sings about a violent relationship between herself and a male lover, with the contemplation of murder as a way to end it.

The song begins with the slow-paced strumming of Eddie Lang's guitar sustaining the melody while Bentley's soft but robust voice makes its way onto the track. She describes her lover's abusive antics with the lyrics of the first verse:

> I heard about your lovers
> Your pimps and girls
> I heard about your Sheiks
> and hand me downs

As she sings in her gravelly voice, she espouses long, deep moans and growls with the lyrics that work to symbolize her emotional frustrations. At the end of the verse, she utilizes the technique of scatting, à la Louis Armstrong, to reproduce the warm sounds of a trumpet that matches the melody of Lang's softly-strummed guitar.[32]

Although Bentley follows in the tradition of black blues singers who rely on manipulations of the voice to reproduce instruments, her adoption of this vocal technique does more in that it connotes a sense of masculinity with her low, husky tones.[33] At the same time, however, the replication of the trumpet, with its muted and soft tone, connotes an implied vulnerability that her voice and lyrics elide. As the trumpet has historically functioned as the backbone of African American jazz ensembles, Bentley's trumpet as a secondary fugue voice, further signals toward vulnerability, as it does not occupy the majority of the sonic space. As such, its subordinate presence can be interpreted as harboring feminine qualities. On the one hand, this contrast between Bentley's "masculine" voice and the "feminine" voices of the strummed guitar and muted trumpet produce a compelling tension of identity that works to challenge perceptions of the "strong black woman." On the other hand, the duality of voices signals toward a possible queer tonality as the shifting of positions from person to instrument and back places Bentley beyond a simplistic identification of gender. Thus, "How Much Can I Stand," with its destabilization of voice, presents a sapphonic appeal that influences perceptions of queer desire.

The shifting of identity, which suggests the subversiveness of alternative gender embodiment, is further exemplified through the tense nature of the song. Throughout the majority of the song, Bentley restricts the tonal range of the verses between the repetitious "how much can I stand" line. By the final verse, nevertheless, Bentley's voice changes as she alludes to an imagined future with her next lover—"The next man I get/It must be guaranteed/When I walk down the aisle/Gonna hear me scream."[34] Strong emphasis is placed on the second break as her voice rises into a shout on "guaranteed" but returns to the low gravelly tone in her final delivery of the song's title question. After this, Bentley engages the trumpet imitation one last time in a blues coda that substitutes lyrics for melody. In this particular instance, though, she exercises a range of fast-paced notes set to the same tempo while Lang's guitar playing also shifts to accompany the new melody.

While Bentley's soaring vocals symbolize agency and independence, the voice's return to the lower octave scale demonstrates how such independence for black women is not without restrictions. However, it is the sound of the trumpet that represents a utopian break from this contradictory position, as its perceived masculinity thus reasserts Bentley's power. Again, this vocal back and forth situates Bentley within the in-between space of "appropriate" gender roles, thus further demonstrating their instability. Furthermore, these moments point to the possibilities of queer desire as the fluctuation between gender codes works to suggest the possibilities of a butch-femme dynamic, with Bentley's voice alternating between the butch and the femme, as the same time as Lang's guitar does the same. For one, this does the obvious work of considering blues as a significant site of space of black female same-gender desire, leaving potential for Bentley's abusive partner to be read as female. Ironically, this gesture normalizes black queer identities through an appropriation of domestic abuse as experienced in heterosexual unions.[35] Additionally, through this implied butch-femme sonic aesthetic, Bentley points to the ways in which black women have willfully participated in the construction of black queer identity on heteronormative terms.

Gladys Bentley's call of attention to the masculine attributes perceived to be innate in black women as implied through the strength narrative, along with the compulsory heterosexual identity of the black sissy, fosters a space of endless black queer possibility. Her gender-fluid persona troubles the problematic notion of authenticity that frames respectable enactments of black sexuality and reveals "the slippage between the mask of black masculinity [and femininity] as always already heterosexual and the unacknowledged desire for the homosexual Other."[36] Bentley as sissy paints a portrait of black womanhood that carries with it sexual and gender agency but, most important, shows the prospect of pleasure.

NOTES

1. Evelyn Brooks Higginbotham, *Righteous Discontent: The Women's Movement in the Black Baptist Church, 1880–1920* (Cambridge, MA: Harvard University Press, 1993); Darlene Clark Hine, *Hine Sight: Black Women and the Re-construction of American History* (Bloomington: Indiana University Press, 1994).

2. Gladys Bentley, "I Am a Woman Again," *Ebony*, August 1952, 54.

3. Bentley, "I Am a Woman Again," 54.

4. Eric Garber, "A Spectacle in Color: The Lesbian and Gay Subculture of Jazz Age Harlem," in *Hidden from History: Reclaiming the Gay and Lesbian Past*, eds. Martin Duberman, Martha Vicinus, and George Chauncey Jr. (New York: Meridian Press, 1990), 324.

5. James Wilson, *Bulldaggers, Pansies, and Chocolate Babies: Performance, Race, and Sexuality in the Harlem Renaissance* (Ann Arbor: University of Michigan Press, 2011), 188.

6. Efrat Tseëlon, *Masquerade and Identities: Essays on Gender, Sexuality, and Marginality* (New York: Psychology Press, 2001), 156, 157.

7. Tseëlon, *Masquerade and Identities*, 78.

8. Roland Barthes, *Camera Lucida: Reflections on Photography*, trans. Richard Howard (New York: Hill and Wang, 1981), 3.

9. Barthes, *Camera Lucida*, 4.

10. Michael Keene, *Aspects of Christianity: Jesus of Nazareth* (Cheltenham: Nelson Thomes, 2000).

11. Michele Wallace, *Black Macho and the Myth of the Superwoman* (London: Verso, 1999).

12. Lady English, "Female Domination," *Lady English*, accessed April 1, 2011, http://www.ladyenglish.com/home.htm.

13. Claudia Varrin, *Female Dominance: Rituals and Practices* (New York: Kensington Books, 2005), 64.

14. Institute for Advanced Feminist Research, *Shock and Awe: War on Words* (Santa Cruz, CA: New Pacific Press, 2004), 59.

15. Brilliant, *Portraiture* (London: Reaktion Books, 1991), 92.

16. I do not need to be convinced of the possibility that Bentley might have enjoyed the innate kinkiness of domestic servitude, as Alfred Duckett's 1957 article in the *Chicago Defender* on the notion of the third sex points to her exploration of the realm of kink that challenges the heteronormative relationship she claimed to enjoy in the *Ebony* article. See Alfred Duckett, "The Third Sex," *Chicago Defender* (March 2, 1957), 7. In Duckett's article, printed after Bentley's public marriage, a friend of the journalist noticed two photographs on her bureau: one of a man and one of a woman. When asked about them, Bentley replied, "Oh. That's my husband and that's my wife" (cited in Wilson, *Bulldaggers, Pansies, and Chocolate Babies*, 187). From this example, I find sufficient grounds on which to apply the notion of sissy maid aesthetics that work to position her as an active agent in her own pleasurable domestication.

17. English, "Female Domination."

18. Patricia Hill Collins, *Black Feminist Thought: Knowledge, Consciousness, and the Politics of Empowerment* (New York: Routledge, 1990), 71; Andrea Shaw, *The Embodiment of Disobedience: Fat Black Women's Unruly Political Bodies* (New York: Lexington Books, 2006), 20.

19. Barbara Omolade, *The Rising Song of African American Women* (New York: Routledge, 1994); Barbara Christian, *Black Feminist Criticism: Perspectives on Black Women Writers* (New York: Teachers College Press, 1985), 166.

20. Bentley, "I Am a Woman Again," 97.

21. Bentley, "I Am a Woman Again," 98.

22. Melissa Daniels and Renee Carter, "Forced Feminization 101," accessed March 1, 2006, http://www.lockedinlace.com/essays/forcedfeminization.html.

23. Daniels and Carter, "Forced Feminization 101."

24. Angela Davis, "Reflections on the Black Woman's Role in the Community of Slaves," in *Words of Fire: An Anthology of Black Feminist Thought*, ed. Beverly Guy-Sheftall (New York: The New Press, 1995), 207.

25. Francesca Royster, *Sounding Like a No-No: Queer Sounds and Eccentric Acts in the Post-Soul Era* (Ann Arbor: University of Michigan Press, 2012), 119.

26. Samuel A. Floyd, *The Power of Black Music: Interpreting Its History from Africa to the United States* (Oxford: Oxford University Press, 1996), 37.

27. Josh Kun, *Audiotopia: Music, Race, and America* (Berkeley: University of California Press, 2005).

28. Hazel Carby, *Cultures in Babylon: Black Britain and African America* (London: Verso, 1999), 11.

29. Dossie Easton and Janet Hardy, *The Ethical Slut: A Roadmap for Relationship Pioneers* (Berkeley, CA: Celestial Arts Publishing, 2009).

30. Elizabeth R. Busbee, "Unequal Footing: Goffman's Models for Deference, Demeanor and Face in Dominant/Submissive Communication." Presented at Lavender Languages and Linguistics (American University, Washington, DC, September 23, 2000), 20.

31. Elizabeth Wood, "Sapphonics," in *Queering the Pitch: The New Gay and Lesbian Musicology*, eds. Phillip Bartlett and Elizabeth Wood (New York: CRC Press, 2006), 28.

32. Gladys Bentley, "How Much Can I Stand," *Mean Mothers/Independent Women's Blues*, vol I. Various Artists (Rosetta Records, 1995), compact disc.

33. Hazel V. Carby, *Cultures of Babylon: Black Britain and African America* (London: Verso, 1999).

34. Bentley, "How Much Can I Stand."

35. While this idea might seem problematic, my intention is to argue that the allusion to domestic violence subsequently fixes Bentley's butch-femme relationship in a way that realigns it with dominant categories of sex and gender. In other words, as male-female relationships are not without their instances of abuse, neither are queer ones. Through this reference, then, Bentley's queer relationship can be interpreted as "normal."

36. E. Patrick Johnson, *Appropriating Blackness: Performance and the Politics of Authenticity* (Durham, NC: Duke University Press, 2003), 48.

11

Let's Play

*Exploring Cinematic Black Lesbian Fantasy,
Pleasure, and Pain*

JENNIFER DECLUE

☺

CONTEMPLATING BLACK QUEER SEX AND SEXUALITY at this
historical moment is encumbered by the tumultuous events of the summer of 2013. At that moment, the battle to overturn Proposition 8 was won
when the Supreme Court of the United States deemed same-sex marriage
once again legal in the state of California. During that same week, the Supreme Court also dismantled key elements of the Voting Rights Act, which
unravels legislation that has lessened voter intimidation and discrimination.
Tensions around race, class, and gender privilege become amplified when
marriage equality is celebrated while racial, gender, and class inequality
continue to predominate the lives of many people within the LGBT community. While the inability to marry may have been the single factor preventing
some members of the lesbian and gay community from enjoying equal protection under the law, antiblack and antibrown racism, poverty, inadequate
public education, substandard or nonexistent health care, inaccessibility to
healthy and nutritious food, and now voter discrimination are significant impediments to equality for other members of the lesbian and gay community.

In the wake of those Supreme Court decisions comes the ruling by a Florida court that found George Zimmerman not guilty on all counts for Trayvon Martin's murder. As I write this essay, people are outraged that the value of black life has once again been adjudicated as worthless— worth less than white life or the lives of those protecting the interests of whiteness.[1] Writing from within a moment in history that was initially framed as being postracial, in large part because of the election of the United States's first black president, Barack Obama, makes salient the willful blindness needed to posit a postracial United States, when in fact persistent and escalating racial discrimination, racial violence, and racial bias abounds in neighborhoods, schools, and courtrooms. It is at this moment in time that I turn my attention to sex, and specifically black queer sex.

The contemporary climate of antiblack racism and outrage is relevant to this discussion of black queer sexuality, erotica, and fantasy; the films analyzed in this essay exemplify ways that racial and sexual oppression and violence haunt black lesbian sexuality. In her article "Queer Sociality and Other Sexual Fantasies," Juana María Rodríguez suggests that sexual fantasy, in which racialized bodies are drawn into scenes of domination and subordination, shame, and objectification, may be generative and not simply reinscribe racial and sexual violence. Rodríguez challenges queer studies scholars to lean into the pleasure of "untamed erotics" and asks us to resist shying away from exploring the materiality of sexuality and the problematics of sex play and fantasy among racialized subjectivities.[2]

I take up Rodríguez's challenge by analyzing cinematic depictions of black lesbian fantasy, BDSM play, and sexual pleasure in Cheryl Dunye's hard-core lesbian porn *Mommy Is Coming* (2012), Campbell Ex's feature-length drama *Stud Life* (2012), and the short film *Bottom* (2013), directed by Chinonye Chukwu.[3] This discussion also attends to traumas of racialized sexual violence that are bound up within black women's sexuality and that appear as specters in these films. By examining cinematic representations of black lesbian sexual practice, pleasure, and exploration, I address ways that black queer women's sexuality is encumbered by the politics of visibility and silence. My analysis contends with the haunting presence of both historic and personal traumas that complicate sex, fantasy, and power play within the black lesbian community and make addressing the complexities seem impossible.

Kinky Queer Black Lesbian: Bottom/Top Erotics

During an interview with several prominent African American women scholars, Hortense Spillers remarks upon the impetus to write one of her foundational texts on black women's sexuality, "Interstices: A Small Drama of Words": "I thought, you know what, before I can get to the subject of the sexuality of black women I didn't see a vocabulary that would make it possible to entertain the sexuality of black women in any way that was other than traumatic. Before you could have a conversation about sexuality of black women you had to clear the static, clear the field of static."[4] Spillers's work, as well as the many African American women scholars who examine black womanhood and sexuality, have begun to clear the field of static that has interfered with and impeded discussions about black women's sexuality.[5] The representations of black lesbian sexuality and eroticism that I analyze also work to clear the field of static and visualize the materiality of black lesbian sex through the language of the cinematic. In "Interstices," Spillers asserts that, save for a few literary texts that address black women's sexuality, "Black women are the beached whales of the sexual universe, unvoiced, misseen, not doing, awaiting their verb. Their sexual experiences are depicted, but not often by them, and if and when by the subject herself, often in the guise of vocal music, often in the self-contained accent and sheer romance of the blues."[6]

The black lesbian erotica that I discuss reanimates the beached whales of the sexual universe with cinematic images, sounds, and narratives that contain blues notes but also strike dissonant chords with scenes that put histories of sexual and racial violence into play. Rather than working to free black lesbian sexuality from the legacy of sexual violence and trauma, the films discussed here operate on the plane of the erotic and engage with loss, trauma, and unspoken violence by creating scenarios in which black lesbian characters explore sexual domination and submission, pleasure and pain, as ecstatic modes that can release the trauma of sexual violence and racial oppression.[7] The approaches to visualizing black lesbian sexuality in the films by Dunye, Ex, and Chukwu differ in tone and narrative structure, yet in their cinematic treatment, these black women filmmakers offer a visual vocabulary that does not escape the trauma that haunts black women's desire and sexual practice but moves forcefully through it. As the scholarship on black women's sexuality continues to grow, perhaps trauma will no longer be a requisite threshold to cross, but these three films manage to advance the conversation by pushing boundaries of taboo and sexual fantasy and by enunciating erotic explorations of pleasure, pain, and release with their cinematic grammar.

Cheryl Dunye's hard-core feature-length porn film *Mommy Is Coming* casts the New York–based Black-Boricua porn star Papi Coxxx as the protagonist, Claudia/Claude, who becomes embroiled in an underground white, queer, German sex club.[8] The black British lesbian characters in *Stud Life* meet and fall in love one summer in London. JJ, who identifies as a stud, fills the dominant position when she learns of Elle's desire to experience pain while being bound and blindfolded. The short film *Bottom* captures an intense moment between black girlfriends in which one lover resists experiencing sex from the bottom and eventually convinces her top to assume the bottom position, and with this reversal the specter of trauma is revealed. Each one of these films' engagements with fantasy, sex play, and sexual power dynamics exposes ways that racial and sexual violence haunt black women's sexuality and offer excursions into and through trauma by way of the erotic.

Black feminist theorist and science historian Evelynn M. Hammonds asserts that black women's sexuality is like a void that is perpetually exposed, making black women's bodies "always already colonized."[9] Hammonds contextualizes her use of the void as a metaphor for black women's sexuality: "Historically, Black women have reacted to this repressive force of the hegemonic discourses on race and sex with silence, secrecy, and a partially self-chosen invisibility." Hammonds discusses "the politics of silence" and "the culture of dissemblance" that Reconstruction era black women reformers developed which embraced Victorian moral codes in order to dismantle the construction of black women as immoral and perpetually sexually available. The politics of silence urged black women not to discuss or display their sexuality so as to counter the damaging stereotypes that deemed them overly sexual and wanton, constructions that were used to justify sexual violence and terror during slavery and well after its abolition. As Hammonds asserts, this strategy failed because it developed a seemingly open and earnest expression of morality, but this culture actually made black women's sexuality invisible—the residual effects of which continue to circulate through black women's sexuality and circumvent black women's expressions of desire.[10]

Given the long history of stigmatization and repression that constructs black women as overly sexual while casting a veil over our own desire, the act of embracing black queer erotica can seem antithetical to the objectives that historic codes of behavior and more contemporary black feminist critiques of pornography have striven to achieve.[11] Yet in Dunye's, Ex's, and Chukwu's cinematic depictions of black queer sex play, the traumas that materialize are not debilitating but rather integral elements on the horizon of sexuality that insist on being addressed, engaged with, and passed through. Rodríguez's theorization of sexual practice and fantasy among queer people of color contends that having a history of racialized and sexual violence should not preclude queer people of color from exploring this form of intense sociality and bonding. She writes: "To deny our fantasies because they are too complicated, too painful, or too perverse, to erase their presence or censor their articulation in public life, constitutes a particular kind of insidious violence that threatens to undermine our ability to explore the contours of our psychic lives, and the imaginary possibilities of the social worlds in which we exist."[12]

Rodríguez's discussion of "the untamed erotics of multiply inflected power relations" that create new forms of sociality and bonding rather than pathologize bodies of color comes alive in Coxxx's role as Claude/Claudia in Dunye's *Mommy Is Coming*. This concept adds another fold into the complexity of the erotic as famously theorized by Audre Lorde, who distances the erotic from the pornographic in her deployment of the erotic, which she describes as sensuous power shared between women that is also held within a woman's own subjectivity.[13] Rodríguez's "untamed erotics" enables a discussion of tensions engendered by visualizing black lesbian sex acts. In her analysis of erotic fantasy among women of color, Rodríguez asserts that this kind of sex play "reveal[s] an intimacy with sexual objectification that is intrinsically linked to racialized and classed narratives of the coercive deployment of power. And core to the understanding and practice of communities of sexual play—including queer of color s/m communities—is the dialectic of master and slave, a racialized violation that retains its erotic charge regardless of the embodiment of its defined players."[14]

The problematics of sex play that Rodríguez addresses in queer of color communities are linked to the binds that ensnare black women in hard-core pornography. The work of black feminist scholars currently propelling the field of porn studies makes an intervention by centering black women's desire and pleasure as producers, consumers, and spectators of pornography. Jennifer C. Nash's *The Black Body in Ecstasy: Reading Race, Reading Pornography* and Mireille Miller-Young's *A Taste for Brown Sugar: Black Women in Pornography* are leading the field of black feminist porn studies with their decidedly different approaches to analyzing black women's experiences in and with pornography. While Nash conducts close readings of vintage hard-core porn films that feature black women from the Golden Age (1970s) and the Silver Age (1980s), Miller-Young has produced a history of black women porn producers by conducting interviews with them, along with analyses of erotic visual culture. While acknowledging the groundbreaking work produced by early feminist porn studies, Nash suggests that these analyses of hard-core pornography either overlook race and the eroticization of race entirely or reinforce black women as wounded sexual subjects. Nash contends that both antipornography feminist critiques and feminist scholarship that embraces sex positivity have discounted the pleasure derived by black women viewers of pornographic films.[15] Nash also pushes black feminist critiques of pornography with her reading practice of *racial iconography* that disrupts black feminism's focus on the injurious nature of pornography, arguing that even in nonpornographic imagery black feminism has used the pornographic as a rhetorical trope to describe the violently exploitative way that black women are visualized in culture.[16]

Both Nash and Miller-Young focus their analyses on straight porn films and only tangentially mention lesbian and gay porn. My analysis of hardcore pornography, BDSM, sex play, and fantasy in these films by black women directors contributes a discussion of black lesbian hard-core porn to black feminist porn studies scholarship that focuses on black women in hetero porn. My research introduces a sustained discussion of black lesbian sexuality and erotica into the discourse of black feminist porn studies while engaging with the history of masochism assembled in Amber Musser's *Sensational Flesh: Race, Power, and Masochism*.

Musser's historical analysis of S/M is sweeping in its attention to early sexological confessions of masochism, radical feminist critiques of pornography and S/M, and the relationship between masochism, patriarchy, and colonialism while also discussing the theoretical discourse that frames S/M as a site linked most legibly with white gay male subculture. Musser theorizes sensation and flesh as modes for perceiving and describing difference without fixing difference in place and thereby essentializing racialized experiences and identities. Musser's engagement with Elizabeth Freeman's discussion of S/M in *Time Binds: Queer Temporalities, Queer Histories* informs her "empathetic reading" practice that allows masochism to be understood as relational and foregrounds the flesh in the process of knowledge production.[17] Freeman's discussion of S/M emerges through her analysis of Isaac Julien's film *The Attendant*, in which she contextualizes sadomasochism through the Marquis de Sade and the French Revolution while attending to the specificity of racial violence and the master/slave play that Julien visualizes in this film.[18] While Julien's *The Attendant* materializes the specter of racial slavery in BDSM scenes involving black and white men through the cinematic device of the tableau vivant of F. A. Biard's 1840 painting *The Slave Trade*, the cinescape that Dunye creates in *Mommy Is Coming* is seemingly color-blind—the characters move through the space without any regard for race or the legacy of racial violence that simmers within the sex play scenes that feature Papi Coxxx.[19]

Entering the Dungeon

Mommy Is Coming stages scenes that tacitly enact the problematics of race and power—scenes that visualize the master and slave dialectic and call up dystopic legacies of sexual violence. Unlike Julien's *The Attendant*, Dunye's cinematic work of erotica resists addressing the vulnerability to racial state power and the history of racial violence in which the protagonist is immersed. In this explicit sex caper comedy, Papi Coxxx embodies the dual personas of the protagonist by playing the tough yet sensitive Claudia, who in certain sexual situations dons a moustache and changes demeanor to become the tough yet sensitive Claude. Through Coxxx's embodiment of the gender binary Claudia/Claude, she represents their black/brown, queer, masculine body—an embodiment that undoubtedly amplifies the intensity and perversity of the hard-core BDSM scenes in this film. Claudia/Claude's racialized body performing sexual fantasies raises the specter of chattel slavery that exoticizes their attractiveness and capitalizes on the trope of the hyperviolent black masculine body, but the history of racial violence and fraught contemporary racial dynamics are not made explicit in the film's narrative or the mise-en-scène. In the opening scene of *Mommy Is Coming*, Claudia jumps into the back seat of a cab next to her blond German girlfriend, Dylan. Claudia pulls a gun out of her backpack, slides a condom on it then fucks Dylan with it all over the backseat of the cab. After Claudia whips Dylan into a frenzy making her cum hard, with the cab driver getting turned on looking at them through the rearview mirror, Dylan wants to top Claudia with the prophylactic-adorned firearm.[20] Claudia refuses to allow Dylan to penetrate her. Disappointed with Claudia's refusal, Dylan callously breaks up with Claudia then kicks her out of the cab.[21]

After this blowup with Dylan, Claudia becomes embroiled in an underground queer sex club. Claudia, who moves through this narrative world as "Claude" part of the time, soon finds himself in a dark, seedy sex dungeon that seems to swallow him up. The windowless cold stone basement is crawling with lovers at different stages of pleasure, pain, and climax. Claude spies a trans man deep-fisting a woman who roars with delight. His partner then returns the release by sucking him off while he is perched in a leather swing. Claude moves through the space as, unbeknownst to him, a couple on the prowl for a third checks him out. The bare-chested German butch introduces her trans boyfriend, Tory, who dons a leather vest and cap. She asks Claude if he is "feeling superior" then tells him that he could learn something from them. Tory lays Claude down on his back then glides on a black latex glove. Tory slides his fist and forearm deep into Claude pounding him with escalating speed. As he is being jolted into ecstasy, Claude repeatedly utters, "Thank you, sir." The butch girlfriend kisses Claude while Tory bangs Claude into climax. The pair flips Claude over onto his hands and knees; then Tory brings out the black leather cat-o'-nine-tails and lashes Claude, relatively gently, across his bare ass. Claude repeats the mantra "Thank you, sir" until the couple decides that Claude has had enough. The pair leaves Claude spent and satisfied on the floor of the sex dungeon.

Witnessing Claude willingly submit to Tory and his butch girlfriend, after Claudia expressed discomfort and refused to be penetrated by Dylan in the taxicab scene, forces an array of contentious racial and gender problematics to surface. As Claude, this character is open to being fucked, can enjoy bottoming, can embrace his own masochism in the sex dungeon; yet, as Claudia, this character refuses to be penetrated. It seems that occupying a masculine position creates the space for Claude not only to handle but also to relish being vigorously and forcefully topped, so much so that he incessantly thanks his dominator.[22] I am curious about the way this character's masculinity is coincident with their masochistic interest in BDSM play and his ecstatic experience of the bottom. As Musser has explicated, radical feminists have vilified s/m along with the use of dildos for denying women's agency and perpetrating violence by reproducing patriarchy, colonialism, and white supremacy.[23] Through Judith Butler's analysis of the subversive potential of the lesbian phallus accessed by using an arm or a pelvis or a tongue—acts that decouple the phallus from masculinity—Musser opens up a discussion about the phallus and the dildo as "bridging the distance between masculine and feminine that allows for the subversion."[24] Claude's masochistic masculinity both reproduces and unravels radical feminists' anxiety over S/M and the phallus. Claudia's refusal to be penetrated is in concert with radical feminist ideals of protecting women's spaces and bodies from penises or penis-like surrogates—although Dylan's delight in being fucked with Claudia's gun exemplifies the submission to sadistic violence that radical feminists denounced.

By equating penetration with masculinity and resisting BDSM sex play and fantasy, radical feminists reproduce a homonormative expectation of lesbian sex and gender performance. Claude's relenting to S/M seduction and his submission to Tory's deep German fist unsettles limiting homonormative gender separation and mixes in the complexity of gender, the corporeal cooperation of woman and man, and the mystification of gender. This BDSM ménage à trois scene does not allow the separation of masculine and feminine to be defined by the penis or the fist. The erotics of the bottom for Claude are a complex of gender subversion as a top and a foray in unnamed race play that is left up to the viewer to tap into. Through the intensity of moving beyond a resistance to penetration into an oasis of titillation and release, the trauma of historic racial violence is embarked upon and passed through in this scene. The untamed erotics of this multiply inflected master/slave dialectic are perverse and unspoken, yet in this sensual performance of domination and submission that reproduces phallic gender power and white dominance in a safe space, Claude opens up to the racialized and gendered fantasy and gives over to the experience of discomfort, fear, pleasure, and catharsis—and the viewer is able to voyeuristically join in on the play.

The images of Claudia's queer body of color working a gun inside of a white woman's body and then later Claude being dominated by a white German couple wearing slick leather bondage gear are laden with racial tropes and racist power dynamics. The anxiety that black masculinity will defile white women's purity, which has propelled the white power structure to torture and kill black people, saturates the taxicab scene by reproducing the violent brown/black aggressor image through Claudia's use of the gun as a cock. The racial dynamics of the BDSM dungeon ménage à trois scene bring to mind enslaved bodies that had to submit to their owner's sexual desire as they buried their resistance to the violation, which may well have included a performance of gratitude.[25] The presence of the master/slave dialectic that appears through the positionality of

Claude and Tory coupled with the image of a top, who is uncomfortable with being topped, getting fucked into submission by a German couple compounds the disparity of power between them. Despite the disconcerting images that bring to mind slave-era sexual violence in this scene, the actor Papi Coxxx and the character Claudia/Claude are choosing to be submissive and are experiencing pleasure in that submission. As charged and complex as this scene is with racial violence entangled with sexual pleasure, visualizing Papi Coxxx in ecstasy as Claude and deriving pleasure from witnessing Claude's seduction loosens some of the traumatic historic knots that have foreclosed visualizing black erotic possibilities.

The characters in *Mommy Is Coming* seem completely unaware of the racial implications embedded within their sexual escapades, which leaves blank spaces in the story around race and sex in this film. This narrative and directorial choice avoids having to contend with historic and contemporary complexities of black and white bodies engaging in erotic sex play and BDSM. Dunye's casting of Papi Coxxx, a black Boricua genderqueer switch, as Claude/Claudia makes their body the only black or brown body engaging in sex in the film. Dunye's colorblind approach to visualizing Coxxx's body of color in a sea of white kink forces audience members to make sense of the racialized sexual dynamics in the film by drawing from their own experiences and perceptions of race, rather than out of the narrative and the character's experiences of race and power. Despite Dunye's lack of attention in this film to the complications and tensions that arise from the racially charged position that Claude occupies while being fisted and then whipped for pleasure by a masculine white body, these scenes recall histories of sexual violence embedded within the master/slave dialectic.[26]

I am not suggesting that erotica with black performers needs to incorporate expositional narrative devices that address race, but I do contend that part of the fantasy of Dunye's film lies in producing a world in which race does not have weight or a violent history that impacts the characters in her film. Claudia/Claude's sexual body of color in an otherwise white cinematic landscape does not emerge in the narrative or become an acknowledged part of the power dynamics of BDSM play that the characters bring to life in their scenes.

In *The Black Body in Ecstasy*, Jennifer Nash moves the discussion of black women in pornography away from considering only the damage that porn can inflict upon black women's bodies and sexual lives, toward a consideration of *ecstasy* that can "capture forms of racial-sexual pleasure that have heretofore been unnamed (and some that have been too taboo to name), including blissful performances of hyperbolic racialization and uncomfortable enjoyment in embodied racialization."[27] As both Nash and Rodríguez have described, race is part of sex play, and as perverse and challenging as that may be, the field of sex enables historic and personal racial-sexual trauma to be explored, eroticized, and embodied. Even though the characters in *Mommy Is Coming* do not acknowledge how race impacts their desire or their fantasies, race is part of the kink that is in play in this film.

This sex dungeon scene raises questions about whether visualizing a black body choosing to occupy a submissive position and receiving glowing satisfaction from this positionality subverts the specter of sexual violence suffered during chattel slavery or reinforces black sexuality as perversely able to withstand pain.[28] Certainly, the answers to such questions are subjective and probably include an amalgam of pleasure achieved through subversion and reinforcement of centuries-old racial tropes. The film spectator occupies a position of power by resting safely outside the complexities of the scene.[29] A film like Dunye's not only implicates the subjects engaging in explicit sex on screen but also ensnares viewers who are being titillated or repulsed, or some combination of both, as they watch a racially congested erotic fantasy unfold before them. Thinking along with Nash, I suggest that pleasure is experienced in looking and in performing racially charged sexually explicit scenes, and forcefully occupying positions of domination and submission enables an ecstatic release for the players and the viewers.[30] The pleasure derived from watching a scene like this is mitigated by one's relationship to the trauma of chattel slavery and sexual submission, as well as having the ability to detach images of a white body dominating a black body in erotic sex play from the material reality of that history.

Even though the untamed erotics found in the underground queer sex club taps into a history of slave era sexual violence, the cinematic representation of Papi Coxxx's body producing erotica works to destabilize racial tropes that perpetuate commonsense understandings of black sexuality. In *The Witch's Flight*, Kara Keeling not only conceptualizes the cinematic as proper to celluloid or digital imagery but also considers the cinematic a process through which the world is perceived.[31] Keeling conceives of common sense and its imbrication with the cinematic as not producing universal truths but rather as "the condition of possibility for the emergence of alternate knowledges that are capable of organizing social life and existence in various ways, some of which might constitute a counterhegemonic force."[32] In her discussion of the effort required to perceive cinematic reality and contend with commonsense understandings, Keeling uses the term *affectivity* "to mark the way that a living being's interactions with other images involves a form of labor that has to do with affect, with those sensations and feelings that carve out a subjective perception in things but that cannot be divorced from the mental operations required to make sense of the world."[33] As Keeling notes, perception requires effort, and viewing the world differently from what is suggested by common sense demands an enormous amount of affective labor. Both Keeling and Rodríguez propose new ways of organizing social life in their respective conceptions of common sense, the cinematic, and erotic sex play in queer communities of color. Drawing together the theories of Keeling, Nash, and Rodríguez forges new pathways of seeing and being, which unseat dominant knowledges that shape the perception of black queer sexuality.

Images of Claudia/Claude exploring their sexuality in *Mommy Is Coming* create new ways of seeing black queer sex. New forms of sociality that deviate from commonsense understandings of blackness and black women's sexuality are represented in the dungeon scene, which suggests that queer black sexuality can afford to participate in healthy exciting sexual exploration that plays around with taboo racial power dynamics. Expectations of black comportment inhibit sexual exploration and reinforce the idea that black sexuality is not commensurate with the culture of kink. Rodríguez poses the question, "So how do we begin to make sense of our politically incorrect erotic desires?"[34] Coxxx's performance in the ménage à trois scene reimagines the master/slave dialectic and provides catharsis for the players and perhaps the audience as well. The affective labor required to witness this transgression of politically correct black sexual practice destabilizes commonsense understandings of black sex by placing a black queer body at the center of the mostly white world of kinky sexual exploration.

In a 2010 interview recorded two years before the filming of *Mommy Is Coming*, Papi Coxxx discusses the problematic way that queer people of color are not visible in kinky spaces but insists that these kinds of bodies do exist in queer erotic settings; Coxxx's performances in queer porn bolster the presence of people of color in this genre of erotica.[35] The perception that black and brown bodies do not engage in kinky queer sex culture avoids having to contend with the messiness of racialized power dynamics imbricated within sexuality. If, as Rodríguez suggests, untamed erotics create new forms of sociality and bonding that move past pathology toward freedom of sexual expression, then Claude's erotic abandon in the queer sex club carries histories of sexual exploitation and the politics of silence into ecstatic pleasure. Claude's sexual agency as well as the experience of pleasure and satisfaction visualized in this scene adds some building blocks of cinematic grammar to the lexicon of black queer sexuality, but not without being routed through trauma.

Tapping the Trauma

Beyond the immediate cinematic reminiscence of plantation-era sexual violence that images of black queer kink conjures lies an abyss of politically incorrect erotic exploration and fantasy that has the potential to release the pain of historical trauma through its confrontation with it. Drawing another film directed by a queer black filmmaker into the discussion, we can consider the ways that trauma emerges in Campbell Ex's *Stud Life*, which visualizes black lesbian sexual exploration with BDSM. The tangled love story that courses through Ex's film is fertile ground for an examination of personal unspoken trauma that surfaces through intimacy and sexual bonding. Although the field of trauma studies is dominated by psychoanalytic approaches to understanding the impact of the Holocaust on survivors, Jewish diaspora theories of trauma and repetition offer ways of discussing both historic and personal trauma that impact black queer sexuality, making explorations into erotic fantasy and sex play difficult to engage with or find generative.[36]

In *Unclaimed Experiences: Trauma, Narrative, and History*, Cathy Caruth relies heavily on Freudian psychoanalysis in her discussion of trauma, the etymology of which she traces back to the Greek word meaning "wound."[37] Trauma has come to be understood as a wound of the mind or psyche rather than simply a physical wound.[38] What is most interesting for the purposes of this discussion of the representation of trauma and black queer sexuality in cinema is the aspect of trauma that has to do with repetition. Through Freud, Caruth theorizes repetition as an element of the traumatic experience, asserting that trauma happens in repetition. The initial act of violence or terror does not register as trauma; reliving and repeating that event or events is where the trauma is felt.[39]

In *Stud Life*, the protagonist, JJ, is a gorgeous stud who meets Elle, a stunning West Indian femme, at a queer night club. They later reconnect at a wedding party where JJ is working as a photographer. The chemistry between JJ and Elle is undeniable, and they quickly fall head over heels for each other. One evening when passion is running hot, Elle asks JJ to slap her. JJ is reluctant and worries that she will hurt Elle, but Elle assures JJ that she likes it. The intimacy between them grows, and JJ becomes quite curious about Elle's occupation, a topic that Elle has avoided revealing until this point. Elle introduces JJ to this personal aspect of her life by asking JJ to retrieve a box from her bedroom; the box contains rope, a knife, a blindfold, and a whip. Elle encourages JJ to use them. JJ binds Elle to a chair and blindfolds her then runs the knife along Elle's smooth soft skin, letting the cool metal point press into her cheek and arms. JJ cuts a strap on the teddy that Elle is wearing. Elle begins to cry, JJ stops, but Elle asks her to continue. After this session, as Elle and JJ cuddle on the floor, Elle reveals her work. She tells JJ that she is a dominatrix and sells the fantasy of a dominating black woman to white men. Elle assures JJ that she never lets men do to her what JJ just did. JJ is unprepared and ill-equipped to handle this revelation; she feels betrayed and does not understand how Elle could consider herself a lesbian while being sexual with men for a living. JJ raises herself up from the floor and gathers her things to leave. Elle becomes intensely emotional, sobbing deeply, pleading for JJ to stay, but JJ cannot spend another moment in Elle's presence. JJ leaves and Elle collapses, broken and defeated.

The representation of sexual power in *Stud Life* has different racial dynamics than in *Mommy Is Coming*, because both JJ and Elle are black with West Indian backgrounds. The power dynamics and histories of violence that surface between white and black characters in Dunye's film are not present in *Stud Life*, but what does emerge in Ex's feature film, and the focus of my analysis of this scene, is Elle's wound. I turn again to Keeling, who contends that "the black femme's cinematic appearance might force hegemonic common senses to make space and time for something new."[40] The figure of the black femme who is visualized with Ex's character Elle disrupts commonsense understandings of black lesbians as being uninterested in or resistant to kink or BDSM—a conception directly related to the culture of silence that has historically obfuscated black women's sexual desire. Visualizing kinky black queer women opens up a space in which submission, domination, and sexual fantasy are able to release emotion and pleasure, but not without a sojourn through trauma.

Elle's sexual history and suffering exists in the subtext of the film, and the cavernous sorrow that erupts with JJ's departure points to trauma that is accessed in the reinflicting of her wound. The tears Elle sheds when she gives up control to JJ while being blindfolded and tied to a chair allow her to connect, through submission, to a reservoir of grief that she needs to release. Elle's reluctance to reveal her life as a sex worker is understandable; she waited to share this intimate detail with JJ until she felt that she could trust her, a trust that JJ betrayed. Elle's choice to withhold this aspect of her sexual life created a sense of betrayal and repulsion in JJ, who, as a result, left Elle alone on the floor in her teddy with her trauma and her grief. JJ's inability to love Elle with the knowledge that she is a sex worker exposes the patriarchal possession that JJ felt toward Elle; JJ could not love Elle knowing that Elle gave pleasure to others for a living. JJ's refusal to accept the entirety of Elle's sexual landscape triggers a well of emotion in Elle that appears to be old and deep and hovering just beneath the surface. Elle's wound is reopened by JJ's abandonment, but the initial blow, the originary wound, was clearly dealt long ago. Elle is left with a sorrow that holds within it an unspoken grief in the realm of the sexual. The erotic charge of submitting to a trusted lover enables Elle to tap into prior loss and pain, without having to locate or define the source. The kinky sex play as well as JJ's callous abandonment reignite feelings attached to an undisclosed tragic something that happened before. Through fantasy and sexual submission, Elle re-creates a sensation that makes room for her to experience and release trauma that is unspecified in the narrative but nonetheless palpable in this character. Visualizing black women experiencing sexual pleasure, achieving control in the realm of the erotic through explorations with pain and submission, or accessing frightening quarters of their psyches in which personal trauma and historic violence lives clears the field of static that infiltrates black women's sexuality. That Ex's and Dunye's films both visualize black queer women's erotica and sex play in Europe raises questions about the ability to produce such images within a U.S. context.[41]

The field of sexual desire and fantasy within the United States and abroad is laden with the risk of violating restrictions imposed by the politics of respectability and taboos of race and power. The short film *Bottom*, which is set in the United States, is able to visualize the dynamics of power that protect or expose vulnerabilities to dominant or submissive positionalities in sex. *Bottom* captures an intimate moment between two black girlfriends who engage in a playful exchange of role reversals, each working to take the dominant position on top. They roll around in bed and kiss while negotiating who will be on the bottom. In the end, after some struggle, the girlfriend who usually lands on top relents and takes the bottom position. She crawls onto her hands and knees and asks her girlfriend to get "the thing." Her girlfriend complies and straps on the dildo. Something comes over the bottom upon penetration; she becomes agitated and upset. She uses her hands and knees to forcefully push her body back into her girlfriend who enthusiastically fucks her from behind. The girlfriend on the bottom moans with pleasure but then her cries become intense, and a kind of panicked sobbing overtakes any excitement present in this moment between them.

Unlike Elle's obfuscated wounds in *Stud Life*, a more specified originary traumatic event of sexual violence can be imagined here—an act of incest, date rape, or another kind of violent sexual assault emerges as a specter in this scene. The girlfriend who normally lands on top, who does not usually enjoy penetration, allows her girlfriend to fuck her, and this act of being penetrated opens up a personal wound, and within that space also exists a looming historical suffering. The presence of the trauma that haunts black women's sexuality from chattel slavery to the Jim Crow era, to the Reagan era, to this moment materializes through the practice of sex. The embodied knowledge of historic trauma coupled with personal trauma and sexual violence makes excising the pain of these events through spoken language and the written word daunting and at times impossible. The realm of the erotic produces the space, and playing with dominance and submission between girlfriends is the terrain upon which unspeakable trauma is invited to appear, to be witnessed, and perhaps to be released.

The untamed erotics that permeate Chukwu's *Bottom* emerge in a scene created with the vision of a black woman director between black lesbian characters. The physical reversal of the lover who usually tops and her coercion into taking the bottom position electrifies the field of static of which Spillers spoke. The unrelenting cinematic gaze rather than the minor chords of the blues becomes the landscape upon which black women's sexuality can be discussed, yet this cinematic depiction of black lesbian sexuality does not avoid trauma—trauma is the climax. *Bottom* clears the traumatic field of static that encumbers black women's sexuality by barreling directly into it and through it. Visualizing the sensual pleasure and arousal between these black women lovers as it slowly slips into a discordant act of violent awakening looses the beached whales of the sexual universe. The sounds that emanate from this reanimated state are cavernous cries for losses never grieved and wounds never acknowledged, let alone healed. The action, the verb between these women, commands that the monsters that lurk from the bottom and between the sheets be faced squarely and laid bare. The courage that is summoned in the safe space of their bed wrests the trauma from the unnamed shadowy place through the strokes being levied by the one who wields "the thing." The realm of the erotic entices the bottom to push past her own rigid, safeguarded position on top into the shut-out parts of her sexuality. Through the erotic, the bottom is jolted into her hurt place, and she rides that wake of emotion as it is coaxed out into the light by her lover, at this time, with this thing. Pleasure, play, and pain make this release possible.

Conclusion

Black queer lesbian bodies engaging in hard-core pornography or bondage play or struggling with being on top are all inevitably burdened with racial violence and histories of sexual exploitation. Reenacting wounds of historical proportion while exposing personal experiences of racialized and sexual violence through erotic fantasy, role reversals, and sex play disrupts codes of silence and dissemblance that have historically been used to protect black women.[42] Even though the notion of black queer cinematic erotica is diametrically opposed to public strategies used to protect and achieve equality for black women, these films do acknowledge psychic and sexual wounds of unspeakable rage and intangible loss by using the realm of erotica to engage with trauma through repetition and release.

Dunye, Ex, and Chukwu each enunciate black lesbian sexual practices and release trauma by producing black queer erotica. The work of the black queer women directors discussed in this essay viscerally demonstrates that cinema is a productive forum through which to make sense of our racially charged and sexually perverse erotic desires. The fields of sexuality and sexual practice, when embraced as spaces of possibility and exploration, become the realm through which grief, pleasure, sorrow, ecstasy, abandonment, and reunion coalesce to produce new ways of seeing, being, and being seen. The racialized, violated wound that has encumbered black women's sexuality and desire is worked through in Ex's feature-length drama and Chukwu's short film, but it makes no appearance in Dunye's comedic porn film. As is consistent with Nash's assertion in *The Black Body in Ecstasy*, it seems that pornography is the cinematic genre in which explicit sexual acts are not always encumbered by a need to process racial and sexual violence. This is the fantasy represented in porn, that sex can be had and pleasure can be achieved without needing to contend with racial or sexual violence; the unspoken history of violence produces the erotics of porn.

The affective labor required to actively engage with black lesbian erotica demands relenting to the fantasy of sexual pleasure unimpeded by racialized sexual violence, while also building the capacity to contend with histories of sexual trauma and the palimpsestic images of chattel slavery that appear in scenes of BDSM, sex play, and fantasy within queer communities of color. Disaggregating kink from whiteness and embracing kinky queerness within black lesbian and genderqueer communities of color expand the horizon of sexual possibility. Fantasy and sex play depend on clear communication and sexual agency, both of which bolster ownership of one's queer erotic embodiment as well as shed the residue of sexual exploitation and trauma. Lesbian and genderqueer partners of color who engage in sex play and power erotica, on- and offscreen, carve out spaces in which exploration replaces shame and kink reconnects the silenced with their voices in ways that make pleasure a mode of liberation, loosing stuck, hurt places from the shadows of our sexual selves into the realm of the erotic.

NOTES

1. Since I began writing this article, antiblack violence perpetrated by the police has escalated. In response to the murders of unarmed black men at the hands of police, a nationwide movement, #BlackLivesMatter, founded by Alicia Garza, Patrisse Cullors, and Opal Tometi, has grown to end police brutality and to hold the police accountable for the murders they committed. Mike Brown in St. Louis, Missouri; Eric Garner in Staten Island, New York, New York; Ezell Ford in Los Angeles, California; John Crawford in Beavercreek, Ohio; Tamir Rice in Cleveland, Ohio; Walter Scott in North Charleston, South Carolina; Freddie Gray in Baltimore, Maryland; and Sandra Bland in Waller County, Texas, were each unarmed when they were killed by the police. To date, grand juries have refused to bring indictments against the police officers who killed Mike Brown and Eric Garner, and no criminal charges have been filed for the murders of Ezell Ford and John Crawford. Michael Slager has been indicted for the murder of Walter Scott. Six police offers were indicted for misconduct, illegal arrest, assault, and involuntary manslaughter as a result of the violence that they inflicted on Freddie Gray, which killed him while he was in their custody. Brian Encina, the officer who arrested and assaulted Sandra Bland, was not charged for her death or assault but with perjury, to which he pleaded not guilty. One of the officers who shot Ezell Ford was found to have acted against policy, but the punishment has yet to be determined. Outrage over systemic violence, police murders, and the refusal of grand juries to bring indictments against police officers who have killed black people

produced civil unrest in St. Louis and in Baltimore, and has spawned coordinated actions in cities across the country.

2. Juana María Rodríguez, "Queer Sociality and Other Sexual Fantasies," *GLQ: A Journal of Lesbian and Gay Studies* 17 (2011): 343.

3. Cheryl Dunye, dir., *Mommy Is Coming* (GM Films, 2012); Campbell X, dir., *Stud Life* (Wolf Video, 2013); Chinonye Chukwu, dir., *Bottom* (2013).

4. Hortense Spillers was interviewed in 2007 by leading African American women scholars; see "'Whatcha Gonna Do?'": Revisiting 'Mama's Baby, Papa's Maybe: An American Grammar Book': A Conversation with Hortense Spillers, Saidiya Hartman, Farah Griffin, Shelly Eversley, and Jennifer L. Morgan," *Women's Studies Quarterly* 35, nos. 1–2 (Spring/Summer 2007): 301.

5. Since Spillers published these articles, African American women scholars have produced work that has significantly opened up discussions about black women's sexuality, including but not limited to Kara Keeling, *The Witch's Flight: The Cinematic, the Black Femme, and the Image of Common Sense* (Durham, NC: Duke University Press, 2007); Christina Sharpe, *Monstrous Intimacies: Making Post-Slavery Black Subjects* (Durham, NC: Duke University Press, 2010); and Jennifer Morgan, *Laboring Women: Reproduction and Gender in New World Slavery* (Philadelphia: University of Pennsylvania Press, 2004). Roderick Ferguson's *Aberrations in Black: Toward a Queer of Color Critique* (Minneapolis: University of Minnesota Press, 2004) and *Black Queer Studies: A Critical Anthology* (Durham, NC: Duke University Press, 2005), edited by E. Patrick Johnson and Mae G. Henderson, are also fundamental texts that forward discussions of black queer sexuality. Jennifer C. Nash's *The Black Body in Ecstasy: Reading Race, Reading Pornography* (Durham, NC: Duke University Press, 2014) and Mireille Miller-Young's *A Taste for Brown Sugar: Black Women in Pornography* (Durham, NC: Duke University Press, 2014) push the discourse of black women's sexuality to attend to explicit sexual practices in pornography; I will discuss these texts later in this essay.

6. Hortense Spillers, "Interstices: A Small Drama of Words" in *Black White and In Color: Essays on American Literature and Culture* (Chicago: University of Chicago Press, 2003), 153.

7. My use of the "erotic" and "erotica" signals sexually explicit fantasy and sensual visualizations of sex play and is informed by Juana María Rodríguez's concept of "untamed erotics" that I engage throughout this paper. I also discuss "the erotic" as theorized by Audre Lorde in her article "Uses of the Erotic: The Erotic as Power," which is a decidedly different conception of the term; Lorde's erotic is more of a spiritual knowledge rather than an explicitly sexual expression; see "Uses of the Erotic: The Erotic as Power," in *Sister Outsider: Essays and Speeches*, 53–59 (Freedom, CA: Crossing Press, 1984).

8. Papi Coxxx, also known as Ignacio Rivera, identifies as queer and two-spirit. Rivera's preferred gender pronoun is they. Rivera is a performance artist, porn star, sex worker, and sex educator. They have produced play parties throughout the United States and abroad that provide spaces for queer and trans people of color to explore kink, BDSM, masturbation, and sex play.

9. See Evelynn M. Hammond, "Black (W)holes and the Geometry of Black Female Sexuality," in *Feminism Meets Queer Theory*, eds. Elizabeth Weed and Naomi Schor (Bloomington: Indiana University Press, 1997), 262.

10. Hammond, "Black (W)holes and the Geometry of Black Women's Sexuality," 263–64. The concept of "the politics of silence" is explained and critically engaged by Evelyn Brooks Higginbotham in her article "African-American Women's History and the Metalanguage of Race," *Signs* 17, no. 2 (1992): 251–74. Higginbotham also discusses "the politics of respectability," a term that is linked to "the politics of silence," in her *Righteous Discontent: The Women's Movement in the Black Church, 1880–1920* (Cambridge, MA: Harvard University Press, 1993). "The culture of dissemblance" is examined by Darlene Clark Hine in "Rape and the Inner Lives of Black Women: Thoughts on the Culture of Dissemblance," in *Hine Sight: Black Women and the Re-construction of American History* (Bloomington: Indiana University Press, 1994).

11. In *The Black Body in Ecstasy*, Nash offers an incisive and generous critique of black feminism's deep resistance and condemnation of visualizing black women's sexuality through pornographic images and films.

12. Rodríguez, "Queer Sociality and Other Sexual Fantasies," 343.

13. Rodríguez, "Queer Sociality and Other Sexual Fantasies," 339; Lorde, "Uses of the Erotic," 53–54.

14. Rodríguez, "Queer Sociality and Other Sexual Fantasies," 342.

15. Nash, *Black Body in Ecstasy*, 19–20.

16. Nash, *Black Body in Ecstasy*, 6–7.

17. Musser, *Sensational Flesh: Race, Power, and Masochism* (New York: New York University Press, 2014), 21–22. Darieck Scott's *Extravagant Abjection: Blackness, Power, and Sexuality in the African American Literary Imagination* (New York: New York University Press, 2010) includes a chapter on BDSM, antiblack racism, and gay male pornographic writing that analyzes Samuel Delany's *The Mad Man*. Scott also theorizes Frantz Fanon's discussion of blackness and tensed muscles in *Black Skin, White Masks*, which Amber Musser picks up in *Sensational Flesh*. Whereas Musser uses "S&M," I have chosen to use "S/M" throughout this chapter.

18. Isaac Julien's *The Attendant* takes place in a museum in London and brings to life a canvas that depicts the slave market, F. A. Biard's 1840 painting *The Slave Trade*. A black museum worker, the attendant, and a white museumgoer, the visitor, enact BDSM scenes that involve a host of vibrant, seductive characters.

19. Baird's painting has two other titles: *Scene on the Coast of Africa* and *Slaves on the West Coast of Africa*.

20. The director of the film, Cheryl Dunye, appears in a few scenes as the cab driver and never engages in sexual performances.

21. In *Sensational Flesh*, 39–45, Amber Musser offers a brief history of the relationship between radical feminism, butch bodies, and S/M in which radical lesbians of the 1970s and 1980s find dildos inextricably linked to patriarchy and domination and accuse lesbians who incorporate dildos and the phallus into their sex lives of willingly submitting to patriarchy.

22. Musser links the protectionist stance taken by radical feminists against S/M and their critiques that contend S/M inflicts domination between women on each other by reproducing patriarchy through the use of erotic power play, pain, and the phallus with Frantz Fanon's indictment of colonialism, racism, and masochism that is rooted in white America's sadistic systemic assault against black men (*Sensational Flesh*, 45–48).

23. Musser, *Sensational Flesh*, 39–42.

24. Musser, *Sensational Flesh*, 42–43.

25. In *Scenes of Subjection: Terror, Slavery, and Self-Making in Nineteenth-Century America* (New York: Oxford University Press, 1997), Saidiya Hartman examines performances of pleasure that slaveholders forced enslaved people to participate in. These performances were a way to bolster the slave owner's position of power and to produce a fantasy that enslaved people were actually experiencing pleasure in their positions of enslavement.

26. African American scholars who approach the subject from several different fields have examined the sexual violence, physical torture, and emotional suffering that black women lived through during U.S. chattel slavery. In *Ar'n't I a Woman? Female Slaves in the Plantation South* (New York: W. W. Norton, 1999), historian Deborah Gray White discusses the impact of plantation life on enslaved women in the South, including the sexual violence and physical torture that enslaved black women had to suffer. In *Out of the House of Bondage: The Transformation of the Plantation Household* (Cambridge: Cambridge University Press, 2008), Thavolia Glymph examines the relationship between enslaved and slaveholding women during chattel slavery. In "Reflections on the Black Woman's Role in the Community of Slaves," in *Words of Fire: An Anthology of Black Feminist Thought*, ed. Beverly Guy-Sheftall (New York: The New Press, 1995), Angela Davis makes an intervention into scholarship on slavery by focusing on the role of black women.

27. Nash, *Black Body in Ecstasy*, 2–3. Until this point I have been using *ecstasy* to describe a euphoric feeling achieved through sex play and erotic dynamics visualized

in hard-core porn. Nash's concept of ecstasy attends to the "racial-sexual pleasure" that I have been addressing in my analysis of *Mommy Is Coming*.

28. In *Scenes of Subjection* Saidiya Hartman theorizes the black enslaved body as being perceived as a pained body deserving punishment. She discusses the perverse pleasure slaveholders derived from inflicting pain upon black bodies who had to sing and dance in deference to the slave owners in pastoral antebellum settings as well as perform happiness and docility on the auction block for their masters.

29. The field of reception studies contends with issues of voyeurism and spectatorship. Cultural studies developed out of an impetus to study the impact of media on mass culture. Theodor W. Adorno and Max Horkheimer's "The Culture Industry: Enlightenment as Mass Deception" (in *Media and Cultural Studies: Keyworks*, eds. Meenakshi Gigi Durham and Douglass M. Kellner, 41–72 [New York: Blackwell, 2006]) and Stuart Hall's *Representation: Cultural Representations and Signifying Practices* (London: Sage Publications, 1997) are but two defining texts in the field. Many other cultural studies theorists and film historians have written extensively about reception and mass consumption of media. In her foundational article "Visual Pleasure and Narrative Cinema" (in *Feminism and Film Theory*, ed. Constance Penley, 46–57 [New York: Routledge, 1988]), Laura Mulvey theorizes the scopophilic cinematic gaze from a feminist perspective. In *Migrating to the Movies: Cinema and Black Urban Modernity* (Berkeley: University of California Press, 2005), Jacqueline Stewart focuses on black experiences watching movies and presenting blackness in public urban spaces.

30. Nash, *Black Body in Ecstasy*, 3.

31. In *Selections from the Prison Notebooks* (ed. and trans. Quintin Hoare and Geoffrey Nowell Smith [New York: International Publishers, 1971]), Italian theorist Antonio Gramsci outlines elements of hegemony, which include the notion of common sense. Common sense is an axiomatic understanding of the ways things are or should be that is part of the hegemonic process of coercion and consent that exacts power over subordinate people and communities. Gramsci's theories of hegemony and common sense are integral to Kara Keeling's discussion of black lesbian visibility, images of the black femme, and black queer women's sexuality in cinema in her text *The Witch's Flight*. Keeling's work also engages with Deleuze's theories of cinema, sensory perception, time, and memory to conceptualize the cinematic as a way of perceiving the world that structures how we see race, gender, and sexuality.

32. Keeling, *Witch's Flight*, 19.

33. Keeling, *Witch's Flight*, 24.

34. Rodríguez, "Queer Sociality and Other Sexual Fantasies," 342.

35. The 2010 queerporn.tv interview with Ignacio Rivera (aka Papi Coxxx) can be accessed at http://www.youtube.com/watch?v=EXFDabsdCHQ. Coxxx also discusses

how they consider their work as a queer-trans-identified person of color in the media a form of community building that offers support to other queer and trans people of color who want to explore sex play and fantasy.

36. Some foundational texts in the field of memory and trauma studies are Nicholas Abraham and Maria Torok, *The Shell and the Kernel: Renewals of Psychoanalysis* (Chicago: University of Chicago Press, 1994); Maurice Halbwachs, *On Collective Memory*, ed. and trans. Lewis A. Coser (Chicago: University of Chicago Press, 1992); Henri Bergson, *Matter and Memory* (New York: Cosimo Classics, [1912] 2007); Dominick LaCapra, *Representing the Holocaust: History, Theory, Trauma* (Ithaca, NY: Cornell University Press, 1994); Cathy Caruth, *Trauma: Explorations in Memory* (Baltimore: Johns Hopkins University Press, 1995); Caruth, *Unclaimed Experience: Trauma, Narrative, and History* (Baltimore: Johns Hopkins University Press, 1996); Sigmund Freud, "Remembering, Repeating and Working-Through (Further Recommendations on the Technique of Psycho-Analysis II)," in *The Standard Edition of the Complete Psychological Works of Sigmund Freud, Volume XII (1911–1913): The Case of Schreber, Papers on Technique, and Other Works*, 147–56 (London: Hogarth Press, [1924] 1950).

37. Caruth looks to Freud's *Beyond the Pleasure Principle* and "Moses and Monotheism" as key texts in her theory of trauma.

38. Caruth, *Unclaimed Experience*, 3.

39. Caruth, *Unclaimed Experience*, 60–63.

40. Keeling, *Witch's Flight*, 131–32. Keeling theorizes the figures of the black "butch" and "femme" in this book. The quote appears in her discussion of Cleo's girlfriend, Ursula, who never speaks a word, in F. Gary Gray's film *Set It Off*. For Keeling, the categories of butch and femme are not named to preserve identity categories but more as a way to examine the way these terms work within black lesbian communities.

41. The placement of Ex's and Dunye's films in Europe calls to mind complex narratives of sexual freedom and racial equality that circulated around black artists such as James Baldwin and Josephine Baker during the early to mid-twentieth century which situated Europe as a space of freedom within the black American cultural imaginary.

42. For more on "the culture of dissemblance," see Hine's "Rape and the Inner Lives of Black Women."

12

Black Gay (Raw) Sex

MARLON M. BAILEY

FOR MANY PEOPLE, sexual pleasure is experienced through our apparent contradictions. These contradictions of sexuality are about the difference between what we say—sometimes who we say we are—and what we actually do. My own sexuality has its share of contradictions: I am an out and proud black gay man who loves heterosexual sex, whether it be watching it in porn or live in the flesh, or participating in it. I am radically pro-gay/queer, but I am turned on by straight-identified men, sometimes even the mildly homophobic ones. This is partly because I believe that Alfred Kinsey and his colleagues were correct when they concluded that most people are neither exclusively homosexual nor heterosexual.[1] And, perhaps most surprising, while I am a staunch advocate for HIV prevention, I also "like raw sex," sucking and fucking—topping and bottoming. Although these may seem dangerous and unhealthy contradictions, especially the raw sex, to me they are actually exciting, titillating, pleasurable, and freeing. These contradictions simply make my love and sex life more interesting. Queer cultural theorist Darieck Scott describes it best when, in his essay "Old School Sex," he says "fucking/getting fucked raw" is what life is; it is what living is.[2] But contrary to conventional belief, what I describe here has more to do with the complexities of subjectivity rather than individual sexual behavior or identity. For black gay men like me, both sex and life are complicated and can be contradictory, certainly far more so than how we are represented, discussed, and understood in HIV prevention discourse.

These days, the combination of black gay men and high-risk sex is increasingly becoming a common topic in disease prevention discourse in public health and popular culture. Ostensibly motivated by the epidemic's disproportionate impact on our communities, these discourses scrutinize and penalize black gay men, placing blame on us by constructing us as vectors of disease who should not have sex at all, let alone risky sex. In general, the discussion of the relationship between black gay men's engagement in high-risk sex and the HIV/AIDS epidemic is oversimplified and undertheorized. Hence, this pervasive way in which to discuss, understand, and represent black gay sex has made it difficult to imagine sex for us that is both satisfying and risk reductive, particularly at a time of both high HIV prevalence and extreme public health surveillance among the community.

Part of the problem is that, to date, there has been no cogent theorization of high-risk sexual behavior in black gay communities; instead, there has mostly been epidemiological surveillance of it. Albeit preliminary, here, I propose a black queer theoretical framework as a way to understand why black gay men engage in raw sex and semen exchange. A black queer theorization can provide necessary insight toward a reconceptualization of sexual health for black gay men, one that extends beyond risk and disease and encompasses desire and pleasure, whether risk is a part of that or not.

In this essay, I begin by briefly exploring the extant literature on HIV/AIDS and the discourses that this literature has produced on prevention. In much of the HIV/AIDS prevention literature there is often a reductive causal relationship drawn between black gay men's sexual behavior and their high HIV prevalence. This view is used as justification for increased surveillance and pathologization of black gay men's sexual practices by public health institutions. Here I suggest that a rigorous analysis is needed to explore the complexities of black gay subjectivity, one that accounts for sexual desires and practices—the contradictions between them—and the social factors and conditions that we contend with daily. Hence, high HIV prevalence among our communities should be viewed within a much larger, more complicated context of black gay life: sexual subjectivity.

Secondly, I engage the literature on high-risk sex (i.e., barebacking and raw sex) to suggest that it does not adequately account for the multiple factors that may play a role in why black gay men engage in high-risk sexual behavior, such as race and socioeconomic status. I also examine the literature on raw sex practices of gay men in general, including the limited focus on black gay men, to suggest that much of what has been written about black gay men's sexual practices rarely includes their perspectives on the meaning of sex, let alone raw sex, for them. Therefore, using a black queer theoretical lens, I analyze how some black gay men represent and describe their desire for and practice of raw sex in their profiles on gay sex websites. Finally, I consider ways in which to conceptualize a notion of sexual health for black gay men that is not reduced to disease and the risk thereof. It is critical that HIV prevention research and services that focus on black gay men develop approaches that are appropriate, practical, realistic, effective, and, most important, pleasure and sex affirming,

HIV/AIDS and Black Gay Men in Context

Communities of black gay and non-gay-identified men who have sex with men (MSM) continue to experience tragically high HIV prevalence after more than three decades of the epidemic.[3] In 2005, the Centers for Disease Control and Prevention (CDC) conducted a five-city study and released a startling report concluding that 46 percent of black gay men are infected with HIV, and 67 percent of those infected were unaware of their HIV infection.[4] In 2006, black gay men and MSM accounted for 63 percent of new infections among all black men and 35 percent among all MSM.[5] More recent statistics show no substantial decrease in the prevalence of HIV infection among black gay men.[6] In 2011, for example, black gay men and MSM accounted for the largest percentage of new HIV infections and AIDS diagnoses, both at 39 percent among MSM.[7] Finally, in 2016, a new analysis conducted by researchers at the CDC determined that, if current rates of HIV diagnoses persist, one in two black MSM will be diagnosed with HIV in their lifetime.[8]

While obviously disturbing, these data are used to create a discourse out of which HIV prevention strategies and policies are developed for black gay men. Notwithstanding the many social factors that contribute to high community prevalence, such as small sociosexual networks and barriers to prevention and treatment services, clearly black gay men and MSM are having high-risk sex. These forms of high-risk sex include, but are not limited to, infrequent or no condom use, multiple sexual partners, and the mixing of sex and substance use and abuse, among other practices. Strategies designed to change and reduce these practices, such as promoting consistent condom use, which has been the main focus of prevention efforts, have not proven effective in reducing HIV prevalence among black gay men.

Although it is well known that unprotected anal intercourse is the primary mode of HIV infection for all MSM, the high HIV prevalence among black men is a result of a variety of social factors that interact with sexual behavior and that increase their vulnerability to infection. For example, black researchers such as Greg Millett, David Malebranche, Chandra Ford, and others, in their respective studies of black gay sexual behavior and HIV, argue that while there is no evidence that black gay men engage in high-risk sexual behavior more than white gay men do, there is evidence to suggest that the impact is greater for black gay men because they tend to have sex within small sociosexual networks.[9] There are at least two intersecting factors that contribute to small sociosexual networks among black gay men. First, research shows that black gay men and MSM are the least desired and pursued for romantic and sexual partnerships by gay men and MSM from other racial and ethnic groups. For example, in 2007 through 2008, H. Fisher Raymond and Willi McFarland conducted a study on race mixing, partner selection, and partner preferences among MSM in San Francisco.[10] Out of their multiracial sample of 1,142 MSM in San Francisco, Raymond and McFarland found that black gay men and MSM were the least desirable as romantic and sexual partners.[11] If desired and chosen at all, black gay men and MSM were most likely to be chosen by other black men for dating and sex. As a result, the sociosexual networks of black gay men and MSM are smaller and thus facilitate a more rapid spread of HIV among already very small black MSM communities with high HIV prevalence.[12]

Second, most of the United States is racially and ethnically segregated, which includes gay communities. Therefore, black gay men tend to have sex with other black men in their neighborhoods who patronize the same clubs and who attend the same social events. These spaces and networks facilitate greater sexual contact between black gay men than with gay men from other racial and ethnic groups, since, statistically, nonblack groups of gay men have proportionately lower HIV prevalence among them. And, as stated above, many black gay men who are HIV positive do not know it; this is due in part to the stigma associated with HIV and black gay sex, as well as other barriers to prevention, testing, and treatment services that these men encounter. Therefore, that black gay men are HIV positive and do not know it means they are not receiving viral load suppression treatment. Viral load suppression makes it less likely for someone to infect someone else with HIV. Therefore, when black gay men and MSM have HIV but do not have an undetectable viral load, it vastly increases the likelihood of them infecting someone with HIV. Since black gay men who engage in high-risk sexual behavior tend to do it within small sociosexual networks, and within communities in which viral loads are higher, there is a greater likelihood of their own seroconversion or of them infecting their partners if they are already HIV positive. The point here is that the smallness of black gay men's sociosexual networks is more of a *structural* driver, as opposed to a *behavioral* one, that makes black gay men and MSM more vulnerable and susceptible to HIV infection.

In response to the aforementioned problem, the national HIV/AIDS prevention agenda, developed by the CDC, focuses, primarily, on identifying two "high-risk" groups of MSM: those who are currently HIV negative but who engage in high-risk sexual behavior, and those MSM who are HIV positive. The aim is to identify these groups, get them tested, and treat them if they test positive to lower viral loads among high-risk communities. In some ways, this strategy shifts prevention away from development of cultural and communal interventions to an emphasis on biomedical treatment and prevention—in that order. Although this extends beyond the scope of this essay, it is worth mentioning that there are a couple of structural problems with this approach. First, many poor and working-class black gay men and MSM are dealing with a whole host of issues, such as under- and unemployment, homelessness, hunger, mental health, sexual violence, and so forth, that create social and structural barriers to testing for HIV and treatment if he receives an HIV diagnosis. To de-emphasize cultural and communal interventions is to leave in place these social and structural barriers that would undermine the effectiveness of biomedical approaches. A black transwoman who is an HIV prevention worker and activist in Indianapolis, Indiana, captured the emphasis needed when she said to me, "We have to treat the person, not the disease." Second, this move from the cultural and communal forms of prevention to the biomedical is also about shifting prevention resources and funds from community-based organizations and agencies that are on the frontlines of the struggle against the epidemic, particularly among poor communities of color, to expensive treatment/medication that fills the coffers of pharmaceutical companies.[13] For working-class or poor black gay men, biomedical prevention and treatment services are often cost prohibitive and inaccessible.

In general, the ongoing high prevalence of HIV infection and AIDS diagnoses among black gay men suggests that these prevention efforts are not proving effective. Even as these HIV prevention efforts and the national agenda prioritize reducing sexual risk and disease among black gay men, the other piece to this puzzle—the relationship between pleasure and risk—has been largely ignored. It is essential to consider why black gay men engage in high-risk sexual behavior and what constitutes satisfying and pleasurable sex despite—and in some cases because of—the risk involved. The inclusion of an examination of the linkage between pleasure and risk might reveal important insights into the factors that underpin black gay men's engagement in high-risk sex. These new insights should be the basis of efforts to effect change in HIV prevention policy.

Barebacking and Raw Sex

Research shows that many black gay men report, either frequently or on occasion, engaging in unprotected anal intercourse or what is referred to as "raw sex."[14] A term used by some groups of black gay men, "raw sex" is anal intercourse (insertive and receptive) without a condom and with or without anal receptive ejaculation and semen exchange, or what many of us in the black gay community refer to as "catching nut."[15] These terms are also used in black gay pornography and on social/sexual networking websites, such as Adam4Adam and Black Gay Chat (bgclive.com). However, in the HIV prevention literature, barebacking is most often used to describe unprotected anal intercourse in which a multiracial/multiethnic range of gay men participate. Although the terms "raw sex" and "barebacking" are often used interchangeably to refer to unprotected anal intercourse, the two bear some important differences. These differences largely underpin and reflect qualitative (race and class) disparities between the lives of mainly white gay men and black gay men.

Several studies conducted on mostly white gay men have profiled increased rates of high-risk sexual behavior—barebacking—and highlight the practice as part of the subculture. Barebacking is usually a decisive and deliberate practice that is sometimes associated with indifference toward or outright resistance to regimes of normative sexual regulation.[16] In *Unlimited Intimacy: Reflections on the Subculture of Barebacking*, Tim Dean examines the subcultural meanings that underpin his subjects' desire for bareback sex and semen exchange despite the high risk of seroconversion. The mostly white gay focus of Dean's elaborate interdisciplinary study defines barebacking as a premeditation and eroticization of unprotected anal sex.[17] Furthermore, Dean's study examines barebacking as not only a practice but also an identity and culture, which reflects the view of many gay men, including some who do not identify as barebackers, that condoms are anachronistic and prohibitive to their pursuits of greater erotic and sexual pleasure and deeper intimacy and connection with other gay men.[18] While Dean suggests the above is true for most barebackers, he also highlights groups of gay men for whom the central aim of barebacking is for viral transmission and exchange.[19]

Louise Hogarth's documentary film *The Gift* (2003) examines gift giving and bug chasing, two subcultures that are connected, but not synonymous, to the barebacking communities that Dean discusses in his book. Gift giving and bug chasing are colloquial terms used to describe groups of gay men who engage in bareback sex either to intentionally infect someone with HIV (if they are HIV positive themselves) or to be infected by HIV (if they are HIV negative), respectively.[20] For these small, majority white gay male communities, HIV infection is an agential aim, meaning that barebacking is the explicit and deliberate means through which one either infects or becomes infected with HIV for a variety of reasons, some of which include alleviating fear and survivor's guilt or to forge kinship ties around HIV.[21]

Dave Holmes and Dan Warner's study on, still, mostly white gay men in large cities in Europe and Canada reveals some psychosocial factors that drive mostly the gay men's engagement in barebacking. For instance, skin-to-skin sexual contact represents not only enhanced physical sensation and pleasure but also emotional satisfaction. For these men, the condom symbolizes a barrier that inhibits physical and emotional connections with men; thus, there is pleasure in deliberately excluding condoms from the sex. Simply put, the higher the risk, the greater the pleasure. In addition, for some, condomless sex is a means through which ultimate sexual satisfaction is obtained, which is ejaculation—"taking the load." Holmes and Warner found that semen exchange satisfies a deep psychosocial desire for recognition and affirmation from other gay men.[22]

The few studies on barebacking that include black gay men as a part of their sample show a significant relationship between high HIV prevalence and barebacking. Leo Wilton and his colleagues' exploratory study of bareback sex among black and Latino MSM found that some viewed it as a form of intimacy and emotional connectedness as well as an affirmation of their gay male sexuality.[23] Alex Carballo-Diéguez and his colleagues examined the pivotal role that sexual pleasure and intimacy play in the barebacking experiences of 120 gay men, 28 of whom were black/African American. They found that for the gay men in their study, social norms, including HIV prevention, are often in conflict with their libidinal drives and the expression of sexual desire and satisfaction.[24] The scant research on barebacking that focuses primarily or exclusively on black gay men and MSM finds correlations between high-risk sexual behavior, substance use, and HIV within a context of high stigma and limited social support.[25] Of note, these studies de-emphasize "barebacking" as an intentional practice but focus instead on black gay men's engagement in unprotected anal intercourse, suggesting that it is largely influenced by structural vulnerabilities and social drivers. For example, George Ayala and his colleagues' multisited quantitative study of 2,235 black and Latino MSM found that unprotected anal intercourse is associated with homophobia, racism, financial hardship, and limited social support.[26] Structural vulnerabilities such as racism, classism, homophobia, and heterosexism impact the lives of black gay men daily (differently from other gay men), and the intersecting forms of oppression and the social and material consequences they produce influence their sexual decision making and experiences.[27]

According to what Sonja Mackenzie argues in *Structural Intimacies: Sexual Stories in the Black AIDS Epidemic,* structural vulnerabilities are lived and experienced, creating the possibilities and constraints on the sexual lives of black gay men. For example, for men who practice survival sex or engage in sex work, raw sex is often more desirable by consumers and thus more profitable for these men. If sex work is the means through which these men make a living wage, this kind of sexual risk must be understood to be an integral part of their daily lives, contending with a structural vulnerability, as opposed to an isolated individual choice.

In general, these studies make an important contribution to the knowledge on barebacking as an intentional practice and, for many, an identity and subculture—and sometimes as a means for desired viral transmission. These barebacking communities consist of mostly white gay men with relative social privilege. Conversely, for the most part, black gay men neither use the term "barebacking" to refer to unprotected sex practice nor do they claim it as an identity or culture. In addition, there is no evidence that black gay men engage in bug chasing and gift giving. Hence, in its overemphasis on white gay men, the barebacking literature has paid insufficient attention to the role that unprotected anal intercourse and semen exchange play in the sexual experiences, expressions, and lives of black gay men. Black gay men contend with multiple structural vulnerabilities that largely influence the role and value of sex in their lives in ways different from gay men from other race/ethnic groups, particularly white gay men. This is an important consideration, especially given the different social location black gay men occupy in society and the disproportionate burden of the epidemic they bear.

As a culturally specific term, "raw sex" represents what appears to be different meanings and roles that sex plays among a diverse group of black gay men. In HIV prevention discourse, however, black gay men and their sexual behavior are often viewed, discussed, and understood in homogenous terms. There is limited to no discussion of what a diverse group of black gay men *want* and *can do* to experience desire or sexual pleasure that is satisfying, particularly for those men who are HIV positive. Overall, we must attend to the role that structural vulnerabilities, social factors, libido, pleasure, and risk play in how black gay men ascribe meaning to sex and how this influences the sexual choices they make and the options and experiences they have. Much of the public health research on black gay men's high-risk sexual behavior fails to provide insight into not only the intracultural meanings of sex but also what constitutes desire and pleasure and whether risky sex is indeed desirable and pleasurable for some black gay men specifically and why.

Theorizing Black Gay Raw Sex

What theoretical framework can be used to examine raw sex among black gay men, one that accounts for our complex experiences and lives? In his book *What Do Gay Men Want? An Essay on Sex, Risk, and Subjectivity*, David M. Halperin suggests that it is no accident that, in its thoroughgoing critique of regimes of sexual normativity or heteronormativity, queer theory has been silent on gay male subjectivity, meaning the inner life of male homosexuality and what it is that gay men want.[28] In some ways, queer theory has been preoccupied, and necessarily so, with discrediting and undoing the role that the field of psychology has played in theorizing human sexuality. For a long time, psychology has treated homosexuality and other nonheteronormative sexualities as pathologies. However, drawing from French theorist Michel Foucault, queer theorists have convincingly argued that normative regimes of sexuality and prescriptions of sexual desire and practice are produced and naturalized through seemingly innocuous societal institutions such as science, education, religion, and so forth. These discursive productions of sexuality are internalized by socially disqualified sectors of society, and their seemingly successful efforts to overthrow or be included in oppressive institutions end up producing new ways and forms of naturalizing normative sexuality.[29] Halperin further argues that this queer critique has also been integral to gay and lesbian resistance to the national repathologization of homosexuality in the advent of the HIV/AIDS epidemic.[30]

Other queer theorists such as Cindy Patton have challenged ways in which normative sexual knowledge and prescriptions permeate public health HIV prevention research and practice and the messaging around HIV. Dominant HIV prevention discourses are fraught with normative assumptions about gay men and gay sex.[31] Gay men are viewed as promiscuous and in need of sexual management to ensure that members of the general population—coded as heterosexual—do not become infected with HIV or other STDs and STIs, as though heterosexuals do not get HIV and other socially/sexually communicable diseases. Thus, queer theories of HIV/AIDS have effectively examined the ways in which discourses of sexual pathology and disease are mapped onto queer bodies and used as justification for intense sexual regulation of gay men. But what has been lacking in these queer analyses of HIV/AIDS is an examination of the ways in which black gay men are confronted with regimes of racial, gender, and sexual normativity, simultaneously, and how these regimes refract sexual desire and pleasure, and the possibilities thereof for us.

To address these lacunae, I conjoin two black queer theoretical concepts, primarily drawn from work on sexuality and HIV/AIDS in the Caribbean, to offer a way in which to contemplate black gay raw sex and the contexts in which it is engaged. Cultural anthropologist Lyndon Gill coined the concept of *erotic subjectivity* from his ethnographic study of a communal response to the HIV/AIDS epidemic in Trinidad and Tobago. Gill explores what can be learned from an HIV/AIDS prevention program called "the Chatroom" at Friends for Life, a Trinidad-based non-governmental organization. His notion of erotic subjectivity highlights the "relationship between 'the erotic' and the subjectivity that challenges apolitical, passionless, and secular interpretations of how we come to know what we know about ourselves, each other, and our world." For Gill, erotic subjectivity is a theory of black (diasporic) gay subjectivity in the age of AIDS, as well as an epistemological position that highlights the interconnection between the political, sensual, and spiritual dimensions of the struggle against the epidemic in Trinidad and Tobago. He contends that erotic subjectivity is both a way of reading the world and being in it as black gay men. And, as an analytic concept, it provides a postcolonial theoretical response to mechanisms of sexual subjugation through gender and racial difference by which black gay men have been victimized throughout the diaspora.[32]

I want to extend Gill's theorization to black gay men in the United States who not only must withstand the scourge of the AIDS epidemic but who are also coerced, and sometimes forced, to subscribe to erotophobic and homophobic (antigay) rules of sex. Such rules deny us the right to the kind of sex afforded to heterosexuals and often white gay men as well. Furthermore, I am interested in how black gay men navigate the complex relationship between what the regimes of normalization tell us not to do, what we want, and what we do sexually, nonetheless. Informed by Gill's theorization, I suggest an alternative way of thinking about raw sex, one that emerges through an analysis of black gay men who unabashedly claim these desires and practices in their profiles on gay social/sexual websites. Of note, for these black gay men, raw sex is claimed as a sexual practice as opposed to a subcultural identity like barebackers. Yet, one might interpret the content of these profiles as a performative resistance to—or an outright rejection of—normative sexuality (both heteronormative and homonormative). Hence, the raw sex profile presents an alternative epistemology of sex in this age of AIDS for black gay men, specifically. This allows black gay men to imagine sexual possibilities beyond the normative, less stigmatized sexual practices usually availed to them.

A profile on sex websites not only tells a would-be suitor basic information about a person, such as his race/ethnicity, age, height, and weight, but also HIV status and whether or not he uses substances, among other information that someone may find pertinent. Furthermore, the profile reveals a lot, both explicit and implicit, about his sexual desires, practices, endowment, and identity. Consider the profile from a black gay man below taken from a popular gay website:

WHO REAL?? WHERE DA 100% BOTTOMS???

36, 5'11", 175lb, 34w, Average, Black Hair, Smooth, Black, Looking for 1-on-1 Sex, Relationship.

NO PIC NO CHAT!!!! NO WHITE ASIAN OR LATINO MEN UNLESS I HIT U UP!!!

IM NOT INTO SAFE SEX SO IF UR PROFILE SAY SAFE SEX ONLY U WILL B IGNORED!!

IM NOT INTO OLDER AND IM NOT INTO MEN OVER 210[lbs]!!! UNLESS U R HWP [height and weight proportionate]!!

IF U WANT DICK Y A LONG LIST OF DEMANDS?? EITHER U DO OR U DONT!!

IM NOT FREAKIN OR FUCKIN ALL OF MICHIGAN SO I NEED A FUCK PARTNER OR 2 . . . I PREFER 2 DATE!!!

FUCKIN U TIL WE BOTH CUM!!! NO VERS GUYS I NEED A STRAIGHT UP BOTTOM FOR 1 on 1 FUCKIN!!!

Casual, Out No, Smoke Yes, Drink Often, Drugs Occasionally, Zodiac Cancer.

Top, 9.5" Cut, Anything Goes, HIV Negative, Prefer meeting at: Public Place.

Makin us both cum hard!!!

Out of all the information provided, there are two aspects of the profile that are important to my theorization here: his outright rejection of "safe sex" and his claim of a negative HIV status. First, in his profile, this black gay man calls out a kind of hypocrisy for those who hide behind the moniker of safe sex but who do not actually practice it. He requires that men claim raw sex and not say "safe sex only." In my research on raw sex thus far, I have found that while many men will say "safe sex only" on their profiles, when they actually have sex, there ends up being nothing "safe" about their sexual interests and practice at all. Of course this strategy of claiming one thing and doing another may be, in some cases, deployed because of the stigma associated with raw sex. However, in other cases, one may intend on having "safe sex" and end up getting caught up in the desire and pleasure of the moment and end up doing it raw—and loving it, while still regretting it afterward. Conversely, in the above profile, the black gay man's desire and pleasure may derive from not only his simultaneous raw sex proclamation and safe sex rejection (and these are not necessarily binary opposites) but also a political resistance to the hegemony of safe sex that coerces black gay men to concede pleasurable and satisfying sex, if they indeed find risky sex pleasurable and satisfying.

Second, HIV prevention discourse would suggest a glaring contradiction present in the above profile between the black gay man's rejection of safe sex (and no interest in hooking up with anyone who says "safe sex only" in their profile) and his claim to be HIV negative. Yet, this contradiction could also constitute a realm of pleasure for him. For instance, in "Old School Sex," Darieck Scott argues that before the AIDS epidemic there was no perceived risk involved with raw sex, there was nothing really remarkable and risky about it beyond the possibility of catching VD—a venereal disease, as they were called then. According to Scott, this was old-school sex.[33] I would add that old-school sex was not viewed as or called raw sex—it was just sex. However, for many, since the AIDS epidemic, the risk of HIV infection has changed gay sex altogether. One of those changes has been the rise of the hegemony of safe sex, as a community-derived response to the epidemic beginning in the late 1980s and early 1990s. On the one hand, raw sex is indeed remarkable and risky, at least the ways in which it is represented in HIV prevention discourses. On the other hand, the risky nature of raw sex—its potential for causing seroconversion and leading to drastic life changes and possibly premature death—can/does actually enhance sexual pleasure. Thus, even though "old-school sex" may be perceived to be better, to be really good sex for some because there was no AIDS epidemic, current sex in the age of AIDS may be better, really good sex for others exactly because of the heightened pleasure that HIV risk produces.[34] In the case of the latter, being encouraged or required to take risk-reductive measures, such as using condoms, undermines that person's sexual and pleasurable aims. For it is the *risk* of seroconversion created by raw sex that enhances the pleasure, not seroconversion as an *outcome* of raw sex.

My discussion above is a great segue to the second black queer theoretic concept that is useful here: M. Jacqui Alexander's concept of *erotic autonomy*. Mostly focusing on regimes of sexual normativity that impact black women's sexuality in the Caribbean, Alexander's concept of erotic autonomy delineates how marginalized and stigmatized sexual subjects can and do engage in erotic and sexual pleasure on their own terms despite the often institutional, communal, and familial influences against it.[35] Let us explore the possibility that some black gay men's pursuit and engagement in raw sex and sexual pleasure that are expressed on their terms may represent an autonomous practice for these men despite the cacophony of "finger wagging" pronouncements against it. As writer Herukhuti puts it, black gay men "have the right to fuck" and fuck raw if they want, because, after all, "whose booty is this?"[36] For my purposes here, I add *sexual* to Alexander's concept of erotic autonomy to emphasize both the erotic and sexual dimensions of raw sex. Taking this point into account, I examine the profile below as a discursive move toward erotic (sexual) autonomy:

i jus wanna fuck raw . . .

    33, 6'0", 190lb, 34w, Athletic, Black Hair, Some Body Hair, Black, Looking for 1-on-1 Sex, 3some/ Group Sex, Misc. Fetishes, Cam2Cam. I like to fuck raw only . . . get at me . . .

    Conservative, Out No, Smoke Yes, Drink Occasionally, Drugs No, Zodiac Taurus.

    Top, 9" Cut, Anything Goes, HIV Positive, Prefer meeting at: My Place.

First, for this website, entitling one's profile with the proclamation, "i just wanna fuck raw . . ." is a radical claim, because while many men desire and engage in raw sex, most will not admit it.[37] He also reveals his positive HIV status, which is also nonnormative for these websites, as many men who are HIV positive either falsely represent themselves as HIV negative or they occlude the status from their profile altogether because of the extreme stigma associated with HIV. This black MSM (who is not out) is a sexual top, implying that he fucks bottoms raw and that he is into group sex and not interested in a relationship (marked as romantic and monogamous). His claim to engage in this panoply of nonhomonormative sexual practices in the gay domain of this website can be viewed as a radical position and practice of sexual autonomy.

Furthermore, when reading a profile like this, it is important to situate behavior within the larger context of black gay subjectivity and grapple with the contradictions and complexities, similar to my own, which I highlight at the beginning of this essay. For black gay men who engage in raw sex, for example, sexual pleasure and desire are often in conflict with social norms and gay identity. These men are not only stigmatized by larger society, particularly public health institutions, they are also stigmatized by other black gay men. In larger society, those black gay men who engage in raw sex are viewed as reckless, dangerous, and uncivilized and in need of punitive social management and ridicule. According to some black gay men—who see themselves as the respectable and moral stewards of black gay life and representation—those who have raw sex are deeply retrograde and demonstrative of black gay men's self-hatred and self-destruction. As Drew-Shane Daniels argues in his July 2013 article in *Mused*, because of the disproportionate impact of the HIV/AIDS epidemic on black gay men, '"barebacking' [assuming he means raw sex too] is never a safe bet for Black gay men."[38]

But let us consider the social context (the subjectivity) in which this black gay man, who is HIV positive, has raw sex. Because of his status, he lives with a multiple social disqualification: he is black, gay, and HIV positive and he has raw sex. This multiple disqualification constitutes the constraints under which he lives, and for him the emphasis is placed on what he should not do sexually, or the hegemony of safe sex. However, another dimension of his subjectivity is about his desire and pleasure—what he wants in terms of sex. Thus, the politics of desire that may inform this black gay man's erotic (sexual) subjectivity is a sociopolitical resistance to the hegemony of safe sex that produces shame and self-hatred for those who do not comply, combined with the sensual and tactical pleasure of skin-to-skin sexual contact. Not only does skin-to-skin sex and catching nut feel better, as many of the black gay men in my research have stated, it also satisfies a craving for, what I call, a deep intimacy, a closeness and a "being desired and wanted" in a world in which black gay men are rarely desired and wanted.[39] One can assume that this is constrained by his HIV status, meaning that many people will not want to have any kind of sex with him, let alone raw sex, because he is openly HIV positive. Nonetheless, this black gay man's profile represents an erotically and sexually autonomous articulation of black gay sex.

Certainly this is not the case for all men, but these profiles reflect these black gay men's efforts to claim and practice erotic (sexual) autonomy as M. Jacqui Alexander uses it in her work. Erotic (sexual) autonomy should be considered as an important aspect of black gay men's erotic subjectivity. Likewise, Gill's theory accounts for the contradictions between one's identity and erotic and sexual desires and the social norms and conditions under which sexual pleasure and satisfaction are pursued and engaged.[40] Both Gill's and Alexander's concepts of erotic subjectivity and erotic (sexual) autonomy, respectively, do theoretical work for black gay men that Halperin says queer theory does not do for male homosexuality, and that is to examine gay subjectivity—what gay men want—in the HIV/AIDS crisis.

What If Raw Sex Is Sexually Healthy?

I will address this question by beginning with a scenario described to me by one of my research participants from the raw sex project. Nick is a black gay man (living in Detroit at the time) who is HIV positive and engages in raw sex with a guy who is also HIV positive—basically this is a seroconcordant sexual relationship. On a previous visit to his doctor for a checkup, he informed her of this relationship.[41] Nick explained his interaction with his doctor during a subsequent visit as such: "With a stern parental look on her face she asked, 'Are you having unprotected sex?' 'Yes,' I responded. 'Aaaah! You've probably already been reinfected with another strain of the virus.' I threw a piercing look at her, and then she said, 'I didn't mean to be so flip, but I just don't understand why you continue to have unprotected sex.'"

Nick describes the practice of serosorting, the strategy of having unprotected sex with someone who is already HIV positive. While not foolproof, serosorting is a common risk-reductive strategy used among HIV positive men. And there is no compelling evidence to suggest that "reinfection with another strain of the virus" actually occurs, especially if both of them are on viral load suppression medication. Nick's experience is all too common; what appears to be his doctor's concern for his health in actuality does harm to Nick and his sexual selfhood, stoking further the mistrust, fear, and frustration with public health that many black gay men hold.

Nick's doctor takes a common public health approach that is designed to address the relationship between high HIV prevalence and high-risk sexual behavior among black gay men by urging individual behavioral change and scolding him in the process.[42] The individual behavioral change approach encourages an inherent problematization of raw sex and semen exchange, whether it be serosorting or not, and aims to reduce these behaviors.[43] However, what is usually not taken into consideration are the negative consequences caused by the hegemony of safe sex for those black gay men for whom raw sex is crucial to their sexual satisfaction. Psychologist and activist Raphael Díaz's *Latino Gay Men and HIV* offers a fecund example for black gay men. In his research on Latino gay men and "risky sex," Díaz found that, for many men in his study, "safe sex," particularly condoms, interrupt and inhibit the pleasure and connection that Latino gay men experience through sex that involves "flesh-to-flesh, mucous-membrane-to-mucous-membrane," along with all the hardness, softness, warmth, and wetness of sex.[44] Similarly, for black gay men, condom use presents a *barrier* to pleasurable and satisfying sex that may be a source of deep intimacy, connection, and self-affirmation that run counter to their experiences of social disqualification, marginalization, alienation, and deprivation. For these men, the lack of a pleasurable and satisfying sex life can lead to unhealthy, life-threatening outcomes.[45]

One of the impediments to conducting research on and developing a holistic definition and approach to sexual health is the reliance on outmoded and ineffective models for HIV prevention. For instance, Raphael Díaz also observes that the "deficit knowledge" command/compliance approach assumes that these men are generally incapable of self-direction and efficacy around HIV prevention, and once an individual is informed of risk, his behavior will change. The *deficit approach* can at times be counterproductive to the prevention and sexual health aims that interventions are designed to undertake because they lack cultural appropriateness and fail to take into account the meanings of high-risk sex for intragroup communities.[46] In other words, what it means to engage in raw sex for some black gay men is not the same as for others, and to assume it is the same not only inadequately addresses our behavior but also does not deal with our needs.

As national HIV prevention efforts move toward strategies such as "find (HIV positives), test, and treat," to lower viral loads to reduce infection rates, concurrently there is also a global discussion, which influences HIV prevention and treatment policy in the United States, around the meaning of "sexual health." According to the World Health Organization, sexual health is the state of physical, emotional, mental, and social well-being in relation to sexuality.[47] Furthermore, the World Health Organization emphasizes that fundamental to sexual health is the right to information and pleasure.[48] Understanding how black gay men think about, negotiate, and make decisions around risk and pleasure can help public health institutions devise prevention strategies that promote their sexual health, while simultaneously addressing the structural vulnerabilities that create unhealthy life conditions. Research and service providers must advocate for more holistic and comprehensive approaches to the study of sexual health for black gay men so as to produce services that promote it. Clearly, a definition of sexual health has to consist of more than reducing the risk of STD/STI infections, particularly HIV.

To gain a greater understanding of the meaning of sex for black gay men and the diverse ways through which they gain sexual pleasure should include an investigation of the spaces and situations in which some black gay men have sex.[49] As some of the studies cited above suggest, black gay men's engagement in high-risk sexual behavior is associated with the structural vulnerabilities, such as homophobia, racism, and stigma. However, the discussion of these social factors and vulnerabilities in the literature rarely considers the ways in which space can be a structural vulnerability for black gay men. Hence, if black gay men have limited access to spaces in which to have sex, let alone engage in stigmatized sexual behavior, particularly in cities in which they live, public/private sex venues and events are important sites to explore as a facilitator for sexual health. Black gay men engage in raw sex and other high-risk sexual behavior at sex clubs and parties where they are able not only to explore different kinds of sexual pleasure more freely—in a relatively safe spatial environment—but also to overcome the inability to have sex at home in many cases. In this sense, space and social environments play a critical role in how black gay men define and experience sex, particularly raw sex, in the midst of socioeconomic challenges, such as spatial exclusion or marginalization, and other forms of discrimination that they endure.

Although, increasingly, the public health literature examines the overall sexual health of MSM rather than just focusing on HIV, limited work has been done that considers the sexual health of black gay men beyond a focus on sexual risk. As the World Health Organization suggests, sexual health promotion requires an understanding of the complex factors that shape human sexuality, which include both risk and pleasure and simultaneous barriers to and facilitators of sexual satisfaction.[50] Simply put, if the meaning of sex requires a consideration of risk, pleasure, and satisfaction, then these aspects should also be a part of how we understand sexual health. In this regard, the perspectives of black gay men and the meanings they ascribe to sex and their perspectives on the sexual behaviors in which they engage are important to their sexual health.

In our HIV/AIDS prevention zeal, we as a society, including our public health institutions and community-based organizations, have forgotten the old adage that says that injunctions help to produce the very practices and actions they aim to prohibit. But beyond this point, I believe that raw sex is more than just about sexual behavior; rather, it is about subjectivity, or what black gay men want, within a context and under conditions of multiple social disqualification, management/surveillance, and exclusion that we navigate and negotiate daily. Raw sex and catching nut is a way to deal with or alleviate the alienation and feelings of worthlessness and ultimately to create a livable life.

Sexual desire, practice, and identity do not exist and happen outside the context and conditions of disqualification; instead, they are produced and emerge within and through them. Thus, as HIV prevention research and policy move toward a conceptualization of and an emphasis on sexual health, it is essential to include what this means for not only black gay men but also others who engage in risky sex. The concept of sexual health should take into account what black gay men want in terms of sexual pleasure and practice and inform a set of strategies through which they can negotiate between pleasure and risk. However, we should not be asked or required to completely forgo pleasure *for* "safe sex." We can get to this point only through learning and understanding black gay men's desires, perspectives, and experiences as opposed to overly focusing on their behaviors, in isolation. For it is from these black gay men that we will understand better the full dimensions of what sexual health really means in the context of our lives so that a more holistic conceptualization can be derived and operationalized.

NOTES

1. Alfred C. Kinsey, Wardell R. Pomeroy, and Clyde E. Martin, "Sexual Behavior in the Human Male," *American Journal of Public Health* 93, no. 6 (June 2003): 896.

2. Darieck Scott, "Old School Sex," *Corpus* 3, no. 1 (2005): 87.

3. Men who have sex with men (MSM) is a public health term used to include men who do not identify as gay but who have sex with men nonetheless.

4. Centers for Disease Control and Prevention, "HIV Prevalence, Unrecognized Infection, and HIV Testing among Men Who Have Sex with Men—Five U.S. Cities, June 2004–April 2005," *Morbidity and Mortality Weekly Report* 54, no. 24 (June 24, 2005).

5. Henry Kaiser Family Foundation, "Fact Sheet: Black Americans and HIV/AIDS," *HIV/AIDS Policy*, November 2010, www.kff.org.

6. Centers for Disease Control and Prevention, "Fact Sheet: HIV and AIDS among Gay and Bisexual Men, Atlanta 2012," updated June 2012, accessed July 12, 2012, http://www.cdc.gov/nchhstp/newsroom/docs/2012/CDC-MSM-0612-508.pdf.

7. Centers for Disease Control and Prevention, "Fast Facts: HIV among Black/African American Gay, Bisexual, and Other Men Who Have Sex with Men," May 2013, http://www.cdc.gov/hiv/pdf/risk_HIV_among_AA_Gay_other.pdf.

8. Center for Disease Control and Prevention, "NCHHSTP Newsroom: Half of Black Gay Men and a Quarter of Latino Gay Men Projected to Be Diagnosed within Their Lifetime," February 2016, http://www.cdc.gov/nchhstp/newsroom/2016/croi-press-release-risk.html.

9. Gregorio A. Millett, John L. Peterson, Richard J. Wolitski, and Ron Stall, "Greater Risk for HIV Infection of Black Men Who Have Sex with Men: A Critical Literature

Review," *American Journal of Public Health* 96, no. 6 (2006): 1007–19. For more on this point, see Gregario Millett, David Malebranche, Byron Mason, and Pilgram Spikes, "Focusing 'Down Low': Bisexual Black Men, HIV Risk and Heterosexual Transmission," *Journal of the American Medical Associations* 97, no. 7 (2005); and Chandra Ford, Kathryn Whetten, Susan A. Hall, Jay S. Kaufman, and Angela D. Thrasher, "Black Sexuality, Social Construction, and Research Targeting 'The Down Low' ('The DL')," *Annals of Epidemiology* 17, no. 3 (March 2007): 209–16.

10. H. Fisher Raymond and Willi McFarland, "Racial Mixing and HIV Risk among Men Who Have Sex with Men," *AIDS Behavior* 13 (2009): 630–37.

11. The racial breakdown for this study sample of 1,142 MSM was 56 percent white, 22 percent Latino, 14 percent Asian, and 9 percent black. I note that the percentages add up to more than 100 percent, but I believe it is a typographical error rather than a flaw with the study.

12. Clearly, many black gay men prefer other black gay men and MSM for romantic and sexual partners over gay men and MSM from other race/ethnic groups. Nonetheless, Raymond and McFarland suggest that "the racial disparity in HIV observed for more than a decade will not disappear until the challenges posed by a legacy of racism towards Blacks in the U.S. are addressed" ("Racial Mixing and HIV Risk," 630).

13. Neils van Doorn, "Between Hope and Abandonment: Black Queer Collectivity and the Affective Labour of Biomedicalized HIV Prevention," *Culture, Health, and Sexuality* 14, no. 7 (August 2012): 827–40.

14. Leo Wilton, Perry N. Halkitis, Gary English, and Michael Roberson, "An Exploratory Study of Barebacking, Club Drug Use, and Meanings of Sex in Black and Latino Gay and Bisexual Men in the Age of AIDS," in *Barebacking: Psychological and Public Health Approaches*, ed. Perry N. Halkitis, Leo Wilton, and Jack Drescher, 49–72 (New York: Haworth Medical Press, 2005).

15. Wilton et al., "Exploratory Study of Barebacking," 51. Black gay men say "catching nut," "taking kids," and "gimme them kids" to describe someone ejaculating inside them or acts of semen exchange. I have learned this from my own sexual experiences, as well as from my research. For instance, I conducted a pilot ethnographic study of twenty-four black gay men's engagement in raw sex, semen exchange, and group sex. This ethnographic data reveal that the terms used to describe particular sex acts, especially during sex, play a role in creating and enhancing sexual desire and pleasure. This point extends beyond the scope of this essay, but in my larger project on black gay sex and subjectivity, I am interested in examining the role that language and sound play in black gay sex.

16. Tim Dean, *Unlimited Intimacy: Reflections on the Subculture of Barebacking* (Chicago: University of Chicago Press 2009). For more studies on barebacking, see Dave

Holmes and Dan Warner, "The Anatomy of a Forbidden Desire: Men, Penetration and Semen Exchange," *Nursing Inquiry* 12, no. 1 (2005): 10–20; Maria L. Ekstrand, Ron D. Stall, Jay P. Paul, et al., "Gay Men Report High Rates of Unprotected Anal Sex with Partners of Unknown or Discordant HIV Status," *AIDS* 13 (1999): 1525–33; David Holmes, Patrick O'Byme, and Denise Gastaldo, "Raw Sex as Limit Experience: A Foucauldian Analysis of Unsafe Anal Sex between Men," *Social Theory & Health* 4 (2006): 319–33; Jeffrey T. Parsons and David S. Bimbi, "Intentional Unprotected Anal Intercourse among Men Who Have Sex with Men: Barebacking—Behavior to Identity," *AIDS Behavior* 11 (2007): 277–87.

17. Dean, *Unlimited Intimacy*, 1.

18. Dean, *Unlimited Intimacy*, xii.

19. Dean, *Unlimited Intimacy*, 17.

20. Christian Grov and Jeffrey T. Parsons, "Bug Chasing and Gift Giving: The Potential for HIV Infection among Barebackers on the Internet," Abstract, *AIDS Education and Prevention* 18, no. 6 (2006): 490.

21. Louise Hogarth, dir., *The Gift* (Dream Out Loud Productions, 2003), DVD.

22. Holmes and Warner, "Anatomy of a Forbidden Desire," 10, 11.

23. Wilton et al., "Exploratory Study of Barebacking," 63.

24. Alex Carballo-Diéguez, Ana Bentuneac, Gary W. Dowsett, Ivan Balan, Jose Bauermeister, Robert H. Remien, Curtis Dolezal, Rebecca Giguere, and Marina Mabragana, "Sexual Pleasure and Intimacy among Men Who Engage in 'Bareback Sex,'" *AIDS Behavior* 15, no. 1 (April 2011): S57–65.

25. Mance E. Buttram, Steven P. Kurtz, and Hilary L. Surratt, "Substance Use and Sexual Risk Mediated by Social Support among Black Men," *Journal of Community Health* 38, no. 1 (2013): 62–69.

26. George Ayala, Trista Bingham, Junyeop Kim, Darrell P. Wheeler, and Gregorio A. Millett, "Modeling the Impact of Social Discrimination and Financial Hardship on the Sexual Risk of HIV among Latino and Black Men Who Have Sex with Men," *American Journal of Public Health* 102, suppl. 2 (2012): S242–49.

27. Sonja Mackenzie, *Structural Intimacies: Sexual Stories in the Black AIDS Epidemic* (New Brunswick, NJ: Rutgers University Press, 2013), 3.

28. David Halperin, *What Do Gay Men Want? An Essay on Sex, Risk, and Subjectivity* (Ann Arbor: University of Michigan Press, 2007), 1.

29. Halperin, *What Do Gay Men Want?*, 3.

30. Halperin, *What Do Gay Men Want?*, 4.

31. See books by Cindy Patton, such as *Fatal Advice: How Safe-Sex Education Went Wrong* (Durham, NC: Duke University Press, 1996), and *Sex and Germs: The Politics of AIDS* (Boston: South End Press, 1985).

32. Lyndon K. Gill, "Chatting Back an Epidemic: Caribbean Gay Men, HIV/AIDS,

and the Use of Erotic Subjectivity," GLQ: *Journal of Lesbian and Gay Studies* 18, no. 2–3 (2012): 278.

33. Scott, "Old School Sex," 85.

34. Scott, "Old School Sex," 86.

35. M. Jacqui Alexander, "Erotic Autonomy as a Politics of Decolonization: An Anatomy of Feminist and State Practice in the Bahamas Tourist Economy," in *Feminist Genealogies, Colonial Legacies, Democratic Futures*, ed. M. Jacqui Alexander and Chandra Talpade Mohanty (New York: Routledge, 1997).

36. Herukhuti, "Whose Booty Is This? Barebacking, Advocacy, and the Right to Fuck," in *Conjuring Black Funk: Notes on Culture, Sexuality, and Spirituality*, vol. 1, ed. H. Sharif Williams (New York: Vintage Entity Press, 2007): 101.

37. This is also very radical and risky because in some states, particularly the one in which this person lives, "Duty to Warn" laws or compulsory disclosure laws require that anyone who is HIV positive must reveal his/her status before having sex with anyone, protected or not.

38. Drew-Shane Daniels, "Barebacking Is Never a Safe Bet for Black Gay Men," *Mused*, July 2013, accessed November 7, 2013, http://www.musedmagonline.com/2013 /07/barebacking-is-never-the-safest-sex-especially-for-black-gay-men/. For another example of the stigma around raw sex, see Sean Kennedy, "'They're Peddling Death': Profiting from Unsafe Sex," *Advocate*, August 29, 2006, 44–48, accessed November 7, 2013, http://www.thefreelibrary.com/%22They%27re+peddling+death%22%3A+profit ing+from+unsafe+sex—an+Advocate . . . -a0150864898.

39. Thomas Glave, "Meditation on 'Barebacking,'" in *Among the Bloodpeople: Politics and Flesh* (New York: Akashic Books, 2013), 156.

40. Gill, "Chatting Back an Epidemic."

41. "Seroconcordant" means that two people knowingly share or believe they share the same HIV status, either negative or positive. This notion is the basis of serosorting, a practice in which gay men forge romantic/sexual relationships with other gay men who share their status as a risk-reductive strategy.

42. Susan M. Kegeles, Robert B. Hays, and Thomas J. Coates, "The Mpowerment Project: A Community-Level HIV Prevention Interventions for Young Gay Men," *American Journal of Public Health* 86, no. 8 (1996): 1129–36.

43. UCSF AIDS Health Project, "Sex without Condoms," *HIV Counselors Perspectives* 10, no. 2 (2001): 1–8.

44. Rafael M. Díaz, *Latino Gay Men and HIV: Culture, Sexuality and Risk Behavior* (New York: Routledge, 1998), 11.

45. Another approach that some public health providers take is the harm-reduction approach or to "start from where the person is" and aim to reduce high-risk sexual behavior by offering a hierarchical risk-reduction schema as a means through which

men can negotiate risk for greater sexual pleasure. While important, neither the conventional nor the harm-reduction approach is effective for men for whom high-risk behavior such as raw sex is central to sexual desire and pleasure and their overall sexual pleasure and satisfaction. For more on this, see Allen Kwabena Frimpong and Michael Terry Everett, "When Condoms Ain't Enuf . . . What to Do with a Sex-Phobic Society in a 'Post-AIDS' Era?," *The Body: A Complete HIV/AIDS Resource,* November 28, 2011, http://www.thebody.com/content/64865/when-condoms-aint -enuf—what-to-do-with-a-sex-phob.html.

46. Díaz, *Latino Gay Men and HIV.*

47. World Health Organization, "Defining Sexual Health: Report of a Technical Consultation on Sexual Health," January 28–31, 2006, Geneva, 5.

48. World Health Organization, "Defining Sexual Health," 1.

49. Patrick Wilson, Rafael M. Díaz, Hirokazu Yoshikawa, and Patrick E. Shrout, "Drug Use, Interpersonal Attraction, and Community: Situational Factors as Predictors of Episodes of Unprotected Anal Intercourse among Latino Gay Men," *AIDS Behavior* 13 (2009): 691–99.

50. World Health Organization, "Defining Sexual Health," 1.

13

Black Data

SHAKA MCGLOTTEN

᳃

#howblackareyou

COMEDIAN, GEEK, AND AUTHOR Baratunde Thurston began his 2009 South by Southwest slide show "How to Be Black (Online)" with a very brief explanation of why black people are important: "we look good / history proves black people are the future / e.g. rock n roll / e.g. hip hop / e.g. ass/lip injections."[1] His playful intro led into a more sophisticated, if also still comical, analysis of black online life. He noted in particular the waning "digital divide." Blacks are online as much as whites if both tethered and wireless access are considered, and both groups tend to use the same sites, with a few exceptions.[2] Thurston also noted the persistence of racism on the web, a point also underlined by numerous scholars of race and the Internet.[3] Thurston focused specifically on black use of Twitter, which he links to the call-and-response game of insults known as the dozens.[4] Of course, tweeting blacks cause consternation among some whites: "Wow!! too many negros in the trending topics for me. I may be done with this whole twitter thing."[5]

Thurston's work on race and technology provides a template for my own efforts here. In this essay, I engage in a black queer call-and-response with a few key concepts circulating in network theories and cultures.

I use an eclectic group of artifacts—Thurston's slide show, an interview with Barack Obama in the wake of the National Security Agency (NSA) surveillance scandal, the artwork of Zach Blas, and a music video about technology and gentrification—to proffer the heuristic, "black data." This heuristic, I suggest, offers some initial analytic and political orientations for black queer studies to more fully engage with the theories, effects, and affects of network cultures. Although there are significant bodies of literature in science and technology, as well as cultural and media studies, that grapple with race and a handful of works that address sexuality and new media technologies, black queer studies, itself still a developing, loosely organized group of scholars and cultural practitioners, has not generated many analyses of the particular ways black queer people are interpolated by or employ new media and other technologies.[6] Here, I use black data to think through some of the historical and contemporary ways black queer people, like other people of African descent and people of color more broadly, are hailed by big data, in which *technés* of race and racism reduce our lives to mere numbers: we appear as commodities, revenue streams, statistical deviations, or vectors of risk.[7] Big data also refers to the various efforts of states and corporations to capture, predict, and control political and consumer behavior. Black data is, then, a response to big data's call, and here I offer readings that outline some possible political and affective vectors, some ways to refuse the call or perhaps even to hang up.

Black queer lives are often reduced to forms of accounting that are variously intended to elicit alarm or direct highly circumscribed forms of care. Statistics are used to mobilize people to fight HIV/AIDS—such as the fact that blacks account for 44 percent of new HIV infections.[8] They are used to direct attention to the omnipresence of violence in black life or to the specific forms of violence directed against black LGBTQ people, as in the National Coalition of Anti-Violence Programs' 2012 report, which notes that LGBTQ people of color are nearly twice as likely to experience physical violence as their white counterparts and that transgender people of color are two and a half times as likely to experience police violence as their white cisgender counterparts.[9] Assigning numerical or financial value to black life, transforming experience into information or data, is nothing new; rather, it is caught up with the history of enslavement and the racist regimes that sought to justify its barbarities. Between the sixteenth and nineteenth centuries, more than twelve and a half million Africans were transported from Africa to the New World. Two million, and likely many more, died during the Middle Passage.[10] A typical slave ship could carry more than three hundred slaves arranged like sardines; the sick and dead would be thrown overboard, their loss claimed for insurance money, as in the infamous Zong massacre. Other, more recent data circulate in the wake of the ongoing global recession and the protests against George Zimmerman's exoneration in the killing of seventeen-year-old Trayvon Martin: black families saw their wealth drop 31 percent between 2007 and 2010;[11] in 2012, police and security guards killed 136 unarmed black men.[12] In the wake of a spate of police violence in 2014 and the failed indictments of the police who killed Michael Brown and Eric Garner, an analysis by the investigative journalism site *ProPublica* showed that black males were twenty-one times more likely to be fatally shot than young white males.[13] These realities have contributed to the growth of the Black Lives Matter movement.

It is tempting to ascribe these racialized accountings to the cruel systems of value established by capitalism, which seeks to encode—quantify and order—life and matter into categories of commodity, labor, exchange value, and profit. Indeed, race itself functions as such as commodity in the era of genomics—a simple oral swab test can help you answer Thurston's question #howblackareyou, and you can watch others' reactions to their results on *Faces of America*, a popular show about genealogical testing. Yet as Lisa Nakamura, Peter Chow-White, and Wendy Chun observe, race is not merely an effect of capitalism's objectifying systems; rather, race is itself a co-constituting technology that made such forms of accounting possible in the first place.[14] "Race *as* technology," Chun notes, helps us understand "how race functions as the 'as,' how it facilitates comparisons between entities classed as similar or dissimilar."[15] Race is a tool, and it was intrinsic, not anterior, to constructions of capital, as well as to ideas about biology and culture. As Mel Chen puts it, race is an animate hierarchy, in which the liveliness and the value of some things (whiteness, smart technology) are established via a proximity to other things positioned lower or further away (blackness, dumb matter).[16] "Wow!! too many negros in the trending topics for me" simply reiterates in the realm of microblogging hierarchical technés of racism that see black people as polluting and therefore as distasteful or dangerous or that would deny information/technology to the subjects of discrimination.[17]

Of course, the above statistics are familiar, and while useful, they tell only very partial stories, reducing black experience to an effect of capitalism (a vulgar Marxism if ever there was one) or to a kind of numerology of bare life. In what follows I sketch a few different trajectories for black data. I performatively enact black data as a kind of informatics of black queer life, as reading and throwing shade, to grapple with the NSA surveillance scandal, new biometric technologies, and the tech-fueled gentrification of San Francisco. These readings (actings out?) also help to illustrate the ways black queer theories, practices, and lives might be made to matter in relation to some of the organizing tensions of contemporary network cultures: privacy, surveillance, capture, and exclusion. Black queers frame what is at stake in these debates insofar as we quite literally embody struggles between surveillance and capture, between the seen and unseen. Moreover, we have developed rogue epistemologies which often rely on an array of technological media and which help us to make ourselves present and to make ourselves disappear. In the reads that follow, I also gesture toward the virtual affinities black queer theoretical or political projects might share with cryptographic and anarchist activisms.

Obama's Face and Black Opacities

Ima read.[18] In this context, my black queer call-and-response takes the specific form of reading and shade, critical performative practices wielded by queers of color and made famous in the film *Paris Is Burning*. Reading is an artfully delivered insult, while shade refers to disrespectful behaviors or gestures, which can be subtly or not so subtly communicated. In *Paris Is Burning*, Dorian Corey describes it this way: "Shade is, 'I don't tell you you're ugly, but I don't have to tell you because you know you're ugly.' And that's shade."[19] Academics know how to be shady, but they usually dress it up in ideology or jargon. Part of my intervention here has to do with how I seek to occasionally sidestep some of these professional niceties.

Obama was raised by white people, not drag queens, but he knows how to give good face. But in the moments before a 2013 interview with PBS's Charlie Rose, Obama's signature smile cracked, revealing instead an ugly mask. This mask held a tense set of ironies. The United States' first black president defended his unprecedented expansion of surveillance programs of the National Security Agency (NSA) to include the collection of the metadata of millions of Americans' and global citizens' telephone and e-mail correspondence. He accused Edward Snowden, a former NSA contractor turned whistleblower, of spying and called for his arrest, continuing a pattern of aggressively prosecuting leakers of governmental overreach.[20] The racial melodrama is striking: a black man authorizes the capture and arrest of a young white man, who by revealing the

spying program directly challenged the hegemony of U.S. imperialism, a project historically and presently tied to the control, domination, torture, and murder of brown and black people around the world.[21]

Obama's grin is a failed mask or the slippery gap that hosts the mask before its radiant, populist actualization: "Charlie, let me tell you ... I want to assure all Americans ..." In another era, and maybe still in this one, Obama's grin might embody the racist fantasy that all black people are animated by an animalistic desire to please or reassure white people. But here the mask is a more familiar code, a politician's lie—"don't worry, everything's fine, carry on." Although brief, Obama's expression arrested my attention, an attention shared with other queers and people of color, one that is always attuned, through calibrated and diffused looks, specu-lations, and modes of attention, to "the evidence of felt intuition," to the subtle or not-so-subtle gestures that indicate shared desire or the threat of violence.[22] My cynical intuition—Ima read—collides with nostalgia for a scene of optimism. I cannot help but juxtapose this rictus grin with Shephard Fairey's famous image of Obama gazing hopefully into the distance. To this juxtaposition we can add a meme that emerged in the wake of the NSA scandal—Yes We Scan.

For Giorgio Agamben and Emmanuel Levinas, faces condition our ethical encounters with one another. Agamben writes, "Only where I find a face do I encounter an exteriority and does an outside happen to me."[23] In the work of Gilles Deleuze and Félix Guattari, however, the face is something more ambivalent; it is operationalized as a regulating function

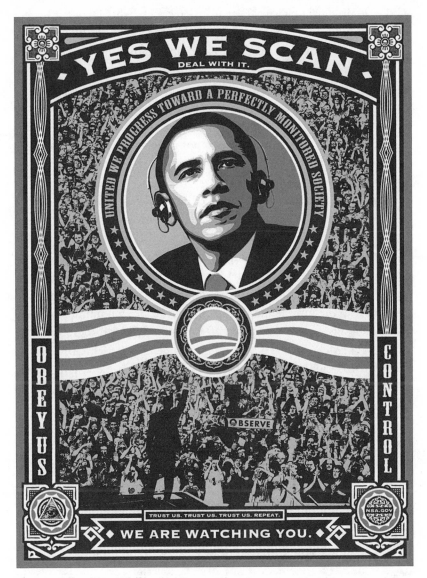

FIGS 13.1 AND 13.2. Two different faces of America's first postracial president: awkward and potentially all-seeing. Opposite: a screengrab by the author. Above: "Yes We Scan," courtesy of Rene Walter.

whose origins lay in racism. "Faciality" determines what faces can be recognized or tolerated.[24] The dozens, and black queer reading practices in particular, are uncanny inversions of faciality. Rather than serve to hierarchically order bodies into viscous clumps, dominating "by comparison to a model or a norm,"[25] reading Obama's face in this way might yield a comic finality—"you're so ugly, even Hello Kitty says goodbye" or "your grin is such a lie that not even your white grandmother would believe you." But Obama's grimacing mask is not merely a sign to be decoded, a truth to be unveiled. A read is a punctum that is also always an invitation, a salvo in a call-and-response.

Edward Snowden unmasked himself in part because he believed that by stepping out from the veil of anonymity, by revealing his identity and giving face, he might effect some degree of control over the representation of his decision to confirm the unprecedented scale of the NSA's programs and to encourage others to come forward.[26] In addition, and unsurprisingly, he believed that his anonymity might endanger him, making him vulnerable to the intimidation, kidnapping, torture, and murder he knew the U.S. government was capable of. By coming forward/out, Snowden curiously mimicked some black and queer practices, which mix a performative hypervisibility (an awareness of one's difference and visibility) with invisibility or opacity (an indifference or even hostility to the norm or to being read properly). James Baldwin, riffing on Ralph Ellison, expressed it somewhat differently in a 1961 interview in which he linked black in/visibility to whiteness: "What white people see when they look at you is not visible. What they *do* see when they *do* look at you is what they have invested you with. What they have invested you with is all the agony, and pain, and the danger, and the passion, and the torment—you know, sin, death, and hell—of which everyone in this country is terrified."[27]

Snowden had gone stealth for years, passing as a mild-mannered analyst, keeping his civil libertarian streak on the down low. Snowden appeared, *carried it*, and then vanished.[28] Currently, Snowden remains in Russia, which has extended his asylum until 2017, while the United States continues to bully other nations into denying him egress. Snowden's face (like that of convicted U.S. Army whistleblower Chelsea Manning) now appears on the placards of thousands of protestors around the world. Their faces have become screens and masks, standing in for or projecting a generalizable face—my face, your face, all our faces. And increasingly, as at a summer 2013 protest in Germany, the faces of these figures are worn as masks, barring access to an individual or specific face while calling into existence a shared or collective one.[29] These faces/masks make a dual demand: transparency from the government, opacity for the rest of us.

In her study of the transatlantic performances of black women, historian and performance studies scholar Daphne Brooks uses the concept of "spectacular opacity" to retool colonial tropes of darkness, which have "historically been made to envelop bodies and geographical territories in the shadows of global and hegemonic domination."[30] Like some uses of masks, or going stealth, darkness and opacity have the capacity to resist the violent will-to-know, the will-to-transparency. Martinican critic and poet Édouard Glissant says that "a person has a right to be opaque,"[31] a point echoed, in different contexts, by cypherpunks like Julian Assange and the hacktivist group Anonymous. For Assange, Anonymous, and others such as the Electronic Frontier Foundation (EFF), developing cryptographic literacies is essential. This may involve using an anonymizing browser such as TOR, an array of browser add-ons, secure file transfer services, and encrypted chat, among many other techniques.[32] Encryption transforms information into codes that are unreadable by anyone without the appropriate cipher. Learning how to make oneself opaque is a practical necessity and a political tactic in this moment of big data's ascendancy, in which clickstreams, RFID tags, the GPS capacities of our cell phones, CCTV, and new biometric technologies are employed by states and corporations to digitally log our movements and virtually every technologically mediated interaction. Yet states and corporations have made encryption more difficult, describing cryptographic tools as weapons and encrypted communications as threats to national security.[33] How can citizens challenge state and corporate power when those powers demand we accede to total surveillance, while also criminalizing dissent? How do we resist such demands when journalists, whistleblowers, activists, and artists are increasingly labeled as traitors or terrorists?[34]

Network theorist Alexander Galloway provides some conceptual and political starting points in his essay "Black Box, Black Bloc."[35] In the essay he considers the ways the black bloc, an anarchist tactic of anonymity and massification, and the black box, a technological device for which only inputs and outputs are known, but not the contents, collide in the new millennium.[36] The black box provides a model for the individual and collective black bloc to survive: using an array of technological and political tools, we might turn to black-boxing ourselves to make ourselves illegible to the surveillance state and big data. To resist the hegemony of the transparent, we (a "we" I imagine as loosely comprising people opposed to the unholy marriage of militarism, corporatocracy, manufactured consent, and neoliberal economic voodoo) will need to embrace techniques of becoming dark or opaque to better become present, to assert our agency and autonomy, or merely to engage in truly private interactions, without being seen or apprehended. We too can employ masks that lie, but unlike Obama's mask, these masks might help produce a sense of camaraderie. In the black bloc, or among the real-world protests organized by Anonymous and others, a mask anonymizes while also representing a shared collectivity, as evidenced by the ways the Guy Fawkes mask popularized by Anonymous is being taken up in contexts around the world: in the student protests in Quebec in 2014, as well as in protest movements in Europe and Brazil. In these contexts masks operate as part of a new politics of opacity, a form of black data that help make identities or identifying information go dark or disappear while simultaneously hailing an incipient multitude. Such a multitude is also reflected in mobilizations in the wake of George Zimmerman's acquittal in which protesters were arrayed in hoodies that declared, "I am Trayvon Martin."

Reading Obama's mask, or trying to decipher his real character or intentions, invites us to reflect on our own desires for transparency, for knowing or settling on a truth in an era in which transparency is always already staged. In an era of pervasive surveillance—by the NSA, Google, Apple, Microsoft, and Facebook, but also by our bosses, colleagues, students, parents, friends, and lovers—masks can offer a layer of protection rather than hide a real essence. A good mask, one resistant to efforts to decode it, may in fact provide us with a little room to maneuver, a little room outside the grasp of our "control society."

Black Skin, Queer Masks

While the collection and interpretation of metadata—data about data—has become increasingly sophisticated, other racial and sexual profiling techniques remain crude. Currently, most of these techniques rely on the visual apprehension of another's difference. Stop-and-Frisk, the New York City Police program that began in 2002 and has resulted in four million stops, nearly 90 percent of them involving blacks and Latinos, is one example. The wanton murder of queers of color is another.

More recent work in biometrics and the study of movement presage new technologies for capturing and recording the body. Scientific research in facial recognition, for example, provides a basis for a biometrics of queerness. On its surface the research gives credence to the concept of gaydar; a series of studies show that people are able to make very fast, above-chance judgments about sexual orientation.[37] How soon might these abilities be coded into facial recognition software? How difficult might passing become?

Christoph Bregler, a professor of computer science at New York University and director of its Movement Lab, is among the leaders of this research. In an interview with NPR's *On the Media* in the wake of the Boston Marathon bombing, he described the coming technologies. He began by noting his ability to identify other Germans while walking in New York City. This quasi-intuitive form of accounting happens almost automatically. A barely audible snippet of language, a person's gait, and body language all contribute to nearly subliminal processes of identification. He used this personal example to describe problems with identifying the Boston bombing suspects, Tamerlan and Dzhokhar Tsarnaev. Surveillance camera footage demanded that law enforcement spend many hundreds of hours combing through the footage.[38] Bregler believes that this work can, should, and will be automated. His own research teams can already identify national identity with 80 percent accuracy.[39]

Bregler imagines a world in which these technologies are more widely available and automated, making the identification of criminals or terrorists easier for law enforcement. Shoshana Magnet and Simone Browne, however, address some of the many problems with such approaches, emphasizing in particular the ways biometric technologies reproduce social stereotypes and inequalities. Magnet notes how biometrics works differently for different groups. Many biometric technologies, for example, rely on false ideas about race, such as the association of particular facial features with racial groups, and these technologies also reproduce the marginalization of transgender people. Browne links contemporary biometrics to a history of identification documents shaping "human mobility, security applications and consumer transactions," as well as to racializing surveillance technologies such as slave passes and patrols, wanted posters, and branding.[40] Details about a person's life, his or her experience and embodiment, are coded as data that do not, strictly speaking, belong to them and which are put to use by states and corporations in ways over which that person may have little control.

Magnet and Browne thereby underscore the ethical dilemmas related to social stratification and intellectual property. They, and others, also describe the ways these technologies represent a desire for unerring precision

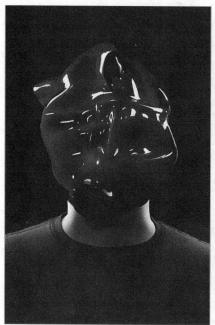

FIGS 13.3 AND 13.4. Masks derived from biometric data by artist Zach Blas. Images courtesy of Zach Blas.

and control that is and can never be achieved. As Wendy Chun notes, this control is first bound, paradoxically, to ideas that technologies will help us be free.[41] Second, the control represented by automated processes is not infallible; they fail. Magnet's work in particular underscores biometric failures, and she argues that "biometrics do real damage to vulnerable people and groups, to the fabric of democracy, and to the possibility of a better understanding of the bodies and identities these technologies are supposedly intended to protect."[42]

In recent and upcoming projects, artist-theorist Zach Blas offers creative hacks that disrupt new biometric technologies of the face. The collaborative *Facial Weaponization Suite* contests the ideological and technical underpinnings of face-based surveillance. In this community-based project, masks are collectively produced "from the aggregated facial data of participants" (Figure 13.4). His *Fag Face Mask* responds directly to the above studies on sexual orientation and facial cue recognition and offers ways to induce failures into these technologies. *Fag Face Mask* uses facial data from queer men, creating a composite that is then rendered by a 3D printer. The resulting mask is a blob, an unreadable map. Thus far, two masks have been printed, one pink, the other black. In video documentation for the work, which self-consciously echoes the aesthetics of the videos released by Anonymous, a figure wearing the pink mask describes the ways biometric technologies seek to read identity from the body, reproducing in the process the notion that one could have a stable identity at all. A few moments into the video, the mask itself, now a pulsing animation, recounts in a synthetic voice the failures of biometrics: "Biometric technologies rely heavily on stable and normative conceptions of identity, and thus, structural failures are encoded in biometrics that discriminate against race, class, gender, sex, and disability. For example, fingerprint devices often fail to scan the hands of Asian women, and iris scans work poorly if an eye has cataracts. Biometric failure exposes the inequalities that emerge when normative categories are forced upon populations."[43] Blas goes on to ask, "What are the tactics and techniques for making our faces nonexistent? How do we flee this visibility into the fog of a queerness that refuses to be recognized?"

Fag Face Mask uses masks, aggregated faces of fags, as weapons to evade or escape capture. Explicitly linked to the masked, communal figures of the black bloc, the Zapatistas, and Anonymous, Blas's project invites us to share in an air of "deliberate mystery," an opaque queer fog.[44] Yet resisting biometric technologies of the face or introducing disruptions into this field of surveillance can also result in law enforcement agencies using yet more extreme approaches. As Blas observes in the video missive, Occupy activists and Afghan civilians alike became the object of biometric data collection, and the NYPD has criminalized the wearing of masks in public. And recently the *Washington Post* revealed that more than 120 million people have been unwittingly added to facial recognition databases when, for example, they obtained a driver's license.[45]

Techniques of refusal, such as anonymous massification vis-à-vis masks, are unevenly available. There are some for whom flight may not be possible and/or for whom it may be forced. For example, becoming clandestine or deserting are not really options for populations already subject to spatialized forms of control.[46] The Stop-and-Frisk program takes place almost entirely in black and brown neighborhoods, contexts in which people yearn to escape police harassment and violence but where efforts to evade surveillance or to contest it only result in heightened forms of scrutiny—hoodies and baggy pants or mascara and glitter are already sufficient to attract dangerous forms of attention. In these contexts, young black and brown men and queers might be better served by technologies that could help them to pass, that would make them white, a dark wish encoded in the song I turn to next.

Google Google Apps Apps

Queers, all the queers
Queers, all the queers
We're on the move
Hey girl, where the fuck you moving to?
Moving to the East Bay
Living life the broke way

The Black Glitter Collective's 2013 music video "Google Google Apps Apps" is an angry lament for the death of queer San Francisco.[47] Latina drag queen Persia, together with collective members DADDIE$ PLA$TIK, work it to an up-tempo beat, but the song itself is depressing. If the first two sections of this essay are concerned with the relationship between masks and the political possibilities represented by darkness figured as opacity, this last section employs the darkness of "black data" in a different way. I focus on the material effects those companies whose business is data have had on the spatialization of dark or unseen people, focusing in particular on the ways queers and people of color have been forced to flee the gentrifying processes effected by San Francisco's most recent tech boom. Here black data takes the form of "black ops,"[48] an angry, ambivalent, even masochistic queer of color response to the entwined logics of white supremacy and the "values" of the high-tech industry.

Persia wrote the song in response to the stress of her imminent unemployment. She was about to lose her job at the San Francisco Museum of Modern Art, and Esta Noche, the gay Latino bar where she performed in San Francisco, was having trouble paying its bills.[49] In the song, she responds to the most recent wave of tech-fueled gentrification in San Francisco, which has resulted in astronomical increases in rents: the median rent for a one-bedroom apartment is now $2,764 per month.[50] Unsurprisingly, these increases have disproportionately impacted already vulnerable populations, such as the poor, people of color, underemployed queers, activists, and a host of community organizations and nonprofits.

New technologies seek to transmute the base matter of bodies into code, into digital forms of information that are intended to enhance communication and sociability, as well as, to borrow a category from Apple's apps, "productivity." They thereby also aid in the biopolitical management of populations and profit corporations like Google, Apple, Facebook, and Twitter, giants in a region also saturated with other smaller and midsize tech businesses and the venture capitalists who support them. Here we see the results of their success without requiring any complicated decryption algorithms; this is simple addition: they reap record profits, they work with city governments to bring jobs to the region and to "develop" city districts, rents go up.

Persia shouts, "SF keep your money/Fuck your money!" The song underscores the material effects the growth of digital technologies and economies have had on real-world spaces, in this case the forced exodus of the people and cultures that helped make San Francisco a political and creative laboratory, that made it home to so many freaks, artists, and sexual adventurers. In a now famous account, Richard Florida noted the appeal of quirky, diverse cities to high-tech companies, forward-looking entrepreneurs, and the "creative class."[51] Florida did not, however, account for the ways the emigration of white-collar creatives and geeks tends to fundamentally alter the very things that made the destination so appealing in the first instance. Persia's resentment, like that of the working class more broadly, does not figure into his analyses.[52] In a discussion about Silicon Valley's recent awkward and usually selfish forays into politics, the *New Yorker*'s George Packer observes, "The technology industry . . . has transformed the Bay Area without being changed by it—in a sense, without getting its hands dirty."[53]

Importantly, the song's refrain links these processes of gentrification and displacement, as well as the underlying ideologies and practices of neoliberal capitalism, to whiteness. Persia and her crew sing:

> Google Google Apps Apps
> Google Google Apps Apps
> Gringa Gringa Apps Apps
> Gringa Gringa Apps Apps
> I just wanna wanna be white!

The technological giants that aim to connect people everywhere are intimately tied to new surveillance regimes, something the song acknowledges early on when Persia tells her audience to "Twitter, Twitter me / Facebook, Facebook me." They are also linked to white privilege and class domination.[54] The new arrivals to San Francisco, these gringos and gringas, terms that refer to English-speaking nonnatives, reproduce the violent fantasies of white manifest destiny. They are bringing civilization, in the forms of design-savvy gadgets, tweets, instant picture sharing, cat videos, augmented reality, biometric tagging, commercial data mining, and apps for everything, to the unwashed hippies and queers of San Francisco, as well as to billions of needy people around the world. Although they might give the impression of being insensitive—if such comments as "adapt or move to Oakland" are any indication—they do not have it out for any-one in particular.[55] They are rational self-evident social actors, self-evident because their motives are pure and transparent: technological mastery, professional achievement, economic success, white-collar comforts (like living in the Bay Area).

Their privilege is evident as well in the alarm and discomfort they feel in the wake of recent protests against their presence in the Bay Area. In a much-discussed Twitter image, protesters at a May 2013 antigentrifica-tion event smashed a piñata of a Google bus, a paper mache avatar of the cushy luxury bus shuttle service Google provides to its San Francisco employees. The buses (also used by other companies) transport workers to the Google offices and are equipped with high-speed Wi-Fi so that they can stay connected 24-7, so that they can optimize their workflows or gos-sip or sleep en route to work without having to mix it up with the masses.

In the video, DADDIE$ PLA$TIK members Tyler Holmes and Vain Hein comically reflect on their own chances of becoming white:

> How does one become white?
> A little bleach might do the trick
> Well I bleach my asshole—
> Does that count?

In this instance, the song ties bleached assholes, a trend that involves depigmentation of the skin around the anus, to whiteness more broadly. While this is a satirical jab at perceived white sexual hangups, the wish that underlies the chorus "I just wanna wanna be white" is nonetheless powerful and real. Whites want to become whiter (all over), but so too do many people of color. Whatever their political orientation, few queers of color can escape the lure of whiteness. Who doesn't want to be beautiful, rich, and white? Who doesn't want to possess technological, financial, and social power? Who doesn't want to control space? Who doesn't want to escape the darkness of violence, poverty, and exclusion? Why wouldn't one opt instead for translucency, transparency, and technological control

FIG. 13.5. Vain Hein and Persia dance in whiteface against a digital backdrop of San Francisco.

and power? Venus Xtravaganza was not alone in the wish she expressed in *Paris Is Burning*: "I would like to be a spoiled rich white girl."[56]

The song ambivalently expresses this wish. First, it articulates an erotics of gentrification that mixes sexual desire with domination through the ironic lyrics that link BDSM play to gentrification vis-à-vis an ode to Madonna's "Justify My Love"—"Techies, take the mission / Techies, gentrify me / Gentrify me / Gentrify my love."[57] Second, however, it underscores the grotesquerie that results when the cast-outs, the freaks and queers of color, do try to become white. Near the end of the video, Persia and her crew smear white paintstick over their faces and don blond wigs, while Vain Hein adds a Leigh Bowery–style doll mask over his already clownish white face. The chorus now takes on another meaning—one that makes the violence of the wish and the impossibility of its realization— more palpable. I wanna be white, but obviously, I never will be, not if that means having money or the ability to influence the shape of particular technologies or urban spaces rather than be the target consumers of high-tech firms or the chaff cities are trying to cull in their obsequious efforts to please tech companies.

Of course, this critique of the marriage of high-tech, gentrification, and whiteness is struck through with ironies. Persia wrote the lyrics to the song on her phone (I wrote most of this essay on a seven-year-old

MacBook Pro, if you're wondering). The song and video required considerable technical manipulation—audio engineering and video editing. It appears on YouTube, a Google property, and it has been circulated widely on Facebook and Twitter (where I found it), all in an effort to achieve some traction in network culture in which traction equals attention equals hits equals, Persia hopes, some form of remuneration. Maybe just enough to help her put down a deposit on her new East Bay gigs.

In the comments section of the video, an inevitable troll remarked on some of these ironies: "interesting that the lyrics of this song hostile to the tech industry were written on a phone." To which another poster sarcastically replied, "It's interesting how all those blacks wanted out of slavery even though they got free food, and home [*sic*]."[58]

The desire to become white is a shadow that haunts the lives of queers of color. Perhaps the most common reaction to such a wish is to deny it or to deconstruct it. But, following Jack Halberstam's more recent work on "shadow feminisms," I wonder if the urge to challenge the logic of whiteness in ourselves—the internalized and not-so-internalized violences engendered in us by white settler colonialisms—does not itself reproduce another set of violences, for racial authenticity or purity, for example.[59] Instead, we might embrace those forms of darkness in which identity is obscured or rendered opaque. There are no coherent, rational, self-knowing subjects here, just furious refusals. These refusals are a kind of black ops, a form of black data that encrypts without hope of a coherent or positive output. Queers and people of color might tactically redeploy black ops as techniques of masking, secrecy, or evasion. Rather than follow the logic of the "Black Hole," the government contractor Electronic Warfare Associates' wireless traffic intercept tool,[60] black ops imagines a world in which our identities and movement are our own, opaque to the securitized gazes of states and corporations. New black ops technologies might help us all play out our masochistic fantasies of becoming white, becoming animal, becoming other, or just pure private becoming.

Persia embraces a darkness that responds to the antisociality engendered by the tech giants with an ambivalent queer antisociality in turn. Her face morphs; masked, she affirms, yes, I want to be white like you. Twitter me, Facebook me, gentrify my love. I'll become white, jerky, stumbling, angry, cruel. Her crew's transformation parodies the awkwardness and unsublimated violence of whiteness (and at least some white people). Their black ops is both a refusal and a rearticulation of the stuck frustrations activists, queers of color, and others feel in the wake of gentrification and neoliberal economic policies more generally. This ambivalence is even present in their name, The Black Glitter Collective: black is for mourning (or encrypting), glitter is for queer fun (it gets *everywhere*).

Conclusion

I have sought to enact a form of black data that is different from discussions of black life that reduce it to lists of bare accountings, which are incomplete and misleadingly suggest that black queer life must always and only be subtended to historical and contemporary traumas or victimization. Instead, I have used interpretive and performative black queer practices—reading and throwing shade—to cultivate a notion of black data tied to defacement, opacity, and encryption. Black queer reads can shame a face (in this case, Obama's), and they can also articulate an opaque, encrypted point of view, one that resists being fully apprehended or made transparent. Throwing shade, in the context of drag and Kiki Balls, for instance, does not require any specific enunciation to deliver an insult; rather, it uses looks, bodily gestures, and tones to deliver a message at once clear ("ratchet") and open-endedly sneaky ("I didn't *say* anything"). I have suggested that such black queer practices, figured here as "black data," might be usefully brought to bear on discussions about network culture, especially those related to surveillance and the relationship and impact of communication technologies on spaces and mobilities. I have moreover allied the political possibilities of a black queer conception of black data with the orientations of anarchists and cryptographers. I hope that these perhaps unlikely alliances might yield new, creative, and viable forms of black ops, encrypted forms of regnant reading and refusal imbued with a dark optimism toward the present, in which political and corporate interests collude to produce an ever-expanding web of ruin, a vast system of surveillance and capture that seeks to transform us all into code.[61]

NOTES

I am grateful to E. Patrick Johnson for the invitation to participate in this volume and for his thoughtful feedback on earlier versions of this essay. Two anonymous reviewers also made suggestions that improved my discussion here. Key ideas in this essay emerged from discussions with Zach Blas. Other readers who offered important insights include Hentyle Yapp, Amit Gilutz, and Bill Baskin. This essay was completed in part through the support of a fellowship provided by the Alexander von Humboldt Foundation.

1. Baratunde Thurston, "How to Be Black (Online)," *Slideshare.net,* accessed July 1, 2013, http://www.slideshare.net/baratunde/how-to-be-black-online-by-baratunde.

2. At the time of Thurston's presentation, for example, blacks tended to use Yahoo! and MySpace more than whites. Thurston, "How To Be Black (Online)."

3. For an extended but not exhaustive list, see Beth E. Kolko, Lisa Nakamura, and Gilbert B. Rodman, eds., *Race in Cyberspace* (New York: Routledge, 1999); Lisa Nakamura, *Cybertypes: Race, Ethnicity, and Identity on the Internet* (New York: Routledge, 2002); Nakamura, *Digitizing Race: Visual Cultures of the Internet* (Minneapolis: University of Minnesota Press, 2008); Nakamura and Peter Chow-White, eds. *Race after the Internet* (New York: Routledge, 2011); Cameron Bailey, "Virtual Skin: Articulating Race in Cyberspace," in *Immersed in Technology: Art and Virtual Environments,* ed. Mary Ann Moser and Douglas MacLeod, 29–49 (Cambridge: MIT Press, 1996); Mark B. N. Hansen, "Digitizing the Racialized Body or The Politics of Universal Address," *SubStance* 33, no. 2 (2004): 107–33; Jennifer González, "The Face and the Public: Race, Secrecy, and Digital Art Practice," *Camera Obscura* 24, no. 1 (2009): 37–65; Andil Gosine, "Brown to Blonde at Gay.com: Passing White in Queer Cyberspace" in *Queer Online: Media Technology and Sexuality,* eds. Kate O'Riordan and David Phillips, 139–53 (New York: Peter Lang, 2007); Shaka McGlotten, "Ordinary Intersections: Speculations on Difference, Justice, and Utopia in Black Queer Life," *Transforming Anthropology* 20, no. 1 (2012): 123–37.

4. For recent treatments of the dozens, see Ali Colleen Neff's discussions in *Let the World Listen Right: The Mississippi Delta Hip Hop Story* (Jackson: University of Mississippi Press, 2009); and Elijah Wald, *The Dozens: A History of Rap's Mama* (New York: Oxford University Press, 2012). For discussions of black Twitter, see Farhad Manjoo's (in)famous "How Black People Use Twitter," *Slate,* August 10, 2010, accessed July 1, 2013, http://www.slate.com/articles/technology/technology/2010/08/how_black_people_use_twitter.html; and Shani Hilton, "The Secret Power of Black Twitter," *Buzzfeed,* accessed July 16, 2013, http://www.buzzfeed.com/shani/the-secret-power-of-black-twitter. For an excellent critical account, see Sanjay Sharma, "Black Twitter? Racial Hashtags, Networks, and Contagion," *New Formations* 78 (2013): 46–64.

5. "OMG! Black People!," last updated July 1, 2009, http://omgblackpeople.wordpress.com/.

6. For a few notable examples of literature in science and technology that addresses race, see Donna Haraway, *Modest Witness@Second-Millennium.FemaleMan-Meets-OncoMouse: Feminism and Technoscience* (New York: Routledge, 1997); Thomas Foster, *Souls of Cyberfolk: Posthumanism as Vernacular Theory* (Minneapolis: University of Minnesota Press, 2005); Wendy Chun, "Introduction: Race and/as Technology; or How to Do Things to Race," *Camera Obscura* 24, no. 1 (2009): 7–35; Chun, *Programmed Visions: Software and Memory* (Cambridge, MA: MIT Press, 2011). On sexuality and new media technologies, see Campbell, *Getting It On Online.* Also see the essays in

O'Riordan and Phillips, *Queer Online*. For recent discussions in black queer studies, see Allen, "Introduction," and Shaka McGlotten and Dana-ain Davis, eds., *Black Genders and Sexualities* (New York: Palgrave, 2012). Also see E. Patrick Johnson and Mae G. Henderson, *Black Queer Studies: A Critical Anthology* (Durham, NC: Duke University Press, 2005). For exceptions to the lack of studies on the ways black queer people are interpolated by or employ new media and other technologies, see Dwight McBride, *Why I Hate Abercrombie & Fitch: Essays on Race and Sexuality* (New York: New York University Press, 2005), 88–133; Shaka McGlotten, *Virtual Intimacies: Media, Affect, and Queer Sociality* (New York: State University of New York Press, 2013); McGlotten, "Ordinary Intersections"; Herukhuti, *Conjuring Black Funk: Notes on Culture, Sexuality, and Spirituality*, vol. 1 (New York: Vintage Entity Press, 2007).

7. The notion of race as a technology is discussed by Lisa Nakumara and Peter Chow-White, Wendy Chun, and Beth Coleman, among others. Nakamura and Chow-White, for example, discuss the "enforced forgetting" that deprived slaves of information (data) about their pasts: racism is a technology, "a systematic way of doing things that operates by mediating between users and techniques to create specific forms of oppression and discrimination" (3). Beth Coleman makes the connection to *techné* more explicit (and also thereby echoing Foucault). For Coleman, *techné* refers to an applied, reproducible skill; race thus emerges as a productive technique of power. See Nakamura and Chow-White, "Introduction—Race and Digital Technology: Code, the Color Line, and the Information Society," *Race after the Internet*, 1–18; Coleman, "Race as Technology," *Camera Obscura* 24, no. 1 (2009): 176–207. See also Chun, "Introduction: Race and/as Technology." For a discussion of discriminatory social costs that result from data mining, see Anthony Danna and Oscar H. Gandy, Jr., "All That Glitters Is Not Gold: Digging Beneath the Surface of Data Mining," *Journal of Business Ethics* 40 (2002): 373–86.

8. "New HIV Infections in the United States, 2010," *Centers for Disease Control*, accessed June 1, 2013, http://www.cdc.gov/hiv/pdf/HIV_infographic_11X17_HR.pdf.

9. "Lesbian, Gay, Bisexual, Transgendered, and HIV-Affected Hate Violence in 2012," *National Coalition of Anti-Violence Programs*, accessed June 4, 2013, http://www.avp.org/storage/documents/ncavp_2012_hvreport_final.pdf, 9.

10. See the important and rich resources available at the Trans-Atlantic Slave Trade Database, accessed June 4, 2013, http://www.slavevoyages.org/tast/index.faces.

11. Signe-Mary McKernan, Caroline Ratcliffe, C. Eugene Steuerle, and Sisi Zhang, "Less Than Equal: Racial Disparities in Wealth Accumulation," *The Urban Institute*, April 26, 2013, http://www.urban.org/UploadedPDF/412802-Less-Than-Equal-Racial-Disparities-in-Wealth-Accumulation.pdf.

12. Arlene Eisen, "Operation Ghetto Storm: 2012 Annual Report on the Extrajudicial Killing of 313 Black People," *Malcolm X Grassroots Movement*, April 7, 2013,

http://mxgm.org/operation-ghetto-storm-2012-annual-report-on-the-extrajudicial
-killing-of-313-black-people/.

13. Ryan Gabrieleson, Ryann Grochowski Jones, and Eric Sagara, "Deadly Force,
in Black and White," *ProPublica*, October 10, 2014, http://www.propublica.org/article
/deadly-force-in-black-and-white#update-note.

14. Nakamura and Chow-White, "Introduction—Race and Digital Technology";
Chun, "Race and/as Technology."

15. Chun, "Race and/as Technology," 8.

16. Mel Chen, *Animacies: Biopolitics, Racial Mattering, and Queer Affect* (Durham,
NC: Duke University Press, 2012).

17. Nakamura and Chow-White, "Introduction—Race and Digital Technology," 3.

18. Zebra Katz, "Ima Read" (Mad Decent, 2012), https://www.youtube.com/watch
?v=5a7toRopm1g. Black queer rapper Zebra Katz explicitly links his song to the art of
insult developed in the queer black and Latino Harlem ball scene and popularized in
Jennie Livingston's *Paris Is Burning* (1990, Miramax Films).

19. Livingston, *Paris Is Burning*.

20. More accurately, the Obama administration has aggressively pursued *unauthor-
ized* leakers. The administration, like others before it, itself leaks information to the
media in order to influence public opinion. As has been widely reported, Obama's administration has leveled charges against seven people, including convicted U.S. Army
private Chelsea (then Bradley) Manning, for leaking information to news media; all
previous administrations totaled three such prosecutions. As a candidate, Obama had
promised to protect leakers and whistleblowers.

21. A long list of historical examples comes to mind, from the legal techniques
employed to turn black people into chattel, to Jim Crow, COINTELPRO, the Wars
on Drugs and Poverty, as well as extrajudicial murder. Terroristic "antiterrorism" programs have a long history of field testing within the United States and across the
globe. The new drone wars in Afghanistan, Pakistan, and Yemen are only the most
recent expressions of these policies.

22. Phillip Brian Harper, "The Evidence of Felt Intuition: Minority Experience,
Everyday Life, and Critical Speculative Knowledge," in *Black Queer Studies*, 106–23.

23. Giorgio Agamben, *Means without End: Notes on Politics,* trans. Vincenzo Binetti
and Cesare Casarino (Minneapolis: University of Minnesota Press, 2000), 100; Em-
manuel Levinas, *Totality and Infinity: An Essay on Exteriority* (Pittsburgh, PA: Duquesne
University Press, 1969). For related discussions, see Arun Saldanha, *Psychedelic White: Goa
Trance and the Viscosity of Race* (Minneapolis: University of Minnesota Press, 2007); and
Mel Y. Chen, "Masked States and the 'Screen' between Security and Disability," *WSQ:
Women's Studies Quarterly* 40, nos. 1–2 (2012): 76–96.

24. Gilles Deleuze and Félix Guattari, *A Thousand Plateaus: Capitalism and Schizophrenia*, trans. Brian Massumi (Minneapolis: University of Minnesota Press, 1987).

25. Janell Watson, "Theorizing European Ethnic Politics with Deleuze and Guattari," in *Deleuze and Politics*, eds., Ian Buchanan and Nicholas Thoburn (Edinburgh: Edinburgh University Press, 2008), 209.

26. Others, including such news organizations as the *Guardian* and WikiLeaks, had already gleaned many insights and published information about these programs. As an insider, Snowden was uniquely positioned to confirm them. See Julian Assange, *Cypherpunks: Freedom and the Future of the Internet* (New York: OR Books, 2012).

27. Fred L. Stanley and Louis H. Pratt, eds., *Conversations with James Baldwin* (Jackson: University Press of Mississippi, 1989), 6.

28. To carry is to work it. See the explanation of Leo Gugu, artist, stylist, and performer, "Speaking with Distinction," accessed June 4, 2013, http://www.youtube.com/watch?v=UX3BrPe4dxc.

29. Chen, "Masked States and the 'Screen' between Security and Disability," 77. Chen's discussion also underscores the relationship between masks and screens and "securitized, nondisabled whiteness," a compelling reading I nonetheless do not pursue here.

30. Daphne Brooks, *Bodies in Dissent: Spectacular Performances of Race and Freedom, 1850–1910* (Durham, NC: Duke University Press), 8.

31. Quoted in Manthia Diawara, "Conversation with Édouard Glissant aboard the Queen Mary II," August 2009, accessed August 1, 2013, http://www.liv.ac.uk/media/livacuk/csis-2/blackatlantic/research/Diawara_text_defined.pdf, 6.

32. For a discussion of these techniques and tips on how to use them, see Seth Schoen, "Technology to Protect against Mass Surveillance (Part I)," *Electronic Frontier Foundation*, July 17, 2013, https://www.eff.org/deeplinks/2013/07/technology-protect-against-mass-surveillance-part-1.

33. See the discussion between Jacob Appelbaum, Andy Müller-Maguhn, and Jérémie Zimmerman in the chapter "The Militarization of Cyberspace," in Assange, *Cypherpunks*, 33–40.

34. See, for example, Glenn Greenwald, *No Place to Hide: Edward Snowden, the NSA, and the U.S. Surveillance State* (New York: Metropolitan Books, 2014).

35. Alexander Galloway, "Black Box, Black Block," in *Communization and Its Discontents: Contestation, Critique, and Contemporary Struggles*, ed. Benjamin Noys (New York: Minor Compositions, 2011).

36. For the last few decades the anarchist "black bloc" has been both hypervisible and absent. Governments and mainstream media have ignored anarchists' emphasis on mutual aid, self-organization, and voluntary association and have instead presented

anarchists as terroristic threats to state power. The black bloc is unfailingly represented as hoodlums intent on the wanton destruction of property. But the black bloc's origins lay in social protest movements in Germany in the 1970s and 1980s, where members sought to protect demonstrators from police violence and arrest. Their black clothing and masks were meant to help other protesters identify them while maintaining their own anonymity, a fact exploited in the 1999 WTO protests when law enforcement themselves donned similar clothing to infiltrate and discredit the protestors (a technique widely employed since). The black bloc's secondary role, the contours of which are hotly contested in anarchist communities, is to act as the militant direct action wing, which can include precisely the sort of destruction of property with which anarchism is synonymous in mainstream media. For refreshing anarchist indymedia, see http://stimulator.tv/.

37. See Nicholas O. Rule and Nalini Ambady, "Brief Exposures: Male Sexual Orientation Is Accurately Perceived at 50 ms.," *Journal of Experimental Social Psychology* 44 (2008): 1100–1105; and Nicholas O. Rule, Keiko Ishii, Nalini Ambady, Katherine S. Rosen, and Katherine C. Hallett, "Found in Translation: Cross-Cultural Consensus in the Accurate Categorization of Male Sexual Orientation," *Personality and Social Psychology Bulletin* 37, no. 11 (2011): 1499–1507.

38. Although there was a widespread effort to crowdsource the Boston Bombing suspects, this ultimately proved fruitless, with epic racial profiling fails, as well as ever more shameful missteps by the *New York Post*, which published the images of two Arab-looking men as suspects—they were a local coach and a high school athlete.

39. Bob Garfield, "The Future of Surveillance," *On the Media*, April 26, 2013.

40. Shoshana Magnet, *When Biometrics Fail: Gender, Race, and the Technology of Identity* (Durham, NC: Duke University Press, 2011); Simone Browne, "Digital Epidermalization: Race, Identity, and Biometrics," *Critical Sociology* 36, no. 1 (2010): 132.

41. Wendy Chun, *Control and Freedom: Power and Paranoia in the Age of Fiber Optics* (Cambridge: MIT Press, 2006).

42. Magnet, *When Biometrics Fail*, 3.

43. Zach Blas, "Facial Weaponization Suite," accessed July 7, 2013, http://www .zachblas.info/projects/facial-weaponization-suite/.

44. Gabriella Coleman, "Anonymous—From the Lulz to Collective Action," *The New Significance*, May 9, 2011, http://www.thenewsignificance.com/2011/05/09 /gabriella-coleman-anonymous-from-the-lulz-to-collective-action/. See also G. Coleman, *Hacker, Hoaxer, Whistleblower, Spy: The Many Faces of Anonymous* (New York: Verso: 2014).

45. Craig Timburg and Ellen Nakashima, "State Photo-ID Databases Become Troves for Police," *Washington Post*, June 16, 2013, http://www.washingtonpost.com

/business/technology/state-photo-id-databases-become-troves-for-police/2013/06
/16/6f014bd4-ced5-11e2-8845-d970ccb04497_story.html.

46. The radical left French journal *Tiqqun* advocates forms of autonomous secession through the creation of an imaginary politics, clandestinity, and a politics of refusal. For a sympathetic critique, see John Cunningham, "Clandestinity and Appearance," *Mute* 2, no. 16 (2010), http://www.metamute.org/editorial/articles/clandestinity-and -appearance. Such a politics of secessionist refusal served as part of the rationale for the arrest of the Tarnac 9, a group of French anarchists who had taken up in a grocery in a small village. They were accused of sabotaging the French rail network (there were no injuries). One of the rationales provided for their arrest is that the group were "pre-terrorists"—their anarcho-autonomist tendencies were reason enough for suspicion. Michèle Alliot-Marie, then interior minister, said, "They have adopted underground methods. They never use mobile telephones, and they live in areas where it is very difficult for the police to gather information without being spotted. They have managed to have, in the village of Tarnac, friendly relations with people who can warn them of the presence of strangers." Quoted in Alberto Toscano, "Criminalising Dissent," *Guardian*, January 28, 2009, http://www.theguardian.com/commentisfree /libertycentral/2009/jan/28/human-rights-tarnac-nine. Toscano goes on to observe: "The very fact of collective living, of rejecting an astoundingly restrictive notion of normality (using a mobile, living in cities, being easily observable by the police) has itself become incriminating." See also "Tarnac Nine," *Wikipedia*, last modified June 13, 2013, http://en.wikipedia.org/wiki/Tarnac_9.

47. Persia and DADDIE$ PLA$TIK, "Google Google Apps Apps," https://www .youtube.com/watch?v=5xyqbc7SQ4w.

48. I am riffing here on Fred Moten's sketch of a fugitive black imagination in "Black Optimism/Black Operation," unpublished conference paper, 2007, http:// lucian.uchicago.edu/blogs/politicalfeeling/files/2007/12/moten-black-optimism.doc.

49. Marke B., "Gentrification-Eviction-Displacement Electro Theme Song," *San Francisco Bay Guardian Online*, May 29, 2013, http://www.sfbg.com/noise/2013/05/29 /heres-your-gentrification-theme-song.

50. Kuchar, Sally, "Mapping the Average Rental Rate of a One and Two Bedroom in San Francisco," *Curbed SF*, May 23, 2013, http://sf.curbed.com/archives/2013/05/23 /mapping_the_average_rental_rate_of_a_one_and_two_bedroom_in_san_francisco .php.

51. Richard Florida, *The Rise of the Creative Class (and How It's Transforming Work, Leisure, Community and Everyday Life)* (New York: Basic Books, 2004).

52. For a critique of Florida and an analysis of the effects the creative class can have on urban environments, see Joshua Long, *Weird City: A Sense of Place and Creative Resistance in Austin, Texas* (Austin: University of Texas Press, 2010).

53. George Packer, "Change the World," *New Yorker*, May 27, 2013, e-version.

54. This statement is complicated, but not undermined, by the fact that half of high-tech workers in California are Asian. Asian Americans hold slightly more jobs in the Bay Area. See Dan Nakaso, "Asian-American Citizens Hold Slight Edge over Non-citizen Asians in Bay Area Tech Jobs," *San Jose Mercury News*, December 9, 2012, http://www.mercurynews.com/business/ci_22147394/citizen-asians-hold-slight -edge-over-non-citizen. The presence of people of color in the tech industry does not fundamentally alter the organizing ideologies of Silicon Valley, insofar as the owners, managers, and venture capitalists who shape the industry are overwhelmingly white.

55. See the comment thread in response to Rebecca Bowe, "Vanishing City," *San Francisco Bay Guardian Online,* May 21, 2013, http://www.sfbg.com/2013/05/21 /vanishing-city?page=0,0.

56. Livingston, *Paris Is Burning*.

57. Persia and DADDIE$ PLA$TIK, "Google Google Apps Apps."

58. See the comments section for Persia and DADDIE$ PLA$TIK, "Google Google Apps Apps."

59. Judith Halberstam, *The Queer Art of Failure* (Durham, NC: Duke University Press, 2011).

60. "Black Hole: Wireless Traffic Intercept, Reconstruction and Analysis," EWA *Government Systems,* http://www.ewa-gsi.com/Fact%20Sheets/Black%20Hole%20 Fact%20Sheet.pdf. Electronic Warfare Associates is a leading contractor in the development of new biometric facial recognition technologies.

61. Alexander Galloway, "Networks," in *Critical Terms for Media Studies,* eds. W. J. T. Mitchell and Mark Hansen (Chicago: University of Chicago Press, 2010), 283.

14

Boystown

Gay Neighborhoods, Social Media, and
the (Re)production of Racism

ZACHARY BLAIR

᠗

IN *BLACK QUEER STUDIES: A CRITICAL ANTHOLOGY*, Charles I. Nero asks
the question, "Why are gay ghettos white?" and proposes that the answer to this question has to do with two interdependent areas that have
historically reinforced each other: gay strategies that have focused on
integrating into the middle classes, and white hostility toward African
Americans.[1] Recent studies have expanded Nero's analysis by looking at
how various gentrification and anticrime projects create exclusionary gay
neighborhoods, particularly in New York City.[2] These studies have looked
at urban development, LGBT activism in the streets, and larger political
economic factors but have largely ignored the role of digital engagements
in the (re)production of the white gay neighborhood. Based on five years
of field research and media ethnography on Boystown, a designated gay
neighborhood in Chicago, this essay reexamines the question, "Why are
gay ghettos white?" and analyzes how neighborhood residents reproduce
racism by constructing homonormative urban space through both digital
and social neighborhood practices. More specifically, I analyze how digital social networking—a medium that has been regarded as a vehicle to

build community and advance social justice—also functions as a vehicle for segregation and a means of reproducing homonormativity.[3] Furthermore, I argue that digital engagements through social networks and sociospatial practices "on the ground" are mutually constituted and that to understand why gay ghettos continue to be white we must understand both these practices as a dialectic that shapes the meaning and experience of urban space.

In the context of neighborhood crime, I employ theories on the social production of space to understand how practices in digital, material, and lived spaces concurrently reinforce and reproduce racist, classist, homophobic, and transphobic notions of place and belonging. Specifically, I explore how neighborhood residents collectively criminalized and policed poor queer black and brown youth through digital interactions on Facebook and everyday practices "on the ground" in an effort to secure an exclusive sense of place. I utilize the concept of homonormativity to analyze and expand upon the two areas Nero originally defined, as well as a way of analyzing how racism, sexism, classism, and transphobia operate together to create exclusionary neighborhoods from a political economic perspective.

The Social Geography of a Gay Neighborhood

Boystown is geographically located in the north side of the most segregated city in the nation.[4] Before Boystown became a thriving gay neighborhood, it was an area that—like much of the city of Chicago—showed the effects of the geographic restructuring of the economy that began in the 1950s. Postindustrial Chicago was defined by white flight, the development of suburbia, and disinvestments in the urban core.[5] While it remained a majority white neighborhood, the eastern part of Lakeview where Boystown is now located was home to significant populations of ethnic minorities in its recent history, including Jewish, Japanese, and Latino residents.[6] During the 1950s and 1960s, Clark Street separated wealthy white lakefront residents from poor Puerto Rican residents to the west, while Irving Park Road separated them from poor Appalachian white and Native American residents to the north.[7] During the 1970s, the area became known as a center for artistic production and leftist activism.[8] It soon attracted young urban professionals who were moving back to the city as well as a large number of gay men and lesbians who were brought together socially and politically by a new gay rights movement

FIG. 14.1. This photograph shows one of the 25-foot-tall art deco rainbow pylons erected as part of the North Halsted Streetscape Project. Twenty of these line North Halsted Street located in the middle of each block. This one stands at 3444 North Halsted Street, south of West Cornelia Avenue. This picture is facing southeast. Photo courtesy of Zachary Blair.

and geographically as they were pushed north out of the city center owing to development. By the 1990s, Boystown was a thriving gay entertainment district and residential neighborhood, with numerous gay bars and nightclubs, a bathhouse, gay-owned retail businesses, condominiums, and renovated apartments. On November 15, 1998, Mayor Richard M. Daley officially designated Boystown as a gay neighborhood, with the construction of twenty rainbow-ringed, art deco pylons that still line the North Halsted Streetscape Project and mark the neighborhood as gay.

Data from the U.S. Census Bureau's 2008–2012 American Community Survey shows that decades of segregation and gentrification have continued to keep the majority of neighborhood residents white and middle class.[9] With available census data, it is difficult to track with any precision the number of gay men (and women) who live in the neighborhood.

However, data suggest that the highest concentration of gay men who live in Boystown dwell along North Halsted Street in the center of the neighborhood's gay entertainment zone.[10] The visibility of gay men and gay male sexuality through the numerous male-centered bars, clubs, and businesses that have anchored and defined the Boystown as Chicago's gay neighborhood over the past 25 years has also created an environment that is dominantly male. This male prominence remains despite the fact that the majority of Boystown residents are actually female and heterosexual.[11]

While Boystown is considered to be home or a popular nightspot for some, for others it is a vital resource. As the city's gay neighborhood, Boystown has the highest concentration of organizations in the city that provide services specifically for the Chicago's LGBT population. As a result, LGBT people come to Boystown from all over the city to access the resources provided by these organizations. A number of these groups have services designed to meet the specific needs of Chicago's LGBT youth. Most prominent, the Center on Halsted—which in 2012 was the city's newest, largest, and best-funded gay community center—offers a youth program, cultural activities, and free anonymous HIV testing. The Broadway Youth Center continues to be an advocate in the neighborhood for the city's LGBT youth and provides services that include STD testing, workshops and support groups, primary medical care, a GED program, and a violence recovery program. Also, the Night Ministry has a van that parks on the corner of Belmont Avenue and Halsted Street that serves food, distributes personal hygiene products and condoms, and provides HIV testing and support services to homeless LGBT youth. These relatively accessible and abundant resources makes Boystown a crucial destination for LGBT people in need.

In addition to the neighborhood's social services, Boystown also provides a relatively safe space for LGBT people to publicly socialize, which is especially important for those living on the streets. In some cases, the social networks that are created on the streets of Boystown were key resources for survival. While the neighborhood is not free of anti-LGBT violence, it is considerably safer than the south and west sides of the city, which are statistically some of the most violent areas in the country.[12] To escape this geography of violence, many of Boystown's LGBT "street youth" travel around forty-five minutes or more by bus or train to this gay-centric destination with one of the lowest crime rates in the city.[13] For some LGBT teenagers who frequent Boystown, being on the streets is safer than being in their homes.

Over the past 10 years, a transient street culture grew among African American and Latino LGBT people in Boystown. The intersection of Belmont Avenue and North Clark Street was the epicenter for this culture, which was most visible during Chicago's warmer months. While neighborhood residents and community organizations referred to this population as the "LGBT street youth," both understood this population to include adults over the age of eighteen. However with many not old enough to be admitted into the neighborhood bars and nightclubs, the social scene was on the streets. On warm summer nights, hundreds of people would gather along Belmont Avenue, for socializing, networking, partying, and dancing. Voguing up North Halsted Street or listening to music and talking to friends in the open doors of parked cars were common activities on Friday nights.

Crime Comes to the Neighborhood

On August 3, 2009, two gay men were violently assaulted right in the center of Boystown's entertainment district within two blocks and ten minutes of each other. At around 4:50 a.m., one of the victims was beaten with brass knuckles and a brick, and the other was beaten unconscious and robbed of his cell phone. The perpetrators were described as a group of four young black men, between the ages of twenty and thirty, with one being light skinned and possibly Hispanic.

These two assaults occurred only days after five men were beaten and robbed in neighboring Lincoln Park, all within four days, one of the victims seriously injured with a broken jaw. A media frenzy pursued, in which local headlines reported "spikes in violence" threatening Chicago's North Side and "a wave of violence" that was engulfing North Side neighborhoods.[14] They also occurred less than 48 hours before Beat 2331's monthly Chicago Alternative Policing Strategy (CAPS) meeting. Word quickly spread that this meeting would be the opportunity for residents to confront the police together about controlling Boystown's crime.

On August 5, 2009, over two hundred people crammed into Nookies Tree—a popular restaurant located at 3334 North Halsted Street—to vehemently confront the local police about the neighborhood's crime problem. This was the largest crowd ever to show up to a CAPS meeting in Boystown, which usually attracts only around a half-dozen people. Resident after resident asked Commander Kathleen Boehmer and the officers who accompanied her how they planned to keep the streets safe. Others shared the stories of their own experiences with assaults and muggings in the neighborhood, most of which were never reported. They were frustrated, angry, and a potential fire hazard, so the meeting was rushed and cut short.

The police assured everyone that they were doing everything possible to find the perpetrators of the muggings and to protect the neighborhood from criminal activity. They also tried to ease worries that the Chicago Police Department was understaffed due to budget cuts resulting from the economic recession and told everyone they had ample resources to keep the streets safe. They pointed to the city's statistics, which showed that (reported) neighborhood crime had gone down from previous years. Still, meeting attendees left unsatisfied with police responses, even more concerned about crime and safety in the neighborhood, and inspired to take it upon themselves to make the neighborhood safe again.

Following the CAPS meeting, residents and business owners met outside of Nookies Tree and began to organize and speak to various news stations that were lined up on the sidewalk outside. An e-mail list was passed around so that residents could start their own meetings, in addition to their own police-led citizen street patrol that would deter crime during peak late-night hours. Another was created for a Facebook page that would allow residents to instantaneously share information about criminal activity going on in the neighborhood—a sort of digital neighborhood watch. Within 48 hours, people were already posting to the Lakeview 9-1-1 Facebook page. In less than a month, there were over thirteen hundred members who contributed to the page's content. It quickly became the central hub for the neighborhood's anticrime movement.

Inspired by the Pink Angels of the early 1990s, the street patrols—dubbed "community walks"—were primarily organized online through the Lakeview 9–1-1 page.[15] Initially, they were scheduled to take place on Fridays and Saturdays (the busiest nights of the week) at two different times. We were to meet in the parking lot of the 7-Eleven on North Halsted Street and West Roscoe Street. The first one occurred at midnight on August 8, 2009, and over fifty people showed up for it. Although white men and women made up the majority of those in attendance, people of color and varying nonnormative gender identities also participated in the walk to "take back the streets." A few of the neighborhood's prominent drag queens even showed up in eye-catching glittering ensembles to support the walks.

Since there were so many of us, we were split up into two groups. There was an overall sense of excitement because so many neighbors showed up to work together for a good cause—to make the neighborhood a safer place. People were meeting their neighbors for the first time. As we walked down the crowded North Halsted Street, people exchanged stories about the crimes in the neighborhood they had personally witnessed or had been victim to.

By the time the walking group passed the nightclub Spin at the intersection of Belmont Avenue and North Halsted Street, it had transformed. We walked right through the center of the neighborhood's dominantly African American LGBT street culture, which during the warmer months was at the strip of Belmont Avenue between North Halsted Street and Clark Street. Smartphones, which up until this point had been used primarily to exchange contact information, quickly became cameras photographing the LGBT people of color hanging out in the street. People were running away from the walking group, with their hands covering their faces. "Don't photograph us!" someone shouted at a fifty-five-year-old gay white man who jumped up on a lamppost with his large Nikon camera to get a better shot. "This is a public space!" he angrily shouted back. "If you do not like being photographed, then leave and go someplace private." Afterward, he told me he used to work for a couple of the local gay news publications and was completely knowledgeable about the laws for taking photographs in public. Jason, a twenty-three-year-old gay white man who moved to Boystown from Indiana, was walking next to me and turned and said, "These stupid niggers. We should shoot them all."

After that, I stayed back to observe how the entire walking group interacted with those on the streets. Most of them were telling people to keep walking and that they were not allowed to loiter in the streets. I noticed that surrounding restaurants that were closed for the night had poured ice over their doorsteps to prevent those out in the street from sitting down in front of their businesses.

We turned down an alley that was behind one of the neighborhood's larger, newer condominium buildings. Jonathan, a forty-eight-year-old white man who was resident there, told the crowd, "Now be careful. There are people here at all hours of the day and night, all doing drugs and prostituting. I know because my apartment is right there, so this is my view every night. I won't even come back here by myself because it just isn't safe, and the smell of urine is overwhelming."

As we walked a little further we interrupted an African American transgender sex worker performing oral sex on one of her customers in the alley. The police officer who was with us stopped her and asked for her ID as her client walked toward Clark Street. While some of the walking group continued forward, most stood there and watched like they were watching a television show, with numerous people in the group photographing and filming the incident. After a short and inaudible conversation between the woman and the officer, she walked away. "See, this is what I'm talking about," Jonathan said, as the rest of the walking group continued their way back to the 7-Eleven.

It was clear that Boystown residents and business owners had named the neighborhood's LGBT street youth and transgender women of color (presumed to be engaged in prostitution) as the problem behind the neighborhood's violent crime. Within hours, photographs from the walk were showing up on blogs, residents' personal Facebook pages, and Lakeview 9–1–1. Boystown residents and business owners were soon assembling an online spectacle, where LGBT youth and transgender women of color were disproportionately represented, making them symbols of crime, undesirable behavior, and violence.

Pictures were posted of LGBT street youth of color fighting with each other on neighborhood streets, with people calling them "delinquent troublemakers" and "future murders." Coded in the language of anti-violence, postings expanded to include nonviolent "crime" like loitering, noise pollution, defiling public and private property, drug dealing, and prostitution. A white condo owner posted a video of African American LGBT street youth voguing up and down the streets late at night, loudly laughing and encouraging one another to strike the best pose. People responded to the post, calling them "gaggles of hoodlums" and talking about how they are unable to sleep at night because of them. Jonathan from the community walk posted a series of photos of a homeless transgender women going through garbage cans in the alley. People responded in posts calling her a "useless nigger," "tranny hooker," and "filthy and nasty."

With so many residents armed with smartphones and instant access to cameras, pictures and videos were constantly being added to Lakeview 9–1–1 and personal Facebook pages as well. A Boystown resident and prominent white drag queen posted a video of African Americans hanging outside the neighborhood's late-night Subway sandwich shop across the street from his apartment and wrote, "Garbage ghetto Whores . . . allowed to litter up our neighborhood. I wonder if the press would be interested? What is so great about subway? This is EVERY NIGHT. . . . GO HOME. It's raining you loud mouthed idiots." Absent were videos of drunk white bar patrons screaming outside of Hydrate, which happens at least on a weekly basis. There were no photographs of the well-known white drug dealers who stroll up and down North Halsted Street or hang out in front of the businesses on Belmont Avenue.

For years, residents continued to monitor, racialize, and criminalize the neighborhood's LGBT street youth and transgender women of color by posting degrading, racializing, and criminalizing photographs, videos, and comments online. The owner of the Lakeview 9-1-1 page tried to censor racist content, but there was so much content that one person alone could not manage the page. In 2011, it was succeeded by the Take Back Boystown page, which functioned as the similar platform for perpetuating racism, homonormativity, and Boystown's exclusivity through social media. As of September 2012, the page had 4,219 followers.

Lived Experiences of Racism in Boystown

A week after the Boystown attacks that changed the course of the neighborhood, Katrina got off at the Belmont Red Line stop as she did nearly every weekday during the warmer months. She was making her trek from her part-time retail job downtown to her apartment at North Pine Grove Avenue and West Sheridan Road. It would be more convenient for her to get off at Addison Street, but during the spring and summer months when crowds of Cubs fans and Wrigleyville patrons pack the Addison stop, she felt safer getting off at Belmont. This way, she would avoid hearing the usual comments white women made to their boyfriends or husbands: "Is that a man or a woman?"; the sexual advances of drunken straight guys leaving the game, "Hey! Wanna suck my dick?"; or the physical threats of violence shouted from across the street, "I'll beat your ass tranny whore." However, on this Monday, August 10, 2009, she did not feel any better off as she made her way up North Halsted Street through the gay neighborhood.

What was usually a pleasant experience for Katrina, where familiar and smiling faces greeted her outside different businesses as she walked past, was an unusually hostile one. Just as she passed Steamworks—the neighborhood's gay bathhouse—a car full of white gay men headed southbound shouted "Go back to your own neighborhood, nigger!" as they drove past her. She recognized one man from Cocktail, her favorite bar on the North Halsted Strip. She continued her walk. As she approached the intersection of North Halsted Street and Addison Street, she had to stop at the crosswalk in front of the Shell station until it was safe for her to cross. While she stood there waiting, another car passed by with a white male in the passenger side screaming "Tranny nigger!" as it drove toward the lake. Rather than give these men a reaction, she ignored her antagonizers and continued her walk home. When she got there, she took off her heels, grabbed two Pond's makeup removal wipes off her bathroom countertop, wiped down her face, and hopped into bed—a queen-size mattress laid on the floor.

What Katrina experienced on her walk home that day was not something new to her, but it felt out of the norm—especially for Boystown. Katrina never felt such intense hostility within the borders of her own neighborhood. Discrimination and threats of violence were not foreign to her. Katrina was someone who naturally stood out in a crowd and she knew it, especially growing up in North Dakota and serving time in the United States Army. She was, as she described herself, "in the middle of her transition." Over six feet tall, with a large athletic build, she had a deep skin tone that she would often refer to as "dark chocolate."

"I'm used to gays saying things under their breath when I walk by or maybe to their friends when I leave the room, but never with such hostility and screaming out in public like that. That stuff usually only happens when I am outside of Boystown. Whenever I'm downtown or on the West Side, that kind of stuff is normal and expected. I can usually pass as a natural female, but when I'm in Boystown I guess people just assume that I'm trans because of my size. Still, it's crazy that it happened to me twice, within 10 minutes and on Halsted Street of all places. Boystown is supposed to be welcoming and diverse and safe, and it's my neighborhood too. Like they think it's okay to do that. Like they ain't gonna see me this weekend at the bars. Like I'm not gonna see them. Girl, please."

A few days later, on August 13, 2009, I had a follow-up conversation with Katrina and her friend Shauna at my apartment. Shauna, who self-identified as black and trans, was an undergraduate student at DePaul University, said, "The fear and the hatred in the air is so thick now, you can cut it with a knife. It never used to be like this. We aren't scared, but all these white people walking around here sure as hell are. They don't know what to do. They need to just go home and lock their doors."

The next day, I sat at Caribou Coffee on Cornelia Avenue and North Halsted Street—affectionately nicknamed "Cruise-a-boo" and "Care-a-boy," depending on whom you talk to. I was reviewing my interview notes and preparing for an interview I had later that evening at the Center on Halsted. On my table I had a book about conspiracy theories that a boyfriend of mine was obsessed with.

"Did you read that book yet?" I heard someone say to me. I looked in the direction of the voice, and someone standing in line to get a coffee was analyzing the papers on my desk. "I was just at the Center, reading all about the illuminati on their little computers. That shit is crazy. Look, I have print outs." She handed me a pile of papers about different conspiracies: reptilians, the illuminati, and the hollow earth theory. "You can go ahead and look at my research, just give it back to me before you leave. They control the world. That's why it's going to shit. I'm Shaadi, by the way."

During the three-hour-long conversation that ensued, I learned that Shaadi was a Chicago native from a suburb on the South Side. She identified as trans but never fully transitioned. She was black and homeless and had been living on and off the streets for the past three years. Once I told her about my project, all she could talk about was how different Boystown was now, compared with the early 1990s. In her nostalgic recollection, she made it clear that she preferred the Boystown from a decade ago, but she also discussed how her experiences in and of the neighborhood have changed in the past week.

"I'm only here temporarily this time—for a couple of months. I don't want to be here any longer than that. People used to be so friendly. When I would go to a coffee shop back then, people would love to socialize and talk to each other. Now look at them," she paused and pointed to the customers sitting in Caribou Coffee. "Everyone is looking down on their laptops and their phones. They do not even want to talk. Especially to someone like me. I think they are afraid I'm going to mug them or somethin'. I don't get it. I don't want anything they got. And it has only gotten worse in the past week since these crimes happened, people have gotten so uptight and on edge. They are turning against each other."

Digital Subjectivities and the Social Construction of Urban Space

The experiences of Katrina, Shauna, and Shaadi portray the tension, violence, and racist practices that erupted in the summer of 2009. The shift that they experienced on the streets was a direct result of the hostility toward people of color that was being structurally (re)produced in Boystown following the crimes of August 3, 2009, in both physical and digital neighborhood spaces. The community walks and digital interactions like those on Lakeview 9-1-1 and Take Back Boystown legitimized racism by providing Boystown residents and business owners with social experiences that supported degrading and criminalizing people of color. All three of these black transwomen felt a shift in neighborhood race relations that occurred after the crimes were committed and that only worsened after subsequent violent crimes were committed within the boundaries of Boystown. As Facebook users, they were constantly bombarded with their neighbors' racist interactions and practices.

As products of the sociospatial practices of neighborhood residents, the digital photographs, videos, and dialogues that were posted to Lakeview 9-1-1 and Take Back Boystown provided Boystown residents with evidence and a sense of common ground that supported problematic efforts to curtail crime, like video surveillance, community walks, and even efforts to shut down youth services provided by local LGBT organizations. Through these digital practices and engagements, primarily white Boystown residents redefined crime and criminalized the unwanted population of people of color. Noise ordinances and nonexistent loitering laws were often cited to support blaming Boystown's minority street population for neighborhood crimes and to justify the surveillance and policing of people of color. As such, Boystown residents produced and practiced race-based, class-inflected, gendered, and age-specific methods of social control.

Not only did Lakeview 9–1-1 and Take Back Boystown become platforms and conduits for residents to engage in attempts at social control, but they also created spaces where socially unacceptable, racist views could be voiced, shared, and legitimized. The digital spaces of Lakeview 9–1-1 and Take Back Boystown allowed residents to publicly produce and engage with bigoted attitudes, ideologies, and discourses through photographs, videos, and concurrent threaded comments. As a result, Boystown was transformed into an environment where the racist, classist, and transphobic subjectivities that proliferated online could be easily reproduced and publicly displayed.

In "Regarding the Torture of Others," Susan Sontag wrote about the photographs of torture in Abu Ghraib that surfaced in 2004. In this essay, she made the point that photographs are becoming less objects to be saved than messages to be disseminated. According to Sontag, the digital dissemination of photographs marks a shift in the ways people publicly organize their subjectivities vis-à-vis the struggles and suffering of others. When this idea is combined with Setha M. Low's theoretical use of the social construction of space, we can see how space is actually transformed through social exchanges, images, and the daily use of the material setting—into scenes and actions that convey symbolic meaning and experience.[16]

In addition to these perspectives, considerable work has been done on how social media and digital visual rhetoric work in tandem to shape lives in the physical world. Political movements in Colombia, protests in Iran, the Arab Spring, and Egypt's Revolution of 2011 have led scholars to investigate and debate the role of social media in communication, collective action, and political change.[17] From large collective social movements to personal relationships, the digital sphere and social networks have been shown to play an increasing role in shaping our daily lives.[18] As a largely visual social experience, when social networking sites and digital culture are considered in conjunction with perspectives from media studies, we can investigate how imagery is an integral component of the digital social experience. There are numerous studies across disciplines in the social sciences that look at how media produces, constructs, and perpetuates racism and other forms of bigotry, as well as identity politics in general, and how portrayals of ethnicity, gender, and race relations correlate with intergroup conflict and power clashes.[19]

The photographs and videos posted to Lakeview 9-1-1 and Take Back Boystown were taken in a range of neighborhood settings—from late-night community walks down crowded streets to private condominium balconies that provided a bird's-eye view of the neighborhood. However, it was through their dissemination on Facebook that they became instruments for reproducing racism and transforming the neighborhood. It was through both the neighborhood experiences and the digital engagements around these experiences that Boystown became constructed as a space of violence, division, and fear—even while city statistics and reports showed that crime was statistically lower than in previous years.

The visibility of these subjectivities exacerbated social tensions in Boystown and fortified the neighborhood as the site of multiple conflicts over difference.[20] Residents across racial identities became increasingly afraid of LGBT racial minorities like Katrina, Shauna, and Shaadi, not just in terms of physical safety but also in terms of economic security. Specifically, they feared that the presence of "these trannies and their Homey G's" would lower property value and drive down business for making the neighborhood appear "ghetto and unsafe" to visitors. What was earlier in the year seen as a booming neighborhood whose rising rent prices would displace the neighborhood's middle-class LGBT population became constructed as a neighborhood in decline caused by an unruly population of African American and Latino LGBT "street youth." The effects of the Great Recession (2007 to 2009 in the United States), which wreaked havoc on the local economy, were forgotten, and blame for decreased profits was pushed onto Boystown's vulnerable street population.

Katrina, Shauna, and Shaadi were not the only people to experience this change in the neighborhood. One hundred and twenty-three people I interviewed or surveyed after August 1, 2009, talked about or mentioned how the neighborhood's racial tensions had increased and how Boystown had become increasingly racist. This does not suggest that racism was previously unknown to Boystown. Each of these women (and many other participants) experienced racism in Boystown prior to the anticrime movements of 2009. There is also a recorded history of neighborhood bars and businesses being boycotted or singled out in local media outlets for racist practices.[21] Rather, these violent attacks and subsequent neighborhood crime had an effect on the social dynamics of the neighborhood in a way that racism and transphobia began to be expressed and (re)produced in new and intense ways, highlighting the fragility of the veneer of racial equality.

The racism experienced by all three women during this time influenced their decision to leave Boystown, showing how these practices work to exclude people of color, transgender women, and the poor. Katrina moved north to Rogers Park. She still socializes in the neighborhood but consciously avoids the Belmont strip and only associates with the neighborhood's hippest bars and clubs. Now, she uses only the Addison Street Red Line stop when visiting Boystown's North Halsted Street strip. Shauna moved to San Francisco and never plans on coming back to Chicago. Shaadi headed back to the South Side in November 2009 and moved in with friends of hers. I lost contact with her after she left the neighborhood.

Boystown's neighborhood-based digital practices on Facebook and neighborhood sociospatial practices (that is, community walks to curtail crime) not only constitute each other but also together create an exclusionary heteronormative environment where racism can flourish. Embedded within these practices are gay strategies that have focused on integrating into the middle classes and white hostility toward African Americans. It is through these mutually constitutive social practices that gay neighborhoods remain white.[22] If we are to combat racism, segregation, gender inequality, class inequality, identity-based discrimination, and homonormativity, we must attend to both digital engagements and practices "on the ground." If we are to create neighborhoods that are inclusive, diverse, and indiscriminate, then we must be actively antiracist in both digital and real environments.

NOTES

1. Charles I. Nero, "Why Are Gay Ghettos White?" In *Black Queer Studies: A Critical Anthology*, eds. E. Patrick Johnson and Mae G. Henderson, 228–45 (Durham, NC: Duke University Press, 2005).

2. Christina B. Hanhardt, *Safe Space: Gay Neighborhood History and the Politics of Violence* (Durham, NC: Duke University Press, 2013); and Martin F. Manalansan, "Race, Violence, and Neoliberal Spatial Politics in the Global City," *Social Text* 23 (2005): 141–55.

3. Lisa Duggan, *The Twilight of Equality: Neoliberalism, Cultural Politics, and the Attack on Democracy* (Boston: Beacon Press, 2003).

4. Darnell Little and Azam Ahmed, "Chicago, America's Most Segregated Big City: Racial Lines Were Drawn over the City's History and Remain Entrenched by People's Choice, Economics," *Chicago Tribune*, December 26, 2008; and Edward Glaeser and Jacob Vigdor, "The End of the Segregated Century: Racial Separation in America's Neighborhoods, 1890–2010," *Manhattan Institute for Policy Research Civic Report* 66 (2012), accessed September 1, 2013, http://www.manhattan-institute.org /html/cr_66.htm.

5. John P. Koval, "An Overview and Point of View," in *The New Chicago: A Social and Cultural Analysis*, eds. John P. Koval, Larry Bennett et. al. (Philadelphia: Temple University Press, 2006), 3–15.

6. Stephen Bedell Clark, *The Lake View Saga, 1837–2007* (Chicago: Lake View Citizens Council, 2007).

7. Roger Guy, *From Diversity to Unity: Southern and Appalachian Migrants in Uptown Chicago, 1950–1970* (Lanham, MD: Lexington Books, 2007).

8. Anne Enke, *Finding the Movement: Sexuality, Contested Space, and Feminist Activism* (Durham, NC: Duke University Press, 2007).

9. Available block-by-block census data shows that median household incomes in the neighborhood range from around $60,000 to $151,000. See U.S. Census Bureau, 2008–2012 American Community Survey, Table S1901, generated by Zachary Blair using American Fact Finder, http://factfinder.census.gov.

10. Data used to estimate a gay/lesbian sexual identity is typically inferred from U.S. census data on same-sex cohabitating couples. U.S. Census Bureau, 2008–2012 American Community Survey.

11. U.S. Census Bureau, 2008–2012 American Community Survey.

12. Alden Loury, "If Chicago's West and South Sides Were Their Own Cities, They'd Be the Deadliest and Most Violent in America," *Chicago Reporter*, June 17, 2010.

13. In 2011, the 23rd Police District (which includes Boystown) reported the second lowest crime rate in the city. It usually accounts for a little over 2 percent of the city's total crime and has some of the lowest murder, arson, motor vehicle theft, and burglary rates in the city. See Erica Demarest, "Lakeview Crime: The Numbers," *Windy City Times*, July 27, 2011. See also Kate Sosin, "Generation Halsted: An Overview," *Windy City Times*, November, 14, 2012.

14. Mark J. Konkol, "Crime Hot Spots Shifting: New Trends—Citywide Rate Is Down, but W. Side, N. Side Districts Are Seeing Spikes in Murders, Other Violence," *Chicago Sun-Times*, August 3, 2009; and Don Lemon, "First Family on Vacation; Chicago's Deadly Streets; Tackling Chicago Violence Nationally," *CNN Newsroom*, August 23, 2009, accessed December 20, 2010, http://transcripts.cnn.com /TRANSCRIPTS/0908/23/cnr.03.html.

15. Tracy Baim, ed., *Out and Proud in Chicago: An Overview of the City's Gay Community* (Chicago: Surrey Books, 2008).

16. Susan Sontag, "Regarding the Torture of Others," *New York Times Magazine*, May 23, 2004; and Setha M. Low, ed., *Theorizing the City: The New Urban Anthropology Reader* (New Brunswick, NJ: Rutgers University Press, 2005).

17. Kirkpatrick 2010; Evgeny Morosov, *The Net Delusion: The Dark Side of Internet Freedom* (New York: Public Affairs, 2012); Dubai School of Government, "Civil Movements: The Impact of Facebook and Twitter," *Arab Social Media Report* 1 (2011): 1–30.

18. Ilana Gershon, *The Breakup 2.0: Disconnecting over New Media* (Ithaca, NY: Cornell University Press, 2010); Steven Shaviro, *Connected, or What It Means to Live in the Network Society* (Minneapolis: University of Minnesota Press, 2003).

19. Anthony Cortese, *Provocateur: Images of Women and Minorities in Advertising* (Lanham, MD: Rowman and Littlefield, 1999); Richard Dyer, "The Matter of Whiteness," in *Theories of Race and Racism: A Reader*, eds. Les Black and John Solomos, 9–14 (New York: Routledge, 2002); Robert M. Entman, *The Black Image in the White Mind: Media and Race in America* (Chicago: University of Chicago Press, 2001); Larry Gross and James D. Woods, *Columbia Reader on Lesbians and Gay Men in Media, Society, and Politics* (New York: Columbia University Press, 1999).

20. Ruth Fincher and Jane Jacobs, *Cities of Difference* (New York: Guilford Press, 1998).

21. Baim, *Out and Proud in Chicago*.

22. It is important to note that not only do gay neighborhoods remain white, but the kind of white that they stay is also largely that of the upper-middle-class white consumer. See Alan Bérubé, "How Gay Stays White and What Kind of White It Stays," in *The Making and Unmaking of Whiteness*, eds. Birgit Rasmussen, Eric Klineberg, Irene Nexica, and Matt Wray (Durham, NC: Duke University Press, 2001).

15

Beyond the Flames

Queering the History of the 1968 D.C. Riot

KWAME HOLMES

☙

QUIET AS IT HAS BEEN KEPT, the Washington, D.C., riot of 1968 started in a vice district. On April 4, less than two hours after the national news wires reported the assassination of Martin Luther King Jr., an unidentified black youth chucked a brick through the front windowpane of the Peoples Drug store near the intersection of 14th and U Streets NW, in Washington's Shaw neighborhood. A temporary alliance between civil rights icon Rev. Walter Fauntroy and Black Power advocate Stokely Carmichael was able to disperse the crowd's momentum that evening, but by 1 p.m. on April 5, hundreds of black Washingtonians, men and women, reconvened on 14th Street NW and promptly set it ablaze.[1] The riot soon spread to two other commercial corridors in black Washington: H Street NE and the section of 7th Street/Georgia Avenue NW that feeds into Howard University's campus. But the violence began at 14th and U Streets, and while published narratives of the riot would frame the intersection as the nexus for local civil rights organizing—at the time, it was home to local branches of the Southern Christian Leadership Conference (SCLC) and the Student Nonviolent Coordinating Committee (SNCC)—other sources reveal the area was rife with hallmarks of social and sexual deviance.

In a 1967 exposé on 14th Street NW, *Washington Post* reporter Leon Dash described the people who frequented the street as "female solicitors and impersonators," "junkies," "rough trade," "butches," and "bootleggers"; he also noted that their presence drew a cadre of "arrogant college boys," "country boys," and "suburban policemen" to the corridor.[2] Moreover, while the D.C. city council, in scheduling a slate of public hearings to investigate the origins of "the civil disturbances," declared the riots "a great shock" to those who "live in and love this city," Dash's article quoted Metropolitan Police Department Lieutenant Jack Lockhart: "If there's a riot in Washington, it will be here."[3] Why was Lockhart in tune with the inevitability that black rage would gather and explode in the heart of Washington's vice district, while the council—a government body charged with assessing and responding to black citizens' grievances—declared itself caught unawares? If black riots are an expression of previously articulated civil rights issues, concerns that the state—if willing—is capable of resolving, then what explains the gulf in understanding between the city council and Lieutenant Lockhart? Or, more pointedly, how might centering an archive of the sexual cosmology of ghettoization bring us closer to understanding the seemingly illegible animus behind black Washingtonians' move from the ballot box to the brick in April 1968?

Rather than a continuation of an articulated civil rights agenda, this essay reads black riots as communicating an anger that could not speak its name within the limited public sphere available to African American activists at mid-century—an anger that only comes into view when examining the gender and sexual valences of ghettoization. In what follows, I illuminate the queer history of three sources of structural inequity in the 1960s—discriminatory policing directed at black men, inadequate housing, and nonresident control of commercial areas in black neighborhoods—and argue that black rage emerged in response to assault of these factors on the reproduction of black masculinity and heteronormativity, and to their penetration of the black body politic with speculative and sexual desires deemed unfit for the nation's suburbs. Similar to Mindy Fullilove's work on the psychological consequences of post-World War II urban development and displacement, this essay positions postwar ghettoization as a site of collective sexualized trauma that—unlike concerns about structural inequities—had few outlets within either civil rights or Black Power discourse.[4]

A Case for Riots, or Black Queer Theory's Contribution to Black Political History

By centering the sexual cosmology of ghettoization in the history of black riots, I ask that we return to the fraught terrain of the nature of black communal violence in the 1960s and its implications for popular assessment of the political subjectivity of black citizens. As indicated in this essay's title, and throughout the essay, I eschew contemporary moves within African American history and politics to describe these events as "rebellions" rather than riots. Widespread arson, looting, and violent assaults on whites during the 329 riots in 257 U.S. cities between 1965 and 1968 left historians of the Civil Rights–Black Power era with something of a representational quagmire. Given the right wing's cynical exploitation of black riots as a rationale for a "law and order" political movement that delivered Richard Nixon to the White House and ushered in a sharp nationwide turn toward punishment and incarceration as treatments for the symptoms of black poverty, early histories of the civil rights movement avoided paying serious attention to the riots. Because the punitive turn is understood as an effort to delegitimize black citizenship, historians who believed their discipline helped document African American's commitment to liberal democracy could not fold the raucous chaos and wanton excess of riots into narratives of the "nonviolent" and "pragmatic" civil rights struggle.

More recently, African Americanist historians have rehabilitated the image of urban riots by rebranding them as black "rebellions." Doing so incorporates them into a broader historical constituency of strategic, and therefore legitimate, working-class politics. As Ashley Howard writes, "Urban rebellions, both in the contemporary moment and the 1960s must be understood as a continuation of previous political jockeying and protest through so-called 'legitimate' channels."[5] If earlier iterations of movement scholarship engaged the black past as evidence of African American claims to full citizenship, contemporary historiography acquits rioters of the "social pathology," "random violence," and other irrationalities that have bulwarked anti-black ideologues' arguments that black people are congenitally unfit for citizenship.

However, while this rebellious reframing rightly responds to the reactionary respectability of early movement scholarship, narrating urban riots as a strategic response to structural inequity privileges historical actors invested in the possibility of an equitable racial future. By contrast, black queer theory demands that we halt the mechanistic incorporation of black subjects into alignment with liberal democracy and capitalism via African Americanist historicism. Indeed, black feminist/queer thought from Hortense Spillers to Christina Sharpe draws our attention to the uncomfortable fact that the political and juridical institutions designed to respond to citizen concerns in the United States are incapable of registering, let alone responding to, black people's pain.[6] For these scholars, literary scenes of ritualized sexual violence perpetrated against black bodies across time and space reveal the ways black people experience, witness, and even scream in response to anti-blackness, but—to paraphrase Frank Wilderson—are unable to speak back to its gratuitous violence.[7] In that vein, this essay investigates the riot as a scream and scrounges through traditional archives of riot history—federal housing policy, media coverage of urban decline, and transcripts of post-riot hearings—to illuminate heretofore illegible motivations behind some African Americans' decision to turn from the ballot box to the brick.

Policing and Black Male Heterosexuality on "the Strip"

The findings of the National Advisory Commission on Civil Disorders (the Kerner Report) were released in March 1968, only a month before Dr. King's assassination. Drawn from extensive surveys of hundreds of riots between 1965 and the "hot" summer of 1967, the Kerner Report seems to offer an acute dissection of the anatomy of black rage, emphasizing inner-city residents' frustrations with inadequate housing, economic opportunity, and police brutality. Yet, often cobbled together from locally produced assessments of the riot, the report fails to illuminate the sexual politics of ghettoization, leaving out a critical part of the emotional history of these events. For example, the problem of police brutality, which headed a list of twelve grievances black residents held against the state, was more than a metaphor for black people's overall excision from the constitutional protections of citizenship. In the wake of the 1968 riot, the D.C. Human Rights Council compiled dozens of stories of police brutality that reportedly occurred between 1966 and 1968. Their report emphasized instances of discrimination suffered by black men on the Metropolitan Police force or between police officers and "innocent" black men, with no references to black women as victims of police violence.[8] Yet, a closer examination of the activism and rhetoric against police brutality in Washington suggests that policing also stood in for racialized contests between black and white male heterosexuality over access to women's bodies in the city's commercialized sex zones.

Of the three commercial zones affected by the 1968 riot, the 14th Street NW corridor, also known as "the Strip," doubled as the city's most notorious vice hub during the 1960s. According to the *Washington Post*'s description of the riot, 14th Street NW was "the spot to pick up a woman, purchase narcotics, make a deal."[9] Indeed, heroin and women drew a diverse cadre of heterosexual men; black men from the city, white men from the city and suburbs, federal employees and congressmen, and white police officers hailing from Maryland, Virginia, and Appalachia came for access to black and white female sex workers. While sex commerce was never entirely absent from the 14th Street NW area before the 1960s, the explosion of the heroin epidemic in the city during the mid-1960s increased the number of women and men willing to traffic in sex to subsidize their addiction.[10] Prior to the development of formal anti-heroin interdiction efforts in the 1970s, police behavior on 14th Street NW was only casually concerned with halting either the heroin or the sex commerce trade. Instead, according to a study from 1968 by the ACLU, "the attitude that is pervasive among the 77 percent of the police officers who are white, is that of an occupying army in alien territory. These police officers do not identify with or feel responsible to the black community in Washington, D.C. They view their jobs as those of lion tamers, and they view their forum of operation as a jungle."[11] Indeed, members of the Metropolitan Police Department were mostly concerned with harassing, assaulting, and jailing black men who "kept company" with the white women they believed were their own.

Evidence for these confrontations exists on the margins of the local struggle for civil rights and self-determination in the District of Columbia. For example, in 1965, onetime D.C. Congress of Racial Equality (CORE) president Julius Hobson abandoned the classic liberalism of the postwar movement for atheism, socialism, and a call for D.C. statehood. Hobson was particularly invested in abolishing police brutality in black neighborhoods. Highly critical of the city's civil rights establishment, Hobson's papers contain a series of affidavits and interviews with victims of police violence whose stories had been ignored by the D.C. Human Rights Council. One such affidavit was supplied by Ronald B. Murray, whose testimony speaks to the obsession of police with limiting black men's access to white women.[12] According to the affidavit, Murray and his friend Leonard Williams were sitting with two "business associates" in his 1964 Fleetwood Cadillac in the spring of 1965 when they were approached by a police officer with whom Murray had an extensive and unpleasant personal history. Murray explained, "This ill feeling that he has toward me all came about because of some company that I used to keep before I learned what I now know about the policemen and the women on 14th Street NW." Confessing that he "used to be overmuch involved with a white woman that was a friend of [the officer] (so you can use your imagination from there)," Murray believed that "all the police officers on 14th Street NW know my name and face" and that he was "marked" because of his relationships with "white women." On that particular evening, the officer who harbored "ill feelings" against Murray aggressively greeted him—"hey you"—eventually asking, "Boy didn't you hear me calling you?" This tense verbal exchange quickly escalated into a physical assault as a number of officers watched and Murray took pains to ensure "whoever was looking could witness that I was not resisting arrest and not touching him in any manner, shape or form."

The excision of Murray's testimony from the public record of police brutality may speak to the late 1960s civil rights establishment's concern with combating the increasingly militant Black Power movement by continuing to emphasize idealized victims of racialized state violence. To cast 14th Street NW as a site where black Washingtonians were regularly beaten and even killed by state agents imagines the ghetto as an uncomplicated victim of the state's aggression. By contrast, imagining 14th Street NW as a zone of racialized sexual conflict and contestation over white women's bodies between black men and white police officers risked evoking the language of such black radicals as Eldridge Cleaver, who framed the sexual assault of white women as a site of revolutionary liberation.[13]

Though only one narrative, Murray's testimony gestures toward widespread knowledge among black men of policemen's proprietary relationship to the women on 14th Street NW. Indeed, in 1965, Murray had only been out a few months after a four-year sentence on a trumped-up assault charge involving the same officer and his partner in 1960, which Murray also credited to competition over white women. The ritualistic aspect of the officer's behavior, the invocation of the southern vernacular "boy," and Murray's belief that he was "marked" by other officers all suggest that competing male heterosexualities contributed to the explosion of black communal violence in the riot era.

Some heterosexual black men in Washington were also painfully aware that white men faced few restrictions in their pursuit of black women sex workers. Again, these grievances were not part of the Human Rights Council's report on police brutality. Instead, they emerge under the cover of anonymity within interviews conducted by the Howard University Civil Rights Documentation Project (CRDP) in the wake of the 1968 riot. Because riot participants faced potential criminal charges, the CRDP promised them anonymity if they agreed to testify to their motivations for becoming involved in the violence. The interviewee marked as "Anonymous B" indicated that he had attacked white men during the riot due to his anger at those traveling to 14th Street NW "looking for some chicks to buy." For Anonymous B, the racially unequal sexual geography of the supposedly desegregated capital city emphasized the extent to which black manhood was hemmed in by the invisible lines of the ghetto. Of white men he witnessed driving through 14th Street NW during the riot, Anonymous B said, "I tried to off a couple myself . . . you know they piss me off coming in here. If I go up on Wisconsin [Avenue], I'm expecting to get an ass whipping; it's as simple as that. But see, these are the same cats, for the most part during the riot . . . who drive around 14th and T and 14th and U trying to buy our women. I don't know, they must have a fantastic sexual drive because they come rolling through here every night trying to buy these same old broads."[14] Here again, women's bodies are signposts in a racialized competition between heterosexual men over control and access to the city as a whole. For black men like Ronald Murray or Anonymous B, white men's desires were securitized by police power or suburban mobility. Utterly divorced from a rationalist discourse surrounding "rights" or the proper functioning of the state, these testimonies excavate the affective economy animating black rage against discriminatory policing in the 1960s city.

Strictly understanding police–citizen interactions as a metaphor for the relationship between the state and the citizen risks evacuating the sexual regulatory mechanisms built into state power that black Washingtonians and the occupying police force acknowledged and operated within. Preliminary evidence suggests that sexualized territoriality played out in the lead-up to racialized mob violence in other cities and even abroad. While the Cincinnati riot in 1967 exploded after an act of police brutality, black and white communities were primed for violence in that city by the controversial arrest and conviction of Posteal Laskey for a series of gruesome rapes and murders attributed to the Cincinnati Strangler.[15] In London, England, the Notting Hill riot in 1958—the first major race riot between working-class whites and West Indian immigrants in that city—was sparked after members of the White Defence League assaulted Swedish sex worker Marjoritte Robinson, who was married to a Jamaican immigrant.[16] These sources also indicate the impossibility of pulling apart police brutality's threat to black masculinity from its threat to the projection of black male heterosexuality within the urban landscape.

Two Societies: The Sexual Politics of Overcrowding and Ownership in the Riot Era

If police brutality tended to spark riots, inadequate housing and non-resident ownership of commercial land within the inner city represented the tinder that racial capitalism piled higher with each year. As Clayton Howard's work indicates, the nationalization of housing policy during and after World War II engineered heteronormative suburban land-scapes, down to the spatial layout of the suburban ranch home, in commuter communities around the country.[17] Manifested in white suburban communities, both public and privately financed residential development incentivized white families' material landholdings and a sense of shared ownership over the "character" of their communities. That sense of ownership that, Gillian Frank points out, animated resistance to both racial integration and the expansion of sexual liberation during the busing crises of the 1970s.[18] By contrast, as Beryl Satter's and Nathan Connolly's work indicates, inner-city neighborhoods were understood by powerful real estate interests as sites of resource extraction in the form of monthly rental payments; residential development in black neighborhoods would maximize profit for landowners or "slumlords."[19] Here, then, are the material building blocks for the Kerner Report's oft-cited warning that the nation was splitting into "two societies," divided between white suburbs and black ghettos.

However, despite universal agreement that poverty had devastated the Negro family, neither the Kerner Report nor the widely distributed Moynihan Report adequately addressed black urban activists' sense that the same discriminatory lending and real estate practices that denied African Americans access to the federally subsidized wealth transfer of suburban home ownership also blocked their access to heteronormativity securitized from the influence of increasingly queer cities between World War II and the riots. In this section, I explore how the "two societies," and specifically the exigencies of race and land in the inner city, produced differing notions of sexual deviance within white and black communities leading into the wave of urban riots.

By the 1960s, white suburban moral crusaders "on guard" for the proliferation of sexual deviance were deeply concerned with the potential infiltration of suburbia by perversions that would go unmarked but for the vigilance of parents and children. For example, in Sid Davis's social hygiene film, *Boys Beware* (1961), white suburban boys were warned against the threat of "the homosexual" who preys on young men in a range of otherwise idyllic suburban locales: the public park, the basketball court, and by a fishing lake. Ralph, the film's homosexual antagonist, also offers rides in a new Cadillac, a key marker of suburban normativity. Most telling, when the film narrates Ralph's encounter with an unsuspecting Jimmy, it describes the imminent threat in this way: "What Jimmy didn't know is that Ralph was sick, a sickness that was not visible like smallpox, but no less dangerous and contagious, a sickness of the mind. You see, Ralph was a homosexual."[20] In gesturing toward the "invisibility" of Ralph's sickness in early 1960s Inglewood, California, a community on the verge of racial integration, *Boys Beware* reveals the way 1960s homophobia was conditioned by the racial dynamics of suburban areas.

However, if white children were warned about the sexual dangers that existed between the home and the schoolhouse, the overcrowding crisis in the nation's ghettos made the home a site where black children might encounter sexual dysfunction within normative family units. Across the nation, land speculators in inner-city neighborhoods in the postwar decades worked to maximize profits by dividing apartment buildings and single-family homes into smaller and smaller housing units marketed to working-class black families, many of them new migrants to larger cities. Within a wide range of academic and popular literature, housing overcrowding became the primary metonym of black deprivation within U.S. racism. In the Shaw neighborhood, housing overcrowding was engineered by a cadre of twelve "slumlords," who, between 1963 and 1968, purchased 75 percent, or over seven hundred, of the neighborhood's properties.[21] Nearly half of those properties were owned by George Basiliko, one of a number of second- and third-generation Greek immigrants based in Falls Church, Virginia, who owned acres of land in majority black communities. Together, Basiliko and his associates pocketed hundreds of thousands of dollars in federal loans designed to incentivize residential rehabilitation in the inner city, only to allow inadequate housing conditions to flourish.[22]

The problem of overcrowding made normative black heterosexuality into a pornographic spectacle that threatened the proper moral development of black children. For example, in the wake of the 1968 riot, the National Urban League tapped Sterling Tucker, head of the D.C. branch, to lead the New Thrust campaign, a national effort designed to increase the notoriously conservative organization's relationship with "ghetto blacks."[23] Within the league, Tucker was one of the strongest voices for black community control over housing policy, and in his manifesto, *Beyond the Burning* (1968), he argued that overcrowding lay at the root of the sexual pathology that plagued working-class communities. "Overcrowding," he wrote, "viciously destroys families, for it intensifies problems by making privacy impossible. Husband and wife have no time alone. They share their bedroom or living room with several youngsters each night. Parents resign themselves to an impossible situation and stop trying to muffle and hide what young ears will hear anyway, what curious eyes will manage to see."[24] Speculators' demand for maximum profits produced a set of spatial arrangements that, for Tucker, warped marital sexual relations, necessary for the reproduction of the black community, into deviance that reproduces the culture of poverty among black children. Tucker wrote, "They know their acts cause early experimentation and a permissive attitude toward sex and morality, but there is nothing they feel they can do in these circumstances to stem the idea."[25] Tucker's words complicate our understanding that black activists were concerned about the "black matriarch's" influence on the proper development of black masculinity. Here, it was the material conditions of the ghetto that reframed black heterosexuality into perversion.

Were Black Riots Homophobic?

As mentioned earlier, the D.C. city council held a series of hearings in the immediate wake of the violence, hoping to assess the source of black anger, and prevent similar upheavals in the future. Dozens of civil rights and Black Power activists participated in the hearings and shared their understandings of what fomented black rage. In proposing massive redistribution of land to Shaw residents, then Black Power activist Marion Barry warned the council, "There is a black city and a white city. There are black values and there are white values and let there be no mistake about it, the two are not the same and therefore you can't plan the same way, you can't plan for black people like you do for white people because there is a difference."[26] One black nationalist group succinctly summarized the problem by declaring, "The chickens have come to roost. The black community has started urban renewal on a crash scale. The message is clear. We will make the decisions about our community."[27] If we take the Community Urban Renewal Action Council seriously, how should scholars interpret the riot's impact on Shaw's queer geographies? By the time the smoke had cleared in mid-April, seven of the nine establishments that catered to a queer clientele in black Washington had been destroyed or were so damaged that they would soon close.

Unquestionably, the fact of absentee commercial landownership contributed to the way black Washingtonians understood homosexuality as a social problem. Rather than universally homophobic, black Washingtonians' relationship to homosexuality was determined by the racial and economic dynamics that produced hypervisible homosexuality as a constituent of urban decline during the 1960s. While a diverse cadre of gay men and lesbians traveled to and through Shaw to socialize and find sex during the 1960s, their differing routes and the locations of their establishments of choice generated different meanings within a community experiencing a rapid decline in black landownership.

Black gay middle-class residents like Juicy Coleman, a native Washingtonian, and Jim Harvey, who moved to D.C. in 1968 to work for Marion Barry's PRIDE Inc., were more likely to socialize in black-owned businesses that catered to sexually diverse, racially homogenous populations.[28] For black gay men and lesbians in Shaw, social life was rooted in gay supper club Nob Hill. Coleman recalls walking into Nob Hill—a black-owned gay bar—in 1965 and realizing that his life already included a number of gay and lesbian people: "I remember that there were two of my teachers from McKinley Tech at the party. And one lady that lived next door to my parents on Swann Street, so when I walked in the door these people were like frantic."[29] For Harvey, who was introduced to Nob Hill after cruising a black gay man in the white gay ghetto of Dupont Circle, the bar served as a home away from his Chicago home during his "formative years." Harvey also spoke of the way Nob Hill became an intersection between the Shaw's queer scene and "mainstream" black institutions, particularly the church. "I met a lot of interesting people.

Met a lot of the old gospel queens. You know, who would play at Nob Hill on Sundays after they'd made their money playing and singing at the church."[30] Harvey's remembrances speak to the cultural dialectic between black queer clubs and musical performance traditions within the black church identified by E. Patrick Johnson.[31] Nestled within a relatively stable residential area, Nob Hill offered a secure home base for groups of black gay men who would fan out and circulate through other queer and nonqueer nightspots in the city. Natives such as Coleman were particularly attracted to the ostensibly straight nightlife establishments along the 7th Street NW/Georgia Avenue NW commercial corridor. According to Coleman, he and his friends would, in modern parlance, queer the space of respectable institutions like Cecilia's or the Kenyon Street Bar and Grille, with other patrons relatively unaware of their presence.[32]

By contrast, bars that catered to racially and economically diverse clientele attracted negative media coverage. Near 7th Street NW and T Street NW, also the locale of the illustrious Howard Theater, stood the "straight downstairs and gay upstairs" Cozy Corner, which drew "a largely black clientele, but whites who were interested in African-Americans would go there too."[33] Less illustrious than Cecilia's or the Kenyon Street Bar and Grill, the nearby Bus Stop Deli was also known as a "late-night hangout for black gay men and lesbians." The temporal specificity of these 7th Street NW spaces, "late-night," inevitably meant that black and white homosexual men found themselves congregating on the streets, producing a visible social problem. In a *Washington Post* feature on the Howard Theater's decline, the theater's black general manager, Shep Allen, told the paper that that respectable customers are "all afraid of the same thing." The *Post* then clarified Allen's statement: "'The thing,' in this case, is the danger of being mugged or held up on a nearby dark side street where most patrons must park to get to the theater at 620 T st nw [*sic*]. The deterioration in the area since 1960 is obvious. Drug addicts, winos, homosexuals and hangers-on crowd the sidewalks. Bars and restaurants that once appealed to the black middle class have shifted gears for a different clientele."[34] Urban anthropologist Uli Hannerz agreed, noting in 1968 that around "7th and U" certain bars "have become established in the public knowledge as hangouts for more specialized clienteles: gamblers, 'gorillas,' homosexuals."[35] It seems likely that that Cozy Corner's popularity with white gay men explains the increased incorporation of "homosexuals" into descriptions of neighborhood decline around 7th Street NW in the 1960s.

Indeed, evidence suggests that white gay men, like white heroin addicts and female sex workers, were collectively understood as outsiders who dumped unwanted desires in the inner city's backyard.

These trends were brought into even starker relief on "the Strip" on 14th Street NW. There, the police's permissive attitude toward heroin and sex commerce produced opportunities for male sex workers, ranging from hustlers to "female impersonators," to trade their wares. The Strip was also home to a few explicitly queer establishments, including Rosetta's Golden Nugget (also known as the "Black Nugget") and Bob's Inn, the original performance home of Avis Pendavis. Black Nugget was particularly popular with transgender and cross-dressing homeless youth, contributing to its reputation as, in the words of Jim Harvey, one of the "seediest" establishments in the District. Indeed, for Shaw-area residents engaged with black activist discourse around the multifaceted racisms of the ghetto, these public exhibitions of nonnormative sexuality along the 14th Street Strip became entangled with critiques of white exploitation of black communities and bodies. Isaac Ruffin, a native Washingtonian and ex-convict involved with local Black Power struggles, wrote a widely published poem entitled "14th Street: Stories of Poverty and Lost Youth":

> 14th St. Wash., D.C., is a dance of
> dashikis and African bushes, rhythm
> and blues and flare bottom trousers
> whores and homosexuals all participating
> in the feast of wings and things
> pig feet, fat meat swimming in bean soup
> nodding occasionally while complimenting
> whoever had the best pill of doogee today,
> people whose occupation is getting high
> everyday all day long.

> 14th Street Washington, D.C.,
> dark, dim underground where the
> hustlers meet and the whores prey
> on whitey's sexual hangup and walk
> away with his wallet and on occasion
> his life.[36]

Ruffin's poem suggested that the problem of 14th Street NW and the ghetto in general was its queer or heterogeneous character: the intermixing of black cultural nationalisms of the Black Power era; black southern culturalisms, such as pig feet; and various modes of deviance, such as nodding addicts, "whores," and "homosexuals." Yet, here again, the words "whitey's sexual hangups," which no doubt referred to both white men's desire for black women and same-sex desires, operate as a metaphor for outsiders' willingness to use the inner city to express desires untenable within the suburbs.

At the city council hearings, black civil rights activists hoped to replace deviant commercial territory with more wholesome sources of entertainment. While no speaker at the council hearings made explicit mention of queer establishments, some, like Calvin Rolark, president of Washington Highlands Civic Association, hoped that "meaningful recreation be established in this area—that is where all members of the family can participate such as bowling alleys, pool halls, tennis courts etc." Bernard George, manager of the Bobby Foster Youth Council, a boxing gym, requested that the council finance the rehabilitation of his facility on the notion that sports training produced a pathway to both "success" and "dignity."[37] For some, then, the post-riot push for community control offered an opportunity to manufacture a more heteronormative and masculinist landscape in the queer ghetto.

Still, a close look at the owners of legible queer establishments in Shaw makes it difficult to argue that suburban outsiders were responsible for the proliferation of dens of ill repute in the 1960s. Bob's Inn, Rosetta's Golden Nugget, and the Cozy Corner were all owned by black Washingtonians. Indeed, Cozy Corner's owner, Walker Weaver, was a founding member of the National Negro Licensed Beverage Owners Association, a group designed, in part, to promote black-owned businesses in the nation's inner cities.[38] Moreover, despite their racial allegiances, black-owned queer establishments took advantage of the systemic municipal neglect that animated black anger leading into the 1968 riot. Had city licensing and zoning regulations been properly enforced, bars like the Cozy Corner may have been shut down because, as one anonymous narrator indicated, it "was one of those places that looked like it could burn down easily."[39] Popular black queer bar Zodiac's Den came into existence owing to lax enforcement of liquor license policy in Shaw. Zodiac Den founder Aundrea Scott recalled, "We needed more space so we found this little, abandoned honky-tonk, country and western club at Riggs Road and South Dakota Ave. We moved into the basement apartment and operated off the [absent] owner's liquor license."[40] In this sense, black entrepreneurs, be they gay or straight, took advantage of general disinterest in the maintenance of black heteronormativity and fulfilled the needs of the sexual marketplace that was allowed to flourish within Shaw—even as their establishments contributed to the decline of Shaw's reputation and animated black anger about white exploitation. Ironically, the one gay bar in Shaw owned by absentee Greek landlords, the Brass Rail, survived the 1968 rebellion due to its location on 13th Street NW and proximity to downtown.

Importantly, though, the reality of landownership in Shaw was often considered immaterial to the political message of the riot itself. As Black Power activist R. H. Booker told the city council, "Black businessmen got burned out . . . because of the fact that black people did not know they were owned by black people . . . you and I know a lot of these places where you see nothing but black people working in them . . . are only fronts for the exploiters who live in Maryland and Virginia."[41] Booker's comment again speaks to the way the queer character of the ghetto obscures a rationalist reading of black politics. Whatever the actual state of landownership, the problem was the unfettered access of white desire to black people and communities—whether the speculative desires of landowners or the sexual desires of both heterosexual and homosexual men.

In turn, it may be easy to assume that black queer Washingtonians like those who sang gospel at Nob Hill on Saturdays and Bethel Baptist on Sundays or who socialized at Cecilia's were sexually invisible to their heterosexual counterparts, that "tolerance" requires the incorporation of an explicitly expressed difference within or outside a given population. Moreover, readers may conclude that my argument sublimates the importance of sexual identity to racial identity, reproducing the rationale for the sexuality studies lacuna within the majority of African American history scholarship. However, these arguments assume African Americans, particularly within hyperstigmatized neighborhoods like Shaw in the 1960s, operate within similar economies of subjectivity and identification as majority white communities do. As Kevin Mumford has argued, neatly "untangling" African Americans' concerns about homosexuality from their concerns about single motherhood and poverty generally in the 1960s is not only impossible but also does little to help us understand the unique ways black intellectuals and activists understood what they opposed when they organized against interlocking forms of structural racism.[42] Historians of black political and sexual subjectivity, then, must embrace the seeming contradictions inherent within black sexual subjectivity as the starting point for new histories of blackness as manifested within "black politics," "black activism," and "black radicalism."

Conclusion

Without a clear understanding of the affective and material pressures placed on the construction of blackness, particularly within the postwar era—pressures that themselves were often contradictory—it becomes impossible to understand the intellectual architecture of black political ideology in either the past or the present, in regard to issues of sexuality or other emotionally charged issues. The discipline's concern with folding black subjects into an uncomplicated, idealized rationalist or strategic politics leaves the histories of many African Americans unattended to. Further research is needed on what Cathy Cohen might describe as the queer constituency of African American communities, those who lay outside the bounds of political normativity. In the District of Columbia, this is in fact a measurable population and includes the majority of African American residents, who have avoided local elections since the establishment of partial home rule in 1973 or who forward conspiracy theories like "The Plan"—a post-riot discourse that presciently claimed land developers had a secret agenda to push all blacks out of the District by the year 2000. These residents represent folk whose experience of anti-blackness inures them from the fantasy of racial equity in the United States. Centering an archive of sexualized indignities within the narration of the 1968 riot offers an essential first step in making plain black political formations too raucous and unruly to be disciplined into either civil rights or Black Power activisms and archives.[43]

NOTES

1. "The City's Turmoil: The Night It Began: How the Violence Began: Chronology of a Night of Turmoil," *Washington Post*, April 14, 1968, A1.

2. Leon Dash, "'The Strip' Is Where the Action Is in D.C.: 14th Street 'Strip' Is Where the Action Is, Vice Hub of City," *Washington Post*, February 12, 1967, C1.

3. U.S. Senate, Subcommittee on Business and Commerce of the Committee on the District of Columbia, *Rehabilitation of District of Columbia Areas Damaged by Civil Disorders*, 90th Cong., 2nd sess. (1968), 257.

4. Mindy Thompson Fullilove, *Root Shock: How Tearing Up City Neighborhoods Hurts America, and What We Can Do About It* (New York: One World/Ballantine Books, 2004).

5. Ashley Howard, "Why Ferguson Isn't the Tale of Two Protests," August 18, 2014, accessed March 20, 2016, http://www.theblackscholar.org/why-ferguson-isnt-the-tale-of-two-protests/.

6. Hortense J. Spillers, "Mama's Baby, Papa's Maybe: An American Grammar Book," *Diacritics* 17, no. 2 (1987); Saidiya Hartman, *Scenes of Subjection: Terror, Slavery, and Self-Making in Nineteenth-Century America* (Oxford: Oxford University Press, 1997); Christina Sharpe, *Monstrous Intimacies: Making Post-Slavery Subjects* (New York: New York University Press, 2010).

7. Frank Wilderson, *Red, White, and Black: Cinema and the Structure of U.S. Antagonisms* (Durham, NC: Duke University Press, 2010).

8. Government of the District of Columbia Commissioner's Council on Human Relations, "Police-Community Relations in the Nation's Capital," July 15, 1968, 1–8. Julius Hobson Papers, Dr. Martin Luther King Jr. Memorial Library, Washingtoniana Collection, Box X, folder Y.

9. Ben W. Gilbert, *Ten Blocks from the White House: An Anatomy of the Washington Riots of 1968* (New York: Frederick A. Praeger, 1968).

10. Robert DuPont and R. N. Katon, "Development of a Heroin-Addiction Treatment Program: Effect on Urban Crime," *Journal of the American Medical Association* 216, no. 8 (1971): 1320–24.

11. "A Police Department in Trouble: Racial Discrimination and Misconduct in the Police Department of Washington, D.C., Report and Recommendations of the National Capital ACLU," August 1968, Julius Hobson Papers, Series 2, Box 4, Dr. Martin Luther King Jr. Memorial Library, Washingtoniana Collection.

12. Ronald B. Murray, "Police Brutality within the Nation's Capital," Julius Hobson Papers, Series 2, Box 4, Dr. Martin Luther King Jr. Memorial Library, Washingtoniana Collection.

13. Eldridge Cleaver, *Soul on Ice* (New York: McGraw-Hill, 1968).

14. "Anonymous B" interviewed by James M. Mosby Jr. on April 24, 1968, for the Howard University Civil Rights Documentation Project. Collections housed in the Manuscript Division of Moorland-Spingarn Library at Howard University.

15. "Hold Negro Suspect for Questioning in Strangulation Deaths," *Call and Post*, December 17, 1966, 12A.

16. Mark Olden, "White Riot: The Week Notting Hill Exploded," accessed March 24, 2016, http://www.independent.co.uk/news/uk/home-news/white-riot-the -week-notting-hill-exploded-912105.html.

17. Clayton Howard, "Building a 'Family-Friendly' Metropolis: Sexuality, the State, and Postwar Housing Policy," *Journal of Urban History* 39, no. 5 (2013): 933–55.

18. Gillian Frank, "'The Civil Rights of Parents': Race and Conservative Politics in Anita Bryant's Campaign against Gay Rights in 1970s Florida," *Journal of the History of Sexuality* 22, no. 1 (2013): 126–60.

19. N. D. B. Connolly, *A World More Concrete: Real Estate and the Remaking of Jim Crow South Florida* (Chicago: University of Chicago Press, 2014); Beryl Satter, *Family*

Properties: How the Struggle over Race and Real Estate Transformed Chicago and Urban America (New York: Picador, 2010).

20. Sid Davis, dir., *Boys Beware* (Sidney Davis Productions, 1961), accessed September 1, 2013, https://www.youtube.com/watch?v=ECilAeLLATc.

21. Leonard Downie Jr., "Slum Landlords Buy Up Shaw Houses: Slum Landlords Quietly Buying Up Shaw Houses," *Washington Post*, March 24, 1968, A1.

22. Downie, "Slum Landlords," A24.

23. Jean M. White, "Urban League to Build 'Ghetto Power': Tucker Gets New Post," *Washington Post*, July 30, 1968, A1.

24. Sterling Tucker, *Beyond the Burning: Life and Death of the Ghetto* (New York: Association Press, 1968), 18.

25. Tucker, *Beyond the Burning*, 19.

26. U.S. Senate, *Rehabilitation of District of Columbia Areas*, 312.

27. Carol Honsa, "Shaw Unit Asks Renewal Voice; Closing of White Businesses Demanded," *Washington Post*, April 14, 1968, C2.

28. Jim Harvey to Mark Meinke, August 10, 2004, Rainbow History Project Oral History Collection, 6–7. The Rainbow History Project (RHP) is an all-volunteer, not-for-profit organization dedicated to collecting and preserving LGBT history in metropolitan Washington, D.C. Transcripts and audio files for RHP oral interviews are not housed within a physical collection, but are available to researchers on request. The oral histories in this essay were collected and recorded by Mark Meinke, one of the project's founding members. For more information on RHP and its collections, see http://rainbowhistory.org.

29. Juicy Coleman to Mark Meinke, August 20, 2001, RHP Oral History Collection, 2.

30. Harvey to Meinke, 8.

31. E. Patrick Johnson, "Feeling the Spirit in the Dark: Expanding Notions of the Sacred in the African-American Gay Community," *Callaloo* 21, no. 2 (April 1, 1998): 399–416.

32. Coleman to Meinke, 3.

33. Mark Meinke, "Places and Spaces: Clubs, Bars, Community Centers, etc. of Washington, DC's LGBT Community (1920 to the present)," 2002, accessed January 17, 2009, http://www.rainbowhistory.org/clubs.pdf, 8.

34. Hollie I. West, "Howard Theater: Often a Silent House," *Washington Post*, January 29, 1969, B1.

35. Uli Hannerz, *Soulside: Inquiries into Ghetto Culture and Community* (New York: Columbia University Press, 1969), 29.

36. Isaac Ruffin, "14th Street: Stories of Poverty and Lost Youth," *Washington Post*, December 24, 1969, C2.

37. U.S. Senate, *Rehabilitation of District of Columbia Areas*, 322.

38. Bob Queen, "Negro Licensed Beverage Owners Launch Powerful Nation-Wide Organization; Membership Soars," *New Pittsburgh*, February 13, 1960, 4.

39. Meinke, "Places and Spaces," 6.

40. Meinke, "Places and Spaces," 30.

41. U.S. Senate, *Rehabilitation of District of Columbia Areas*, 388.

42. Kevin J. Mumford, "Untangling Pathology: The Moynihan Report and Homosexual Damage, 1965–1975," *Journal of Policy History* 24, no. 1 (2012): 53-73.

43. Meinke, "Places and Spaces," 3–5, 17, 24.

16

The Strangeness of Progress and the Uncertainty of Blackness

TREVA ELLISON

◔

The queer thing is that we are still alive. —ALEXIS PAULINE GUMBS

THE JUNE 2013 SUPREME COURT RULINGS on the legalization of gay marriage and the overturning of Section 4 of the Voting Rights Act have animated ongoing conversations about the tensions between black and LGBT social and political organizing in the United States. This essay adds to scholarship that theorizes the coconstitutive nature of racial, sexual, and gender difference by tracing how single-issue federal reforms around identity-based injury have reproduced carceral geographies and relations at the same time as they have been productive of rights and legal protections for various identities. I analyze the congressional hearings of the 1994 Violent Crime Control and Law Enforcement Act (VCCLEA) to understand how identity-based claims of injury are organized and managed under the discursive logic of neoliberal multiculturalism. I argue that gender- and sexuality-based inclusion functioned alongside antiblack racism to expand carceral geographies and infrastructure as a part of a state-sanctioned antiracist, antisexist, and antihomophobic project. This analysis underscores how the legal management of harm under neoliberal multiculturalism bears strange fruit. This strange fruit takes shape as the spatial and ideological expansion of systems of surveillance, policing, and incarceration that exploit black vulnerability. Black vulnerability is sustained through an economic system of racial capitalism, in which racial difference functions as a material force or "valorized ideological domain" of capitalism.[1] This strange fruit also forms a persistent and unruly archive of the violence associated with what many would term "progress." This analysis provides a view of progress, or the post–World War II ascendancy of race and racism to the official concern of the state, as inherently strange. The discursive construction of the protected citizen through the VCCLEA not only obscures how harm and violence circulate around black queer or black LGBT embodiment but also abstracts the spatial relationship between harm, violence, and multiple embodiments of blackness. This essay concludes with a meditation on the problem of legal redress as a means of attending to black injury, noting the uncertainty of blackness as a legal category. I consider what a politics of scale could offer our political-intellectual projects aimed at unsettling the relations and structures that sustain antiblack racism through the tactics of surveillance, policing, and incarceration.

The current moment is particularly apt to consider these questions, as political and intellectual organizing around the state-sanctioned and extrajudicial murders of black people has reached a fever pitch following the murders of Eric Garner, Mike Brown, Jordan Davis, Trayvon Martin, Oscar Grant, Troy Davis, Ramarley Graham, and many others. National and local advocacy groups have called for filing federal charges against George Zimmerman and the reform of Stand Your Ground laws in the wake of his acquittal for Trayvon Martin's murder. Considering the ways the Violent Crime Control and Law Enforcement Act encodes the expansion of policing, incarceration, and criminalization as an official antiracist, antisexist, and antihomophobic project underscores the limits of using legal redress as a strategy for unsettling the death-dealing relations that produce racism, what Ruth Wilson Gilmore defines as "state-sanctioned and/or extralegal production and exploitation of group-differentiated vulnerability to premature death."[2] We have to ask how and when it is possible for blackness to appear before the law in ways that do not reproduce the logics that organize space, power, knowledge, and being in ways that reinstitute white, heterosexual, and bourgeois embodiment as the most legitimate and intelligible instantiation of the human.

Notably missing from the conversation about extrajudicial and statesanctioned violence is a discussion of how harm and violence impacts various embodiments of blackness, particularly black women and black LGBT people who were also murdered through legal and extralegal violence. This is not because people have not organized around or claimed these people. Family members, journalists, activists, intellectuals, and everyday people have worked tirelessly to call attention to and demand accountability for the murders of Aiyana Stanley-Jones by Detroit police officers, Rekia Boyd by Chicago police, the assault of 13 black women by an Oklahoma City police officer, the prosecution of Marissa Alexander in Florida for surviving a domestic assault, the murders of Islan Nettles in New York and Deshawnda Bradley in Los Angeles, and so many more. However, these names and the lives they represent are devalued in a social order that devalues the everyday existence of black women and black LGBT people, particularly black transwomen. For example, the 2012 National Transgender Discrimination Survey notes that 34 percent of black transgender respondents reported living on less than $10,000 a year.[3] A research project being funded by the MacArthur Foundation based on housing research in Milwaukee likens evictions to an extracorrectional punishment for black women, noting that black women in Milwaukee make up 9.6 percent of the population but 30 percent of evictions.[4] These statistics cannot account for the interpersonal and communal violence that circumscribe the experiences of black women and black LGBT people.[5] The same networks of power, resources, and belonging that attempt to make our lives unlivable shape the difficulty of translating violence against black women and black LGBT people into intelligible national outrage. The routines and networks of antiblack violence that characterize American life are upheld by a precarious relationship between blackness and representation in the post–civil rights era in which the quantity of black representation (political, legal, and social visibility rights and privileges) is diffused from the quality of black representation or the character of prevailing socially and institutionally sedimented value system.[6] It is this contradiction that confounds normative models of democratic redress, such as the legal system, when they are used to affirm an existence that is already socially, economically, and politically devalued. The limit of official modes of juridical representation to register black injury has re-ignited a long-standing social and political critique of law and order, currently organized under the banner of #blacklivesmatter.

"Operation Ghetto Storm," a report released by the Malcolm X Grassroots Movement, has received considerable attention by activists and advocacy groups organized around the murders of young black men.[7] The report details the murders of black people by law enforcement, security guards, and vigilantes, noting a black person is murdered every 28 hours by one of these groups of people. I am concerned about how the definition of "extrajudicial" in this report obscures the circulation of harm through violence and vulnerability that enables the murders of black women and black queer and LGBT people, particularly black transwomen. These murders are rendered as not only outside the realm of legal and ethical concern but also outside the purview of antiblack racism. This positioning misses the ways that the multiple and sometimes conflicting experiences of black cisgendered men, black women, and black transwomen are conditioned by similar contexts of discursive power and modes of spatial differentiation (namely, neoliberal multiculturalism and racial capitalism). Racial capitalism is an economic system through which the built environment, ideas, and knowledge, as well as sign systems and feelings, are organized into different kinds of places to facilitate the extraction of surplus value, which, transformed into capital, has concentrated in the hands of white people, men, and property owners operating under the auspices of multinational corporations, national and international governance, and banking entities (the International Monetary Fund and the World Bank). The "racial" in racial capitalism underscores the historically accrued symbiosis between racial difference and capitalism, as racial difference has been the logic that upholds the regimes of human and spatial differentiation that created flexible pathways for the private and public accumulation of surplus value.

In this essay I use the term "carceral geographies" to describe the spatial network of the prison industrial complex, including the built environment, labor, capital, and human capacity, as well as knowledge, signs, symbols, images, and representational forms and modes that are appropriated for domination and control. Carceral geographies include formal institutions, processes, and developments such as prisons and jails, gang injunction zones, mental health hospitals, policing, surveillance, and unemployment, poverty, and wealth polarization. The term also includes knowledge production about and representations of crime and criminals, laws, and ideas about safety, as well as nonverbal signs, symbols, and feelings. I am choosing to focus on the representational modes that attempt to suture penal democracy at the level of law and discourse, noting that this is but one of many registers from which to critique and imagine alternatives to carceral geographies.

I am thinking about a representational mode as the manner through which something or someone is described, defined, or comes into resolution. In that sense, a representational mode can also be thought of as a type of social imaginary,[8] something that is created and cohered around a particular set of conditions that also contains an evacuation. Sylvia Wynter gives important insight in terms of outlining the stakes of representational modes:

> The Argument proposes that the struggle of our new millennium will be one between the ongoing imperative of securing the well-being of our present ethnoclass (i.e., Western bourgeois) conception of the human, Man, which overrepresents itself as if it were the human itself, and that of securing the well-being, and therefore the full cognitive and behavioral autonomy of the human species itself/ourselves. Because of this overrepresentation, which is defined in the first part of the title as the Coloniality of Being/Power/Truth/Freedom, any attempt to unsettle the coloniality of power will call for the unsettling of this overrepresentation as the second and now purely secular form of what Aníbal Quijano identifies as the "Racism/Ethnicism complex," on whose basis the world of modernity was brought into existence from the fifteenth/sixteenth centuries onwards.[9]

In Wynter's formulation, racialized, heteropatriarchal, classed, and other forms of violence do the work of re-presenting Man or the interests of the dominant ethnoclass (white, heteronormative, property-owning) as the singular genre of the human. Wynter traces specific moments and iterations of Man as the overrepresentation of the human outlining specific representational modes that function to reinvent Man as human. Through the Enlightenment period, for example, Man is reiterated as biocentric Man as new representational modes emerge, such as the social and natural sciences.[10] Because a representational mode always produces an absence or excess, I use the term "ethical absence" to describe the normalized and routinized lapse of legally encoded and/or socially accepted ideals such as freedom, rights, justice, due process, bodily autonomy, and self-determination.[11] Ethical absence is also the historically accrued mismatch between the putative values and legally encoded rights and protections associated with modern subjectivity and group-differentiated vulnerability to premature death.[12] Sites of ethical absence help us to locate the limit of any way of knowing or mode of representation, because these are places where claims to universal rights are and *can be* routinely disavowed. For example, the modern prison has developed as a site of ethical absence. Upheld by racialized and classed vulnerabilities to changes in sites of capital accumulation, it is both institutionally and ideologically rooted to the extent that the volume of injury it produces has not been enough to displace incarceration as a commonsense policy solution.

Multiculturalism names one dominant representational mode of neoliberal capitalism in the mid-1990s, the time period when the Violent Crime Control and Law Enforcement Act was enacted. Multiculturalism is one representational mode that developed in the late 1980s and through the 1990s partly in response to the anti-imperial and antiracist social movements and knowledge production that emerged in the middle of the twentieth century. Multiculturalism marks the recalibration of racial difference into cultural difference and the appropriation of cultural difference into a matrix of legal inclusions and protections. Just as the black radical tradition comes into being as one of the representational modes of abolition democracy,[13] anti-imperialist and antiracist social movements and knowledge production in both a U.S. and global context generated a number of representational modes that attempt to intervene on the overrepresentation of Man (read: white and property owning) as the singular genre of human, such as negritude, black power, and black feminism, to name a few. These representational forms operated on and made use of categories such as worker, woman, black, gay, and lesbian as an attempt to negate Man as the overrepresentation of human or what is also called "heteropatriarchal white supremacy."

Neoliberalism is often described as a paradigm that organizes social, economic, and political life, with an emphasis on austerity measures, the dismantling of welfare and other public institutions, the commodification of money, also known as "financialization," as well as the expansion of flexible pathways for capital through the production of special economic zones. Jodi Melamed describes neoliberalism "as a term for a world historic organization of economy, governance, and biological and social life."[14] Melamed employs the term "neoliberal multiculturalism" to discuss how multiculturalism as a representational mode of neoliberalism operates on and reconfigures racial categories to produce a distinct kind of racism, one that "deploys economic, ideological, cultural, and religious distinctions to produce lesser personhoods, laying these new categories of privilege and stigma across conventional racial categories, fracturing them into differential status groups."[15] The appropriation of oppositional cultural forms and representational modes into the discursive matrix of neoliberal multiculturalism requires a reorientation of our insurgent political and intellectual formations toward a politics of scale that pays attention to the ways that racial differentiation and cultural appropriation are underwritten by spatial differentiation and vice versa.

The Strangeness of Progress: Safety through Enforcement

The Violent Crime Control and Law Enforcement Act and the Prison Industrial Complex

The Violent Crime Control and Law Enforcement Act of 1994 was an omnibus crime bill authored by then Delaware senator Joseph Biden and sponsored by Jack Brooks, a House representative from Texas. Among many other things, the bill provided funding for over 100,000 new police officers, $9.7 billion in funding for prisons, and $6.1 billion in funding for crime prevention programs. Upon signing the bill, on September 13, President Clinton hailed it as a bipartisan triumph: "Without responsibility, without order, without lawfulness, there is no freedom. Today the will of the American people has triumphed over a generation of division and paralysis. We've won a chance to work together."[16] The Violent Crime Control and Law Enforcement Act increases the life and scope of the prison industrial complex in several ways: the bill created new crimes and enhanced sentences for preexisting crimes, allocating billions of dollars to expand law enforcement infrastructure. In terms of new crimes and sentencing enhancements, the bill created sixty new death penalty crimes, made gang membership illegal, established a federal three-strikes policy,[17] created federal penalties for repeat sex offenders, authorized the U.S. Sentencing Committee to create enhancements for hate crimes, and authorized the prosecution of minors being tried for violent crimes as adults. The bill also ended federal Pell grants for prisoners seeking postsecondary education during their term of incarceration.

The VCCLEA also heavily subsidized the expansion of law enforcement infrastructure by providing grants to state and local law enforcement agencies for police hiring, sensitivity training, scholarships for programs for students agreeing to work in law enforcement, and funding for state and local courts to mitigate the anticipated increased load of new crimes and over 100,000 new police officers. The bill also allocated federal funds for the construction, expansion, and improvement of prisons and jails.

A portion of these funds are allocated through a "Truth in Sentencing" grant that makes funding conditional on violent offenders' being required to serve no less than 85 percent of their sentences. The bill also created the Community Oriented Policing Program, or COPS Program, which gives a variety of grants for law enforcement, including funding for new police officers, school resource officers, sheriff's deputies, expansion of tribal police forces, and law enforcement technology. Although originally established to expand the police force by 100,000 between 1995 and 2000, the COPS Program still receives funding. For the fiscal year 2011, the COPS Program was awarded over $349 million to give grants to state and local law enforcement agencies.[18] Funding for most law enforcement programs was guaranteed starting fiscal year 1995 to fiscal year 2000, independent of crime rates, and thus guaranteed the swelling of state and federal prisons. Lawmakers may have anticipated prison growth, as the bill also mandates that prison overcrowding is constitutional so long as living conditions are not "cruel and unusual."

Rendering the LGBT Subject and the
Failure of the Racial Justice Act

One of the provisions of the VCCLEA was to appoint the U.S. Sentencing Commission to establish enhanced sentencing guidelines for hate crimes that fall under federal jurisdiction. This provision was the result of several attempts to establish sentencing specific to hate crimes after the passage of the 1990 Hate Crimes Statistics Act, which was the first federal act to name sexual orientation as a protected category in the framework of bias crimes. The Hate Crimes Sentencing Act, a title act under VCCLEA, was supported and lobbied for by national and state LGBT advocacy groups such as the Human Rights Commission, the National Gay and Lesbian Task Force, and the New York City Gay and Lesbian Anti-Violence Project. The National Gay and Lesbian Task Force also lobbied for VCCLEA and continues to name it as a victory in hate crimes legislation, despite noting that the law as a whole has been criticized for its focus on enforcement, which disproportionately affects low-income people and people of color.[19] For these groups, sentencing enhancement at the federal level was cited as a step toward more localized legislation. However, the representational tactics deployed to render LGBT people as a legitimate protected category work through the delinking of sexuality from race and other categories of difference.

The Subcommittee on Crime and Criminal Justice convened two hearings on hate/bias crimes in May and July of 1992. During the hearings, speakers from several not-for-profit agencies provided evidence on the upsurge of bias crimes for different legally protected categories such as gender, sexual orientation, and race, with speakers acting as specialized representatives for a particular type of violence. For example, the Anti-Defamation League focused on anti-Semitism, while the Asian American Defense League and Education Fund covered violence against different Asian American ethnic groups. Toward the latter part of this hearing, Congressman James Sensenbrenner expressed his discomfort with legislating sentencing enhancements for bias crimes based on sexual orientation: "Our civil rights laws have protected people based upon status that they really have no control of: Their race, their creed, their national origins, their gender, and in certain cases, disabilities as well. Sexual activity, however, is voluntary. Most people engage in it. Some do not. And we never have extended the protection of civil rights laws to activity that is voluntary and at the choice of the individual. The protection has been extended to things that they basically were born with or can't help or in the case of disability."[20]

Howard Katz, Bias Bill coordinator for the New York City Gay and Lesbian Anti-Violence Project, after providing charts and maps demonstrating that one of every three bias crimes occurs in the Chelsea and East/West Village neighborhoods of New York, remarked: "This proves once again that the pattern of antigay and antilesbian crimes is different from other forms of hate crimes. For us, perpetrators come into neighborhoods perceived to be lesbian or gay to seek out victims. It's not a question of crossing into someone else's turf. But rather, in many instances, gay bashers go out hunting for sport, to beat up some faggots, to get some queers."[21] Violence due to "turf wars" is implicitly coded as racial violence and taken up in the congressional hearings on youth and gangs, while the unprotected domestic sphere functions as the primary place of gendered violence. The landscape of antigay and antilesbian violence in this account does not overlay that of racial violence. The separation of race, gender, and sexuality also helps to cohere the production of different kinds of places: the home or domestic sphere in need of protection, the gay neighborhood in need of protection, and the streets in need of regulation.

We can understand Katz's emphasis on the uniqueness of antigay and antilesbian violence in relation to Sensenbrenner's skepticism about sexual orientation as a protected category because sexual orientation is "voluntary." For harm and violence based on sexual orientation to be legible, it is delinked from other types of violence. Racialized sexualities are produced as the excess of sexual orientation rendered through multiculturalism. The protection of sexual orientation is accomplished through increased law enforcement and enhanced sentencing, as sexuality becomes overrepresented by "sexual orientation," which is narrated as racially neutral. The coding of sexuality as racially neutral (white) in this legislation is especially troubling, given that violence and harm that is reported as anti-LGBT is most often directed toward people of color, particularly black people. A 2013 report from the National Coalition of Anti-Violence Programs found that 53.8 percent of reported anti-LGBT homicides were of black people and that 73 percent of murders were of LGBT people of color.[22] Both Hanhardt and Manalansan have detailed how the production of gay neighborhoods, through quality-of-life policing, results in the routine police harassment of queer and LGBT people of color.[23] This dynamic between LGBT legibility and antiblack racism constitutes queer people of color not just as unprotectable but also as continuously out of place. Katherine McKittrick writes: "Racism and sexism produce attendant geographies that are bound up in human disempowerment and dispossession."[24] The production of the West Village as a gay (white) neighborhood, then, is bound up in a discourse wherein protected sexual orientation is overrepresented as nonblack and queer of color embodiment is placeless: somewhere between racialized "turf" and gay neighborhood.

The only hearings in which antiblack racism is addressed directly through proposed legislation is in the death penalty hearings before the Subcommittee on Civil and Constitutional Rights of the Senate Committee on the Judiciary, during which Julius Chambers, of the NAACP Legal Defense Fund; Joseph Lowery, president of the Southern Christian Leadership Conference; David Baldus, professor of law at the University of Iowa; and Ronald Tabak of the Death Penalty Committee attempted to persuade the committee members that "it is indisputably true that race is the single most important factor influencing life or death decisions in courtrooms across these United States."[25] The Racial Justice Act was introduced by John Conyers and provides death row inmates, at the state and federal levels, a legal basis on which to challenge their death sentences if statistics suggest that the race of either defendants or victims had affected past death-sentencing decisions in the jurisdiction where the crime was committed. During the hearing, Chambers presented data and findings from a study David Baldus conducted that concluded "offenders who kill whites are far more likely to be sentenced to death than offenders who kill blacks."[26] The act, as well as Baldus's study, met with strong opposition and eventually was dropped in conference. Various prosecutors and scholars argued that there was, in fact, no evidence to support discrimination against blacks in regard to the application of the death penalty. William B. Hill, deputy attorney general for the State of Georgia, noted, "The Racial Justice Act imposes a burden on prosecution, on the Government that cannot be carried . . . . The Racial Justice Act simply abolishes the death penalty."[27] Hill argued that the racial injustice as modeled statistically by Baldus was merely a representation of jury unpredictability. The fact that two different juries can make two different rulings given the same facts, for Hill, meant that the Racial Justice Act had the potential to invalidate every application of the death sentence. While I am not interested in glorifying the Racial Justice Act as a piece of liberatory legislation, I am interested the ways that "racial justice" posited here as one attempt at remedy for black injury—a very limited and incomplete remedy— disrupts not only the protection through an enforcement scheme that is the driving paradigm of the Violent Crime Control and Law Enforcement Act but also the very exercise of the law itself. Racial protection is only legible when represented as an issue to be solved by policing and punitive legislation.[28] For example, in his remarks to law enforcement agents in London, Ohio, about the need for an omnibus crime bill, Clinton links at-risk blackness to nonnormative sexuality:

> The other day I flew into Shreveport, Louisiana, and the front page of the newspaper had a letter that a teenage girl had written to me. So she came out to meet me at the airport, this young girl. And her letter said this: "If I could meet the President, I would ask him to make his top priority crime. Crime is so bad I'm afraid to go outside. I really didn't pay attention to crime until someone shot and killed my friend who was one of my church members. My concern is,"—listen to this—"My concern is I won't have anyone to marry because all the nice young men will have been killed, incarcerated, or in a gang." . . . And let me say, when I see what has happened in the crime area: 3 times as many murders today as in 1960; 3 times as many violent crimes per police officer as there were 30 years ago; and 3 times as many births outside marriage, where there has never been a marriage, also related to the ultimate crime problem.[29]

Clinton's comments reiterate a narrative, which has persisted since the War on Poverty, that blames rising youth violence on the increase of women-headed, single-parent families, children born out of wedlock, father absence, a "soft" juvenile court system, and welfare programs that deincentivize work. The now infamous Moynihan Report of 1964 and Ronald Reagan's figure of the "welfare queen"—two narratives that blame black women for urban poverty—were updated in the 1990s by Princeton political scientist John Dilulio in the essay "The Coming of the Superpredator."[30] During congressional hearings addressing hate crimes, racism represented through the language of hate crimes was acknowledged and validated by committee members, although none of the presented incidents and testimonials about racially motivated hate crimes involved black people as "victims" of bias. Protecting black people, in the case of the Violent Crime Control and Law Enforcement Act, fell under the auspices of curbing youth violence by criminalizing gang membership, lowering the legal age of adult prosecution for certain violent felonies, and imposing stiffer penalties for drug distribution in protected zones such as parks, schools, and churches: white men saving black people from black people. The specter of the 1992 Uprisings in Los Angeles and sensationalized new reports about young black killers in Chicago displaced a serious discussion of antiblack racism with conversations about youth violence and youth superpredators, in which "gang member" operated as metonym for all black youth. Blackness is rendered via multiculturalism as "at risk," "endangered," and in need of regulation, which resonates with current events today. We can think of the law as a visioning archive because it sediments a way of seeing particular people (as combatant or citizen). The visioning archive of VCCLEA is one in which black injury does not exist.

Protecting Women/Projecting the Man

The Violence against Women Act (VAWA) was one of the most heavily discussed components of the Violent Crime Control and Law Enforcement Act.[31] Out of the fifty-seven congressional hearings that took place around the VCCLEA, on a broad range of topics from insurance fraud to counterterrorism, the death penalty to youth violence, ten congressional hearings addressed the Violence against Women Act, the most for any of the title acts of the bill. The Violence against Women Act revises and expands protections for women against violent crime, mandating a series of penalty enhancements for sex and domestic violence crimes and allocating funding for local law enforcement agencies for extra services and training, as well as funding for domestic violence shelters and programs, including establishing a national domestic violence hotline. Lauded as a feminist triumph, the bill was endorsed by a variety of national women's advocacy groups, such as the National Organization for Women, Fund for the Feminist Majority, and the National Coalition against Sexual Assault.

Senator Strom Thurmond convened the first congressional hearing for the act: "The simple fact that our daughters and wives fear walking down city streets alone or entering their homes at night reminds us of the reality of violent crime. . . . Justice demands that vicious acts against women be dealt with by enacting tough criminal penalties."[32] With the exception of Elizabeth Symonds, from the American Civil Liberties Union, who said, "We [the ACLU] unequivocally oppose the numerous criminal justice provisions that appear in the Senate (or potentially) House versions of this legislation. These include increased sentences for repeat offenders, the expansion of pre-trial detention and a section that provides grants to governments that use mandatory arrest policies,"[33] the majority of the witnesses that included survivors of sexual violence, psychologists, doctors, and attorneys demanded that the state elevate women from second-class citizenship status through criminalization and enforcement. The emphasis on enforcement refixed the punitive optics of the state on women of color through a variety of mechanisms. Although the law is titled "Violence against Women Act," it evacuates the "fatal couplings of power and difference" that produce gendered violence.[34] That is to say, gendered violence is reconfigured in this act strictly as an interpersonal and not structural problem, the consequences of which can be witnessed in mandatory dual arrest policies, in which both parties are arrested in domestic violence incidents. These policies further criminalize poor women and women of color by increasing contact with law enforcement. Increased punitive intervention owing to domestic violence laws has prompted investigations into other potential criminal offenses, child welfare department investigations, and the risk of deportation.[35]

Although Sally Goldfarb, from the NOW Legal Defense and Educational Fund, among many others noted that violence against black women comprised the majority of reported incidents of sexual violence, antiblack racism is not discussed in any of the hearings as a contributing factor to gendered violence.[36] The report that NOW entered as a part of Sally Goldfarb's congressional testimony emphasizes this: "Women are targets for many types of violence *because of their sex*," and "Women of all walks of life are at risk.[37] Although black women figure into the discussion as "victims" of gender violence, ignoring the racialized dimensions of sexual violence situates racialized gender positions as the excess of gender as it is configured through the act. The overrepresentation of stranger rape and domestic violence as the primary forms of gendered (and not racialized) violence ignores a whole range of gendered violence by falsely territorializing it. Joseph Biden, chairman of the Committee on the Judiciary, one of the major authors and proponents of the Violence against Women Act, readily notes this territorialization: "One of the criticisms of my legislation is that I am delving into family matters too much and that government should stay out of that—a laudable concern, I think. I mean it is a genuine concern, one that I think we should cross in this case."[38] The primacy of domestic violence as the most legible form of gendered violence ignores a host of other forms of gendered violence, including state-sanctioned violence such as prison and police strip searches, rape, and harassment by Border Patrol and Department of Homeland Security agents, violence against sex workers, and childhood abuse.[39] Gendered violence comes into resolution through the VAWA only to the extent that regulating it becomes a means of reproducing the relations of production that depend on governable units of association like families.

The types of gendered violence made legible through the act already assume a certain degree of gender normativity. The debate around Title III, the civil rights clause of VAWA, circulated around the legal difficulties of defining and proving "gender animus" or that the motivation of a crime is based on the victim's gender.[40] The issue was not defining gender but defining and proving intent and motivation, a discourse that already assumes a knowable gender binary. Although the abbreviation LGBT is employed throughout the hearings to talk about sexual orientation, transgender people and gender nonconforming people are a present absence in the congressional hearings on hate crimes, as antigay and antilesbian violence was presented as the sole type of violence that occurs based on sexual orientation and violence against women (cisgendered) as the primary manifestation of gendered violence.

The issues of sex worker harassment, childhood abuse, and poverty as forms of gendered violence were taken up in the congressional hearing titled, "Women in Prison: Programs and Alternatives." During this hearing, the National Women's Law Center presented a report describing the systemic issues facing women prisoners, noting that women are being increasingly incarcerated owing to the War on Drugs and because they are prosecuted for "non-violent economic crimes" and prostitution.[41] The report also notes that most incarcerated women are low-income women of color and survivors of domestic and child abuse. The hearing on women in prison focused on the introduction of the Family Unity Demonstration Project Act, a bill that did not get incorporated into the larger act but one that would have provided grants for federal and state prisons to implement community custody programs for women with children. This law attempted to fix the disruption to the normative nuclear family that mass incarceration of mothers creates by developing "gender-responsive" prisons, thereby expanding carceral geographies under the guise of protecting women.[42] Separating the concerns of women in prison from the hearings on violence against women makes it difficult to center an analysis of gendered violence that includes state-sanctioned violence. The multiple and complex experiences that could be represented through the terms "gender" and "woman" are limited to a fixed set of legible positions that reinstate the neoliberal state as the purveyor of social order. The infrastructure of the bill itself, a collection of category-specific title acts, enables multiculturalist management by organizing groups of people and organizations with intersecting interests into discrete subgroups, so as to obtain limited legal reforms. Antiracism, antisexism, and antihomophobia are sutured into state policy as discrete, nonoverlapping phenomena in order to reproduce the commonsense of carceral relations.

Scale and the Uncertainty of Blackness

Black scholars have theorized the uncertainty of blackness as a foundational component of modern systems of representation and spatial production. The occasion of humanities and the sciences was also the occasion of the coming into being of the post-Enlightenment self-determined subject of universality and the articulation of racial difference as a product of the difference between places on the globe.[43] In Denise da Silva's account of modern subjectivity, racial difference is instituted through the articulation of regions of ethical absence and the representation of post-Enlightenment Europe as the origin place of the universal, self-determined subject. This formulation in which racial difference is accomplished through spatial differentiation begs a consideration of the kinds of places that the Violent Crime Control and Law Enforcement Act reproduces. The focus on domestic violence as the primary form of gendered violence privileges the private home as a place of social reproduction and renders street harassment and street attacks as a social problem rather than a legal problem. In a 1993 congressional hearing on violence against women in Utah, Dr. John Nelson, then deputy director of the Department of Public Health in Salt Lake City, declared that domestic violence was a public health concern, noting, "I'd like to point out that this [domestic violence] is not just the problem of other people. This is a problem of all people, Senator. This goes across all social or economic stratum, all walks of life, all races, everything you could think of demographically it goes across the stratum."[44] These kinds of appeals help reinstitute places of ethical concern and ethical absence. Domestic violence becomes legible as a legal issue rather than social problem only as it is delinked from racial and class pathology and articulated as general national crisis. In this case, racial and class difference compose the boundary between moral crisis and pathology. Despite congressional skepticism about extending legal protections to gays and lesbians, the passage of the Hate Crimes Sentencing Act under VCCLEA and the 2009 passage of the Matthew Shepard and James Byrd Jr. Hate Crimes Prevention Act have functioned alongside local quality-of-life policing as a tool of urban renewal in cities across the United States.[45] The production of affluent, white, gay urban neighborhoods has not entailed increased safety for LGBT youth of color, as racial difference forms the criterion of spatial ownership in a so-called gay ghettos. The development of middle- and upper-class housing markets in the West Village, for example, has led to increased police and extrajudicial harassment of queer youth of color.[46] The Racial Justice Act, on the other hand, failed because black injury failed as a convincing law-and-order narrative—it pointed to a problem of the carceral state itself rather than presenting a problem for the state to solve. The attempt to apply ethical and legal concern to black people on death row disrupted the idea of state-sanctioned punishment as a commonsense safety strategy.

Blackness functions as both central to and in excess of what is legible under such systems of representation as the law. By demonstrating how blackness vexes canonical notions of gender and sexuality as an uncertain and incomplete process of becoming, black feminist scholars have theorized how the combination of blackness with other categories like gender and sexuality works to constitute subjects outside the realm of legal and ethical concern.[47] To deal with the uncertainty of blackness also calls attention to the uncertain relationship blackness has had to legal universality in the United States. The Dred Scott decision writes blackness outside of juridical universality, arguing that black people have "no rights a white man is bound to respect," because the original architects of the republic did not envision black or any nonwhite people as the subjects of universality.[48] Even when advocacy and activist organizations are able to successfully institute race-based legal protections against violence in the form of hate crimes laws, these laws are of a limited usefulness because proving the existence of hate crime is based on proving intent.[49] The dismantling of rights gained during Reconstruction and the civil rights movement, like public education and voting rights that characterize the current moment, exemplifies the tenuous nature of juridical inclusion. In the recent decision to overturn Section 4 of the Voting Rights Act, the opinion written by Chief Justice Roberts notes, "Things have changed in the South. Voter turnout and registration rates now approach parity. Blatantly discriminatory evasions of federal decrees are rare. And minority candidates hold office at unprecedented levels."[50] This statement highlights the overseen/unknown character of racial difference; black participation in representational democracy becomes metonymic for black well-being and the South, overrepresented as the place of the production of racial discrimination. This statement frames racism as an antiquated regional bias instead of an effect of the foundational premises of Western civilization, again highlighting the productive tension between spatial differentiation and racial differentiation and its management.

If racial differentiation is cohered through the production of certain kinds of places—places of ethical absence, such places as prisons, abandoned neighborhoods, homeless encampments, and underfunded public schools—what could treating race as a scalar category do for insurgent political-intellectual work? Scale is a level of representation or resolution that analytically delimits what patterns, trends, and relationships are discernible. In the discipline of geography, scale is a concept that is used to understand how social relations and processes produce different types of places (spatial differentiation) and, in turn, how spatial differentiation influences social relations and processes.[51] The concept of scale presupposes that capitalist development has entailed and is supported by particular and shifting arrangements of the built environment and people. Considering how the kinds of places that have endured over time, such as the nuclear family, the planned city, or the neighborhood, have shaped and are shaped by the movement of capital, power, ideas, and resources helps us understand how space is constitutive of social life and vice versa. Geographer Neil Smith argues that scale forms the criterion of difference between kinds of places.[52] In the VCCLEA, race functions as a scalar category because it is the criterion of difference between the places of juridical and legislative concern and places of ethical absence. In the Violence against Women Act line-item bill, racial and class differences form the criterion of difference between what kinds of gendered violence are legislatively actionable and which are not, in this case domestic violence versus street harassment. A politics of scale draws into relief the multiple and contradictory social, economic, and political processes that collide to constitute different kinds of places. The discursive power of senators, policy analysts, lobbyists, and advocacy groups to define violent crime as largely an interpersonal rather than a structural problem circumscribes the ability of young black cisgendered men, black women, and black queer and LGBT people to successfully obtain legal or official redress for various kinds of injury. In the case of the murders of young black cisgendered men, black women, and black LGBT people, any intellectual analysis or political narrative that attempts to treat these deaths as separate misses the ways that the streets, as a site of the organization of various forms of social life, are both hypersurveilled and policed and, in the case of black injury, constituted as a geography of ethical absence. Thinking about how blackness is materially and ideologically produced as a kind of place, as the criteria of difference between places, necessarily recalibrates any analysis that over-represents any single configuration of race, gender, and sexuality as more or most abject. The way representations of racist, sexist, and homophobic violence in the VCCLEA are delinked from blackness such that injury is not a legible narrative for black people creates an opportunity to think about how our political intellectual projects that deal with antiblack violence can become more flexible.

NOTES

Alexis Pauline Gumbs, "M/Other Ourselves: A Black Feminist Genealogy (or, the Queer Thing)," make/shift 1, no. 8 (fall/winter 2010/2011).

1. Jodi Melamed, *Represent and Destroy: Rationalizing Violence in the New Racial Capitalism* (Minneapolis: University of Minnesota Press, 2011), 7; Stuart Hall, "Race, Articulation, and Societies Structured in Dominance," in *Black British Cultural Studies: A Reader*, ed. Houston A. Baker Jr., Manthia Diawara, and Ruth H. Lindeborg (Chicago: University of Chicago Press, 1996), 16–60.

2. Ruth Wilson Gilmore, *Golden Gulag: Prisons, Surplus, Crisis, and Opposition in Globalizing California* (Berkeley: University of California Press, 2007), 28.

3. It is important to note that of the more than 6,000 respondents to the survey, only 381 were black; therefore, the stability of these statistics is undermined by the relatively small sample size. See "Injustice at Every Turn: A Look at the Black Respondents in the National Transgender Discrimination Survey," November 2012, accessed August 10, 2013, http://transequality.org/PDFs/BlackTransFactsheetFINAL_090811.pdf.

4. Matthew Desmond, "Poor Black Women Are Evicted at Alarming Rates, Setting Off a Chain of Hardship," Policy Research Brief, MacArthur Foundation, 2014, accessed January 10, 2014, http://www.macfound.org/media/files/HHM_-_Poor_Black_Women_Are_Evicted_at_Alarming_Rates.pdf.

5. In *Compelled to Crime*, Beth Richie mobilizes the concept of battering to characterize the abuse experienced by black women institutionally and communally. See Richie, *Compelled to Crime: The Gender Entrapment of Battered Black Women* (New York: Psychology Press, 1996). While a similarly rigorous study does not exist for black LGBT people, organizations that serve black LGBT people, like the Audre Lorde Project in New York, for example, frame communal violence against black LGBT people as a product of antiblack policing in general. For example, a December 2014 statement issued by the Audre Lorde Project titled "Wake Up, Rise Up" connects police brutality, false arrest, and detainment to communal violence by placing the names of black trans and gender nonconforming people who have died due to interpersonal violence alongside the names of black people killed by the police and black people who were detained, arrested, or imprisoned for self-defense. Accessed January 10, 2014, http://alp.org/wake-rise.

6. In 2012 the Associated Press conducted a survey through a third-party research firm, GFK, on racial attitudes in the United States and found that the majority of the over 2,000 survey respondents expressed antiblack attitudes when asked questions to measure both explicit and implicit racism; 59 percent of white respondents expressed implicit antiblack attitudes. This report is interesting because it illustrates the complexity of racism, noting that 43 percent of black respondents expressed antiblack attitudes. Associated Press, Racial Attitudes Survey, October 29, 2012, accessed August 20, 2014, http://surveys.ap.org/data%5CGfK%5CAP_Racial_Attitudes_Topline_09182012.pdf.

7. "Operation Ghetto Storm: 2012 Annual Report on the Extrajudicial Killings of Black People by Police, Security Guards, and Vigilantes," Malcolm X Grassroots Movement, 2013, accessed August 20, 2013, http://mxgm.org/wp-content/uploads/2013/04/Operation-Ghetto-Storm.pdf.

8. Norman M. Klein, *The History of Forgetting: Los Angeles and the Erasure of Memory* (London: Verso, 1997), 10.

9. Sylvia Wynter, "Unsettling the Coloniality of Being/Power/Truth/Freedom: Towards the Human, after Man, Its Overrepresentation—An Argument," *CR: The New Centennial Review* 3, no. 3 (2003): 260.

10. Wynter, "Unsettling the Coloniality," 267.

11. The idea of ethical absence comes from Denise Ferreira da Silva's argument in *Toward a Global Idea of Race* (Minneapolis: University of Minnesota Press, 2007) that race functions as a global organizing concept because part of the project of Western Enlightenment was the triumph of reason and logic, which privileged Europe and Europeans as modern subjects, simultaneously rendering non-European people and places as outside the realm of rational subjecthood and universal ethical ideals of self-determination and self-actualization.

12. I am working here through Ruth Wilson Gilmore's definition of "racism," which she defines as the state-sanctioned and/or extralegal production and exploitation of group-differentiated vulnerability to premature death. See Gilmore, *Golden Gulag*.

13. See William Edward Burghardt Du Bois, *Black Reconstruction in America, 1860–1880* (New York: Simon and Schuster, 1999); and Cedric J. Robinson, *Black Marxism: The Making of the Black Radical Tradition* (Chapel Hill: University of North Carolina Press, 1983).

14. Jodi Melamed, "The Spirit of Neoliberalism from Racial Liberalism to Neoliberal Multiculturalism," *Social Text* 24, no. 4 89 (2006): 14.

15. Melamed, "Spirit of Neoliberalism," 14.

16. William J. Clinton, "Remarks on Signing the Violent Crime Control and Law Enforcement Act," September 13, 1993. Retrieved from the United States Government Printing Office, August 20, 2013, https://www.gpo.gov/fdsys/pkg/PPP-1994-book2/pdf/PPP-1994-book2-doc-pg1539.pdf.

17. Three-strikes laws make twenty-five years to life a mandatory sentence upon the conviction of a third felony.

18. Community Oriented Policing Services (COPS), accessed August 20, 2013, http://cops.usdoj.gov.

19. "Hate Crimes Protection Historical Overview," accessed August 20, 2013, http://www.thetaskforce.org/issues/hate_crimes_main_page/overview.

20. *Violent Crime Control and Law Enforcement Act of 1996: Bias Crime Hearings before the Subcommittee on Crime and Criminal Justice of the Committee on the Judiciary, House of Representatives,* 102nd Congress, 59-169 (May 11, 1992). Statement of Jim Sensenbrenner, Committee on the Judiciary, accessed August 10, 2013, http://congressional.proquest.com/congressional/docview/t33.d34.103_pl_322?accountid=14572.

21. *Violent Crime Control and Law Enforcement Act of 1996: Bias Crimes Hearing before the Subcommittee on Crime and Criminal Justice of the Committee of the Judiciary, House of Representatives,* 102nd Congress, 59-169 (May 11, 1992). Howard Katz, New York Gay and Lesbian Anti-Violence Project, accessed August 10, 2013, http://congressional.proquest.com/congressional/docview/t33.d34.103_pl_322?accountid=1457.

22. National Coalition of Anti-Violence Projects, "Lesbian, Gay, Bisexual, Transgender, Queer, and HIV-Affected Hate Violence in 2012," June 4, 2013, http://www.avp.org/storage/documents/ncavp_2012_hvreport_final.pdf.

23. Martin F. Manalansan IV, "Race, Violence, and Neoliberal Spatial Politics in the Global City," *Social Text* 23, nos. 3–4 (2005): 141–55; and Christina B. Hanhardt, "Butterflies, Whistles, and Fists: Gay Safe Streets Patrols and the New Gay Ghetto, 1976–1981," *Radical History Review* 100 (2008): 61–85.

24. Katherine McKittrick, *Demonic Grounds: Black Women and the Cartographies of Struggle* (Minneapolis: University of Minnesota Press, 2006), 3.

25. *Violent Crime Control and Law Enforcement Act of 1996: Death Penalty Hearing before the Committee on the Judiciary, Senate,* 101st Congress, 643-902 (October 2, 1989). Prepared Statement of Joseph Lowery, Southern Christian Leadership Conference, accessed August 10, 2014, http://congressional.proquest.com/congressional/docview/t33.d34.103_pl_322?accountid=1457.

26. *Violent Crime Control and Law Enforcement Act of 1996: Death Penalty Hearing before the Committee on the Judiciary, Senate,* 101st Congress, 643-902 (October 2, 1989). Prepared Statement of Julius Chambers, NAACP Legal Defense and Educational Fund, accessed August 10, 2014, http://congressional.proquest.com/congressional/docview/t33.d34.103_pl_322?.

27. *Violent Crime Control and Law Enforcement Act of 1996: Death Penalty Hearing before the Committee on the Judiciary, Senate,* 101st Congress, 979-1084 (October 2, 1989). Prepared Statement of William Hill, Deputy Attorney General, Georgia, accessed August 10, 2014, http://congressional.proquest.com/congressional/docview/t33.d34.103_pl_322?.

28. The Racial Justice Act did pass in North Carolina in 2009 and was repealed by the GOP-dominated North Carolina legislature in June 2013.

29. William J. Clinton, "Remarks to Law Enforcement Community in London, Ohio," February 15, 1994, http://www.presidency.ucsb.edu/ws/?pid=49656.

30. John Dilulio, "The Coming of the Superpredator," *The Weekly Standard,* November 27, 1995, accessed August 10, 2014, http://www.weeklystandard.com/the-coming-of-the-super-predator/article/8160.

31. The use of "Man" in the section title follows Sylvia Wynter's description of Man as the overrepresentation of the human, the figure of the interests of the dominant ethnoclass (white, property owning, bourgeois). Wynter, "Unsettling the Coloniality of Being."

32. *Violent Crime Control and Law Enforcement Act of 1996: Death Penalty Hearing before the Committee on the Judiciary, Senate,* 101st Congress, 19-20 (June 20, 1990). Strom Thurman, Senator, South Carolina, accessed August 10, 2014, http://congressional.proquest.com/congressional/docview/t33.d34.103_pl_322?accountid=1457.

33. *Violent Crime Control and Law Enforcement Act of 1996: Death Penalty Hearing before the Committee on the Judiciary, Senate,* 101st Congress, 59-169 (November 16, 1993). Elizabeth Symonds, Legislative Council, ACLU, accessed August 10, 2013, http://congressional.proquest.com/congressional/docview/t33.d34.103_pl_322?accountid=1457.

34. Ruth Wilson Gilmore, "Fatal Couplings of Power and Difference: Notes on Racism and Geography," *Professional Geographer* 54, no. 1 (2002): 15–24.

35. Kristin Bumiller, *In an Abusive State: How Neoliberalism Appropriated the Feminist Movement against Sexual Violence* (Durham, NC: Duke University Press, 2009), 12.

36. *Violent Crime Control and Law Enforcement Act of 1996: "Women and Violence Part 2" Hearing before the Committee on the Judiciary, Senate,* 101st Congress, 2-29 (November 16, 1993). NOW Legal Defense and Education Fund, submitted report, accessed August 10, 2013, http://congressional.proquest.com/congressional/docview/t33.d34.103_pl_322?accountid=1457.

37. *Violent Crime Control and Law Enforcement Act of 1996: "Women and Violence Part 2" Hearing before the Committee on the Judiciary, Senate,* 101st Congress, 2-29 (November 16, 1993). NOW Legal Defense and Education Fund, submitted report, accessed August 10, 2013, http://congressional.proquest.com/congressional/docview/t33.d34.103_pl_322?accountid=1457.

38. *Violent Crime Control and Law Enforcement Act of 1996: "Women and Violence Part 2" Hearing before the Committee on the Judiciary, Senate,* 101st Congress, 105-106 (August 29, 1990). Senator Joseph Biden, Committee Chairman, accessed August 10, 2014, http://congressional.proquest.com/congressional/docview/t33.d34.103_pl_322?accountid=1457.

39. Andrea Smith, *Conquest: Sexual Violence and American Indian Genocide* (Durham, NC: Duke University Press, 2015), 29.

40. *Violent Crime Control and Law Enforcement Act of 1996: "Women and Violence Part 2" Hearing before the Committee on the Judiciary, Senate,* 101st Congress, 33-69 (November 16, 1993). ACLU, submitted report, accessed August 10, 2013, http://congressional.proquest.com/congressional/docview/t33.d34.103_pl_322?accountid=1457.

41. *Violent Crime Control and Law Enforcement Act of 1996: "Women and Violence Part 2" Hearing before the Committee on the Judiciary, Senate,* 101st Congress, 2-29 (June 29, 1993). National Women's Law Center, submitted report, accessed August 10, 2014, http://congressional.proquest.com/congressional/docview/t33.d34.103_pl_322?accountid=1457.

42. Rose Braz, "Kinder, Gentler, Gender Responsive Cages: Prison Expansion Is Not Prison Reform," *Women, Girls and Criminal Justice* (October/November 2006): 87–91.

43. Da Silva, *Toward a Global Idea of Race*; Siobhan B. Somerville, *Queering the Color Line: Race and the Invention of Homosexuality in American Culture* (Durham,

NC: Duke University Press, 2000; Anne Fausto-Sterling, "Gender, Race, and Nation: The Comparative Anatomy of Women in Europe, 1815–1817," in *Deviant Bodies: Critical Perspectives on Difference in Science and Popular Culture*, eds. Jennifer Terry and Jacqueline L. Urla (Bloomington: Indiana University Press, 1995), 19–48.

44. *Violent Crime Control and Law Enforcement Act of 1996: "Women and Violence Part 2" Hearing before the Committee on the Judiciary, Senate,* 103rd Congress, 47-84 (April 13, 1993). John Nelson, MD, Deputy Director, Department of Health, Salt Lake City, Utah, accessed August 10, 2013, http://congressional/docview/t33.d34.103 _pl_322?accountid=1457.

45. David Bell and Jon Binnie, "Authenticating Queer Space: Citizenship, Urbanism and Governance," *Urban Studies* 41, no. 9 (2004): 1807–20.

46. Rickke Mananzala, "The fierce Fight for Power and the Preservation of Public Space in the West Village," *Scholar and Feminist Online* 10, no. 1 (2012), accessed August 20, 2013, http://sfonline.barnard.edu/a-new-queer-agenda/the-fierce-fight-for -power-and-the-preservation-of-public-space-in-the-west-village/.

47. Kimberle Crenshaw, "Mapping the Margins: Intersectionality, Identity Politics, and Violence against Women of Color," *Stanford Law Review* 43 (1991): 1241–99; Patricia Hill Collins, "The Tie That Binds: Race, Gender and US Violence," *Ethnic and Racial Studies* 21, no. 5 (1998): 917–38; Hortense J. Spillers, "Mama's Baby, Papa's Maybe: An American Grammar Book," *diacritics* 17, no. 2 (1987): 65–81.

48. Scott v. Sandford, 60 U.S. 393 (1856), *Justia US Supreme Court Center*, accessed August 16, 2013, https://supreme.justia.com/cases/federal/us/60/393/case.html.

49. Dean Spade, "Trans Law and Politics on a Neoliberal Landscape," *Temple Political and Civil Rights Law Review* 18 (2009), accessed August 10, 2013, http://papers .ssrn.com/abstract=1426230.

50. Shelby County v. Holder, 12-96 (2013), *Justia US Supreme Court Center*, accessed August 16, 2013, http://www.supremecourt.gov/opinions/12pdf/12-96_6k47.pdf.

51. Neil Smith, "Contours of a Spatialized Politics: Homeless Vehicles and the Production of Geographical Scale," *Social Text* 33 (1992): 55–81.

52. Smith, "Contours of a Spatialized Politics."

17

Re-membering Audre

Adding Lesbian Feminist Mother Poet to Black

AMBER JAMILLA MUSSER

(Black) Woman

I CAME TO AUDRE LORDE through Gilles Deleuze and Frantz Fanon. I wanted to consider the postmodern fragmentation of subjectivity that Deleuze favored and Fanon abhorred through a gendered perspective. Lorde, who frequently began her readings by saying that she was a "woman, a black lesbian feminist mother lover poet," offered an entry point into poststructuralism from a very different perspective.[1] As I worked through what it means to think about bodies and difference, her theories of selfhood and collectivity were intoxicating. Her concept of the erotic in particular seemed to give answers to urgent political questions: How to attend to difference, but work together for change? How to work through the body while acknowledging structural difference? Yes, Lorde's words seemed to promise the elusive brown queer utopia that I had been searching for.

I am not alone in my admiration of Lorde; the eightieth anniversary of her birth was celebrated by numerous essays and tributes, many of which focused on Lorde's intellectual and political legacy. Linda Garber writes that Lorde "stands historically and rhetorically at the crux of the so-called generation gap between lesbian-feminist and queer theoretical notions of identity."[2] In Garber's description of Lorde as a point of inter-section between different historical moments and theoretical orientations, we can begin to understand that this fascination with Lorde has as much to do with her philosophies of community and difference as her role as a forerunner to contemporary queer theory. But lately, I have begun to wonder if claiming Lorde as queer has somehow erased her identity as a black lesbian feminist. This hyphenated identity is more than a means toward upending patriarchy and racism; these identities meant something to Lorde. In addition to teasing out her appeal, I aim to unearth the impact of Lorde's black lesbian feminist identity in her theorization of the erotic. In focusing on black lesbians, I am also working toward new theorizations of queer female sexuality.

(Black) Warrior

In "A Litany for Survival," Audre Lorde hails the marginalized. "For those of us who live at the shoreline," she begins; "those of who were imprinted with fear," she continues; "we were never meant to survive," she finishes.[3] As one of Lorde's most cited poems from *Black Unicorn* (1978), it functions as an invitation to think and feel with Lorde. The use of "us" and "we" collectivizes pain, struggle, and futility in a system that is geared toward the oppression of difference. For many, especially those who expe-rience life vis-à-vis an estranged relationship to the state, Lorde's words have acted as a lifeline, a reminder that struggle is not singular and that community is central to existing.

Lorde insists that her life is political because it is in opposition to patriarchal and racist forms of structural violence: "I am a Black woman in a world that defines human as white and male for starters. Everything I do including survival is political."[4] In a speech to commemorate the twenti-eth anniversary of Lorde's death, Aishah Shahidah Simmons expands upon these words to bring other marginalized identities into conversation with Lorde: "I am a Black woman. I am a trans woman. I am a trans man. I am an Asian woman. I am an Arab woman. I am a Native American woman. I am an Aboriginal woman. I am a Latina. I am a Pacific Islander woman. I am a Palestinian woman. I am a Roma woman. I am a Central/Southwest Asian woman in a world that defines human as white and male for starters. Everything We Do Including Survival Is Political."[5] Simmons's move to link Lorde's statement about the difficulty of being a black woman to the struggles of a wide range of identities is in keeping with the sentiment behind "A Litany for Survival," one that brings many different people to worship at Lorde's altar. During her life and especially after her death, Lorde has become an important political figure and resource to talk about marginalization, violence, community, and difference.

This space of community through (or despite) difference has been one of Lorde's enduring legacies, and it is articulated most clearly in her discussion of the erotic. She elaborates on this idea most extensively in her essay "Uses of the Erotic," which was first delivered as a paper at the Berkshires Conference on the history of women in 1978. In the essay, Lorde names the amorphous erotic ("a resource within each of us that lies in a deeply female and spiritual plane firmly rooted in the power of our unexpressed or unrecognized feeling") as that which had been disavowed by white patriarchal society and produces a theory of the erotic as that which must be reclaimed in order to move away from objectification and toward a robust community of women.[6] Her essay, then, makes two primary claims: that the route to subjecthood is community, and that objectification is experienced as a form of antisociality. Further, objectification does not just impact the individual; by shutting off possibilities of sociality, it also prevents communities from forming, thereby eliminating bonds between women and avenues for nurturing and collaboration. "Uses of the Erotic" is a critique of white, capitalist society, a statement about the potential of feminism, and a rallying cry for action.

Lorde views the erotic as working toward a particular antiracist, antisexist community. She argues that women must learn to find the erotic within themselves so that they can come together despite the oppressive forces keeping them apart. The erotic, for Lorde, is a space for women to form bonds with each other to repair the damage done by patriarchy and racism and to formulate ways of moving beyond those systems. Lorde is also explicit about framing the erotic as something that can help women form a feminist community that is inclusive and respectful of difference. She elaborates on this commitment to a feminism comprised of many different types of women in "The Master's Tools Will Never Dismantle the Master's House," writing that change can occur through "learning . . . how to make common cause with those others identified as outside the structures in order to define and seek a world in which we can all flourish. It is learning how to take our differences and make them strengths."[7] Here we see that Lorde's formulation of a feminism based on the erotic is explicit in its desire to develop solidarity through difference. The erotic offers a way to be with others through difference because the erotic "provid[es] the power which comes from sharing deeply any pursuit with another person." Importantly, the erotic is based on communal affective bonds—specifically joy—outside the parameters of identity: "The sharing of joy, whether physical, emotional, psychic, or intellectual, forms a bridge between the sharers which can be the basis for understanding much of what is not shared between them, and lessens the threat of their difference."[8] The erotic does not dismantle difference as much as open space for its examination within the context of feminist community.

However, Lorde's politics of the erotic are often read as a universal form of politics around marginality. In the *Feminist Wire's* two-week commemoration of Lorde's eightieth birthday, Darnell Moore argues that Lorde's rallying call for collectivity has contemporary import at a moment when neoliberalism works to isolate people: "Lorde's words, which were as prophetic and timely now as they were in 1978, beckon us to consider the uses of the erotic in these times: temporal moments when intimate connection between friend and stranger is seemingly obstructed by a type of capitalist individualism that refuses community. . . . When we say no to connection, to *eros*, we might easily miss THE movement, that is, the movement that moves us toward each other."[9] Moore's adaptation of Lorde for the contemporary moment dwells more on the process of coming together than on Lorde's specific invocation of feminism. Likewise, in making the connection between past and present and branding Lorde the formulator of an expansive notion of community, E. Patrick Johnson writes, "Lorde suggests that until women—and I would argue, all marginalized people—embrace those pieces of our creative and erotic energy that have been repressed, colonized, or otherwise curtailed, we cannot stand within our own truth or exploit the fullness of who we are so that we may effect change in the world."[10] In this linkage of community and the erotic, we see a move outside of identity politics and feminism in particular toward thinking about possibilities for coalition, solidarity, and affect. Importantly, this marks the erotic as a binding force that supersedes differences of race and gender.

This version of the erotic as a form of understanding affective connection through marginalization has been useful for scholars working within queer studies to theorize community. As Rinaldo Walcott notes, Lorde is indispensable for those working to understand black queer diasporic formations.[11] Jafari Allen's ethnography, *¡Venceremos? The Erotics of Black Self-making in Cuba*, uses the erotic to develop both an individual project of subject-making and a politics of friendship (reading Lorde through Foucault). The erotic helps him politicize the acts of survival that black queer Cubans perform as they negotiate their sense of self and resistance to the daily violence that attends to their lives. Allen argues that the erotic operates on multiple levels at once—individual, interpersonal, and social— which he describes as a "politics of erotic transcendence experienced in flashes of self-awareness, communities, love relationships, or 'Heiligeweg,' to transgression of the hegemonic rules of a particular public, to actual transformation of the standard practices of the public."[12] From here Allen moves toward theorizing erotic subjectivity, which encompasses "exercises of individual agency toward developing *who we are* in changing worlds, despite who we are told we are or *ought to be*—is thus *political* because it challenges the status quo allocation of social and material capital, moving the individual toward improving her or his own felt/lived experience by critically reading one's own experiences and objective relations to the world."[13] As we can see, the erotic here is a space of selfhood, community, *and* critique. Lyndon Gill also draws on Lorde's version of the erotic, though Gill is careful to note that his investment is in suturing the political, spiritual, and sensual: "Following Lorde, I propose that the erotic must be reconceptualized as a perspectival trinity that holds together the political-sensual-spiritual at their most abstract; in other words, 'the erotic' describes various formal and informal power hierarchies (the political), sexual as well as nonsexual intimacy (the sensual), and sacred metaphysics (the spiritual) simultaneously."[14] In his research on queer male communities in Trinidad and Tobago, Gill uses the concept of the erotic to tease out both systems of colonial domination and "postcolonial theoretical response to this mechanism of subjugation."[15]

Allen and Gill's work is exciting in the ways that it seeks to apply Lorde's concept of the erotic to contemporary social and political forms of resistance. Both draw on the idea of the erotic as sensual and political (though, as he notes, Gill emphasizes the spiritual dimension more heavily), but, notably, neither conceives of Lorde's erotic as a feminine or feminist space. Gill's decision to broaden the scope of the erotic is deliberate. Reading historically, Gill argues that the all-female setting of the Berkshires Conference explains the specificity of Lorde's comments: "While it may be the case that Lorde conceived of the erotic as the exclusive domain of women, I contend instead that we must read

Lorde for the audience gathered and not presume that she would reject the proposition that eros as a principle be allowed to retain the widest possible applicability—without losing its necessary attention to the ground of lived experience (of women, men, trans people, heterosexuals, queers, and people of color, etc.)."[16] This impulse to have Lorde's words embrace as many people as possible speaks to an optimism about coalitional politics and community that honors Lorde's legacy in an important way. Yet, I would like to read further into what we might gain from taking the erotic as a specific site of feminist resistance for black queer women. In some ways this modification builds on work from other scholars of black queer diasporas, notably Omise'eke Tinsley, who writes in *Thiefing Sugar* that women of color's same-sex eroticism serves "as a wellspring of resistance to colonial symbolic and economic orders."[17] In the next sections of the essay, I ask how we might incorporate theorizations of black feminism and black female queerness into our understanding of the erotic.

(Black) Lesbian Feminist

While Lorde was unapologetic about claiming a multiplicity of identities—mother, poet, warrior, lesbian, feminist, black—these identities made her aware of multiple forms of marginalization and enabled her to imagine a feminism robust enough to tackle difference and create authentic community. We might describe Lorde's writing toward community as a response to the exclusion she felt as a black lesbian feminist. It is no accident that the collection of essays in which "Uses of the Erotic" appears is titled *Sister Outsider*. She writes passionately against racism within feminist circles in "The Master's Tools Will Never Dismantle the Master's House" and "An Open Letter to Mary Daly." Yet, Lorde was also deeply troubled by the problem of homophobia within the black community. The separation of black lesbians from the space of community and politics is an important aspect of Lorde's desire to write against patriarchy and racism.

In a 1978 essay in *The Black Scholar*, Lorde argues that racism, sexism, heterosexism, and homophobia stem from "an inability to recognize the notion of difference as a dynamic human force."[18] She writes that the black community's demonization of black lesbians is a distraction from the structural forms of discrimination that the community faced *and* that it is a denial of a long tradition of close female friendships: "Instead of keeping our attention focused upon our real needs, enormous energy is being wasted in the Black community today in antilesbian hysteria. Yet women-identified women—those who sought their own destinies and attempted to execute them in the absence of male support—have been around in all of our communities for a long time." The black lesbian, Lorde argues, "is an emotional threat only to those Black women whose feeling of kinship and love for other Black women are problematic in some way."[19] Fear of difference was keeping women from working together toward solutions for gender and race-based discrimination. Reflecting on this essay in a 1979 interview with Adrienne Rich, Lorde describes the vulnerability of inhabiting a shared marginality: "When people share a common oppression, certain kinds of skills and joint defenses are developed. And if you survive you survive because those skills and defenses have worked. When you come into conflict over other existing differences, there is a vulnerability to each other which is desperate and very deep."[20] While Lorde's essay ends with a call to collectivity that echoes the one she would issue in "The Uses of the Erotic"—"As Black women we have the right and responsibility to define ourselves and to seek our allies in common cause: with Black men against racism, and with each other and white women against sexism"—this tension between vulnerability and survival stems from her recognition of the particular oppressions that face not only black lesbians but also all black women.[21] Though "Uses of the Erotic" hails all women, Lorde is especially optimistic that black female inclusion into this feminist collectivity would allow for acceptance of black lesbianism because black women could "recognize each other without fear and . . . love where we choose."[22] She makes this argument again in "Sexism: An American Disease in Blackface," which she begins by writing, "Black women have particular and legitimate issues which affect our lives as Black women, and addressing those issues does not make us any less Black."[23]

As we can see, Lorde's black lesbian feminism makes her aware of the intersecting nodes of oppression and the need to be part of a community that could speak to all of these issues. The major force that works against community is fragmentation, because it imagines only one source of oppression: "I cannot afford the luxury of fighting one form of oppression only."[24] Lorde's insight into multiple marginalizations is not only a reminder of the specific positionality of black lesbian difference but also marks a particular form of feminist theorizing that arises from that space, what Roderick Ferguson would describe as a critique of heteropatriarchy from which he articulates a queer of color critique. In *Aberrations in Black,* Ferguson describes black lesbian difference as bearing traces of "the attempt to negate the normalization of heteropatriarchal culture and agency by the inchoate global economy."[25] In other words, black lesbian difference makes visible the ills perpetuated by neoliberalism, patriarchy, and heterosexism.

Lorde's investment in a community that could accommodate difference also meant that she situated many of her critiques of capitalism, patriarchy, and racism at the level of community. In addition to the overt inequalities that these systems of domination perpetuate, Lorde argued that their ability to isolate people and prevent community was equally pernicious because it prevented change. We see this in "Uses of the Erotic" where Lorde writes that racism and sexism keep people enmeshed in "the confused, the trivial, the psychotic, the plasticized sensation."[26] Sensation, in Lorde's telling, is the antithesis of an authentic erotic connection; it is what Lorde describes as the pornographic, which "represents the suppression of true feeling ... [it] emphasizes sensation without feeling."[27] In offering flesh without connection, pornography produces antisociality, objectification, and fragmentation. Without an affective connection, the feelings of others are not shared, but used, "and use without consent of the used is abuse."[28] Additionally Lorde classifies this *use* of the feelings of others as a form of objectification, which "is to deny a large part of the experience, and to allow ourselves to be reduced to the pornographic, the abused, and the absurd."[29] These statements allow us to understand Lorde's division of feelings from sensations—feelings can be shared, while sensation (and pleasure without emotion) is individuating. Sensation, then, is not only a province of the individual but is also cultivated by an inappropriate relationship to the other. These affective modes directly hinder the possibility of community and change.

Here, we are given a choice as to how to interpret Lorde's distrust of pornography and sensation. We can read it as emblematic of the antipornography stance that preoccupied many feminists in the late 1970s and early 1980s. If we are reading for black lesbian difference, however, we can also follow Sharon Holland and read these statements as a moment where black feminism illuminates the importance of thinking about different types of relationships to history—that is, objectification impacts women differently depending on their material conditions. Holland emphasizes the importance of black feminist thought for thinking through the erotic by using this antipornography moment as a mark of the specificity of the black female body's experience. In positioning difference at the center of the erotic, Holland wants to show how it has been erased by queer theory and in ways that it need not be. She writes, "Absenting *these* somewhat conservative black feminist opinions from the women of color intellectual project performs damaging work."[30] In citing this moment as a rupture between sexuality studies and black feminism (and lesbian feminism), it is easy to see where conflict might occur. However, there are benefits to reading this moment into queer theory because it complicates our understanding of desire and helps to work against much of queer theory's tendency to be colorblind. Acknowledging these histories actually opens up a different type of relationship between queer studies and black queer bodies.[31] We also see that Lorde's lesbian feminist investment in community also represents a revaluation of what femininity and feminism could look like. It is a space where femininity is not shaped by patriarchy and objectification. In this it is not prescriptive of what the feminine should be other than that it is manifest through an authentic relationship to the self and to others. In the following sections I will explore the alternate spaces that Lorde opens up through the erotic that are specifically tied to her black lesbian feminism—the realm of maternal connection and female sensuality.

(Black) Mother

Lorde's discussion of the erotic and black femininity brings us to an unexpected place: the maternal. Her investment in mothering is clearly stated by her identification as a mother, but beyond the fact that she raised two children, the maternal is a central, often-overlooked component of Lorde's black lesbian feminist erotic. In part, Lorde's turn to the maternal is emblematic of the broader movement within 1970s feminism to explore and politicize relationships between women—both sexual and not. Historian Jane Gerhard argued that "as more and more cultural feminists rejected the idea that exploring women's sexual desires could lead to women's empowerment, the movement looked for and found in abstracted notions of motherhood a potential rallying point for all feminists."[32] Here, I want to suggest that Lorde's invocation of the maternal works to produce a particular mode of community formation across difference.

Lorde's attachment to the maternal is not only about her role as a mother to two children but also about a link to a future with less suffering. We hear this when Lorde evokes the maternal into her rallying cry for community in "Uses of the Erotic"; recall that she says, "The aim of each thing which we do is to make our lives and the lives of our children richer and more possible."[33] It is easy to focus on the affective community that Lorde summons with these words, but we also want to remember

that she uses the trope of children to produce the possibility of a different future. This moment of optimism, figured through the trope of the
child, signals Lorde's use of the maternal as both actual (experiential) and
virtual (abstract) modes of being.

We also see Lorde's invocation of the virtual maternal in "Eye to Eye"
when she forges a link between herself, the Amazons of Dahomey, and
the Queen Mothers of Benin. By connecting herself with these African
female leaders, Lorde inserts herself into a narrative beyond her individual
existence. This framing establishes a continuum between contemporary
black women and their African ancestors, thereby stretching the bounds of
kinship away from the strictly biological toward an imagined female community. Michelle Wright argues that this move to incorporate African and
American heritages underscores Lorde's deployment of "diaspora as the
new collective model for Black subjectivity."[34] In this way we can see that
Lorde's concept of the maternal is also racialized, not only in terms of her
choice of black African ancestors but also through her elastic understanding of who a mother might be.

This elasticity is complicated because Lorde must also think through
the institution of slavery and its distortions of kinship. Hortense Spillers argues that kinship for African Americans has been compromised
by the conflation of people and property, leaving African Americans
effectively orphaned because they were disowned by fathers and usually
raised by women with whom they had no biological connection.[35] In contemporary America, this legacy persists, producing the idea of the black
mother as simultaneously omnipresent and absent. Spillers connects this
to a larger structural problematization of theorizing kinship and family in
which this legacy of parental (both paternal and maternal) absence is mis-
recognized as matriarchy. She writes, "Even though we are not even talking
about any of the matriarchal features of social production/reproduction—
matrifocality, matrilinearity, matriarchy—when we speak of the enslaved
person, we perceive that the dominant culture, in a fatal misunderstand-
ing, assigns a matriarchist value where it does not belong; actually *mis-
names* the power of the female regarding the enslaved community. Such
naming is false because the female could not, in fact, claim her child, and
false, once again, because 'motherhood' is not perceived in the prevailing
social climate as a legitimate procedure of cultural inheritance."[36] While
the institution of chattel slavery complicated kinship for African Americans,
Lorde writes against that rupture. The historic loss of the maternal makes
it important for Lorde to theorize these African ancestors as part of her

trajectory, and it politicizes her claiming of black motherhood as a space of particular power. This move simultaneously recuperates matrilinearity and the figure of the black mother.

In this racialization of the maternal, Lorde evokes the absent/present black mother, lineages that stretch from Africa to America, which suggests that the maternal is a mode of care that is not only about the literal. Rather, I posit that she sees it as a mode of embodying the erotic. Thus, Lorde works to nuance a position that is frequently overdetermined with the language of essentialism. Lorde shows us the possibilities of maternity and femininity as articulating modes of being and connecting that have to do with optimism, care, and eccentric kinship. This maternal is feminine, but not necessarily connected to the act of carrying a child. Alexis P. Gumbs elaborates on the importance of mothering as a political, pedagogical act in *We Can Learn to Mother Ourselves: The Queer Survival of Black Feminism, 1968–1996*: "The pedagogical work of mothering is exactly the site where a narrative will either be reproduced or interrupted. The work of black mothering, the teaching of a set of social values that challenge a social logic which believes that we, the children of black mothers, the queer, the deviant should not exist, is queer work. Therefore, as a queer theorist, I theorize that work."[37] This politicization of mothering is a vital component of recognizing the work that emerges from Lorde's position as a black feminist lesbian. It does not, however, lead us to sex, which is another important component, not just of the erotic but also of conceptualizing what it means to theorize Lorde as a lesbian.

(Black) Lover, Poet

"When I say I am a Black Lesbian, I mean I am a woman whose primary focus of loving, physical as well as emotional, is directed to women."[38] Lorde's love of women was very much on display in the way that she lived her life. She had long partnerships with Frances Clayton and Gloria Joseph and numerous shorter affairs with other women. In describing Lorde's attitude toward love and friendship, Alexis De Veaux argues that "Lorde believed she didn't really know a person unless she slept with them; she bedded, or attempted to bed, women she knew or was attracted to 'as part of the challenge of friendship.' Her sexual aggressiveness was part of a need to control every aspect of her connection to other women."[39] Though this assertiveness is very much on display in *Zami: A New Spelling of My*

Name, the 1982 "biomythography" loosely based on Lorde's life in which Audre, the protagonist, has numerous sexual encounters with women, Lorde only offers mention, but not description, of this side of herself in her prose. Lorde's discussion of women loving women *is* radical, however, not just because she was writing in a moment before widespread acceptance of homosexuality but also because she is insistent on the overlapping terrain of the black lesbian and black mother. Stereotypically these categories have not been thought together; the black mother is imagined to be either overly fecund or a version of an asexual black mammy, and if the lesbian is considered, she is vilified. Lorde's insistence that lesbianism is political and sexual and (sometimes) maternal opens conversations about what woman loving might mean. Into the vacuum of theorization on black female sexuality that Evelynn Hammonds and Hortense Spillers decry, Lorde describes a sexual, political black lesbianism.[40]

To find Lorde's articulations of this woman loving, I suggest we turn to her poetry. *Black Unicorn*, Lorde's volume of 67 poems, including "Litany for Survival," describes what De Veaux calls Lorde's "bonds with women as intersections of the political, personal, and erotic."[41] Written in the same burst of productivity (1977–79) that also ushered in her famous essays, including "Uses of the Erotic," Lorde viewed *The Black Unicorn* as an important and accomplished volume of her poetry. De Veaux writes that "the publication of *The Black Unicorn* in 1978 had not only marked the production of a significant body of work, it presented a challenge. She had viewed the poems as awesome."[42] Linda Garber argues that *The Black Unicorn* presents a case study in Lorde's "identity poetics" in that "the poems, parallel to Lorde's multiple positioning, are often made of up layer upon layer of undone, transcended, and incorporated dualisms. In the end Lorde does not seek to leave identity behind, but to put it in its place—or rather places, plural."[43] The poems in the volume draw heavily on Lorde's interest in African culture and mythology, but they also speak to her lesbianism and political commitments. The conversation that Lorde created within the poems (and one that she was reluctant to divide for later volumes of her collected works) was transnational and explicit about the importance of bonds with women for sustenance and political change.

Interspersed between poems about the agony of slow black death, Lorde dwells on different forms of touch between women. In "Woman," Lorde writes, "I dream of a place between your breasts / to build my house like a haven / where I plant crops / in your body."[44] In another poem, "Meet," which follows "A Litany for Survival," Lorde writes, "Tasting your ruff down to sweetness" and "Or the taste of each other's skin as it hung / From our childhood mouths."[45] These moments of call and response are strikingly different from the "we" and "our" of "A Litany for Survival." In "Woman," the "I" desires touch, to sow; it desires to make "you" productive. In "Meet," the "you" is devoured through the mouth. In these moments where Lorde calls up hands and tongues and textures and tastes, she is calling forth a sexuality that is embodied, active, and sensual.

Sarah Chinn argues that Lorde's explicit descriptions of lesbian sex are a direct manifestation of what Lorde describes in "Uses of the Erotic" in that they are "about a sensory connection with others, 'the sharing of joy, whether physical, emotional, psychic, or intellectual,' that embraces the entire body, that 'flows through and colors . . . life with a kind of energy that heightens and sensitizes and strengthens all . . . experience.' The erotic infuses and intensifies the experience of the body, linking the sensory with the spiritual."[46] Like Chinn, I agree that these are important moments in Lorde's oeuvre, especially since analysis of her poetry has been overlooked in considerations of her legacy. These spaces suggest alternative ways to consider what it is to be a black lesbian feminist poet mother. In "Meet," for example, Lorde interrupts descriptions of sex to reference children: "as our hands touch and learn / from each others hurt. / Taste my milk in the ditches of Chile and Ouagadougou . . . now you are my child and my mother," thus bringing together the mother and the black lesbian in an unexpected way.[47]

Lorde's insistence on having sensuality, desire, woman loving, and politics meet in the same space is deliberate. It speaks both to the different facets of her identity and their inextricability because Lorde's experience of marginalization and her politicization come from these intersecting nodes of identity. Further, the radicality of insisting on a language of sex for queer black female bodies rescripts the ways that coalition might be enacted; it renders touch sexual and sensual in political ways. While I do not aim to use Lorde to make a sweeping statement about the experiences of all black lesbian feminists, Lorde's insistence that theory come from the body adds a necessary corporeal undertone to queer conversations about fragmentation. Remembering the bodies behind theory reminds us that ideas are often more radical and nuanced when we think about them as responding to particular oppressions using already established languages. Coalition through difference and marginalization is one thing, but remembering Lorde's black lesbian feminism breathes different and important life into that space.

Lorde's insistence on touch, on coalition, on politics, on difference is not incidental. It is the product of her embrace of her identity as a black, lesbian, feminist, mother, and poet. Remembering these parts of her identity complicates Lorde's legacy and our imagination of who should inhabit each of these territories. It offers a way to think through the erotic as not only a useful political tool but also a response to very particular experiences of racism, patriarchy, and capitalism. Given Lorde's explicit writing against fragmentation and toward community, it behooves us to remember Lorde by re-membering her.

NOTES

1. Audre Lorde, *The Cancer Journals* (New York: Aunt Lute Books, 1995), 25.

2. Linda Garber, *Identity Poetics: Race, Class, and the Lesbian-Feminist Roots of Queer Theory* (New York: Columbia University Press, 2001), 97.

3. Audre Lorde, "A Litany for Survival," in *The Black Unicorn* (New York: Norton, 1978), 31–32.

4. Audre Lorde, "What I Do When I Write," *Women's Review of Books* 6 (October 1989): 27.

5. Aishah Shahidah Simmons, "Excerpts from *Silence . . . Broken:* Audre Lorde's Indelible Imprint on My Life," *Feminist Studies* 40, no. 1 (2014): 198.

6. Audre Lorde, "Uses of the Erotic: The Erotic as Power," in *Sister Outsider: Essays and Speeches* (Berkeley, CA: Crossing Press, 2007), 53–59, 53.

7. Lorde, "The Master's Tools Will Never Dismantle the Master's House," in *Sister Outsider*, 112.

8. Lorde, "Uses of the Erotic," 56.

9. Darnell L. Moore, "Using the Erotic to Do Our Work," *Feminist Wire*, February 25, 2014, accessed March 14, 2016, http://thefeministwire.com/2014/02/using-erotic-work/.

10. E. Patrick Johnson, "A Revelatory Distillation of Experience," *WSQ: Women's Studies Quarterly* 40, no. 3 (2013): 312.

11. Rinaldo Walcott, "Outside in Black Studies: Reading from a Queer Place in the Diaspora," in *Black Queer Studies: A Critical Anthology*, eds. E. Patrick Johnson and Mae G. Henderson, 90–105 (Durham, NC: Duke University Press, 2005).

12. Jafari S. Allen, *¡Venceremos? The Erotics of Black Self-making in Cuba* (Durham, NC: Duke University Press, 2011), 96.

13. Allen, *¡Venceremos?*, 97.

14. Lyndon Gill, "In the Realm of Our Lorde: Eros and the Poet Philosopher," *Feminist Studies* 40, no. 1 (2014): 187.

15. Lyndon K. Gill, "Chatting Back an Epidemic: Caribbean Gay Men, HIV/AIDS, and the Uses of Erotic Subjectivity," GLQ: *Journal of Lesbian and Gay Studies* 18, nos. 2–3 (2012): 280.

16. Gill, "In the Realm of Our Lorde," 185.

17. Omise'eke Natasha Tinsley, *Thiefing Sugar: Eroticism between Women in Caribbean Literature* (Durham, NC: Duke University Press, 2010), 20.

18. Republished in Audre Lorde, "Scratching the Surface," in *Sister Outsider*, 45.

19. Lorde, "Scratching the Surface," 49.

20. "An Interview: Audre Lorde with Adrienne Rich," in *Sister Outsider*, 99.

21. Lorde, "Scratching the Surface," 52.

22. Lorde, "Scratching the Surface," 52.

23. Audre Lorde, "Sexism: An American Disease in Blackface," in *Sister Outsider*, 60.

24. Audre Lorde "There Is No Hierarchy of Survival," in *I Am Your Sister: Collected and Unpublished Writings of Audre Lorde,* eds. Rudolph P. Byrd, Johnnetta Betsch Cole, and Beverly Guy-Sheftall (Oxford: Oxford University Press, 2009), 219.

25. Roderick Ferguson, *Aberrations in Black: Towards a Queer of Color Critique* (Minneapolis: University of Minnesota Press, 2003), 118.

26. Lorde, "Uses of the Erotic," 54.

27. Lorde, "Uses of the Erotic," 54.

28. Lorde, "Uses of the Erotic," 58.

29. Lorde, "Uses of the Erotic," 59.

30. Sharon Patricia Holland, *The Erotic Life of Racism* (Durham, NC: Duke University Press, 2012), 59.

31. We see continuations of this impulse in work from Jennifer Nash, LaMonda Horton-Stallings, and Arianne Cruz.

32. Jane Gerhard, *Desiring Revolution: Second Wave Feminism and the Rewriting of American Sexual Thought, 1920 to 1982* (New York: Columbia University Press, 2001), 164.

33. Lorde, "Uses of the Erotic," 55.

34. Michelle Wright, *Becoming Black: Creating Identity in the African Diaspora* (Durham, NC: Duke University Press, 2004), 142.

35. Hortense J. Spillers, "Mama's Baby, Papa's Maybe: An American Grammar Book," *Diacritics* 17, no. 2 (1987): 64–81.

36. Spillers, "Mama's Baby, Papa's Maybe," 80.

37. Alexis Pauline Gumbs, "We Can Learn to Mother Ourselves: The Queer Survival of Black Feminism 1968–1996" (PhD diss., Duke University, 2010), 51.

38. Audre Lorde, "I Am Your Sister: Black Women Organizing across Sexualities," in *I Am Your Sister,* 58.

39. Alexis De Veaux, *Warrior Poet: A Biography of Audre Lorde* (New York; London: W.W. Norton, 2004), 129.

40. Evelynn Hammonds, "Black (W)holes and the Geometry of Black Sexual Difference," *differences* (1994): 126–26; and Hortense Spillers, "Interstices: A Small Drama of Words," in *Pleasure and Danger: Exploring Female Sexuality,* ed. Carole Vance, 73–100 (New York: Routledge, 1984).

41. De Veaux, *Warrior Poet,* 216.

42. De Veaux, *Warrior Poet,* 302.

43. Garber, *Identity Poetics,* 106.

44. Audre Lorde, "Woman," in *The Black Unicorn* (New York: Norton, 1978), 82.

45. Lorde, "Meet," in *The Black Unicorn,* 33–34.

46. Sarah E. Chinn, "Feeling Her Way: Audre Lorde and the Power of Touch," *GLQ: A Journal of Lesbian and Gay Studies* 9, no. 1 (2003): 188.

47. Lorde, "Meet," 33.

18

On the Cusp of Deviance

Respectability Politics and the Cultural Marketplace of Sameness

KAILA ADIA STORY

◎

I name myself "lesbian" because this culture oppresses, silences, and destroys lesbians, even lesbians who don't call themselves "lesbians." I name myself "lesbian" because I want to be visible to other black lesbians. I name myself "lesbian" because I do not subscribe to predatory/institutionalized heterosexuality. I name myself lesbian because I want to be with women (and they don't all have to call themselves "lesbians"). I name myself "lesbian" because being woman-identified has kept me sane. I call myself "Black," too, because Black is my perspective, my aesthetic, my politics, my vision, my sanity. —CHERYL CLARKE, from "New Notes on Lesbianism"

IN THE EPIGRAPH ABOVE, Cheryl Clarke's words recall a bygone era of black lesbian feminism that was unabashed in its radicalism, forthrightness, and, dare I say, pride. As part of a generation of other feminist lesbians of color who came of age in the early 1970s, Clarke, in proclaiming, "I name myself 'lesbian,'" reflects her commitment to a set of radical politics—both black and queer—that intervened in what had otherwise been a mostly straight and/or white second-wave feminist movement. The writings of Clarke, Audre Lorde, Barbara Smith, and a host of others empowered me to also proclaim my lesbianism to my mother at the age of sixteen. I told her I was gay after I had made out with a girl at a track meet. "Well how do you know you're gay, if you've never slept with a woman?" my mom questioned. I told her that I just knew and compared it with the adolescent crushes she had had in school. "You were a virgin until you were nineteen, but up until that point you knew you liked boys, right?" She understood, and that was that. As a high femme black lesbian, I had to continuously "out" myself, as many people would often connect my gender performance with my race and often unintentionally label me "straight." But, like Clarke, identifying as lesbian was and is more than a *sexual* orientation, though that is part of that identity for me; it is also a *political* orientation that speaks to my position as black woman in a country that "oppresses, silences, and destroys lesbians, even lesbians who don't call themselves 'lesbians.'"[1]

Alas, the identity-based politics of such folks as Clarke and others was diminished with the purportedly more radical queer theory explosion of the 1990s. And while one cannot argue that the theoretical intervention of gender (or race for that matter) as citational rather than essential ushered in a productive way of rethinking our relationship to "identity," it also undermined some of the strategies that people of color had developed to speak to the materiality of their condition. Furthermore, (white) queer theorists' myopic focus on sexuality without attending equally to interlocking oppressions such as race and class radicalized a new generation of queer scholars of color who picked up where Clarke and others left off. There were two watershed moments: 1995, when the Black Nations/Queer Nations Conference occurred, and 2000, when the Black Queer Studies in the Millennium Conference convened. The latter led to the *Black Queer Studies* volume in 2005, which gave me life! Indeed, it was in that volume that I first discovered the theoretical language for who I was/am. I began to see myself as the corporeal interanimation of racialized sexuality and black feminist praxis. For the first time in my academic career, queer theory/studies was not white, and for the first time black studies was not straight.

One step forward, two steps back. For all the progress brought on by the advent of black queer studies, currently, we seem to be experiencing yet another watershed moment within queer and black cultures. Indeed, the quick move to have a "kumbaya" moment across racial difference that disavows difference altogether, coupled with a move toward racial normativity, has created a culture in which taglines such as "Gay

Is the New Black" or "Gay Civil Rights" flourish and in which blackness becomes synonymous with heteronormative social relations vis-à-vis representations in popular culture.[2] The ahistorical collapse of civil rights and gay rights in this context serves to obscure the racism within white queer communities and elide other attendant issues for queer people of color beyond marriage. Alternatively, black male celebrities disseminate heteronormative discourse through their television programs and films that further instantiate patriarchy, misogyny, and homophobia. Ultimately, white queers and black straights continue to silence our voices and/or sanitize our images in an attempt to make our lived experiences more palatable or respectable to the larger public. The common theme that binds these two discourses is marriage in all its heteronormative trappings. Whether it be the overwhelming push for marriage equality by white queers over and above other equally important issues facing queer people (and particularly queer people of color) or the creation of hegemonic forms of sexual representation by black straight male celebrities, homonormativity and heteronormativity reign supreme in today's cultural marketplace of sameness. My desire, then, is to return to a more radical form of political struggle in which we do not "subscribe to predatory/institutionalized heterosexuality" and where we dance in the delight of difference. Indeed, I want to throw shade on normativity, sashay away from a politics of respectability, and get my life from a politics of deviance.

Drawing on Cathy Cohen's essay "Deviancy as Resistance: A New Research Agenda for the Study of Black Politics," Evelyn Brooks Higginbotham's notion of "the politics of respectability," and in the spirit of the first Black Queer Studies volume, I argue that there remains a sociopolitical and ideological need for black sexual deviance as a legitimate expression of sexuality and desire that resists a retrograde return to respectability.[3] I analyze the visual and rhetorical strategies of Tyler Perry and Steve Harvey, both self-appointed relationship and self-help gurus who disseminate heteronormative discourse through their films, television shows, and books that further instantiate patriarchy, misogyny, and homophobia. I also critique the mainstream white queer marriage movement and the way it marginalizes black queer people, making blackness and queerness appear mutually exclusive; it also forecloses the possibility of intentional black sexual deviance as an avenue for change and empowerment. In this essay I first examine the works of Steve Harvey and Tyler Perry to show the sexual erasure of black queer people within black popular culture. Next, I discuss the consequences of whiteness within the marriage equality movement to demonstrate how its rhetoric perpetuates heterosexual privilege due to its emphasis on whiteness. Lastly, I illuminate the ways in which queer people of color resist these representations and social movements through their practices of deviance and difference.

(Re)visiting Respectability: Tyler Perry and Steve Harvey's Heteronormative Playhouse

Men go out and get jobs and hustle to make money because of women.
We drive fancy cars because of women. We dress nice, put on cologne,
get haircuts and try to look all shiny and new for you.
—STEVE HARVEY, *Act Like a Lady, Think Like a Man:*
What Men Really Think about Love, Relationships,
Intimacy, and Commitment

I think it's important to show a husband and a wife together,
in a room, raising children, because you don't see that anymore.
—TYLER PERRY, "AMC Q&A: Tyler Perry Defends
the Schizophrenia of Why Did I Get Married Too?"

Steve Harvey, known to most as an African American comic, became an overnight relationship guru in 2009 with his *New York Times* bestseller, *Act Like a Lady, Think Like a Man: What Men Really Think about Love, Relationships, Intimacy, and Commitment*. Harvey appeared on *The Oprah Winfrey Show*, and in 2012 Sony Pictures released a major motion picture based on the principles of the book.[4] Tyler Perry, who has now become a household name owing to his success as a playwright, filmmaker, and television producer, has echoed Harvey's sentiments on black relationships within his productions.[5] Most of Perry's plays, films, and situation comedies, as well as Harvey's bestseller, portray and are dependent on a heteronormative trajectory of black sexuality. More often than not, this trajectory, which ends in a "legally recognized marriage" or a "happily ever after" motif, reinforces the old-fashioned and apolitical notion that the only viable, sustainable, and normative dating and/or relationship schema is one that is based on the heteronormative, patriarchal, and racist institutions of marriage and heterosexuality. African American women and their sexual desires, ultimately, become the focus of these representations because of their societal position as a racialized and gendered other. Both Harvey and Perry deploy the rhetorical and visual strategies of the "the politics of respectability."

In *Righteous Discontent: The Women's Movement in the Black Baptist Church, 1880–1920*, Evelyn Higginbotham recovers the neglected story of black women's activism within and outside the institution of the black church. In discussing the myriad of motivations behind the American Baptist Home Mission Society, or the "Female Talented Tenth," as she refers to them, Higginbotham argues that central to the organization's work was racial uplift in conjunction with creating a social and cultural sentiment of respect for African Americans by white Americans. Further, various members of the organization believed that African Americans' lack of adherence to the social and cultural norms of white society was the real barrier to racial advancement and progress. Many believed that to gain respect from white America as individuals, and to achieve racial uplift as a collective, "required changes in religious beliefs, speech patterns, and manners and morals."[6] Ultimately, Higginbotham argues, black women's "adherence to respectability enabled [them] to counter racist images and structures."[7]

But the advances of middle-class black women came at a cost to working-class and sexual dissident members of the black community. Indeed, the Mission Society's pandering to the social and cultural norms of white America occurred simultaneously with the shaming of the black community's most vulnerable—that is, the poor and queer folk—for "the black Baptist women condemned what they perceived to be negative practices and attitudes among their own people."[8] The legacy of black respectability politics remains today and manifests in various forms, from political discourse to popular culture. Popular culture in particular is a site where some of the most pernicious forms of respectability politics flourish because they get a pass as a solely "entertainment" art form, rather than being seen as hegemonic ideology. Building on the legacy of Higginbotham's "Female Talented Tenth," both Tyler Perry and Steve Harvey posit black respectability generally, and black female respectability specifically, as a way of demonstrating that black Americans are in fact no different from white Americans. They go through the same mishaps in life and love, and in the end, one need only adhere to a respectability politic to access full citizenship. Through their productions, both insist on "blacks' conformity to the dominant society's norms of manners and morals," inevitably perpetuating the myth of black sexuality as pathological.[9] Neither Perry nor Harvey views black sexual expression and desire that exists outside of heteronormative marriage as legitimate, moral, or empowering because such sexual desire exists outside of the Judeo-Christian faith. This is especially true for Perry, whose plays and films are imbued with fundamentalist didacticism on the topics of love, faith, and marriage. Perhaps even more troubling is Perry's own embodiment of misogynist performances of drag.[10]

The formerly homeless playwright initially struggled to garner audiences for his plays in New Orleans and Atlanta because of their focus on adult survivors of child abuse. In 1998, however, after Perry created the character "Madea," a Mammy-meets-Sapphire figure, his plays became an overnight success. Audiences loved learning life-changing lessons from the hilarious and outrageous "grandmother" Mabel Simmons. Perry's southern-themed stage plays soon turned into film productions, and he made appearances on *The Oprah Winfrey Show* and wrote a *New York Times* bestselling book as his alter ego, Madea.

Similar to those of black male comedians who came before him, Perry's drag persona, Madea, presents the black woman's body as denigrated spectacle—as an object of mockery, objectification, and abjection—and does nothing to disrupt popular notions of "natural" blackness and femaleness.[11] Similar to the Video Vixen imaginary of the early 1990s, Perry's depictions come to stand in for real black women's bodies in the minds of moviegoers, who leave the theater commenting how their grandmothers are "just like Madea." Indeed, the black female body in Perry's productions remains what Patricia Hill Collins calls a "controlling image."[12] Because the controlling images of Mammy and Sapphire that Perry and others depict in their drag are already asexual and serve as a tabula rasa to overlay any depiction the actor may choose, the result is the heteronormalizing of an otherwise potentially transgressive queer performance. Judith Butler actually discusses this form of drag in *Bodies That Matter* when she argues that such performances "are functional in providing a ritualistic release for a heterosexual economy that must constantly police its own boundaries against the invasion of queerness, and . . . this displaced production and resolution of homosexual panic actually fortifies the heterosexual regime in its self-perpetuating task."[13] Perry deploys drag within this "heterosexual regime" by foreclosing the possibility of Madea engaging in sex or intimacy with a presumably heterosexual partner. To do so would unravel the heteronormative logic upon which the drag performance rests by calling into question the heterosexuality (that is, queerness) of the performer himself. While Perry has been unable to contain the queer excess that his drag and real life evince, according to Butler his films and performances nonetheless serve as "high net entertainment" and lack in subversive potential.[14]

Perry's Medea character becomes the foil for his larger project of constricting black love to heteronormative representations. Although Perry's films and stage plays center on "the experiences of those who stand on the (out)side of state sanctioned, normalized White, middle- and upper-class, male heterosexuality," he cannot imagine a world in which his audiences or main characters deliberately choose nonnormative cultural and/or sexual mores in an attempt to resist the state's "reification of the nuclear family, the conformity to institutionally prescribed and informally regulated gender roles and intimate sexual relations." Perry perpetually focuses his attention on poor black women in these films and plays as "morally wanting by both dominant society and other indigenous group members."[15] Indeed, Perry's female characters rarely possess sexual agency; rather, they are in need of a male savior, God "himself," or both. And when they do acquire some kind of sexual agency, it is always already tethered to normative heterosexual relations. Despite engaging in provocative and timely topics such as HIV/AIDS, family disputes, molestation, rape, infidelity, and so forth, Perry's solution to these issues becomes formulaic: faith in God and heteronormative marriage are the salve for the ills of the black community. And, according to Perry, this conservative life trajectory is particularly a "cure" for what is ailing black women. Two films that highlight these machinations are *I Can Do Bad All by Myself* and *Temptation*.

Written, produced, and directed by Tyler Perry, *I Can Do Bad All by Myself* was released in 2009, the same year as Harvey's bestseller. Many of the sexist themes about heterosexual relationships and advice to women found in Harvey's book mirror the trials and tribulations endured by Perry's protagonist, April (played by Taraji P. Henson), in her pursuit to "get her life together" and "find a good man." April, "a heavy-drinking nightclub singer who lives off Raymond, her married boyfriend," wants nothing to do with her sister's children, sixteen-year-old Jennifer and her two younger brothers, who have been unwillingly placed with April by Madea. April's attitude toward the children begins to change "when Sandino, a handsome Colombian immigrant looking for work, moves into April's basement room. Making amends for his own troubled past, Sandino challenges April to open her heart."[16] Ultimately, Perry's main character has two choices: remain stagnant and unfulfilled in her relationship with her married, abusive boyfriend, Raymond, or begin to explore the possibilities of faith in God and love with Sandino. As in all Perry films, in *I Can Do Bad All by Myself*, April and Sandino get married in an over-the-top community wedding, with the children in tow, and begin to pursue a life filled with faith and love for God.

Certainly, as an artist and auteur, Perry has the right to create the kinds of entertainment he wishes. And in the black film canon there should be room for storybook fairy tales and "happily-ever-after" endings. Nonetheless, ideology undergirds all forms of representation, and as cultural consumers and critics we must be attuned to the ways in which "innocent" and "feel good" films and other forms of representation collude with hegemonic forms of oppression. In this regard, Perry's films repackage old tropes that traffic in misogyny, sexism, and homophobia in the guise of racial uplift—ones no different, I might add, from previous forms promulgated by systems of white supremacist capitalist patriarchy—rather than offering a progressive view of racial or gender relations. Instead, Perry's films update the politics of black respectability for contemporary times, as there exists no room for characters to make choices outside a Judeo-Christian sexual moral code. As such, those who live outside that code either have to be "saved" or are punished. Unlike Cathy Cohen, Perry has yet to take seriously the idea that "these so-called deviants have chosen and acted differently, situating their lives in direct contrast to dominant normalized understandings of family, desire, and sex."[17] Instead, his poor and black female protagonists become pawns of his black respectability rhetoric in the cultural marketplace of sameness where he shops and barters for his own cultural capital.

On July 19, 2013, Perry gave fans a sneak preview of his film *Temptation: Confessions of a Marriage Counselor* on the *Steve Harvey Show*. *Temptation*, which was adapted from a play of the same name, is about Judith, a woman who becomes restless in her marriage and commits adultery with another man. Her extramarital affair inevitably has a ripple effect on the rest of her life. The film is a cautionary tale to all women who seek sexual independence, professional success, and personal freedom.

As a consequence of her "salacious actions" she is repeatedly berated and beaten by her lover, Harley, and ultimately punished through contracting HIV. It is within this story line that Perry's politics become most dangerous, for not only does the character of Judith embody the "problem" with successful, independent women who express sexual agency, but he also renders her punishment through the figure of the "down low" brother who purportedly preys on unsuspecting women, thereby becoming the source of HIV contagion. Thus, both characters signal to the viewing audience a cautionary tale against deviant behavior. Women should be submissive and cleave to their husbands, and men should not engage in same-sex sex lest they be punished with disease. Deploying the down-low trope in the film is particularly specious because it unabashedly reinforces the myth that men who have sex with men (MSMs) are the cause for the rise in the number of cases of HIV infection among heterosexual black women.[18] Moreover, it demonizes same-sex sex as pathological. In the context of the film, Perry literally demonizes Judith's lover, Harley, the putative down-low brother. Indeed, if the character Sandino in *I Can Do Bad All by Myself* is a proverbial Jesus, then Harley is definitely the embodiment of the devil.

Perry's not-so-subtle titular reference to the biblical Satan's temptation of Eve in the Garden of Eden gets played out through Judith and Harley's relationship. And because Judith yields to temptation, she pays the consequences for her "sins." In biblical terms the "wages of sin is death," which in this film is synonymous with HIV. All of Perry's films and plays are didactic, and *Temptation* is no different in its literal associations of Harley with the devil. Everything in Harley's house is either red or "constantly on fire."[19] Similar to the serpent who convinces Eve to eat the apple, Harley lures Judith away from a Christian and heteronormative life to a life filled with threesomes, cocaine, and, ultimately, HIV. Thus, *Temptation*, through its promulgating uncritical Christian piety, heteronormative monogamy at the expense of one's sexual pleasure, and physical abuse and HIV as the punishment for nonnormative sex, is both personally repugnant and cinematically irresponsible.

Perry is not alone in peddling this particular brand of raced and gendered respectability. Steve Harvey is also insistent in his advice on his morning show and with the publication of his book that black women are the root and cause of their own misfortune and unhappiness. Steve Harvey begins *Act Like a Lady, Think Like a Man* by stating that the impetus for writing his book came from his many call-in queries to his daytime radio show, *The Steve Harvey Morning Show.*[20] Although Harvey suggests that his book is geared to African American women and men, the underlying premise of the book is that the real problem with black relationships is black women. With their irreverent personas and irresponsible sexuality, the women in Harvey's book, much like the women in Perry's films, are desperate to find substantive, lasting, and overall monogamous heteronormative unions so as to have fulfilling lives. While there is nothing inherently problematic in representations that feature heterosexual African Americans pursuing and finding partnership, both Harvey's book and Perry's films render these representations at the expense of black women and those who engage in nonnormative sex. Both men reinforce black sexuality as pathological and in need of rehabilitation, pandering to a white supremacist capitalist patriarchy that always already defines blackness in abject terms.

As proponents of black respectability politics, Tyler Perry and Steve Harvey teamed up in 2014 to do a sweepstakes based on Perry's *Temptation*. In the spirit of helping "couples keep the romance alive," *The Steve Harvey Morning Show* and Tyler Perry's film *Temptation* sought to award five winners up to "$500.00 for the Ultimate Date Night." Contestants were required to answer the question, "How do you keep the passion in your relationship alive and avoid temptation?"[21] Both Harvey and Perry's attempt to position themselves as the moral voices of the black community on black love relationships, thereby policing black sexuality and confining it to heterosexual marriage, effectively erases the myriad of experiences and desires of some black heterosexual women and men, as well as black LGBTQ folks. Their productions also limit the possibilities of racialized and nonnormative sexuality and gender presentation.

However, Perry and Harvey are not the only ones who perpetuate the myth that black sexuality and identity is inherently pathological. The whitening of the marriage equality movement propagated by many white queer activists also perpetuates this myth and inadvertently creates silence around race. For the remainder of the essay, I will explore how such taglines as "Gay Is the New Black" or " Gay Civil Rights," utilized by proponents of the modern-day marriage equality movement, are exemplary of the rhetorical hegemony of "postrace" discourse and demonstrate how it not only silences black voices but through its emphasis on whiteness also perpetuates rhetorical and visual heterosexual privilege.[22]

Gay Is the New Black: The Whitening of the Marriage Equality Movement

"Whiteness is everywhere in U.S. culture, but it is very hard to see. . . . As the unmarked category against which difference is constructed, whiteness never has to speak its name, never has to acknowledge its role as an organizing principle in social and cultural relations . . . the possessive investment in whiteness . . . surreptitiously shapes so much of our public and private lives."
—GEORGE LIPSITZ, *The Possessive Investment in Whiteness: How White People Profit from Identity Politics*

The hegemony of whiteness as "unraced," coupled with white supremacy, allows whites a space to disavow their race privilege while simultaneously reifying people of color as the racial other. Through this racial dynamic whites maintain an economic, social, political, and cultural advantage over people of color. They also maintain their ability to co-opt the political strategies that emerge within communities of color—created to resist the very acts of systemic and institutionalized racism that neoliberal whites disavow but nonetheless perpetuate through acts of benevolent racism. And despite the end of de jure segregation over fifty years ago, the geopolitics of most cities in the United States reflect a country of racial residential silos, whereby whites and people of color, for the most part, self-segregate. Or, to put it a bit more crudely, because people of color disproportionately represent this country's poor, affordable housing is still beyond their reach. This story becomes even more complicated when one considers the effects of gentrification by white queers on historically black neighborhoods as Charles Nero has so eloquently argued.[23] It is this latter connection between white queers and people of color, and specifically black people, that frames the second half of this essay, for it speaks to the ways in which "postracial" discourse in the new millennium actually means that whites are no longer responsible for the consequences of past and current racisms. For many white queer folks involved in the marriage equality movement, their own relationships to race and racism are sadly no different.

Respectability politics are not unique to African Americans, especially when sexual identity becomes a part of the matrix. In other words, just as Perry and Harvey invest in heteronormative representations as a form of racial uplift, white queers have a similar investment in such forms to maintain their status as respectable whites. The institution of marriage has become one of the vehicles through which this ascension to normativity occurs. Such an investment in white respectability does double duty here in that it simultaneously sustains white queers' racial privilege while also sustaining racial and class difference. As George Lipsitz argues, whites' possessive investment in whiteness, despite it being "a delusion, a scientific and cultural fiction that like all racial identities has no valid foundation in biology or anthropology," has to do with its "all-too-real consequences for the distribution of wealth, prestige, and opportunity."[24] The institution of marriage, then, reflects and upholds the tenets of whiteness and Judeo-Christian values, especially since as an institution it was historically codified as a means by which to exchange property—whether that property be women or actual material goods. As such, white queers attempt to de-emphasize homosexuality as nonnormative, cultivating instead a sanitized version of homosexuality that, in its most insidious instantiation, becomes another form of sexual regulation that cultural critic Lisa Duggan has called "homonormativity."[25] The "trouble with normal," to riff off of Michael Warner, is that in this instance sexual normativity undergirds racial supremacy, often blinding many white queers to their privilege. This is why they can afford to myopically focus on sexuality as the only category of oppression, ignoring the ways in which queer people of color are disempowered by the very institution of marriage.

For example, the momentum of the marriage equality movement in the aftermath of September 11 was telling for many queer people of color. During this period white queers, who had long been on the margins of society owing to their sexual orientation, sought allegiance with straight white groups under the auspices of nationalism and white supremacy. September 11 and its aftermath served as a viable connection for the mainstream white gay and lesbian community to unite with white straights based on fears of racial difference. According to Priyanka Jindal, this "unholy" union allowed "white gays and lesbians to assimilate and become part of the white heterosexual nation."[26] Therefore, the activist and intellectual pursuit of legalized marriage and respectability by the marriage equality movement is nothing but a racialized ruse for class ascension linked to racist heteronormative notions of citizenry.

The white face of the marriage equality movement and the continuation of respectability politics within many black communities solidifies the notion that the only "legitimate" gay identity is a white one and the only legitimate black identity is a straight one. Instead of seeing the radical possibilities of intentional racial and sexual deviance as resistance, the marriage equality movement excludes more than it includes. Namely, it privileges marriage over desire, gay and lesbian identity over bisexual and transgender identity, and white queer middle-class men over poor and working-class queer people of color. Concomitantly, Perry's, Harvey's, and others' pandering to conservative notions of racial uplift performs a similar logic as the marriage equality movement by positioning nonheteronormative expressions of sexuality as beyond the "boundaries of blackness."[27] While marriage equality advocates and some black male entertainers-come-spokespersons for the black community may have good intentions, the consequences of such social movements and discourses are not only the disavowal of alternative sexual and racial epistemologies but also the instantiation of structural and symbolic forms of discrimination enacted by the state. Marriage, after all, is not based solely on amorous feelings between two people or merely a religious rite; it is also a legal *contract* facilitated by the state—despite the supposed separation of church and state.

The institution was also established to transfer accumulated wealth from one generation to the next. Given the history of black disenfranchisement, poverty, and subjection to state violence, marriage as an institution has never benefited black folks as much as whites. Indeed, enslaved blacks were not given access to legal marriage until after emancipation. And although blacks did marry during slavery, those marriages were based not on legal definitions of marriage by the state but rather on the cultural values of the slave community. The motivation behind marriage in these instances was to keep families together rather than the accumulation of wealth, since they did not own property, not even their own bodies. Even when blacks were allowed to marry legally, many of the puritan notions about marriage, such as monogamy, were sometimes impractical because of the particular effect slavery had on black families.

Historian Tera Hunter explains that newly freed slaves "created novel solutions for the vexing moral, legal, and practical concerns in resolving marital relations disrupted by forces beyond their control," such as forced separation. According to Hunter, "affections undernourished by hundreds of miles and many years might be supplanted by other relationships. Many ex-slaves faced awkward dilemmas when spouses presumed to be dead or long-lost suddenly reappeared." More interesting are the "novel" solutions to such dilemmas that speak to a nonconformist framework toward marriage and sexual relationships: "One woman lived with each of her two husbands for a two-week trial before making a decision. . . . In one case . . . a wife resumed her relationship with her first husband, while the second husband, a much older man, was brought into the family as a 'poor relation.'"[28] The examples that Hunter provides bolster my argument that deviance as a strategy of resistance is not only more practical for blacks but also speaks to the privileging of desire over the constrictions of institutional marriage, such as, in this instance, serial monogamy or even polygamy. The point I want to emphasize here is that blacks' relationship to the institution of marriage has always already been a queer one. Indeed, it has existed in between the lack of access to legally sanctioned marriage by the state and the culturally sanctioned marriages that they created to keep family together. This history of marriage for blacks informs the current relationship black queers have to the marriage equality movement in significant ways. Namely, similar to the ways that newly emancipated slaves who sought legalized marriage soon discovered that it was not a panacea for the continued oppressions they faced, contemporary black queer people recognize that marriage will not be a salve for ongoing racial, gender, and class oppression.

Deviance and Difference as Sites of Resistance

Reading blackness and queerness as mutually exclusive categories is not only historically inaccurate but also undermines their transgressive potential when they are deployed for the dismantling of oppression. As E. Patrick Johnson and Mae G. Henderson argue, the "interanimation" of queerness and blackness "carries the potential to overcome the myopic theorizing that has too long often sabotaged or subverted long-term and mutually liberatory goals."[29] In the current marriage equality movement, this myopic focus on an institution that disproportionately benefits white queers overlooks other institutionalized forms of oppression, namely racism and classism. And some black folks' narrow view of blackness as always already heterosexual and male undermines the uplifting of all blacks who labor under the sign of blackness. An alternative to these strategies, in addition to interanimating black and queer, is animating the radical potential of deviance and difference.

In her essay "Deviance as Resistance: A New Research Agenda for the Study of Black Politics," Cathy Cohen argues that rather than adopting a political agenda that acquiesces to the respectability politics of white mainstream culture, advocates for racial progress and justice should instead avail themselves to the transformative potential of intentional deviancy as resistance. Drawing on Michel Foucault's thesis of "simultaneous repressive and generative power," Cohen contends that "individuals with little power in society engage in counter normative behaviors," resulting from their limited agency, and consequently create "a new radical politics of deviance," which counters and/or challenges "the presiding normative order with regard to family, sex, and desire." This inevitably engenders "new or counter normative frameworks by which to judge behavior." Thus, even when proponents of the marriage equality movement and/or advocates for racial uplift like Perry and Harvey attempt to sanitize, police, and regulate the behavior of those who live on the margins of society, those same individuals "challenge established norms and rules," by pursuing "basic human goals such as pleasure, desire, recognition, and respect."[30] So important is the pursuit of these goals that marginalized groups do so in the face of ideological and material consequences, such as demonization in the media, employment discrimination, and disenfranchisement, just to name a few.

Because of the history of surveillance and control of black sexuality by whites, it is understandable that one response by blacks to such surveillance and control might be that of capitulating to white notions of sexual morality—even if whites do not uphold those mores themselves. Because queer desire is seen as outside normative sexuality, then, blacks have often frowned upon same-sex desire—at least in public discourse.[31] But black communities have never been monolithic and have always incorporated the nonnormative behavior of their members. I would argue that it has been this confluence of intracultural difference that has been the greatest strength of black social movements in the fight for liberation, whether that difference has been actively acknowledged or not. In discussing the radical possibility of difference in her essay "The Master's Tools Will Never Dismantle the Master's House," Audre Lorde argues that difference within oppressed communities has often been treated with suspicion and separation, instead of a springboard to enact change. Lorde writes:

> Those of us who stand outside the circle of this society's definition of acceptable; those of us who have been forged in the crucible of difference; those of us who are poor ... who are lesbian ... who are black ... know that survival is not an academic skill. It is a learning of how to stand alone, unpopular, and sometimes reviled, and how to make common cause with others identified as outside the structures, in order to define and seek a world in which we can all flourish.[32]

Lorde's essay still serves as an endless reservoir of the many ways in which oppressed communities might mobilize difference as catalysts of change within and outside their respective communities. As Lorde reminds us all, "It is not our differences that divide us. It is our inability to recognize, accept, and celebrate those differences."[33] Neither Lorde nor Cohen imagines a community in which its members conform their beliefs and behaviors to a politics of respectability; rather, they imagine a community that seeks its liberation, empowerment, and ultimately its respect from mainstream society through a praxis of difference and deviance as sites of resistance.

1. Cheryl Clarke, "New Notes on Lesbianism," in *The Days of Good Looks: The Prose and Poetry of Cheryl Clarke, 1980 to 2005* (New York: Da Capo Press, 2006), 81.

2. Paul Butler, "Gay Is the New Black," *New York Times*, accessed October 5, 2013, http://www.nytimes.com/roomfordebate/2013/06/26/is-the-civil-rights-era-over/the -court-should-focus-on-justice-rather-than-rights; "Gay Civil Rights," *Huffington Post*, accessed October 5, 2013, http://www.huffingtonpost.com/tag/gay-civil-rights.

3. Evelyn Brooks Higginbotham, *Righteous Discontent: The Women's Movement in the Black Baptist Church, 1880–1920* (Cambridge, MA: Harvard University Press, 1993).

4. Harvey wrote a follow-up book to his first. *Straight Talk, No Chaser: How to Find, Keep, Understand a Man* (New York: Amistad) was published in 2010 but was not as successful as his first.

5. "Q&A—Tyler Perry Defends the Schizophrenia of Why Did I Get Married Too?," accessed June 25 2015, http://www.amc.com/talk/2010/03/qa-tyler-perr.

6. Higginbotham, *Righteous Discontent*, 54.

7. Higginbotham, *Righteous Discontent*, 187.

8. Higginbotham, *Righteous Discontent*, 187

9. Higginbotham, *Righteous Discontent*, 187

10. I want to be clear here that I am not suggesting, as do some feminists, that all drag is based in misogyny. On the contrary, as I will argue below regarding Perry's drag persona, I posit that not all drag is transgressive and can be put in the service of misogyny and patriarchy. For a discussion of drag as inherently misogynist, see Marilyn Frye, *The Politics of Reality: Essays in Feminist Theory* (Trumansburg, NY: Crossing Press, 1983).

11. Examples include Flip Wilson as Geraldine, Martin Lawrence as Shen-nah and his mother on his show, and Eddie Murphy, most recently as Rasputia in *Norbit* and a slew of other characters in his Nutty Professor trilogy.

12. Patricia Hill Collins, *Black Feminist Thought: Knowledge, Consciousness, and the Politics of Empowerment* (New York: Routledge, 1990).

13. Judith Butler, *Bodies That Matter: On the Discursive Limits of Sex* (New York: Routledge Press, 1993), 126.

14. Perry has been plagued for years by rumors about his (homo)sexuality. Butler, *Bodies That Matter*, 126.

15. Cathy Cohen, "Deviance as Resistance: A New Research Agenda for the Study of Black Politics," *DuBois Review: Social Science Research on Race* 1.1 (Mar 2004): 29.

16. IMDB, "*I Can Do Bad All by Myself*: Plot Summary," accessed October 5, 2013, http://www.imdb.com/title/tt1385912/plotsummary?ref_=tt_ov_pl.

17. Cohen, "Deviance as Resistance," 30.

18. This is, namely, because of the "down low" phenomenon, wherein black men who have sex with men have been falsely cited as the cause for the increased HIV/AIDS rates among African American women ages 18 to 24. As of late, there is no hard evidence that such men are increasing these rates. Men who have sex with men are just seen as being a "high risk" sexual group. CDC, *HIV Surveillance Report*, vol. 23, February 2013. Human immunodeficiency virus diagnosis data are estimates from all 50 states, the District of Columbia, and six U.S. dependent areas. Rates do not include U.S. dependent areas. Also see Jeffery Q. McCune Jr., *Sexual Discretion: Black Masculinity and the Politics of Passing* (Chicago: University of Chicago Press, 2014).

19. Lindy West, "Tyler Perry Isn't Just an Artless Hack, He's a Scary Ideologue," *Jezebel*, August 3, 2013, accessed June 25, 2015, http://jezebel.com/5993523/tyler-perry -isnt-just-an-artless-hack-hes-a-scary-ideologue.

20. Steve Harvey, *Act Like a Lady, Think Like a Man: What Men Really Think about Love, Relationships, Intimacy, and Commitment* (New York: HarperCollins, 2009), 3.

21. "Temptation Sweepstakes," bet.com, http://www.bet.com/celebrities/movies /temptation/temptation-sweepstakes-rules.html (accessed October 5, 2013).

22. Butler, "Gay Is the New Black"; and "Gay Civil Rights."

23. See Charles Nero, "Why Are All the Gay Ghettos White?" in *Black Queer Studies: A Critical Anthology*, eds. E. Patrick Johnson and Mae G. Henderson (Durham, NC: Duke University Press, 2005), 228–45.

24. George Lipsitz, *The Possessive Investment in Whiteness: How White People Profit from Identity Politics* (Philadelphia: Temple University Press, 1998), 3.

25. Lisa Duggan, "The New Homonormativity: The Sexual Politics of Neoliberalism," in *Materializing Democracy: Toward a Revitalized Cultural Politics*, eds. Russ Castronova and Dana Nelson (Durham, NC: Duke University Press, 2002), 175–94.

26. Priyanka Jindal, "Sites of Resistance or Sites of Racism?" in *That's Revolting! Queer Strategies for Resisting Assimilation*, ed. Mattilda Bernstein Sycamore (Brooklyn, NY: Soft Skull Press, 2008), 39–46.

27. See Cathy Cohen, *The Boundaries of Blackness: AIDS and the Breakdown of Black Politics* (Chicago: University of Chicago Press, 1999).

28. Tera Hunter, *To Joy My Freedom: Southern Black Women's Lives and Labors after the Civil War* (Cambridge, MA: Harvard University Press, 1997), 39.

29. Johnson and Henderson, eds., *Black Queer Studies*, 6.

30. Cohen, "Deviance as Resistance," 30.

31. I should note here that black communities' public denunciation of homosexuality does not always indicate private actions. In other words, blacks may be

explicit about their disavowal of homosexuality yet privately condone homosexual relationships.

32. Audre Lorde, "The Master's Tools Will Never Dismantle the Master's House," in *This Bridge Called My Back: Writings by Radical Women of Color,* eds. Cherríe Moraga and Gloria Anzaldúa (New York: Kitchen Table Press, 1981), 100.

33. Audre Lorde, *Our Dead behind Us* (New York: W. W. Norton, 1994), 56.

19

Something Else to Be

Generations of Black Queer Brilliance and the
Mobile Homecoming Experiential Archive

ALEXIS PAULINE GUMBS AND
JULIA ROXANNE WALLACE

◯

An (Intergenerational) Something Else to Be

THE MOBILE HOMECOMING VISION

This is immersion in legacy. This is a celebration of how boldness survives the
moment of its need. This is an intimate embrace with a living herstory that
traces pathways between our lungs, called laughter, called stillness, called sigh.
This is a dance, a prayer, a baptism in hope. This is how we know who we are.
This is how we live forever. —From the Mobile Homecoming website

THE INSPIRATION AND RESOURCES for the Mobile Homecoming, an experiential archive project amplifying generations of black LGBTQ brilliance, spring from a collective desire to witness the lives and loves that are foundational for the survival of participants in a black, LGB, trans, queer, or genderqueer legacy. The form of our journey is poetic and experimental, and it transforms to open itself up to the resources of those innovative geniuses who have come before us and to collectivize those resources with our contemporary and younger community members, all of whom hold us accountable to this labor of love. We are not the first to challenge form (the form of the archive, the form of the movement, the form of the question) in ways that resonate in black queer communities, and we will not be the last. In each community, context, and time the ceremony must be found to activate the medicine necessary for us each to achieve our destinies.[1] Elsewhere we write about the details of how the Mobile Homecoming ceremony functions on critical ethnographic and social movement terms. This essay looks at founding black feminist moments in queer of color critique to present the Mobile Homecoming experiential archive project as a form of reading and writing community, a literary praxis informed by Toni Morrison's *Sula* and Audre Lorde's "A Litany for Survival," key literary moments relevant to an insurgent history of queer black life written across generations.

In 1973, when Toni Morrison published her second novel, *Sula*, she changed black feminist literary criticism forever. Some say that black feminists created black feminist literary criticism to deal with Sula, the character and the text. In partnership with her first novel, *The Bluest Eye*, Morrison's *Sula* does more than insert nuanced black female characters into an existing literary scene. With these two novels Morrison insists that the very form of the novel must bend and bow and breathe and move to witness the experiences of black women and girls.

Sula arrived well placed in time to become the catalyst that it was and is for black feminist literary criticism. The book was published right when the first black women's lit courses were being taught in newly formed black studies and women's studies programs in colleges in the Northeast. The two foundational works of black feminist literary studies, Mae Gwendolyn Henderson's "Speaking in Tongues: Dialectics, Dialogics, and the Black Woman Writer's Literary Tradition" and Barbara Smith's "Toward a Black Feminist Criticism" both read *Sula* as their primary text and as an instance through which to imagine what black feminist literary criticism could be. Audre Lorde mentions in a 1982 interview with Claudia Tate that she doesn't care that it was *Song of Solomon* that Morrison won the National Book of the Month Club selection for, it is *Sula* that "made me light up inside like a Christmas tree"; she adds, "That book is like one long poem."[2]

The passages that cause black feminists to canonize *Sula* are the passages about mutual self-invention that occur between Sula and Nel. The most cited passage is the one where the narrator explains the destined friendship of the two girls, noting that "having long ago realized they were neither white nor male ... they went about creating something else to be."[3] This is a proposition as far reaching as to appear in Afro-Scottish Maud Sulter's description of an art exhibit she curated in England; as long lasting as to reappear as the "different sort of subject" that Hortense Spillers asks for in her 1987 essay "Mama's Baby, Papa's Maybe"; and as genesis moment for queer of color critique in Roderick Ferguson's *Aberrations in Black: Toward a Queer of Color Critique* in 2003. The two other moments of the text that black feminist theorists drew in the sky are Sula's insistence, when her grandmother, Eva, suggests she should settle down and have some babies, that "I don't want to make someone else. I want to make myself."[4] This challenge to motherhood partially constitutes the critique of heteropatriarchy that allows Barbara Smith to claim *Sula* as a "lesbian" text alongside the book's final revelation that the loss of a husband is nothing compared with the loss of a girlfriend.

As queer black feminist researchers and artists seeking a way to amplify black feminist practices in the black LGBTQ community across generations, with a specific focus on those visionaries who, like Nel and Sula, have faced the dilemma of being seen as nonwhite and nonmale (even if they, in fact, are trans men), we decided to look closely at how people in different communities across decades had sustained the practice of being something else both literally and in the vernacular sense that is used in the black community to mark nonconformist behavior and performance (that is, "Now Alexis and Julia are driving around in that Winnebago looking for black queer rituals? They are truly something else."). We have found that even engaging this inquiry requires a queerness in our approach to research, something else to do and something else to be while doing it. Our specific other ways of being are implicated in a theory of survival, what it means for us to survive while doing experiential archive work grounded in the U.S. Southeast, what it means to do this work sustainably and centrally and not as a side project, what it means for the legacy of our elders and ancestors to move through us, and what it means to "[seek] a now that can breed [queer] futures."[5]

Safety, Security, Sustainability, and Survival: Lordeian Routes and Strategic Approaches

"A Litany for Survival," one of Lorde's best-known poems, has fulfilled its own prophecy. It is literally the vehicle through which Audre Lorde's poetry survives. The poem itself has survived much more visibly than other poems in her body of work. In 1988 a radio profile created by Jennifer Abod in honor of Audre Lorde's work began with the sound of drums and Lorde herself reading "A Litany for Survival." The title of the groundbreaking biographical film about Audre Lorde's life by Ada Gay Griffin and Michele Parkerson is entitled *A Litany for Survival*. "A Litany for Survival" is available as a podcast on the Internet. At a rally mourning Amadou Diallo, entitled "A Litany for Survival," Patricia Spear Jones read the poem aloud. One of the sections in *Colonize This!*, one of the landmark texts of contemporary young radical women of color, is entitled "Family and Community: A Litany for Survival." Kara Keeling's *The Witch's Flight* explains its stakes with an essay entitled, "Another Litany for Survival." This poem has indeed survived in many forms and is the major poem for the continuation of Lorde's presence in contemporary discourse. However, the actual life of the word "survival" in Audre Lorde's poetry is undertheorized and often overshadowed by the celebratory resonance of "survival," despite the haunting refrain of the poem itself, which insists, "We were never meant to survive." At the same time, some people have taken the word "survival" to mean subsistence or "mere" survival and opted to counter it with the rhyming word "thrive." For us, the significance of retaining the use of the word "survival" has to do not only with its legacy in black feminist poetics and practice but also with the imperative to remember our existence always in the context of our guardian dead, those ancestors that survive through us and our community, which has suffered differential unjust death because of capitalism, racism, homophobia, and transphobia.

Alexis takes this issue on in depth in her dissertation, "We Can Learn to Mother Ourselves: The Queer Survival of Black Feminism." This concept of survival also informed both of us as we insisted on honoring the survivors in our communities before they become ancestors. We engage in this issue as we navigate moving through the United States as young, queer, black, female, and genderqueer bodied people accountable to our histories and the tangible desire for queer black futures. How do we both survive the journey and sustain our (black queer) lives and accountability along the way?

HOW WE ROLL: A LITANY FOR SUSTAINABILITY

For those of us . . .
who love in doorways coming and going
in the hours between dawns
looking inward and outward
at once before and after
seeking a now that can breed futures
like bread in our children's mouths
— *Audre Lorde,* "A Litany for Survival"

"Who love in doorways coming and going in the hours between dawns . . . ." We are black and queer, so our histories of travel are not only voluntary but also compelled and circumscribed by violence, hate, and inequality. We hold the legacies of people on the run. We come from travelers who did not choose their journey to this continent. We come from travelers who dare not run out of gas because segregation and racial hatred in the South meant they could not stop without risking their lives. We come from travelers who were pushed off their land with the threat of lynching and the sanction of law. We come from travelers whose neighborhoods got trampled by new highway plans. We come from travelers who were kicked out of their homes for daring to love across boundaries.

The legacy of violence, hate, and inequality for black people and queer people was and is so pervasive that publications were necessary to guide travelers across the country. The *Negro Motorist Green Book*, published from 1936 to 1966, provided contacts and information for black travelers in the unsafe territory of the United States. "Contact Dykes," a section in the *Lesbian Connection* magazine founded in 1974, continues to this day to provide contacts and information for lesbian travelers. Those who took to their cars during Jim Crow were not exempt from segregation and violence, though driving was a means of escaping those conditions on public transportation. The literary and filmic history of this country also tells the tale—from Nel's formative experience of traveling south on the segregated train with her mother to the legacy of the Freedom Rides in the 1960s in a film by the same name. Is there an era in the history of this land since "discovery" and colonization that has not been dangerous for those nonwhite, nonmale, or nonheterosexual in this country?

On our Mobile Homecoming journey we faced the reality of this legacy when we were stopped and detained for seeming "odd" to Mississippi Highway Patrol, then separated and questioned while officers called for backup and refused to believe the preposterously true story that we were on the road to document black feminist queer visionaries. We confronted the continued urgency of our work to create intergenerational resources for black queer survival as we met elders with unstable housing who were close to being out on the street with their priceless black queer movement artifacts. For example, Lenn Keller, key photographer and archivist of the lesbian of color presence in the Bay Area, housed us in a space that was serving as a temporary home for her and her decades of photographs and ephemera. When we interviewed her, she didn't know where she would be living next. Ironically, the existence of archives of letters between black feminists is evidence of this same loving between doorways during times when long-distance phone calls were prohibitively expensive for most and isolation as black feminist lesbian, bisexual, gay male, and queer visionaries in far-flung contexts required reaching out. Our journey was tracked through a network of people who have stayed in touch across decades without depending on Facebook or any other digital medium.

The coming and going that we enacted as we journeyed from home to home across the United States is a performance of the space that the visionaries we met have made for each other in their lives as they assisted each other with forced relocations owing to family violence and economic struggles. It was our first cross-country ritual tour with the project that clarified the fact that the need for housing among black LGBTQ organizers, artists, and activists of all ages is urgent and unresolved. This is an issue we face perpetually in our local community and across the country. Currently, Washington, D.C.–based Mobile Homecoming interviewee Imani Woody, who has designed the Living Life Like It's Golden six-part series for LGBTQ elders and is currently creating Mary's House, a residential center for LGBTQ elders, is tackling the expanding need for housing for elders, who, as our listening process on the tour has confirmed, have less financial, familial, and pension-based resources than their age-mates. We are confronted with the need to make new doorways to love each other in and to face the continued reality of homelessness in the black LGBTQ community at every stage of our lives.

Looking inward and outward . . .

On the Mobile Homecoming journey we recognize that our history of travel is not all recreational but that we come from travelers nonetheless, people who needed to be both mobile and at home and who often had to choose between the two.[6] So for us, the "R" in RV stands for Revolutionary, for Resource, for Road-less-traveled, for Respect, for Re-imagining, for Reality. We want our journey to be healing for us and to provide a healing example for others about what movement can mean, where love can live, how home can survive.

The stories our elders have shared redefine and shape what it means to be at home. Imani Rashid, one of the butch-identified elders who inspired us to create the project, shares in our film *No Legacy Let Go* how she experienced the contradictory experiences of enjoying the feminine ritual of watching her mother get dressed, at the same time as she resisted the constriction of her mother's insistence that she attend charm school and ballet classes to become ladylike herself. Imani, along with other comrades in the Salsa Soul Sisters, a lesbian of color organization founded in 1974 in New York, created a new version of home with their child-inclusive events, especially lesbian and gay Kwanzaa, which Imani talks about in our Mobile Homecoming PSA on queer Kwanzaa, a decades-long practice we learned about in New York City and Detroit, Michigan, and have begun to practice annually as an intergenerational community in Durham, North Carolina.

In addition to the organizational homespaces that we have witnessed and learned about, we have also seen that our visionary interviewees have developed what we call spiritual superpowers both as a result of being excluded from dominant religions and as a creative survival practice to create positive energy, community, and strength in a dehumanizing society. From creating safe spaces for queer and trans practitioners of traditional African religions, such as Ifa, to radically inclusive black church practices to astral projection, charging crystals, and the Science of the Mind, we have found that almost every person we have interviewed has deep spiritual grounding. They are grounded even if it is to say, as the late Vera Martin, cofounder of Old Lesbians Organizing for Change (OLOC) said to us in her modular home in a lesbian RV park in Arizona, "I believe in me."

At once before and after . . .

Our RV does not only travel through space, it travels through time, sitting in the untimely place where this anomaly, this miracle, queer black initiates, media makers, adventurers transmitting history and reframing the future in a mobile home, is possible. We see the RV itself as surrounded in two-way windows, as we take in the lessons that the land and the people have to offer and transmit the insights of our journey out to the world. We moved through the world guided by a GPS system donated by Yashna Padamsee from Domestic Workers United, protected by both an amethyst crystal donated by interviewee and former Salsa Soul Sisters member Ed Swan, an AAA membership donated by drum circle member Summer Mason and blessed by prayer flags donated by Queer Black New Orleans based healer Geryll Robinson (aka Dr. Gee Love.) Uncannily, multiple generations of black queer social organizing and community building seem to overlay each place we move through like a palimpsest. As soon as we shared our vision for the project we learned about Lisa Moore's midnineties thesis film of interviews with black lesbian elders, which is now expanding and developing in partnership with Tiona Mc-Clodden and Harriet's Gun Media. We learned about countless photo and documentary projects including one conducted by an elder in Alexis's family who previously had not shared about LGBTQ identity, but was excited to recount a college road trip documenting women's communities in the United States.

We found echoes among the participants and we became echoes the more we participated. Shani Angela, founder of Mixit Tallahassee, explained her community's use of softball as a community building practice among lesbian parents and even a method for doing outreach in local prisons in terms that reminded us of Pat Parker and other Oakland-based lesbians of color using softball as an alternative to the bar scene in response to the discrimination they faced in the 1970s. In Durham, North Carolina, which is our primary home base, Jay, founder of Cedar Chest, a literary and social organization that existed in Durham in the 1990s, pointed out that two of the locations that we used for our 2011 intergenerational retreat Indigo Days (including the duplex we lived in at the time) had previously been sites of black lesbian workshops or parties in decades past. The same elders who founded the Salsa Soul Sisters who used drums to affirm outlaw marriages and to create sacred ritual space host a drum circle every Thursday in Durham and bring a truck full of drums to our local Mobile Homecoming events. We attended retreats for black lesbians in their inaugural year, such as the Shades Retreat in Georgia, and retreats that were in the twenty-fifth year, like Sistafest/ BLU in southern California. In the practice of the experiential archive, it is impossible to imagine that history moves in one direction or ends, and at the same time, history often feels too present to get nostalgic about it.

For those of us who live at the shoreline/
standing upon the constant edges of decision/
crucial and alone . . .

There are times on the road and in our own community that even the choice of the safest bathroom to use or whether to use the bathroom at all is a game time decision. Even whether to be out as our full selves in so-called queer communities is a decision that we do not want our folks to ever have to make. We intend and know as Harriet Tubman knew, "My people are free."[7] Any contrary manifestation is an illusion to be eradicated.

The only choice we consider is the choice of unstoppable love. A large part of our work, particularly with the Mobile Homecoming retreats we are now hosting, is creating safe space for intergenerational groups of queer black folks. Sometimes this means that folks within our community with more privilege have to transform. It also means we, as hosts and facilitators, have to transform and acknowledge our own privileges and ignorance too. The process and prayer to create a space that, as June Jordan wrote in the guidelines for her "Poetry for the People" classes, is "safe enough" for the most oppressed within our oppressed community to be and to be cherished alongside those of us in transformation, is constant.[8]

For example, since its founding, transgender men and women have participated at every level of the project (interviewees, collaborators, donors, and supporters), but it has been a challenge for the Mobile Homecoming project to navigate visibility as a trans-inclusive project while honoring the decisions of many of our elders who experience antitrans violence and exclusion in gay, lesbian, women's, and feminist spaces not to disclose publicly in some spaces that they are trans. It is important for us to acknowledge that some of the organizations that we lift up from feminist lesbian history, like the Salsa Soul Sisters and some current crucial community-building spaces such as the women of color tent at the Michigan Womyn's Festival, actively practiced/practice gender policing and exclusion that has traumatized and continues to traumatize members of our community.

Sometimes creating the safe space for those who feel alone even within LGBT spaces means saying no to our loved ones with more privilege. Sometimes it means being very candid. Always it means we love our queer selves so much that we will let nothing come between us safely being together. The transformation takes place here. At our first official Mobile Homecoming retreat, Indigo Days, during a discussion on gender that Julia overheard from the kitchen while doing dishes, some folks did not fully understand this commitment. Alexis participated in the conversation with many other brilliant black queer folks and black lesbians articulating the relevant history, love, and legacies. Julia came in from the kitchen and made the crucial point: We love and affirm you all as whoever you understand yourself to be and celebrate that knowledge. All of us here are committed to transforming in the ways necessary, including learning to use the preferred pronouns and to the patience necessary when we believe that the transformation is in process but not complete. Anyone not willing to be on board can leave. This is not a negative thing but an ecstatic moment, a healing moment, because now you know we will go to any length to make sure we are all affirmed as who we are.

When the foundation is laid and the crucial point is made, we do not always have to be alone. Our elders can heal from the trauma that has said they can be only a certain type of lesbian or express masculinity only as a butch in a narrow way.

At a retreat on sexuality and the black lesbian community hosted by Imani Rashid Productions in Brooklyn, Imani asked us to specifically address transphobia. Several elders in the community who were butch-identified at the time expressed fear of exploring their masculinity for fear that they would be expelled from the lesbian community and that their partners would leave them if they identified as other than "woman." During the day, as we attended the conference, many people openly expressed that they were nervous and apprehensive about the segment on gender identity and masculinity that we were facilitating at the end of the day. But when we actually facilitated a discussion and panel after a screening of Kortney Zeigler and Awilda Rodriguez's film *Still Black*, we created a context of profound love and reminded our beloved community how long and hard we have all worked to be affirmed and loved on our own terms.

By creating transformative and inclusive space at our retreats and the spaces we attend, we have seen a conversation across age about gender identity in black LGBTQ community that we believe is light years beyond where that conversation is in other communities. Queen Hollins, founder of the Earthlodge in Southern California expressed difficulty and challenges using gender-inclusive "they" at our retreats after a lifetime of womb-affirming, woman-centered healing work and now leads sacred rituals to support transgender people preparing for physical transition at her Earthlodge center.

This is not a safety that we always have on the road. This is not even a safety we have in our families of origin or chosen queer communities where we live. However, it is a safety that we can create intentionally with those that are willing; and by creating the space in more places the gap between one home and the next will become smaller and smaller. By modeling the possibilities we can create the world we want to have and start the evolutionary progression. This is the potential of mobility.

Seeking a now that can breed futures like bread in our children's mouths so their dreams will not reflect the death of ours . . .

We are currently transitioning from our relatively fuel-efficient oil-crisis-era gas-powered Winnebago to a Revolutionary Vehicle that is more fully sustainable. We are accountable to a set of people making a way out of no way, using every resource they had access to toward survival and divine participation in the process through which the universe and the planet affirm and re-create themselves through us. The way we see it, life is already contradictory and experimental. If the content of this journey is about passing on the legacies of black queer visionaries to generate and affirm new life, the *form* of the journey is an experiment in how it is possible to live sustainably and fully on the move, in honor of our ancestors, and in a manner that affirms our children, pointing the way toward a more efficient, loving, responsible relationship with the environment.

We see this approach in the elders by whom we have been inspired on our journey, including Lenn Keller, whose 30 years of documentary photography she has traveled with in order to share the resources of what has happened with those who might yet organize; Queen Hollins and the Earthlodge, which is a center for creating what she calls "Nu Legacy" beyond cycles of trauma; Rose Pulliam and Priscilla Hale, directors at allgo, which is a cultural arts, health, and advocacy programming for queer people of color, who are teaching us about not working all the time (even when we love our work) and the delicate, delightful balance of being organizational collaborators and romantic partners.

We hope that by witnessing and participating in our journey, people who never thought that certain forms of movement were possible or desirable will see how moving life really can be. We hope they discover the possibilities—leave home and make home at the same time, leave a job and practice their own craft primarily, launch their own local community-accountable project, or get on the road themselves.

Safety versus Security: A Queer Black Abolitionist Vision

"For those of us who cannot afford the passing dreams of choice . . . this instant, and this triumph. We were never meant to survive."

We don't look like we're from around here.

What then does it mean for us to be safe on the road? Because we know the limits of the state, and because we CHOOSE to create something different and better for ourselves, we must remember the difference between safety and security.

"Security," to us, means having the upper hand in an unsafe situation. Security, to many, means having access to the violent means that the state uses to defend itself, the police, the national guard, the private security forces that companies use to protect their wealth. For those of us, black, queer, young, radical, and grassroots, who are not often seen as part of the state's project to reproduce itself (except when we are targeted as consumers), those sources of security are not dependable. As far as we can tell, security comes from weapons. And it only works if you have more, faster, bigger weapons than whoever makes you insecure. Our intention is for our journey to be SAFE.

Safety, to us, means being able to be comfortable in our skin, having the freedom to move, being able to sleep restfully and wake renewed and excited about the journey. Safety comes from knowing that we are held by a community that has our backs. Safety comes from knowing that all along the road there are home spaces with comrades who will welcome us and who will answer if we call on them. Safety comes from relationships and people.

And safety comes from having a plan. Our safety plan for this journey involves everyone in our community. Instead of hoping for security in the random parking lots/campsites on which we could accidentally happen along the road, we have decided to plan for safety. We plan never to drive when we should be sleeping, which means stopping often. To stop in safety, we contact loved ones and comrades all over the country so they will know when we are near. We may park in the driveways of loved ones, we may park at campsites nearby, and we let comrades know where we are and that we might call on them if we need any form of help.

Our safety plan is inspired by the legacies of ancestors and elders who navigated road trips through dangerous places and involves a network of comrades and kindred who are aligned with the vision of the project and who affirm our queerness, our genderqueerness, our proud blackness, our youth. Their love and respect are what allow us to feel and be safe.

Our understanding of safety has grown and shifted through our journey and is reflected in our evolving strategy. For example, in every city we visit, we cohost an intergenerational social gathering called "Where Have You Been All My Life," for which the designation of safe space changes based on the local co-organizers in the cities and their definition of safe space based on the history of that community. In some cases it is a black-only gathering; in some cases it is a people of color gathering; in some cases allies (across race or sexuality) are invited; in some cases they are not. Most important, we have shifted our primary focus from documentation to experience, putting the majority of our effort into hosting transformative retreats (three a year!) where queer black intergenerational community happens as a lived experience. We made this shift based on our experiences in some of the many U.S. states where LGBTQ people can be legally evicted from housing and fired from their jobs. In some cities, elders who were happy to attend intergenerational events and share life-changing stories would ask us to "memorize" their words because they did not feel safe being recorded.

This network of kindred draws on and contributes to an ongoing process through which progressive kindred can connect to one another. We share stories, hear stories, make friends, discover commonalities, fall in love, meet our elders' and comrades' children, exchange recipes. We know that our need for one another is mutual and much bigger than the logistical need for places to refuel and rest. We have experienced and continue to hope that as we connect with our national Mobile Homecoming family and allies, and connect them to one another, future travelers will be able to know where there are safe couches to sleep on, people to call if they need help, or folks to connect with if they move to a new town. The world that we want to live in is a community, where needs are shared and met, where difference is affirmed, where people stand up for each other and open themselves up to love and the possibility of life. We invite you to join us in being something else.

NOTES

1. Sylvia Wynter, "The Ceremony Must Be Found: After Humanism," *Boundary 2* 12/13 (1984): 19.

2. Audre Lorde, "Audre Lorde," in *Black Women Writers at Work,* ed. Claudia Tate (New York: Continuum, 1983), 107.

3. Toni Morrison, *Sula* (New York: Plume, 1982), 52.

4. Morrison, *Sula*, 92.

5. Audre Lorde. "A Litany for Survival," in *The Collected Poetry of Audre Lorde* (New York: W. W. Norton, 1997), 255.

6. Headings come from Audre Lorde, "A Litany for Survival," 255.

7. Jean Humez, *Harriet Tubman: The Life and Life Stories* (Madison: University of Wisconsin Press, 2004), 383.

8. *June Jordan's Poetry for the People: A Revolutionary Blueprint*, edited by Lauren Muller and the Blueprint Collective (New York: Routledge, 1995), 16.

SELECTED BIBLIOGRAPHY

Abraham, Nicholas, and Maria Torok. *The Shell and the Kernel: Renewals of Psycho-analysis*. Chicago: University of Chicago Press, 1994.

Adorno, Theodor W., and Max Horkheimer. "The Culture Industry: Enlightenment as Mass Deception." In *Media and Cultural Studies: Keyworks*, edited by Meenakshi Gigi Durham and Douglass M. Kellner, 41–72. New York: Blackwell, 2006.

Agamben, Giorgio. *Means without End: Notes on Politics*. Translated by Vincenzo Binetti and Cesare Casarino. Minneapolis: University of Minnesota Press, 2000.

Agard-Jones, Vanessa. "Le Jeu de Qui? Sexual Politics at Play in the French Caribbean." In *Sex and the Citizen: Interrogating the Caribbean*, edited by Faith Smith, 181–98. Charlottesville: University of Virginia Press, 2011.

———. "What the Sands Remember." *GLQ: A Journal of Lesbian and Gay Studies* 18, nos. 2–3 (2012): 325–46.

Ahmed, Sara. "Declarations of Whiteness: The Non-Performativity of Anti-Racism." *borderlands e-journal* 3, no. 2 (2004): 1–59. http://www.borderlands.net.au/vol3no2 _2004/ahmed_declarations.htm.

Alexander, M. Jacqui. "Erotic Autonomy as a Politics of Decolonization: An Anatomy of Feminist and State Practice in the Bahamas Tourist Economy." In *Feminist Genealogies, Colonial Legacies, Democratic Futures*, edited by M. Jacqui Alexander and Chandra Mohanty, 63–100. New York: Routledge, 1997.

———. *Pedagogies of Crossing: Meditations on Feminism, Sexual Politics, Memory, and the Sacred*. Durham, NC: Duke University Press, 2006.

Allen, Jafari S. "Introduction: Black/Queer/Diaspora at the Current Conjuncture." *GLQ: A Journal of Lesbian and Gay Studies* 18, nos. 2–3 (2012): 211–48.

————. *¡Venceremos? The Erotics of Black Self-making in Cuba*. Durham, NC: Duke University Press, 2011.

Armstead, Ronnie. "Las Krudas, Spatial Practice, and the Performance of Diaspora." *Meridians* 8, no. 1 (2008): 130–43.

Assange, Julian. *Cypherpunks: Freedom and the Future of the Internet*. New York: OR Books, 2012.

Bailey, Cameron. "Virtual Skin: Articulating Race in Cyberspace." In *Immersed in Technology: Art and Virtual Environments*, edited by Mary Ann Moser and Douglas MacLeod, 29–49. Cambridge, MA: MIT Press, 1996.

Baim, Tracy, ed. *Out and Proud in Chicago: An Overview of the City's Gay Community*. Chicago: Surrey Books, 2008.

Baldwin, James. *The Fire Next Time*. [1963]. New York: Vintage, 1993.

————. *Giovanni's Room*. New York: Dial Press, 1956.

Barnard, Ian. *Queer Race: Cultural Interventions in the Racial Politics of Queer Theory*. New York: Peter Lang, 2004.

Barthes, Roland. *Camera Lucida: Reflections on Photography*. Translated by Richard Howard. New York: Macmillan, 1994.

Beam, Joseph. "Brother to Brother: Words from the Heart." In *In the Life*, edited by Joseph Beam. Freedom, CA: Crossing Press, 1984.

Becker, Howard. *Art Worlds*. Berkeley: University of California Press, 2008.

Bergson, Henri. *Matter and Memory*. [1912]. New York: Cosimo Classics, 2007.

Bersani, Leo. "Is the Rectum a Grave?" *October* 43 (1987): 197–222.

Bérubé, Allan. "How Gay Stays White and What Kind of White It Stays." In *The Making and Unmaking of Whiteness*, edited by Birgit Brander Rasmussen, Eric Klineberg, Irene Nexica, and Matt Wray, 234–65. Durham, NC: Duke University Press, 2001.

Black Public Sphere Collective. *The Black Public Sphere: A Public Culture Book*. Chicago: University of Chicago Press, 1995.

Bridgforth, Sharon. *Love Conjure/Blues*. Washington, DC: Red Bone, 2004.

Brilliant, Richard. *Portraiture*. London: Reaktion Books, 1991.

Brooks, Daphne. *Bodies in Dissent: Spectacular Performances of Race and Freedom, 1850–1910*. Durham, NC: Duke University Press, 2006.

Brown, Jayna, Patrick Deer, and Tavia Nyong'o, eds. "Punk and Its Afterlives." Special issue, *Social Text* 31: 3 116 (2013): 1–11.

Browne, Simone. "Digital Epidermalization: Race, Identity, and Biometrics." *Critical Sociology* 36, no. 1 (2010): 131–50.

Busbee, Elizabeth R. "Unequal Footing: Goffman's Models for Deference, Demeanor and Face in Dominant/Submissive Communication." Presented at Lavender Languages and Linguistics, American University, Washington, DC, September 23, 2000.

Campbell, John Edward. *Getting It On Online: Cyberspace, Gay Male Sexuality, and Embodied Identity*. Haworth Gay and Lesbian Studies. New York: Harrington Park Press, 2004.

Carby, Hazel V. "'It Just Be's Dat Way Sometime': The Sexual Politics of Women's Blues." In *Unequal Sisters: A Multicultural Reader in U.S. Women's History*, edited by Ellen Carol DuBois and Vicki L. Ruis, 238–49. New York: Routledge, 1994.

Caruth, Cathy. *Unclaimed Experience: Trauma, Narrative, and History*. Baltimore: Johns Hopkins University Press, 1996.

——, ed. *Trauma: Explorations in Memory*. Baltimore: Johns Hopkins University Press, 1995.

Chapman, Alix. "The Punk Show: Queering Heritage in the Black Diaspora." *Cultural Dynamics* 26, no. 3 (2014): 327–45.

Chen, Mel. *Animacies: Biopolitics, Racial Mattering, and Queer Affect*. Durham, NC: Duke University Press, 2012.

Christian, Barbara. *Black Feminist Criticism: Perspectives on Black Women Writers*. New York: Teachers College Press, 1985.

——. "But Who Do You Really Belong to—Black Studies or Women's Studies?" *Women's Studies: An Inter-disciplinary Journal* 17 (1989): 1–2, 17–23.

Chun, Wendy. *Control and Freedom: Power and Paranoia in the Age of Fiber Optics*. Cambridge, MA: MIT Press, 2006.

——. "Introduction: Race and/as Technology; Or, How to Do Things to Race." *Camera Obscura* 24, no. 1 (2009): 7–35.

——. *Programmed Visions: Software and Memory*. Cambridge, MA: MIT Press, 2011.

Clark, Stephen Bedell. *The Lake View Saga, 1837–2007*. Chicago: Lake View Citizens Council, 2007.

Clarke, Cheryl. *The Days of Good Looks: The Prose and Poetry of Cheryl Clarke, 1980 to 2005*. New York: Da Capo Press, 2006.

Clay, Adreanna. *The Hip-Hop Generation Fights Back: Youth Activism and Post–Civil Rights Politics*. New York: New York University Press, 2012.

——. "'Like an Old Soul Record': Black Feminism, Queer Sexuality, and the Hip-Hop Generation." *Meridians* 8, no. 1 (2008): 53–73.

Cohen, Cathy J. *The Boundaries of Blackness: AIDS and the Breakdown of Black Politics*. Chicago: University of Chicago Press, 1999.

——. "Deviance as Resistance: A New Research Agenda for the Study of Black Politics." *Du Bois Review: Social Science Research on Race* 1, no. 1 (2004): 27–45.

——. "What Is This Movement Doing to My Politics?" *Social Text*, no. 61 (Winter 1999): 111–18.

Coleman, Beth. "Race as Technology." *Camera Obscura* 24, no. 1 (2009): 176–207.

Collins, Patricia Hill. *Black Feminist Thought: Knowledge, Consciousness, and the Politics of Empowerment*. New York: Routledge, 1990.

Combahee River Collective. "The Combahee River Collective Statement: Black Feminist Organizing in the Seventies and Eighties." In *Home Girls: A Black Feminist Anthology*, edited by Barbara Smith, 264–74. New Brunswick, NJ: Rutgers University Press, 2000.

Cooper, Brittney. "Love No Limit: Towards a Black Feminist Future (In Theory)." *The Black Scholar* 45, no. 4 (2015): 7–21.

Cooper, Carolyn. *Sound Clash: Jamaican Dancehall Culture at Large*. New York: Palgrave Macmillan, 2004.

Cortese, Anthony. *Provocateur: Images of Women and Minorities in Advertising*. Lanham, MD: Rowman and Littlefield, 1999.

Cunningham, John. "Clandestinity and Appearance." *Mute* 2, no. 16 (2010). http://www.metamute.org/editorial/articles/clandestinity-and-appearance.

Danna, Anthony, and Oscar H. Gandy Jr. "All That Glitters Is Not Gold: Digging beneath the Surface of Data Mining." *Journal of Business Ethics* 40 (2002): 373–86.

Davis, Angela Y. *Blues Legacies and Black Feminism: Gertrude "Ma" Rainey, Bessie Smith, and Billie Holiday*. New York: Pantheon, 1998.

———. "Reflections on the Black Woman's Role in the Community of Slaves." In *Words of Fire: An Anthology of Black Feminist Thought*, edited by Beverly Guy-Sheftall, 200–218. New York: The New Press, 1995.

———. *Women, Race, and Class*. New York: Random House, 1981.

Davis, Charles T., and Henry Louis Gates. *The Slave's Narrative*. New York: Oxford University Press, 1985.

Delany, Samuel. "Coming/Out." In *Shorter Views: Queer Thoughts and the Politics of the Paraliterary*. Middletown, CT: Wesleyan University Press, 2000.

Deleuze, Gilles, and Félix Guattari. *A Thousand Plateaus: Capitalism and Schizophrenia*. Translated by Brian Massumi. Minneapolis: University of Minnesota Press, 1987.

De Veaux, Alexis. *Warrior Poet: A Biography of Audre Lorde*. New York: W. W. Norton, 2004.

Doan, Petra, and Harrison Higgins. "The Demise of Queer Space? Resurgent Gentrification and the Assimilation of LGBT Neighborhoods." *Journal of Planning Education and Research* 31 (2011): 6–25.

Dubai School of Government. "Civil Movements: The Impact of Facebook and Twitter." *Arab Social Media Report* 1 (2011): 1–30.

Duggan, Lisa. *The Twilight of Equality: Neoliberalism, Cultural Politics, and the Attack on Democracy*. Boston: Beacon Press, 2003.

Durham, Aisha. "Using [Living Hip-Hop] Feminism: Redefining an Answer (to) Rap." In *Home Girls Make Some Noise!: Hip-Hop Feminism Anthology*, edited by Gwendolyn Pough, Elaine Richardson, Aisha Durham, and Rachel Raimist, 304–12. New York: Parker Publishing, 2007.

Dyer, Richard. "The Matter of Whiteness." In *Theories of Race and Racism: A Reader*, edited by Les Black and John Solomos, 9–14. New York: Routledge, 2002.

Easton, Dossie, and Janet W. Hardy. *The Ethical Slut: A Roadmap for Relationship Pioneers*. Berkeley, CA: Celestial Arts, 2009.

Edelman, Lee. "Antagonism, Negativity, and the Subject of Queer Theory." *PMLA* 121, no. 3 (2006): 821–22.

————. *No Future: Queer Theory and the Death Drive.* Durham, NC: Duke University Press, 2004.

El-Tayeb, Fatima. *European Others: Queering Ethnicity in Postnational Europe.* Minneapolis: University of Minnesota Press, 2011.

Enke, Anne. *Finding the Movement: Sexuality, Contested Space, and Feminist Activism.* Durham, NC: Duke University Press, 2007.

Entman, Robert M. *The Black Image in the White Mind: Media and Race in America.* Chicago: University of Chicago Press, 2001.

Fanon, Frantz. *Black Skin, White Masks.* 1952. Translated by Charles Lam Markmann. New York: Grove, 1967.

Ferguson, Roderick A. *Aberrations in Black: Toward a Queer of Color Critique.* Minneapolis: University of Minnesota Press, 2004.

Fernandes, Sujatha. *Cuba Represent! Cuban Arts, State Power, and the Making of New Revolutionary Cultures.* Durham, NC: Duke University Press, 2006.

Fields, Barbara Jeanne. "Slavery, Race, Ideology in the United States of America." *New Left Review* 181 (May/June 1990): 95–118.

Fincher, Ruth, and Jane Jacobs. *Cities of Difference.* New York: Guilford Press, 1998.

Florida, Richard L. *The Rise of the Creative Class, and How It's Transforming Work, Leisure, Community, and Everyday Life.* New York: Basic Books, 2004.

Foster, Thomas. *The Souls of Cyberfolk: Posthumanism as Vernacular Theory.* Minneapolis: University of Minnesota Press, 2005.

Freeman, Elizabeth. *Time Binds: Queer Temporalities, Queer Histories.* Durham, NC: Duke University Press, 2010.

Freud, Sigmund. "Remembering, Repeating and Working-Through (Further Recommendations on the Technique of Psycho-Analysis II)." In *The Standard Edition of the Complete Psychological Works of Sigmund Freud, Volume XII (1911–1913): The Case of Schreber, Papers on Technique, and Other Works,* 147–56. [1924]. London: Hogarth Press, 1950.

Galloway, Alexander. "Black Box, Black Bloc." In *Communization and Its Discontents: Contestation, Critique, and Contemporary Struggles,* edited by Benjamin Noys, 237–49. New York: Minor Compositions, 2011.

————. "Networks." In *Critical Terms for Media Studies,* edited by W. J. T. Mitchell and Mark Hansen, 280–96. Chicago: University of Chicago Press, 2010.

Garber, Eric. "A Spectacle in Color: The Lesbian and Gay Subculture of Jazz Age Harlem." In *Hidden from History: Reclaiming the Gay and Lesbian Past,* edited by Martin Duberman, Martha Vicinus, and George Chauncey Jr., 318–31. New York: Meridian Press, 1990.

Gates, Henry Louis, Jr. "The Fire Last Time." *New Republic* 206, no. 22 (1992): 37–43.

Gershon, Ilana. *The Breakup 2.0: Disconnecting over New Media.* Ithaca, NY: Cornell University Press, 2010.

Gill, Lyndon K. "Chatting Back an Epidemic: Caribbean Gay Men, HIV/AIDS, and the Uses of Erotic Subjectivity." *GLQ: Journal of Lesbian and Gay Studies* 18, nos. 2–3 (2012): 277–95.

Glaeser, Edward, and Jacob Vigdor. "The End of the Segregated Century: Racial Separation in America's Neighborhoods, 1890–2010." *Manhattan Institute for Policy Research Civic Report* 66 (2012). http://www.manhattan-institute.org/html/cr _66.htm.

Glave, Thomas. "Fire and Ink: Toward a Quest for Language, History, and a Moral Imagination." *Callaloo* 26, no. 3 (2003).

———. *Words to Our Now: Imagination and Dissent.* Minneapolis: University of Minnesota Press, 2005.

———, ed. *Our Caribbean: A Gathering of Lesbian and Gay Writing from the Antilles.* Durham, NC: Duke University Press, 2008.

Glymph, Thavolia. *Out of the House of Bondage: The Transformation of the Plantation Household.* Cambridge: Cambridge University Press, 2008.

González, Jennifer. "The Face and the Public: Race, Secrecy, and Digital Art Practice." *Camera Obscura* 24, no. 1 (2009): 37–65.

Gopinath, Gayatri. *Impossible Desires: Queer Diasporas and South Asian Public Cultures.* Durham, NC: Duke University Press, 2005.

Gosine, Andil. "Brown to Blonde at Gay.Com: Passing White in Queer Cyberspace." In *Queer Online: Media Technology and Sexuality,* edited by Kate O'Riordan and David Phillips, 139–53. New York: Peter Lang, 2007.

Gramsci, Antonio. *Selections from the Prison Notebooks,* edited and translated by Quintin Hoare and Geoffrey Nowell Smith. New York: International Publishers, 1971.

Greenwald, Glenn. *No Place to Hide: Edward Snowden, the NSA, and the U.S. Surveillance State.* New York: Metropolitan Books, 2014.

Griffin, G. A. Elmer. "Word Bullets." Review of *Verbal Riddim: The Politics and Aesthetics of African-Caribbean Dub Poetry* by Christian Habekost. *Transition* 66 (1995): 57–65.

Gross, Larry, and James D. Woods. *Columbia Reader on Lesbians and Gay Men in Media, Society, and Politics.* New York: Columbia University Press, 1999.

Gumbs, Alexis Pauline. "We Can Learn to Mother Ourselves: The Queer Survival of Black Feminism, 1968–1996." PhD diss., Duke University, 2010.

Guy, Roger. *From Diversity to Unity: Southern and Appalachian Migrants in Uptown Chicago, 1950–1970.* Lanham, MD: Lexington Books, 2007.

Guy-Sheftall, Beverly. "Introduction: The Evolution of Feminist Consciousness among African American Women." In *Words of Fire: An Anthology of African American Feminist Thought,* edited by Beverly Guy-Sheftall, 1–22. New York: New Press, 1995.

Habekost, Christian. *Verbal Riddim: The Politics and Aesthetics of African-Caribbean Dub Poetry.* Amsterdam: Rodopi, 1993.

Halberstam, Judith. *The Queer Art of Failure.* Durham, NC: Duke University Press, 2011.

Hall, Stuart. "What Is This 'Black' in Black Popular Culture?" In *Stuart Hall: Critical Dialogues in Cultural Studies,* edited by David Morley and Kuan-Hsing Chen, 465–75. New York: Routledge, 1996.

———, ed. *Representation: Cultural Representations and Signifying Practices*. London: Sage, 1997.

Halley, Janet, and Andrew Parker, eds. *After Sex? On Writing since Queer Theory*. Durham, NC: Duke University Press, 2011.

Hammonds, Evelynn M. "Black (W)holes and the Geometry of Black Female Sexuality." In *Feminism Meets Queer Theory*, edited by Elizabeth Weed and Naomi Schor, 136–56. Bloomington: Indiana University Press, 1997.

Hanhardt, Christina B. *Safe Space: Gay Neighborhood History and the Politics of Violence*. Durham, NC: Duke University Press, 2013.

Haraway, Donna. *Modest_Witness@Second_Millennium.FemaleMan_Meets_Onco-Mouse: Feminism and Technoscience*. New York: Routledge, 1997.

Hartman, Farah Jasmine Griffin, Shelly Eversley, and Jennifer Morgan. "The Sexual Body." *Women's Studies Quarterly* 35 (Spring–Summer): 299–309.

Hemphill, Essex. *Ceremonies: Prose and Poetry*. New York: Plume, 1992.

———, ed. *Brother to Brother: New Writings by Black Gay Men*. Boston: Alyson Publications, 1991.

Herukhuti. *Conjuring Black Funk: Notes on Culture, Sexuality, and Spirituality*, vol. 1. New York: Vintage Entity Press, 2007.

Higashida, Cheryl. *Black Internationalist Feminism: Women Writers of the Black Left, 1945–1995*. Champaign: University of Illinois Press, 2011.

Higginbotham, Evelyn Brooks. *Righteous Discontent: The Women's Movement in the Black Baptist Church, 1880–1920*. Cambridge, MA: Harvard University Press, 1993.

Hine, Darlene Clark. *Hine Sight: Black Women and the Re-construction of American History*. Bloomington: Indiana University Press, 1994.

Holland, Sharon Patricia. *Raising the Dead: Readings of Death and (Black) Subjectivity*. Durham, NC: Duke University Press, 2000.

James, Joy. "Radicalizing Feminisms." In *The Black Feminist Reader*, edited by Joy James and T. Denean Shapley-Whiting, 239–60. New York: Wiley-Blackwell, 2000.

Jenkins, Candice M. *Private Lives, Proper Relations: Regulating Black Intimacy*. Minneapolis: University of Minnesota Press, 2007.

Johnson, E. Patrick. *Appropriating Blackness: Performance and the Politics of Authenticity*. Durham, NC: Duke University Press, 2003.

———. "'Quare' Studies, or (Almost) Everything I Know about Queer Studies I Learned from My Grandmother." *Text and Performance Quarterly* 21, no. 1 (2001): 1–25.

———. "Queer Epistemologies: Theorizing the Self from a Writerly Place Called Home." *Biography* 34, no. 3 (2011): 429–46.

———. *Sweet Tea: Black Gay Men of the South*. Chapel Hill: University of North Carolina Press, 2008.

Johnson, E. Patrick, and Mae G. Henderson, eds. *Black Queer Studies: A Critical Anthology*. Durham, NC: Duke University Press, 2005.

Jones, Omi Osun Joni L., Lisa L. Moore, and Sharon Bridgforth. *Experiments in a Jazz Aesthetic Art, Activism, Academia, and the Austin Project*. Austin: University of Texas Press, 2010.

Keeling, Kara. *The Witch's Flight: The Cinematic, the Black Femme, and the Image of Common Sense*. Durham, NC: Duke University Press, 2007.

Keizer, Arlene. *Black Subjects: Identity Formation in the Contemporary Narrative of Slavery*. Ithaca, NY: Cornell University Press, 2004.

Kelley, Robin D. G. *Freedom Dreams: The Black Radical Imagination*. Boston: Beacon, 2002.

Kolko, Beth E., Lisa Nakamura, and Gilbert B. Rodman, eds. *Race in Cyberspace*. New York: Routledge, 1999.

Kun, Josh. *Audiotopia: Music, Race, and America*. Berkeley: University of California Press, 2005.

LaCapra, Dominick. *Representing the Holocaust: History, Theory, Trauma*. Ithaca, NY: Cornell University Press, 1994.

Lane, Nikki. "Black Women Queering the Mic: Missy Elliott Disturbing the Boundaries of Racialized Sexuality and Gender." *Journal of Homosexuality* 58, nos. 6–7 (2011): 775–92.

Lang, Joshua. *Weird City: A Sense of Place and Creative Resistance in Austin, Texas*. Austin: University of Texas Press, 2010.

Lara, Ana-Maurine. "Of Unexplained Presences, Flying Ife Heads, Vampires, Sweat, Zombies, and Legbas: A Meditation on Black Queer Aesthetics." *GLQ: A Journal of Lesbian and Gay Studies* 18, nos. 2–3 (2012): 347–59.

Levinas, Emmanuel. *Totality and Infinity: An Essay on Exteriority*. Translated by Alphonso Lingis. Pittsburgh, PA: Duquesne University Press, 1969.

Lorde, Audre. *Sister Outsider: Essays and Speeches*. Freedom, CA: Crossing Press, 1984.

———. *Zami: A New Spelling of My Name—A Biomythography*. Watertown, MA: Persephone, 1982.

Low, Setha M., ed. *Theorizing the City: The New Urban Anthropology Reader*. New Brunswick, NJ: Rutgers University Press, 2005.

Luhning, Holly. "Accountability, Integrity, and *benu*: An Interview with d'bi.young." *Alt.theatre Magazine* 8 (September 2010).

Lyne, Bill. "God's Black Revolutionary Mouth: James Baldwin's Black Radicalism." *Science and Society* 74, no. 1 (2010): 12–36.

Madison, D. Soyini. "Performing Theory/Embodied Writing." *Text and Performance Quarterly* 19, no. 2 (April 1999): 107–24.

———. "That Was My Occupation: Oral Narrative, Performance, and Black Feminist Thought." In *Exceptional Spaces: Essays in Performance and History*, edited by Della Pollock, 319–42. Chapel Hill: University of North Carolina Press, 1998.

Magnet, Shoshana. *When Biometrics Fail: Gender, Race, and the Technology of Identity*. Durham, NC: Duke University Press, 2011.

Manalansan, Martin F. *Global Divas: Filipino Gay Men in the Diaspora*. Durham, NC: Duke University Press.

———. "Race, Violence, and Neoliberal Spatial Politics in the Global City." *Social Text* 23 (2005): 141–55.

Martín Sevillano, Ana Belén. *Sociedad civil y arte en Cuba: Cuento y artes plásticas en el cambio de siglo* (1980–2000). Madrid: Editorial verbum, 2010.

Martínez, Ernesto Javier. *On Making Sense: Queer Race Narratives of Intelligibility*. Stanford, CA: Stanford University Press, 2012.

Matory, J. Lorand. "The Homeward Ship: Analytic Tropes as Maps of and for African-Diaspora Cultural History." In *Transforming Ethnographic Knowledge*, edited by Rebecca Hardin and Kamari Maxine Clarke, 93–112. Madison: University of Wisconsin Press, 2012.

McDowell, Deborah E. *"The Changing Same": Black Women's Literature, Criticism, and Theory*. Bloomington: Indiana University Press, 1995.

McGlotten, Shaka. "Ordinary Intersections: Speculations on Difference, Justice, and Utopia in Black Queer Life." *Transforming Anthropology* 20, no. 1 (2012): 45–66.

———. "Virtual Intimacies: Love, Addiction, and Identity @ the Matrix." In *Queer Online: Media Technology and Sexuality*, edited by Kate O'Riordan and David Phillips, 123–37. New York: Peter Lang, 2007.

———. *Virtual Intimacies: Media, Affect, and Queer Sociality*. New York: State University of New York Press, 2013.

McGlotten, Shaka, Dána-Ain Davis, and Vanessa Agard-Jones. "Black Gender and Sexuality: Spatial Articulations." *Souls* 11, no. 3 (2009): 225–29.

McKay, Claude. "If We Must Die." In *The Black Poets*, edited by Dudley Randall. New York: Bantam Books, 1971.

Miller-Young, Mireille. *A Taste for Brown Sugar: Black Women in Pornography*. Durham, NC: Duke University Press, 2014.

Moore, Mignon R. *Invisible Families: Gay Identities, Relationships, and Motherhood among Black Women*. Berkeley: University of California Press, 2011.

Morgan, Jennifer L. *Laboring Women: Reproduction and Gender in New World Slavery*. Philadelphia: University of Pennsylvania Press, 2004.

Morgan, Marcyliena, and Dionne Bennett. "Hip Hop and the Global Imprint of a Black Cultural Form." *Daedalus, the Journal of the American Academy of Arts and Sciences* 2 (Spring 2011): 177–96.

Morosov, Evgeny. *The Net Delusion: The Dark Side of Internet Freedom*. New York: Public Affairs, 2012.

Morris, Mervyn. "Dub Poetry?" *Caribbean Quarterly* 43, no. 4 (1997): 1–10.

Morrison, Toni. *Beloved*. New York: Random House, 1987.

———. *Playing in the Dark: Whiteness and the Literary Imagination*. Cambridge, MA: Harvard University Press, 1992.

Moten, Fred. *In the Break: The Aesthetics of the Black Radical Tradition*. Minneapolis: University of Minnesota Press, 2003.

Mulvey, Laura. "Visual Pleasure and Narrative Cinema." In *Feminism and Film Theory,* edited by Constance Penley, 46–57. New York: Routledge, 1988.

Muñoz, Jose Esteban. *Cruising Utopia: The Then and There of Queer Futurity.* New York: New York University Press, 2009.

Musser, Amber Jamilla. *Sensational Flesh: Race, Power, and Masochism.* New York: New York University Press, 2014.

Nakamura, Lisa. *Cybertypes: Race, Ethnicity, and Identity on the Internet.* New York: Routledge, 2002.

———. *Digitizing Race: Visual Cultures of the Internet.* Minneapolis: University of Minnesota Press, 2008.

Nakamura, Lisa, and Peter A. Chow-White, eds. *Race after the Internet.* New York: Routledge, 2011.

Nash, Jennifer C. *The Black Body in Ecstasy: Reading Race, Reading Pornography.* Durham, NC: Duke University Press, 2014.

———. "Black Anality." GLQ: *A Journal of Lesbian and Gay Studies* 20, no. 4 (2014): 439–60.

Neal, Mark Anthony. *What the Music Said: Black Popular Music and Black Public Culture.* New York: Routledge, 1998.

Neff, Ali Colleen. *Let the World Listen Right: The Mississippi Delta Hip Hop Story.* Jackson: University of Mississippi Press, 2009.

Nyong'o, Tavia. "Punk'd Theory." *Social Text* 23, nos. 3–4, 84–85 (2005): 19–34.

Omolade, Barbara. *The Rising Song of African American Women.* New York: Routledge, 1994.

Osumare, Halifu. *The Africanist Aesthetic in Global Hip-Hop: Power Moves.* New York: Palgrave Macmillan, 2008.

Packer, George. "Change the World." *New Yorker,* May 27, 2013. http://www.newyorker.com/magazine/2013/05/27/change-the-world.

Page, Enoch H., and Matt U. Richardson. "On the Fear of Small Numbers: A Twenty-first-Century Prolegomenon of the U.S. Black Transgender Experience." In *Black Sexualities: Probing Powers, Passions, Practices, and Policies,* edited by Juan Battle and Sandra Barnes, 57–81. Newark: Rutgers University Press, 2009.

Painter, Nell Irvin. "Soul Murder and Slavery." Fifteenth Charles Edmondson Historical Lecture, Baylor University, Waco, TX, 1993.

Pardue, Derek. *Brazilian Hip Hoppers Speak from the Margins: We's on Tape.* New York: Palgrave Macmillan, 2011.

Parker, Pat. *Movement in Black.* Expanded ed. Ithaca, NY: Firebrand Books, 1999.

Perez, Hiram. "You Can Have My Brown Body and Eat It, Too!" In "What's Queer about Queer Studies Now?," edited by David L. Eng, Judith Halberstam, and José Esteban Muñoz, special issue, *Social Text* 84–85 (Fall–Winter 2005): 171–92.

Perry, Keisha-Khan Y. *Black Women against the Land Grab: The Fight for Racial Justice in Brazil.* Minneapolis: University of Minnesota Press, 2013.

Phillips, Amanda, and Alison Reed. "Additive Race: Colorblind Discourses of Realism in Performance Capture Technologies." In "Performance Art and Digital Media," edited by Michael Nitsche, special issue, *Digital Creativity* 24, no. 1 (Fall 2013): 1–15.

Phillips, David, and Kate O'Riordan, eds. *Queer Online: Media Technology and Sexuality*. New York: Peter Lang, 2007.

Pinho, Osmundo. "Race Fucker: Representações raciais na pornografia gay." *Cad. Pagu*, no. 38 (January/June 2012).

Pollock, Della. "Marking New Directions in Performance Ethnography." *Text and Performance Quarterly* 26, no. 4 (October 2006): 325–29.

———. "Performing Writing." In *The Ends of Performance*, edited by Peggy Phelan and Jill Lane, 73–103. New York: New York University Press, 1998.

Pough, Gwendolyn D. *Check It while I Wreck It: Black Womanhood, Hip-Hop Culture, and the Public Sphere*. Boston: Northeastern University Press, 2004.

———. "An Introduction of Sorts for Hip-Hop Feminism." In *Home Girls Make Some Noise!: Hip-Hop Feminism Anthology*, edited by Gwendolyn D. Pough, Elaine Richardson, Aisha Durham, and Rachel Raimist, vii–ix. New York: Parker Publishing, 2007.

Puar, Jasbir. *Terrorist Assemblages: Homonationalism in Queer Times*. Durham, NC: Duke University Press, 2007.

Reddy, Chandan. *Freedom with Violence*. Durham, NC: Duke University Press, 2011.

Reid-Pharr, Robert F. *Black Gay Man: Essays*. New York: New York University Press, 2001.

Richardson, Matt. *The Queer Limit of Black Memory: Black Lesbian Literature and Irresolution*. Columbus: Ohio State University Press, 2013.

Rivera-Velázquez, C. "Brincando bordes, Cuestionando el Poder: Cuban Las Krudas' Migration Experience and Their Rearticulation of Sacred Kinships and Hip Hop Feminism." *Letras Femeninas* 34, no. 1 (2008): 97–123.

———, dir. *Queen of Myself: Las Krudas d' Cuba*. Tortuga Productions in association with Krudas CUBENSI, 2010.

Robinson, Cedric. *Forgeries of Memory and Meaning: Blacks and the Regimes of Race in American Theater and Film before World War II*. Chapel Hill: University of North Carolina Press, 2007.

Rodríguez, Juana María. *Queer Latinidad: Identity Practices, Discursive Spaces*. New York: New York University Press, 2003.

———. "Queer Sociality and Other Sexual Fantasies." *GLQ: A Journal of Lesbian and Gay Studies* 17 (2011): 331–48.

———. *Sexual Futures, Queer Gestures, and Other Latina Longings*. New York: New York University Press, 2014.

Rose, Tricia. *Black Noise: Rap Music and Black Culture in Contemporary America*. Middletown, CT: Wesleyan University Press, 1994.

Royster, Francesca. *Sounding Like a No-No: Queer Sounds and Eccentric Acts in the Post-Soul Era*. Ann Arbor: University of Michigan Press, 2012.

Rule, Nicholas O., and Nalini Ambady. "Brief Exposures: Male Sexual Orientation Is Accurately Perceived at 50 Ms." *Journal of Experimental Social Psychology* 44 (2008): 1100–1105.

Rule, Nicholas O., Keiko Ishii, Nalini Ambady, Katherine S. Rosen, and Katherine C. Hallett. "Found in Translation: Cross-Cultural Consensus in the Accurate Categorization of Male Sexual Orientation." *Personality and Social Psychology Bulletin* 37, no. 11 (2011): 1499–1507.

Saldanha, Arun. *Psychedelic White: Goa Trance and the Viscosity of Race.* Minneapolis: University of Minnesota Press, 2007.

Saunders, Tanya. "Black Lesbians and Racial Identity in Contemporary Cuba." *Black Women, Gender and Families* 4, no. 1 (Spring 2010): 9–36.

———. "Grupo OREMI: Black Lesbians and the Struggle for Safe Social Space in Havana." *Souls: A Critical Journal of Black Politics, Culture and Society* 11, no. 2 (2009): 167–85.

———. "La Lucha Mujerista: Krudas CUBENSI and Black Feminist Sexual Politics in Cuba." *Caribbean Review of Gender Studies* 3 (2009): 1–20. http://sta.uwi.edu /crgs/november2009/journals/CRGS%20Las%20Krudas.pdf.

Scott, Darieck. *Extravagant Abjection: Blackness, Power, and Sexuality in the African American Literary Imagination.* New York: New York University Press, 2010.

Sedgwick, Eve Kosofsky. *Epistemology of the Closet.* Berkeley: University of California Press, 1990.

Sharma, Sanjay. "Black Twitter? Racial Hashtags, Networks, and Contagion." *New Formations* 78 (2013): 46–64.

Sharpe, Christina. *Monstrous Intimacies: Making Post-Slavery Black Subjects.* Durham, NC: Duke University Press, 2010.

Shaviro, Steven. *Connected, or What It Means to Live in the Network Society.* Minneapolis: University of Minnesota Press, 2003.

Smith, Barbara, ed. *Home Girls: A Black Feminist Anthology.* New Brunswick, NJ: Rutgers University Press, 2000.

———. *The Truth That Never Hurts: Writings on Race, Gender, and Freedom.* New Brunswick, NJ: Rutgers University Press, 1998.

Snorton, C. Riley. *Nobody Is Supposed to Know: Black Sexuality on the Down Low.* Minneapolis: University of Minnesota Press, 2014.

Somerville, Siobhan B. *Queering the Color Line: Race and the Invention of Homosexuality in American Culture.* Durham, NC: Duke University Press, 2000.

Spillers, Hortense J. *Black, White, and in Color: Essays on American Literature and Culture.* Chicago: University of Chicago Press, 2003.

———. "'Whatcha Gonna Do?': Revisiting 'Mama's Baby, Papa's Maybe: An American Grammar Book': A Conversation with Hortense Spillers, Saidiya Hartman, Farah Griffin, Shelly Eversley, and Jennifer L. Morgan." *Women's Studies Quarterly* 35, nos. 1–2 (Spring–Summer 2007): 299–309.

Stallings, L. H. *Mutha' Is Half A Word: Intersections of Folklore, Vernacular, Myth, and Queerness in Black Female Culture*. Columbus: Ohio State University Press, 2007.

Stanley, Fred L., and Louis H. Pratt, eds. *Conversations with James Baldwin*. Jackson: University Press of Mississippi, 1989.

Stewart, Jacqueline Najuma. *Migrating to the Movies: Cinema and Black Urban Modernity*. Berkeley: University of California Press, 2005.

Stockton, Kathryn Bond. *Beautiful Bottom, Beautiful Shame: Where "Black" Meets "Queer."* Durham, NC: Duke University Press, 2006.

Tinsley, Omise'eke Natasha. *Thiefing Sugar: Eroticism between Women in Caribbean Literature*. Durham, NC: Duke University Press, 2010.

Toop, David. *Oceans of Sound: Aether Talk, Ambient Sound, and Imaginary Worlds*. London: Serpent's Tail, 2001.

Tseëlon, Efrat. *Masquerade and Identities: Essays on Gender, Sexuality, and Marginality*. New York: Psychology Press, 2001.

Veal, Michael. *Dub: Soundscapes and Shattered Songs in Jamaican Reggae*. Middletown, CT: Wesleyan University Press, 2007.

Walcott, Rinaldo. "Queer Returns: Human Rights, the Anglo Caribbean, and Diaspora Politics." *Caribbean Review of Gender Studies* 3 (2009): 1–19. http://sta.uwi .edu/crgs/november2009/journals/Walcott.pdf.

———. "Somewhere Out There: The New Black Queer Theory." *Blackness and Sexualities* 16 (2007): 29.

Wald, Elijah. *The Dozens: A History of Rap's Mama*. New York: Oxford University Press, 2012.

Wallace, Michele. *Black Macho and the Myth of the Superwoman*. Verso Classics. London: Verso, 1999.

Warner, Michael. *Fear of a Queer Planet: Queer Politics and Social Theory*. Minneapolis: University of Minnesota Press, 1993.

———. *The Trouble with Normal: Sex, Politics, and the Ethics of Queer Life*. New York: Free Press, 1999.

Watson, Janell. "Theorizing European Ethnic Politics with Deleuze and Guattari." In *Deleuze and Politics*, edited by Ian Buchanan and Nicholas Thoburn, 196–217. Edinburgh: University of Edinburgh Press, 2008.

Wekker, Gloria. *The Politics of Passion: Women's Sexual Culture in the Afro-Surinamese Diaspora*. New York: Columbia University Press, 2006.

White, Deborah Gray. *Ar'n't I a Woman? Female Slaves in the Plantation South*. New York: W. W. Norton, 1999.

Wiegman, Robyn. *Object Lessons*. Durham, NC: Duke University Press, 2012.

———. "Whiteness Studies and the Paradox of Particularity." *boundary 2* 26, no. 3 (1999): 115–50.

Williams, Patricia. *The Alchemy of Race and Rights*. Cambridge, MA: Harvard University Press, 1991.

Wilson, James. *Bulldaggers, Pansies, and Chocolate Babies: Performance, Race, and Sexuality in the Harlem Renaissance*. Ann Arbor: University of Michigan Press, 2011.

Wood, Elizabeth. "Sapphonics." In *Queering the Pitch: The New Gay and Lesbian Musicology*, edited by Phillip Bartlett and Elizabeth Wood, 27–66. New York: CRC Press, 2006.

Wright, Michelle M., and Antje Schuhmann, eds. *Blackness and Sexualities*. Berlin: LIT Verlag Münster, 2007.

young, d'bi. *art on black*. Toronto: Women's Press, 2006.

———. *benu*. Unpublished performance script, 2009.

———. *blood.claat*. Toronto: Playwrights Canada Press, 2005.

———. *rivers . . . and other blackness . . . between us: (dub) poems of love*. Toronto: Women's Press, 2007.

———. *sankofa: blood.claat, benu, word!sound!powah!* Toronto: Playwrights Canada Press, 2013.

———. *wombanifesto*. Havana: Studio Havana Cuba, 2010.

CONTRIBUTORS

JAFARI S. ALLEN is associate professor in the Department of Anthropology at the University of Miami. He works at the intersections of queer sexuality, gender, and blackness and is a faculty member of Yale's programs in women's, gender, and sexuality studies, LGBT studies, and American studies. A recipient of numerous fellowships, he teaches courses on the cultural politics of race, sexuality and gender in black diasporas; black feminist and queer theory; critical cultural studies; ethnographic methodology and writing; and Cuba and the Caribbean. Professor Allen is the author of the critical ethnography of race, gender, sexuality, and revolution ¡Venceremos? The Erotics of Self-making in Cuba (Duke University Press, 2011); editor of Black/Queer/Diaspora, a special issue of GLQ: A Journal of Lesbian and Gay Studies; and various scholarly and popular articles, book chapters, and blog posts. He is currently working on a new book that traces cultural and political circuits of transnational queer desire in travel, tourism, art, and activism, in and between the Caribbean, South America, Europe, and North America.

MARLON M. BAILEY is associate professor of women's and gender studies in the School of Social Transformation at Arizona State University. He is the author of Butch Queens Up in Pumps: Gender, Performance, and the Ballroom Culture of Detroit (Michigan University Press, 2013), which was a finalist for the Lambda Literary Award. His research interests include African diaspora studies, queer diasporas, race, gender and sexuality, queer theory, black queer studies, theater/performance studies, ethnography, and HIV/AIDS.

ZACHARY BLAIR is a PhD candidate at the University of Illinois at Chicago. He specializes in urban anthropology, with a focus on political economy, violence, and identity. His dissertation research explores the gentrification of Boystown through the lens of political economy, looking specifically at how race, gender, sexuality, and class construct neighborhood experiences.

LA MARR JURELLE BRUCE is assistant professor of American studies at the University of Maryland, College Park. His scholarship concerns blackness and feeling, and how these inflect our expressive cultures. Winner of the Joe Weixlmann Award from *African American Review*, Bruce also has work featured or forthcoming in *American Quarterly, TDR: The Drama Review*, and *Oxford Bibliographies in African American Studies*. His book project in progress, *How to Go Mad without Losing Your Mind: Madness, Blackness, and Radical Creativity*, is a study of black artists who mobilize "madness" in radical literature and performance.

CATHY J. COHEN is the David and Mary Winton Green Professor of Political Science at the University of Chicago. Cohen is the author of two books, *Democracy Remixed: Black Youth and the Future of American Politics* (Oxford University Press, 2010) and *The Boundaries of Blackness: AIDS and the Breakdown of Black Politics* (University of Chicago Press, 1999). She coedited the volume *Women Transforming Politics: An Alternative Reader* (New York University Press, 1997) with K. Jones and J. Tronto. Her articles have been published in numerous journals and edited volumes, including the *American Political Science Review, NOMOS, GLQ, Social Text*, and the *DuBois Review*. Cohen is also politically active. She was a founding board member and former cochair of the board of the Audre Lorde Project. She was also on the boards of Kitchen Table: Women of Color Press, CLAGS, and the Arcus Foundation. Cohen also founded and directs the Black Youth Project.

JENNIFER DECLUE is an assistant professor of women's and gender studies at Smith College. Her research interests include queer studies, black feminism, visual studies, cultural studies, diasporic loss, histories of segregation and miscegenation in the United States, the afterlife of chattel slavery, and the construction, production, and reproduction of blackness in the United States. Her work has been published in *GLQ: A Journal of Lesbian and Gay Studies* and *Spectator*, as well as critical anthologies of race, gender, visuality, and sexuality.

TREVA ELLISON is an assistant professor in geography and women's, gender, and sexuality studies at Dartmouth College. Treva is an interdisciplinary scholar whose research focuses on criminalization, carceral geographies, and social movements in the United States. Treva's writing appears in places such as *Transgender Studies Quarterly, Feminist Wire*, and *Scholar and Feminist Online*. Treva is currently working on their manuscript project, "Towards a Politics of Perfect Disorder: Carceral Geographies, Queer Criminality, and Other Ways to Be," which historicizes the production of and resistance to queer criminality in order to examine the dynamic interplay between criminalization, identity politics, and place-making.

LYNDON K. GILL is an assistant professor in the departments of African and African diaspora studies and anthropology at the University of Texas at Austin. He received his PhD in African American studies and anthropology (with a secondary field in studies of women, gender, and sexuality) from Harvard University. He has held postdoctoral fellowships at Princeton University's Center for African American Studies, the University of Pennsylvania's Department of Anthropology and Center for Africana Studies, and the Ford Foundation. His research interests are queer aesthetics in the African Diaspora, the erotic, LGBT art and activism in Caribbean cultures, subjectivity, and community building. He is currently completing his first book, *Erotic Islands: Art & Activism in the Queer Caribbean* (Duke University Press). He is also an installation artist.

KAI M. GREEN is assistant professor of feminist studies at the University of California, Santa Barbara. Kai is also a poet, performer, musician, and filmmaker dedicated to bringing the stories of the oppressed to forefront through their art and scholarship. Kai was born and raised in Oakland, California. Kai completed their BA in American studies with a minor in Africana studies at Williams College in 2007. Kai's dissertation engages the stories and histories of black queer Los Angeles. Kai has also completed a short documentary entitled "It Gets Messy in Here" that explores the intersections of race, gender, and sexuality via the experiences of transgender men and masculine of center women of color.

ALEXIS PAULINE GUMBS is a queer black troublemaker, a black feminist love evangelist, and a prayer poet priestess and has a PhD in English, African and African American studies and women and gender studies from Duke University. Her critical work on black feminism and queerness appears in many publications from the *Routledge Companion to Anglophone Caribbean Literature* to *Mothering and Hip Hop Culture* and from *Obsidian* to *SIGNS*, and her poetry appears in *Kweli, Vinyl, Reverie,* and *Backbone.* Alexis is the author of *Spill: Scenes of Black Feminist Fugitivity* (Duke University Press, 2016) and the coeditor of *Revolutionary Mothering: Love on the Front Lines* (PM Press). Alexis was named one of *UTNE Reader's* 50 Visionaries Transforming the World in 2009, was awarded a Too Sexy for 501-C3 trophy in 2011, *Advocate's* top 40 under 40 feature in 2012, and one of *GO Magazine's* 100 Women We Love in 2013.

KWAME HOLMES is an assistant professor of ethnic studies at the University of Colorado, Boulder. Holmes earned his PhD in modern American history, with minor fields in African American and comparative gender studies from the University of Illinois at Urbana-Champaign. His research engages the intersection of race, sexuality, class identities, and politics within the history of the modern city. He is currently completing a book manuscript on the production of black and gay identities, politics, and geographies in Washington, D.C., entitled "Chocolate to Rainbow City: Branding Black and Gay in the District of Columbia, 1953–1982."

E. PATRICK JOHNSON is the Carlos Montezuma Professor of Performance Studies and African American Studies at Northwestern University. A scholar, artist, and activist, Johnson has performed nationally and internationally and has published widely in the area of race, gender, sexuality, and performance. Johnson is a prolific performer and scholar and an inspiring teacher whose research and artistry has greatly impacted African American studies, performance studies, and sexuality studies. He is the author of two award-winning books, *Appropriating Blackness: Performance and the Politics of Authenticity* (Duke University Press, 2003) and *Sweet Tea: Black Gay Men of the South—An Oral History* (University of North Carolina Press, 2008). He is the editor of *Cultural Struggles: Performance, Ethnography, Praxis* by Dwight Conquergood (Michigan University Press, 2013) and coeditor (with Mae G. Henderson) of *Black Queer Studies: A Critical Anthology* (Duke University Press, 2005) and (with Ramón Rivera-Servera) of *solo/black/woman: scripts, interviews, and essays* (Northwestern University Press, 2013) and *Blacktino Queer Performance* (Duke University Press, 2016).

SHAKA MCGLOTTEN is associate professor of media, society and the arts at SUNY-Purchase. He is the author of *Virtual Intimacies: Media, Affect, and Queer Sociality* (SUNY Press, 2014) and coeditor (with Dana-Ain Davis) of *Black Genders and Sexualities* (Palgrave, 2012). His writing on gaming, chat rooms, zombies, and porn has appeared in anthologies and journals such as *Transforming Anthropology*.

AMBER JAMILLA MUSSER is assistant professor of women, gender, and sexuality studies at Washington University in St. Louis. Her research interests include queer theory, feminist theory, critical race theory, cultural and critical theory, critical historiography, and the history of psychiatry and medicine. Musser received her PhD in the history of science in 2009 from Harvard University. She has published in or has forthcoming articles in *Social Text, differences, WSQ, GLQ*, and *Women and Performance*. She is the author of *Sensational Flesh: Race, Power, and Masochism* (New York University Press, 2014), which uses masochism as a lens to examine how power structures race, gender, and embodiment in different contexts.

ALISON REED is assistant professor of African American literature and studies of race and ethnicity in the Department of English at Old Dominion University. Her research on performance, identity, power, and social movements has appeared in several journals, including *Lateral: The Journal of the Cultural*

Studies Association, Text and Performance Quarterly, Digital Creativity, Media-N, Women and Performance, and *Margaret Atwood Studies.* She is currently working on two book projects: one, "Traumatic Utopias," on queer abolitionist performance from Black Power to the Borderlands, and another, "Black Sound, White Masks," on the racial and sexual politics of sonic embodiment from minimalist classical music to jazz metal.

RAMÓN H. RIVERA-SERVERA is associate professor of performance studies at Northwestern University. He is author of *Performing Queer Latinidad: Dance, Sexuality, Politics* (University of Michigan Press, 2012). He is coeditor (with E. Patrick Johnson) of *solo/black/woman: scripts, essays, and interviews* (Northwestern University Press, 2013) and *Blacktino Queer Performance* (Duke University Press, 2016); with Henry Godinez, of *Festival Latino: Six Plays from the Goodman Theatre Festival* (Northwestern University Press, 2013); and with Harvey Young, *Performance in the Borderlands* (Pallgrave Macmillan, 2011). He is currently conducting research for two book projects: "Exhibiting Performance: Race, Museum Cultures, and the Live Event," which looks at the ways race has been collected and exhibited in North America and the Caribbean since the mid-1990s, and "Choreographing the Latina/o Post-Modern: Puerto Rican Moves in the New York Dance Avant-Garde," a cultural history of Puerto Rican participation in the New York City experimental dance scene since the 1980s.

TANYA L. SAUNDERS is associate professor in the Center for Latin American Studies and the Center for Gender, Sexualities, and Women's Studies Research at the University of Florida. Her academic interests are in the areas of identity formation, coloniality studies/postcolonial theory, cultural studies, sociology of knowledge, Afro-Latino studies, arts-based social movements, race, gender, and sexuality. She is interested in the ways in which the African Diaspora, throughout the Americas, uses the arts as a central tool for social change. Her book *Cuban Underground Hip Hop: Black Thoughts, Black Revolution and Black Modernity* (2015) is available from the University of Texas Press.

C. RILEY SNORTON is assistant professor of Africana studies and feminist, gender, and sexuality studies at Cornell University. He is the author of *Nobody Is Supposed to Know: Black Sexuality on the Down Low* (University of Minnesota Press, 2014). He is the director of the short documentary *Men at Work: Transitioning on the Job* and has published articles in the *International Journal of Communication, Hypatia: A Journal of Feminist Philosophy,* and *Souls: A Critical Journal of Black Politics, Culture, and Society.* He has also contributed to numerous edited volumes and is currently completing a second monograph on race and trans history.

KAILA ADIA STORY is associate professor and Audre Lorde Chair in Race, Class, Gender and Sexuality in the Departments of Women's and Gender Studies and Pan-African Studies at the University of Louisville. She is the editor of *Patricia Hill Collins: Reconceiving Motherhood* (Demeter Press, 2014) and co-hosts the weekly radio show *Strange Fruit: Musings on Politics, Pop Culture, and Black Gay Life.*

OMISE'EKE NATASHA TINSLEY is an associate professor in the Department of African and African Diaspora Studies at the University of Texas, Austin. Her monograph, *Thiefing Sugar: Desire between Women in Caribbean Literature* (Duke University Press, 2010), examines how expressions of desire between women explore a poetics and politics of decolonization in literature from the Dutch-, French-, and English-speaking Caribbean. She is currently at work on a project that analyzes constellations of racial, national, sexual, and gender identity in recent Caribbean fiction, film, and performance, as well as a work of historical fiction that draws from oral histories to imagine intersections of migration, work, and desire experienced by African/Haitian American women who came from New Orleans, Louisiana, to Richmond, California, to work in Kaiser's shipyards during World War II.

JULIA ROXANNE WALLACE creates media and art intended to heal and transform. Julia is a multimedia artist, filmmaker, musician, composer, and theologian with a degree in multimedia computer science from UNC-Asheville, a masters in divinity from Emory University, and coursework toward a masters in film production at Georgia State University. She is the founder of the Black Feminist Film School and cofounder of Mobile Homecoming, a national inter-generational experiential archive project that seeks to amplify generations of black LGBTQ brilliance by using multimedia and building intergenerational families of choice across time and space.

KORTNEY ZIEGLER is an independent scholar, award-winning filmmaker, writer, and transgender activist. He is the first person to be awarded the PhD in African American studies at Northwestern University. He is the writer and director of the feature-length documentary *Still Black: A Portrait of Black Transmen.*

INDEX

biometric technologies, 265, 269–73, 286n60

biomythography, 121, 357. *See also* Audre Lorde Project; Lorde, Audre

black data, 20, 263–64, 270, 274, 278–79

black feminist porn studies, 10, 219–21, 353

Black Lace (magazine), 16, 67–70, 72, 74, 78

Black Lives Matter movement, 34, 233n1, 325

black queer studies, 8, 54, 55, 57, 80, 281n6, 363; and Audre Lorde, 5, 21, 35; intellectual history of, xi–xiii, 1–6, 11–14, 23, 31, 35; in Latina/o contexts, 97; and new media, 263. *See also* African American studies

black radicals, 37, 59, 318

black studies. *See* African American studies

Blas, Zach, 263, 272–73

Bond, Julian, 4

Bottom, 217–19, 223–24, 230–31

Boystown, 20, 287–300

Brazil, 18, 147, 152; hip hop activism in, 148, 155, 158, 161; protest movements in, 270; race in, 33, 150, 155–56

Brown, Michael, 34, 264

bulldaggers, 29, 35–36

Butler, Judith, 84, 86, 133, 367

capitalism, 150, 160, 264, 307, 353, 359, 383; advanced, 152; corporate, 190n10; neoliberal, 275, 328; post-, 93n7; racial, 32, 57, 62n1, 311, 324, 326; sex and, 73; transnational, 124; U.S. American, 147–48; white supremacist, 369, 371

carceral geographies, 323, 326–37

carceral state, 21, 338

Caribbean epistemology, 13, 17, 18, 134

Caycedo, Carolina, 16, 96, 99, 101–4, 107, 109n5, 110n17

Center on Halsted, 290, 297

Centers for Disease Control and Prevention (CDC), 241, 243

Christian, Barbara, 34, 133

Chukwu, Chinomye, 217–18, 220, 231, 232

cinema, 177, 193n30; American, 18, 170, 185, 187, 190n10; queer black, 26n32, 232

cinematic, the, 176, 217–20, 222, 225–32, 370

cisgender, 18, 33, 36, 67, 73, 77, 81n1, 168–70, 182, 263, 326, 340

Clinton, Bill, 329, 333–34; era of multiculturalism, 168

coalitional politics, 36, 113–14, 349, 351, 359

Cohen, Cathy, 29, 36, 113, 125, 127n2, 128n14, 319, 364, 375

collectivity, 57–58, 115, 270, 346, 349, 352

colorblindness, 49–52, 62n1

Combahee River Collective, 32, 38, 41; statement of, 31, 34

community, 79, 184, 347–55, 359, 376; black, xi, 9, 21, 312–14, 351, 366, 368, 371, 373, 382; *Black Lace*, 72; black LGBTQ, 41–42, 65–66, 217, 244, 381–83, 385–92; building of, 5, 69, 238n35, 288, 387–88; control, 313, 317; dub, 117; heteropatriarchal spectatorial, 108; hip hop, 150–51, 156, 158–59, 162; LGBTQ, 50, 136, 154, 216, 373; organizations, 5, 37, 40, 50, 61, 65–66, 151, 156, 243, 256, 274, 290–92, 298, 387; policing program oriented to, 330, 337; politics of, 59; practices based on, 60–61, 251, 272; sex-based, 10, 240–41; slave, 374; Vodou, 132; walks, 292, 294, 298–300

Cooper, Bernadette, 167, 189n2

Cooper, Brittney, 26n28

Coxxx, Papi, 219–22, 225–27, 235n8, 237n35

Cuba, 147–48, 162; hip hop in, 153–58, 160; lesbians in, 18, 154–55; race in, 33, 150, 152

Cuba's Underground Hip Hop Movement (CUHHM), 150, 154–56. *See also* hip hop

cultural studies, 2, 6, 60, 125, 237n29

Dean, Tim, 10, 24n18, 244–45

deep web, 20

Defense of Marriage Act, 3

Delany, Samuel, 8, 16, 83–84, 89–92, 235n17. See also *Triton*

Deleuze, Gilles, and Félix Guattari, 15, 28, 29–30, 266

D'Emilio, John, 1, 3

desire, xii, 28, 83, 132, 354, 369, 373–76; and agency, 12–13, 19, 107, 213, 375; black, xiii, 13, 229, 266, 371; black gay men and, 20, 250–57; black women and, 69, 71, 218–20, 229, 365–66; black queer, 6, 19, 20, 257; and fantasy, 219, 226, 229–30; female, 13, 143; and gender transgression, 116, 186, 208–10; heterosexual, 183; and HIV/AIDS, 9–10, 19, 24n18, 240, 246–50, 252–53; queer, 5, 212–13, 376; racial, 73, 106, 226, 278; same-sex, 6, 116, 124–26, 128nn13–14, 133, 180; sexual, 6, 106, 258n15, 261n45, 277; sexual and political, 114; and slavery, 10, 13, 219–20, 224, 227; to transition, 6, 89; utopian, 59; white, 49, 310, 316–18

deviance, 36, 114, 305, 312, 317, 364–65, 373–76

diaspora, 23n6, 125, 140, 249; African, 13, 18, 97, 123–25, 131, 133, 141; black, 29, 130n45, 355; black queer, 13, 16, 18, 35, 125, 351; Haitian, 18, 137, 144; Jewish, 228; reading practice, 3

dildo, 69, 72–75, 135, 141, 223–24, 231, 236n21

drag kings, 17, 133–35, 137, 140; black, 134–35, 140–41

drag performance, 139–43, 189n6, 279, 367, 377n10; black, 168, 173, 177–79, 185–87; in film, 170, 174–75, 177–80; by Gladys Bentley, 196, 198, 201–5; Judith Butler on, 16, 84; as site of gender variance, 18

drag performers, 2; in film, 167–72, 176, 181–85, 187–88, 190n8, 191n12

drag queens, 38, 135, 140–41, 265, 274, 293–94; black, 18, 141, 168–70, 195n47

dub music, 17, 116–17, 118, 128n11

dub poetry, 121, 129n26; queerness of, 118

dub theater, 120

Dunye, Cheryl, 217–20, 222, 225–26, 229–30, 232

Durham, Aisha, 151

Ebony (magazine), 198, 200, 207, 214n16

Edelman, Lee, 58–59, 169, 190n11

Electronic Frontier Foundation (EFF), 269

encryption, 269, 278–79

eros, 349, 351

erotic, 69, 219, 224, 230–233; agency of, 104–5, 107; and Audre Lorde, 21–22, 71, 220, 234n7, 346–59; autonomy, 251–53; and race, 11, 74–75; subjectivity of, 248, 253, 350; untamed, 19, 217, 220, 224, 226–27, 231, 234n7

erotica, 218–19, 222, 232. *See also* black feminist porn studies; pornography

Ex, Campbell, 217–20, 227–30, 232

Ezili, 17, 132–34, 137, 139, 142–45

Facebook, 20, 162, 270, 275, 278, 288, 292, 294, 298–300

Fanon, Frantz, 55, 174, 235n17, 236n22, 346

149; and hip hop, 151. *See also* respectability, politics of

injury, 49, 51, 59, 323, 328; black, 21, 324–25, 333–34, 338, 340; pre-white and post-white, 52–53, 60; white queer politics of, 57

interdisciplinarity, 4, 6, 14, 33, 34, 43, 91, 244

Jim Crow, 231, 282n21, 384

Johnson, E. Patrick, xi, 32, 61, 98, 107, 349, 375

Keeling, Kara, 226–27, 229, 237n31, 238n40, 383

Kerner Report, 307, 311

Kinsey, Alfred, 239

Lady Chablis, 168, 182–88

Lane, Alycee, 67, 69–75, 77–79

Las Krudas CUBENSI, 147–48, 153–58, 162–63

Latinidad, 97–98, 109n6, 177

Le Guin, Ursula K., 83

literary studies, 14, 61, 381

Lopez, Jennifer, 105, 108

Lorde, Audre, 27–28, 77, 121, 376, 383–84; and the erotic, 21, 71, 220, 348–51; and feminism, 351–54; and identity politics, 22, 346–48, 357–59; and the maternal, 354–56. *See also* Audre Lorde Project; biomythography

lwa, 132–34, 138–41

mammy, 185, 195n45, 206–8, 357, 367

Manning, Chelsea, 268, 282n20

marriage equality, 22, 36, 50, 216, 364, 371–75. *See also* gay marriage

Martin, Trayvon, 217, 264, 270, 324

masculinity, 141, 178, 196, 206, 208, 212, 223–24; black, 17, 19, 103, 133, 135, 140, 174, 182, 204–5, 213, 305, 311, 313; Latino,

98; women performing, 18, 68, 140, 203–5, 209, 210, 389

masochism, 221, 223, 236n22. *See also* BDSM; sadomasochism

maternal, 345–56

McBride, Dwight, 6, 7–8, 24n18

media, 43, 104, 237n29, 238n35, 265, 282n20, 283n36, 376; corporate, 36; digital, 19; film, 3, 190n10; gay, 38; new, 263, 280n6, 263; popular, 22; print, 163; social, 5–6, 109n5, 295, 299. *See also* gay sex websites

media studies, 6, 263, 299

microagencies, 16, 96, 103, 107, 108

Midnight in the Garden of Good and Evil, 18, 168, 181–88

Mobile Homecoming Project, 22, 380–81, 385–88

Mommy Is Coming, 217, 220, 222, 225–27, 229

Morrison, Toni, 14, 54, 62, 381; *Sula* as lesbian text, 382

nalga-cultura, 96, 99, 108–9

naming, 30, 66, 79, 355; self-naming, 33; re-naming, 76–77

National Advisory Commission on Civil Disorders. *See* Kerner Report

National Organization of Women (NOW), 335

National Security Administration (NSA), 262, 265–66, 268, 270

neoliberalism, 94n31, 349, 353; economic policies of, 270, 275, 279; and multiculturalism, 21, 323, 324, 326, 328; politics of, 34, 35, 37; progress narratives of, 50, 52; rhetoric of, 61; and trends in academia, 15. *See also* political economy

Nero, Charles, 5, 287–88, 372

network cultures, 262–63, 265

North Halsted Streetscape Project, 289

sadomasochism (s/m), 220–21, 223–24, 236nn21–22. *See also* BDSM; masochism

safety, 20, 73, 292, 299, 326, 338, 389–92

Salt-N-Pepa, 167–69, 189n2

same-sex marriage. *See* gay marriage; marriage equality

sankofa trilogy, 17, 116, 118, 120–26, 130n40

Scott, Darieck, 54–55, 239, 251

Sedgwick, Eve Kosofsky, 7, 35, 187

sex: acts, 7–10, 19, 74–75, 220, 258n15; anal, 108, 180, 196; black queer/gay sex, 7–9, 19, 22, 24, 69–71, 216–18, 220, 227, 240, 242, 253, 258n15; change, 83, 85, 89–90; condomless/unprotected, 10, 19–20, 244–46, 254; explicit, 5, 8, 10, 222, 226; gay/same-sex, 8, 13, 28, 251, 358, 370; group, 252; high-risk, 9, 19, 240–47, 254–56, 260n45, 378n18; play, 19, 217, 219–22, 224–28, 230, 232–33, 234n7, 235n8, 236n27, 238n35; raw, 8–10, 25n20, 239–41, 244, 248, 246–56, 258n15, 261n45; safe, 10, 71, 249–51, 253–54, 257; work(ers), 11, 246, 294, 308, 310–11, 316, 336. *See also* barebacking; BDSM; sadomasochism

sexuality, 71, 132, 158, 220, 319, 358, 373; agency over, 13; ambiguous, 169; bi-sexual, 43, 140–41; black, 1, 3–4, 49, 213, 226–27, 365–66, 371, 376; black female, 12, 19, 25n23, 196, 357; black gender and, 66, 80, 85, 92, 98, 338; black lesbian, 68, 217–18, 221, 231, 389; black queer, 8, 19–20, 197, 216–17, 227–28; of black queer women, 237n31, 347; of black women, 73, 217–19, 197, 227, 231–32, 234n5, 251, 370; contradictions of, 239; gay male, 245, 290; gender and, 18, 21, 50, 85, 137, 210, 340; and HIV/AIDS, 248; human, 247, 256; and media, 6, 263; non-normative, 78, 316,

333, 368, 370–71, 373, 376; normative, 247–49, 376; online, 21; race and, 37, 50, 54, 85, 99, 330–32, 340, 392; racial-ized, 22, 51, 363; and sexual health, 255; study of, 1–4, 33, 41–42, 57, 180; trans, 88, 143; white queer, 51. *See also* heterosexuality; homosexuality

sexuality studies, xiii, 1–4, 54, 318, 354

shade, 2, 4, 6, 10, 23, 265; throwing, 23, 265, 279, 364

sissy-play, 18–19, 196–97, 204, 206–10

slavery, 11, 41, 56, 77, 96, 103, 122, 141, 219, 222, 278, 374; afterlife of, 184, 194n4; chattel, 226, 231, 233, 236n26, 307, 355; mental, 144

Snowden, Edward, 265, 268, 283

social geography, 97, 288

solidarity, 21, 114, 124, 169, 349; class-based, 53; performative, 36

Sontag, Susan, 57, 298

Southern Christian Leadership Con-ference (SCLC), 304, 332

spectacular absence, 49, 54, 62

Spillers, Hortense, 12, 41, 175, 218, 355, 382

Stockton, Kathryn Bond, 54–58

Stonewall Rebellion, 3, 38

Stop-and-Frisk, 39, 270, 273

structural vulnerabilities, 246–47, 255–56

Student Nonviolent Coordinating Committee (SNCC), 304–5

Stud Life, 217, 219, 228–31

studium, 201, 203, 208. *See also* punctum

subjectivity, 20, 59, 60, 188, 220, 239, 253, 318, 327, 337, 346; black, xii, 306, 355; black queer/gay, 3, 240, 252–53, 256, 258n15, 318; erotic, 248, 253, 350; gay, 247–48; trans, 16, 67

surveillance, 20, 187, 256, 265, 269–73, 275, 279, 298, 324, 326, 376; public health, 19, 240, 256, 326 survival, xiii, 198, 376, 380–83, 385; black queer, 386; community-based practices of, 60; daily, 108; political, 347; practices of, 31–33, 350, 386; resources for, 290; vulnerability and, 352; of the white body, 180

tea, 2, 4, 6, 23
Thurmond, Strom, 335
Thurston, Baratunde, 262, 264
Timiya. *See* Howard, Qaadir
Tinsley, Omise'eke Natasha, 12, 24n9, 33; *Thiefing Sugar*, 13, 351
To Wong Foo, Thanks for Everything! Julie Newmar, 18, 167–68, 170, 172–75, 183, 186–88
trans, 15, 38, 66; trans*, 67, 79–80
transfemininity, 141
transgender studies, 66–67, 145; black, 14. *See also* gender studies; queer studies; sexuality studies
transphobia, 85, 87, 288, 300, 383, 389
transracial, 84, 87–88
transgression, 116, 171, 186, 208, 227, 350
trauma, 49, 51–52, 54, 279, 305, 389–90; of historic racial violence, 224–26, 228–33; of sexual violence, 19, 217–20
Triton, 16, 83–92. *See also* Delany, Samuel
Twitter, 262, 275, 278

Vazquez, Angie, 95–96, 99–100, 103, 108

vernacular, 118, 382; black/African American, 2, 127n2; black gay/queer, 2, 23n2, 47n37; Southern, 309
Victorian morality, 70, 202, 219
Violence Against Women Act (VAWA), 334, 336
Violent Crime Control and Law Enforcement Act (VCCLEA), 323–24, 329–30, 334, 338–40
Vodou. *See* Haitian Vodou
vogue, 32, 37, 39–40
Voting Rights Act, 216, 323, 339
vulnerability, 51, 204, 211, 222, 242, 246, 256, 326, 342n12, 352

Walcott, Rinaldo, 125, 139, 349
Washington, D.C., riot (1968), 21, 304–8, 310, 312–14, 317–19
Whose Beloved Community conference, xi, 4, 8
womanhood, 69, 74, 171–72, 207, 210; black, 174, 182, 184, 192n22, 203, 205, 213, 218; ideal, 144
women's studies. *See* gender studies; queer studies; sexuality studies; transgender studies
Wynter, Sylvia, 327, 343n31

young, d'bi, 17, 114–16, 119–23, 125–26

Zimmerman, George, 217, 264, 270, 324